Dynamic
Macroeconomic
Theory

Dynamic Macroeconomic Theory

Thomas J. Sargent

Harvard University Press
Cambridge, Massachusetts
and London, England

This book is printed on acid-free paper, and its binding materials
have been chosen for strength and durability.

Library of Congress Cataloging-in-Publication Data

Sargent, Thomas J.
  Dynamic macroeconomic theory.

  Bibliography: p.
  Includes index.
  1. Macroeconomics — Mathematical models.
2. Equilibrium (Economics) — Mathematical models.
I. Title.
HB172.5.S27   1987   339′.0724   86-7601
ISBN 0-674-21877-9 (alk. paper)

This book has been digitally reprinted. The content remains
identical to that of previous printings

For Judy, my daughter

Preface

This book originated in notes for graduate courses in macroeconomics and monetary theory that I taught at the University of Minnesota during the years 1977-1985. My goal has been to introduce some of the methods and results of dynamic macroeconomics and to help the reader apply the methods to concrete problems in macroeconomics and monetary economics. To attain this goal, I sacrificed generality and sometimes also rigor. I hope that the references at the end of each chapter will encourage further and deeper study of the technical material.

This book and the ways in which I have studied and taught macroeconomics have been heavily influenced by the work of Robert E. Lucas, Jr., and Neil Wallace. I have learned much from reading their papers and from hearing their lectures. I have also learned about the subjects in this book from a string of exceptionally able graduate students, including Robert M. Townsend, Lars Peter Hansen, Dan Peled, Randall Wright, Richard Rogerson, Martin Eichenbaum, Charles Whiteman, Rao Aiyagari, Rodolfo Manuelli, and Eugene Yun (all at the University of Minnesota) and from Danny Quah and Patrick Kehoe (both at Harvard University). For their help in reading and criticizing the manuscript, I am grateful to Rodolfo Manuelli, Yong Yoon, Gary Hansen, Marianne Baxter, Patrick Kehoe, and especially Baek In Cha and Eugene Yun. For extensive assistance with typing, I thank Wendy Williamson, Nancy Muth, Linda Dixon, and Judy Andrew. Wendy Williamson provided extensive research assistance in finding and organizing references and in insuring that deadlines be met. Phil Swenson, Kathy Rolfe, and Eugene Yun prepared the graphs.

I also thank Harvard University and the National Bureau of Economic Research, which I visited during the academic year 1981–82, for giving me time to begin writing this book. I am indebted to the Federal Reserve Bank of Minneapolis for its continuing support and for providing me with a perfect place in which to think about macroeconomics. I am grateful to Marcia Brubeck and Jodi Simpson for skillful and constructive editing. The index was prepared by Andrew Atkeson and Jodi Simpson, for which I thank them.

Contents

Dynamic
Macroeconomic
Theory

Introduction

The tasks of macroeconomics are to interpret observations on economic aggregates in terms of the motivations and constraints of economic agents and to predict the consequences of alternative hypothetical ways of administering government economic policy. By "government economic policy" is meant not an isolated government policy action but an entire regime, that is, a consistently spelled-out plan for administering the government's policy instruments over time and across contingencies. General equilibrium models form a convenient context for analyzing such alternative government policies, because their construction requires feasible contingency plans for government actions, explicitly and completely spelled out, as well as a set of consistent assumptions about private agents' perceptions of the government's plans. A related attraction of general equilibrium models is their internal consistency: one is assured that agents' choices are derived from a common set of assumptions about government policy and about the preferences, technology, and endowments in the economy. In the past ten years, these strengths of general equilibrium models, and the corresponding deficiencies of Keynesian and monetarist models of the 1960s, have induced macroeconomists to begin applying general equilibrium models.

This book describes some general equilibrium models that have been built to help interpret time series observations of economic aggregates and to predict the consequences of alternative government interventions. Many of the observations that macroeconomists want to interpret intrinsically involve the passage of time. Interest rates, asset prices, capital accumulation, unemployment, and borrowing and lending are thus all subjects involving the passage of time. Our interest in these subjects impels us to study models that are dynamic.

The general equilibrium models used by macroeconomists are special. They employ particular and drastic restrictions on preferences, technologies, and endowment patterns that are designed to render the models tractable for studying a particular subject. A wide variety of such restrictions can be imagined. Consequently, at this moment there is no one widely accepted, all-purpose model. Instead, different dynamic general equilibrium models are now being used to interpret various macroeconomic phenomena and to experiment with hypothetical government policies. For this reason the present book describes several models and applies each of them to issues of interest to macroeconomists. A good way to appreciate the relative strengths and weaknesses of the different models is to experience the insights that flow from their application.

The restrictions in these models have been inspired by various considerations. Analytical tractability is sometimes the motivation for the adoption of special restrictions, as in the asset-pricing model of Lucas (Chapter 3), where restrictions give the economy a recursive structure. This model is a special case of an Arrow-Debreu economy. A quite different reason for adopting special structures is that there is no room for a valued unbacked fiat currency in the Arrow-Debreu general equilibrium model. For the study of questions involving valued fiat currency, it is necessary to imagine an environment that is not a special case of the Arrow-Debreu model. (The Arrow-Debreu model *is* acceptable as a model for pricing a commodity money but is not useful for explaining velocity observations for a commodity money economy.)

A main goal of this book is to describe and illustrate the method and some of the tools of dynamic general equilibrium models in macroeconomics. One major tool is discounted dynamic programming, to which Chapter 1 gives a nontechnical introduction. Dynamic programming is a recursive method for solving a special class of constrained-optimum problems in which the objective function and the constraints have each been restricted in a particular way. A grasp of the nature of these restrictions and the circumstances under which they fail to hold is the key to understanding the time inconsistency phenomenon that arises in designing optimal government policy interventions in dynamic general equilibrium models. Chapter 1 discusses these matters and provides a variety of examples that may be used to practice the technique of dynamic programming.

Chapter 2 provides an introduction to the theory of search. This material gives the reader further practice in applying dynamic programming. More important, search models have transformed the way in which macroeconomists think about unemployment and the design of interventions to influence it. Chapter 2 stops far short of providing a comprehensive survey of the current literature on search. The chapter aims, however, to provide the reader with some of the tools needed to read that literature and with a taste for some of the results.

Dynamic programming is a tool that has been used to formulate and to solve simple general equilibrium models for determining asset prices, interest rates, and capital accumulation processes. The models typically consist of a single representative private agent and a single government agent, each living the same number of periods, usually infinite in number. Often the equilibrium of the model can be computed by solving a particular dynamic programming problem. Chapter 3 describes the asset-pricing model of Robert E. Lucas, Jr., and uses it to study a variety of issues. The model of Chapter 3 is a real model, there being no role for a government-issued currency that is not backed by future government budget surpluses. Preferences, technology, endowments, and trading opportunities are specified, so that such an unbacked asset would have no value in equilibrium.

The remaining chapters of the book provide an introduction to monetary theory. Chapter 4 first introduces some central issues in monetary theory. After describing why there is no role for an unbacked currency in the Lucas "tree model" of Chapter 3, Chapter 4 shows how preferences in Lucas's model can be altered to attain a version of a currency in the utility function model.

Chapter 5 describes a version of Lucas's cash-in-advance model and puts it to work. This model modifies that of Chapter 3 by restricting the trading opportunities available to agents while retaining the same specification for preferences, technology, and endowments. Agents are prohibited from consuming their own endowment and from exchanging credit for current consumption goods and are constrained to purchase current consumption goods with a government-issued currency that they have previously accumulated. These constraints on trading opportunities give rise to an equilibrium in which government-issued currency is valued although it is not fully backed by prospective government surpluses. The constraints on trading are arranged to keep the model in its real aspects equivalent to that of Chapter 3. This provision builds in "neutrality" with respect to currency variations. Apart from restrictions on the pattern of trades, the cash-in-advance model has private agents who are identically endowed and have identical preferences. When we study the two-country version of this model, we assume that agents are identical across the two countries and are equally endowed and taxed.

The restrictions on trading opportunities that drive the cash-in-advance model are imposed as primitive parts of the model and are not derived from an explicit description of a pattern of spatial separation or technology for trading. The particular details of the cash-in-advance restriction delicately influence the nature of the results that emerge. In the two-country version of the model, for example, we shall see how sensitively the behavior of the exchange rate depends on the precise specification of the cash-in-advance restrictions. In the one-country model, it very much matters that only government-issued currency counts as cash and that evidences of privately issued credit, such as bank notes and checks, do not qualify as cash.

Chapter 6 describes a model of Bewley and Townsend that is distinct from but related to the cash-in-advance model of Chapter 5. In Bewley's model the structure of trading is restricted by prohibiting all private borrowing and lending and insurance. (In the model of chapter 5, some private borrowing and lending are permitted.) Private agents have identical preferences but endowment sequences that vary across time and across people. People would like to smooth their consumption streams over time by borrowing and lending among themselves but are prohibited from doing so. Only by trading a single asset, namely a government-issued unbacked currency, can individuals make their consumption stream smoother than their endowment stream. Because agents want to smooth consumption, currency is valued in equilibrium.

One of Townsend's contributions was to provide an explicit description of an economic environment that in equilibrium endogenously eliminates any opportunities for private borrowing and lending. Townsend described a particular pattern of agents' endowments and of their spatial separation and movements over time that was sufficient to prevent private loan markets from operating. Versions of the economic environment described by Townsend also exist in which local loan markets operate but in which there is still room for a valued unbacked government currency. Potentially, then, this model permits us to think about situations in which "inside money" (evidences of private indebtedness) and "outside money" (government-issued currency that is unbacked by prospective government budget surpluses) coexist.

Townsend's model forms a natural bridge between the cash-in-advance model of infinitely lived agents in Chapter 5 and the overlapping-generations models of Chapters 7 and 8. The overlapping-generations model restricts agents so that they have finite lives (in our case, two periods). By separating agents in time and by restricting their endowment patterns and the technology available to them, we can create room for a valued government-issued currency that coexists with private (intragenerational) borrowing and lending. The intertemporal arrangement of agents in the overlapping-generations model is not identical to the spatial separation and movement pattern in Townsend's model but plays the same role in supplying a friction that prevents private loan markets from eliminating a valued unbacked government currency.

Many issues and doctrines in macroeconomics may be studied in the context of these models. Topics explored in the present book include

- The structure of a variety of "irrelevance theorems" that characterize equivalence classes of government policies that give rise to identical equilibrium consumption allocations; the Ricardian equivalence theorem and the Modigliani-Miller theorems for government open-market operations of Wallace, Chamley and Polemarchakis, and Peled are examples
- The quantity theory of money and the conditions under which movements in the stock of money are neutral
- Aspects of the coordination problem facing the monetary and fiscal authorities
- The sense in which inflation is and is not a "purely monetary phenomenon"
- Whether price-level stability is an appropriate goal for the monetary authority; the discussion will include examples of economies in which the "real bills doctrine" holds (it states that increases in the stock of currency engineered by government open-market purchases of safe private debt are not inflationary) and other examples in which it does not
- Credit controls, "how to pay for the war" efficiently via forced saving, and the dynamic Laffer curve that is associated with inflationary finance
- Alternative schemes for paying interest on reserves of government currency

These and other macroeconomic issues are examined in the context of one or another of the models presented. Once an analysis has been completed with one model, it will usually become evident how the same issue could be treated in terms of the others. Often only one model will be used to study an issue in the text, and parenthetical notes and exercises will indicate how things would work in another. These comparisons help the reader learn which model is most useful for studying a given problem.

The different models will sometimes provide quite different perspectives on a given issue. Their common commitment to dynamic general equilibrium theorizing, however, ensures that some important common themes and messages recur. One common theme is the idea that an equilibrium is a stochastic process (that is, a probability distribution over sequences) for the endogenous variables of the model. An important common message is that policy experiments need to be completely described in terms of alternative feasible stochastic processes for the government's instruments. That is, the entire contingency plan of the government must be spelled out in order for a policy experiment to be well posed and susceptible to analysis. (Macroeconomic models used in the 1960s erroneously purported to supply answers to questions about the effects of isolated government actions at one point in time without completely spelling out the government's contingency plan.) One part of this message is that monetary and fiscal policies must be coordinated. It is not feasible to have both an independent central bank and an independent fiscal authority.

Of the many differences between the overlapping-generations model and the cash-in-advance model with an infinitely lived agent, two deserve mention here. The first is that, in the former model, equilibria can exist in which valued unbacked government currency and evidences of private indebtedness coexist, with no asset dominating another in rate of return. In general, this situation does not occur in the cash-in-advance model. With one exception, the equilibria described in Chapter 5 have the characteristic that government currency is dominated in rate of return but that no other asset is. This difference sensitively conditions the implications of these models for a variety of practical issues, including the nature of Fisher effects on nominal interest rates and the effectiveness of central bank open-market operations.

A second noteworthy difference is that heterogeneity among households with respect to preferences and endowments is tractable within the overlapping-generations model and is more difficult in the context of the infinitely-lived-agent model in the style of Chapter 5. As a result, the overlapping-generations model is easier to work with when observations on quantities of private indebtedness are being addressed. On the other hand, it is difficult to take the overlapping-generations model literally as a model of money in terms of the intergenerational friction that makes room for currency. In this respect, it is more attractive to interpret the overlapping-generations model figuratively, regarding it as a simpler way of embodying the same sort of friction that was modeled by Townsend. With such a figurative interpretation, however, it becomes difficult to motivate the formal econometric interpretation of time series on monetary aggregates within the overlapping-generations model. With respect to issues of timing, models with infinitely lived agents seem more attractive for building formal econometric models of such time series.

The last point reflects a broad tension within the general equilibrium approach to macroeconomics. On the one hand, general equilibrium modeling is founded on the premise that, for explaining one aspect of an economic system, it is important to account for all the other aspects simultaneously. Thus, for example, in a general equilibrium model, the stochastic process for interest rates and the value of currency will each depend on the same specifications about the production technology and the patterns of endowments and preferences that also influence investment, production, and consumption processes. The sense of general equilibrium analysis is that it is important to explain everything at once in a way that adds up (that is, in an internally consistent fashion). Furthermore, if a general equilibrium model is taken seriously econometrically, it naturally instructs the user to fit and test the model employing all of the available data on all of the model's variables via full-system statistical procedures (such as maximum likelihood or generalized method of moments). In other words, the model itself does not say that its predictions are to be taken more seriously in some directions than in others.

On the other hand, in order to make general equilibrium models tractable enough for macroeconomic work, their preferences, technology, and endowments have typically been so simplified, and so much has been abstracted, that it is often difficult to take their predictions in some directions seriously. The internal logic of general equilibrium modeling then creates a difficulty in taking *any* of the model's predictions seriously.

The tension between these two points underlies some of the disagreements between advocates of different models of money, particularly proponents of the overlapping-generations model and of the infinitely-lived-agent cash-in-advance model. Such tension also underlies the distinct approaches to testing and estimation of dynamic general equilibrium macroeconomic models advocated, say, by Kydland and Prescott (1982), on the one hand, and by Hansen and Sargent (1980), on the other hand.

These tensions notwithstanding, researchers keep trying to put general equilibrium models at the service of macroeconomics. This endeavor rests on faith that insights about the laws of motion of economic aggregates can be acquired by building models of economies that are internally consistent. Such faith perseveres despite the fact that internal consistency is always purchased with simplification and abstraction.

The Appendix provides an introduction to functional analysis for macroeconomics. With a minimal investment in this machinery, readers will be able to deepen their understanding of dynamic programming, linear stochastic difference equations, discrete-time calculus of variations, and linear rational expectations models. Apparently disparate results from various areas have a common mathematical structure, as the Appendix endeavors to show. It tries to give the reader a sense of the unity of the mathematical methods, which, together with the book's models, are put to work in the exercises.

References and Suggested Readings

Hansen, Lars P., and Thomas J. Sargent. 1980. Formulating and estimating dynamic linear rational expectations models. *Journal of Economic Dynamics and Control* 2(1):7–46. (Reprinted in *Rational Expectations and Econometric Practice,* ed. R. E. Lucas, Jr., and T. J. Sargent, pp. 91–125. Minneapolis: University of Minnesota Press, 1981.)

Kydland, Finn, and Edward C. Prescott. 1982. Time to build and aggregate fluctuations. *Econometrica* 50(6):1345–1370.

Real Dynamic Macroeconomic Models

I

1 | Dynamic Programming

This chapter introduces the basic ideas and methods of dynamic programming and displays the restrictions on a dynamic system and the objective function that must be met for dynamic programming to be applicable. Where these restrictions are satisfied, dynamic programming provides a powerful method for studying dynamic optimization. The required restrictions permit the analyst to break what is in general a single exceedingly large dimensional optimization problem into a collection of much smaller optimization problems that can be solved sequentially. That step usually affords computational simplicity and often provides analytical insights.

The restrictions on objective functions and the dynamic system required for dynamic programming are satisfied in many formulations of private agents' investment problems. There is a class of multiagent problems (differential games), however, in which the structure of interactions among different agents' decision problems prevents one or more agents' problems from conforming to the restrictions required for dynamic programming. For these agents, therefore, optimal decisions must be computed not sequentially but simultaneously. The inapplicability of sequential methods to such decision problems is called time inconsistency and was first studied in macroeconomic contexts by Kydland and Prescott (1977) and Calvo (1978).

Although the main ideas of dynamic programming are simple, the details can involve sophisticated mathematical arguments. In this chapter things have been kept at a heuristic level of presentation, with the hope of communicating the main ideas quickly and enabling the reader to use these techniques to solve problems. More thorough presentations of the subject are listed at the end of the chapter; in particular see Bertsekas (1976); Bertsekas and Shreve (1978); Lucas, Prescott, and Stokey (forthcoming); Bellman (1957); and Chow (1981).

1.1 A General Intertemporal Problem

Consider the following general intertemporal optimization problem under certainty. Let x_t be an $(n \times 1)$ vector of *state* variables at time t, $t = 0$, $1, \ldots, T + 1$. Let u_t be a $(k \times 1)$ vector of *control* variables at time t, $t = 0, \ldots, T$. (The terms "state" and "control" are ambiguous in the context of the problem of this section. A precise description of them will be postponed, pending consideration of the special problem of Section 1.2, in which they are well motivated.) The problem is to choose $u_0, u_1, \ldots, u_T$, $x_1, \ldots, x_{T+1}$ to maximize an objective function

$$(1.1) \qquad R(x_0, u_0, x_1, u_1, \ldots, x_T, u_T, x_{T+1}),$$

subject to x_0 given and subject to a system of constraints connecting the controls and the states, which we write in the implicit form

$$(1.2) \qquad G(x_0, u_0, x_1, u_1, \ldots, x_T, u_T, x_{T+1}) \geq 0.$$

In (1.2) we imagine that G is a collection of $(T + 1)n$ functions. We imagine that R and G are sufficiently smooth and that R is sufficiently concave to permit the method of Kuhn and Tucker to be applied. We then have a standard classical constrained-optimization problem, which can be solved by forming the following Lagrangian and maximizing with respect to u_0, $u_1, \ldots, u_T, x_1, x_2, \ldots, x_{T+1}$:

$$(1.3) \qquad \begin{aligned} J = {} & R(x_0, u_0, x_1, u_1, \ldots, x_T, u_T, x_{T+1}) \\ & + \mu' G(x_0, u_0, x_1, u_1, \ldots, x_T, u_T, x_{T+1}), \end{aligned}$$

where μ is a $[(T + 1)n \times 1]$ vector of Lagrange multipliers. The solution of this problem can be represented as a set of functions $u_0 = H_0(x_0)$, $u_1 = H_1(x_0), \ldots, u_T = H_T(x_0)$, with the optimal controls expressed as a function of the initial given state x_0, and a set of functions $x_1 = w_1(x_0)$, $x_2 = w_2(x_0), \ldots, x_{T+1} = w_{T+1}(x_0)$, with subsequent states expressed as a function of the initial state x_0. It is a standard feature of this problem that the optimal controls $u_0, u_1, \ldots, u_T$ as functions of x_0 must be determined simultaneously. This feature can be verified by obtaining the first-order necessary conditions for maximizing (1.3) and by studying the structure of the Jacobian matrix for the system of first-order necessary conditions. The system of first-order conditions in general fails to be recursive or block recursive, so that the optimal values for u_t and x_t are simultaneously determined.

1.2 A Recursive Problem

For dynamic problems in which the horizon T is large, it would be convenient if the problem could somehow be specialized to avoid the need to compute all of the controls simultaneously. This consideration has led to the following specialization of (1.1) and (1.2), which permits a recursive approach to the computation of the optimal controls.

We assume that $r_t(x_t, u_t)$ is a concave function and that the set $\{x_{t+1}, x_t, u_t : x_{t+1} \leq g_t(x_t, u_t), u_t \in R^k\}$ is convex and compact. We thus replace (1.1) and (1.2) with the problem of maximizing by choice of $(u_0, x_1, u_1, \ldots, x_{T+1})$ the function

$$(1.4) \qquad r_0(x_0, u_0) + r_1(x_1, u_1) + \ldots + r_T(x_T, u_T) + W_0(x_{T+1}),$$

subject to x_0 given and the "transition" equations

$$(1.5) \qquad \begin{aligned} x_1 &= g_0(x_0, u_0) \\ x_2 &= g_1(x_1, u_1) \end{aligned}$$

$$\cdot$$
$$\cdot$$
$$\cdot$$

$$x_{T+1} = g_T(x_T, u_T).$$

The function $r_t(x_t, u_t)$ is called the one-period return function at t, whereas the function $g_t(x_t, u_t)$ is called the transition function at t. The structure of the transition equations (1.5) motivates the labeling of x_t as state and u_t as control variables. The state vector x_t constitutes a complete description of the current position of the system. As far as the current and future returns $r_s(x_s, u_s)$ for $s \geq t$ are concerned, past values of u_v and x_v for $v < t$ add no information beyond that contained in x_t. This result is a consequence of the particular time separable structure of (1.4) and (1.5). The control vector u_t contains variables under the partial control of the problem solver that impinge on x_{t+1}, given x_t. In general for a given problem, the appropriate definition of the state is not unique, there being alternative ways of completely describing the current position of the system. Many of the admissible definitions of the state will include redundancies.

In (1.4) and (1.5) the functions $r_t(x_t, u_t)$, $W_0(x_{T+1})$, and $g_t(x_t, u_t)$ are assumed to be sufficiently smooth to permit the use of Lagrange's method.

Forming the Lagrangian, we have

(1.6) $L = r_0(x_0, u_0) + r_1(x_1, u_1) + \ldots + r_T(x_T, u_T) + W_0(x_{T+1})$
$+ \lambda_0'[g_0(x_0, u_0) - x_1] + \lambda_1'[g_1(x_1, u_1) - x_2]$
$+ \ldots + \lambda_T'[g_T(x_T, u_T) - x_{T+1}],$

where λ_t is an $(n \times 1)$ vector of Lagrange multipliers for $t = 0, \ldots, T$ and the prime denotes transposition.

The first-order necessary conditions for this problem are

(1.7a) $\dfrac{\partial L}{\partial u_t} = \dfrac{\partial r_t}{\partial u_t}(x_t, u_t) + \dfrac{\partial g_t(x_t, u_t)}{\partial u_t}\lambda_t = 0, \qquad t = 0, \ldots, T$

(1.7b) $\dfrac{\partial L}{\partial x_t} = \dfrac{\partial r_t(x_t, u_t)}{\partial x_t} + \dfrac{\partial g_t}{\partial x_t}(x_t, u_t)\lambda_t - \lambda_{t-1} = 0, \qquad t = 1, \ldots, T$

(1.7c) $\dfrac{\partial L}{\partial x_{T+1}} = W_0'(x_{T+1}) - \lambda_T = 0$

(1.7d) $x_{t+1} = g_t(x_t, u_t), \qquad t = 0, 1, \ldots T.$

Here $\partial r_t/\partial u_t$ is a $(k \times 1)$ vector with $\partial r_t/\partial u_{ti}$ in the ith row, where u_{ti} is the element in the ith row of u_t. Also, $\partial g_t/\partial u_t$ is a $(k \times n)$ matrix with $\partial g_{ti}/\partial u_{th}$ in the ith column and hth row, where g_{ti} is the ith row of g_t and u_{th} is the hth row of u_t. Solving (1.7b) for λ_{t-1} and shifting forward one period, we have

$$\lambda_t = \dfrac{\partial r_{t+1}(x_{t+1}, u_{t+1})}{\partial x_{t+1}} + \dfrac{\partial g_{t+1}(x_{t+1}, u_{t+1})}{\partial x_{t+1}}\lambda_{t+1}.$$

Using this and (1.7c) recursively to eliminate λ_t, $t = 0, \ldots, T$, from (1.7a), we obtain the following system:

(1.8a) $\dfrac{\partial r_t}{\partial u_t}(x_t, u_t) + \dfrac{\partial g_t(x_t, u_t)}{\partial u_t}\left\{ \dfrac{\partial r_{t+1}}{\partial x_{t+1}} + \dfrac{\partial g_{t+1}}{\partial x_{t+1}}\left[\dfrac{\partial r_{t+2}}{\partial x_{t+2}} + \dfrac{\partial g_{t+2}}{\partial x_{t+2}} \right. \right.$
$\left. \left. \cdot \left(\dfrac{\partial r_{t+3}}{\partial x_{t+3}} + \dfrac{\partial g_{t+3}}{\partial x_{t+3}}\left\{ \ldots + \dfrac{\partial g_T}{\partial x_T}[W_0'(x_{T+1})] \right\} \right) \right] \right\} = 0$
$t = 0, \ldots, T - 1$

(1.8b) $x_{t+1} = g_t(x_t, u_t), \qquad t = 0, \ldots, T - 1$

(1.8c) $\dfrac{\partial r_T}{\partial u_T}(x_T, u_T) + \dfrac{\partial g_T(x_T, u_T)}{\partial u_T}W_0'(x_{T+1}) = 0$

(1.8d) $x_{T+1} = g_T(x_T, u_T),$

where in (1.8a) it is understood that g_t and r_t both have arguments (x_t, u_t).

In the special case in which $r_t(x_t, u_t)$ is quadratic, g_t is linear, and $\partial g_t/\partial x_t \equiv 0$, Equations (1.8a)–(1.8b) can be solved to yield a system of second-order difference equations in the vector x_t, subject to the initial condition that x_0 is given, and the terminal conditions (1.8c)–(1.8d). A further specialization results if the functions r_t and g_t are assumed to be time invariant so that (1.8) yields a set of time-invariant linear difference equations. In this case, the equations can be solved using methods similar to those illustrated in Sargent (1986, chap. 9). For more general specifications, however, it is useful to have an alternative method of solving the problem or at least of characterizing the solution, because nonlinear difference equations are generally very difficult to solve directly.

To motivate this method, notice the special structure of system (1.8), which is depicted in Table 1.1. The structure is special because (x_s, u_s) for $s < t$ does not appear directly in the marginal conditions and transition laws dated t and later. This fact makes it feasible to use the following "backward" recursive solution strategy.

Given x_T, the (subsystems of the) last two equations of system (1.8), namely (1.8c) and (1.8d), form a system of $(n + k)$ equations in (x_{T+1}, u_T). We solve these equations for x_{T+1} and u_T as functions of x_T, say,

$$(1.9) \qquad x_{T+1} = f_T(x_T), \qquad u_T = h_T(x_T),$$

where $f_T(x_T) \equiv g_T[x_T, h_T(x_T)]$. Next, use $u_T = h_T(x_T)$ to eliminate u_T from the preceding two (subsystems of) equations in (1.8), namely (1.8a) and

---

Table 1.1 The structure of system (1.8)

Define the implicit functions ϕ_t^1, ϕ_t^2, $t = 0, 1, 2, \ldots, T$, by

$$\phi_t^1(x_t, u_t, x_{t+1}, u_{t+1}, \ldots, x_T, u_T, x_{T+1})$$
$$= \frac{\partial r_t}{\partial u_t} + \frac{\partial g_t}{\partial u_t} \left\{ \frac{\partial r_{t+1}}{\partial x_{t+1}} + \frac{\partial g_{t+1}}{\partial x_{t+1}} \left(\ldots + \frac{\partial g_T}{\partial x_T} \right) [W_0'(x_{T+1})] \right\} = 0$$

and $\phi_t^2(x_t, u_t, x_{t+1}) = x_{t+1} - g_t(x_t, u_t) = 0$, respectively. Then (1.8) can be represented as

$$\phi_0^1(x_0, u_0, x_1, u_1, x_2, \ldots, x_T, u_T, x_{T+1}) = 0$$
$$\phi_0^2(x_0, u_0, x_1) = 0$$
$$\phi_1^1(x_1, u_1, x_2, \ldots, x_T, u_T, x_{T+1}) = 0$$
$$\phi_1^2(x_1, u_1, x_2) = 0$$
$$\phi_T^1(x_T, u_T, x_{T+1}) = 0$$
$$\phi_T^2(x_T, u_T, x_{T+1}) = 0$$

(1.8b) for $t = T - 1$,

(1.10)
$$\frac{\partial r_{T-1}(x_{T-1}, u_{T-1})}{\partial u_{T-1}} + \frac{\partial g_{T-1}(x_{T-1}, u_{T-1})}{\partial u_{T-1}}$$

$$\cdot \left[\frac{\partial r_T}{\partial x_T}(x_T, u_T) + \frac{\partial g_T}{\partial x_T}(x_T, u_T) W_0'(x_{T+1}) \right] = 0$$

$$x_T = g_{T-1}(x_{T-1}, u_{T-1}),$$

and solve these equations for u_{T-1} and x_T each as functions of x_{T-1}:

(1.11) $x_T = f_{T-1}(x_{T-1}),$ $u_{T-1} = h_{T-1}(x_{T-1}).$

One can continue recursively in this way, solving for a collection of feedback rules of the form

(1.12) $u_t = h_t(x_t),$ $t = T, T - 1, T - 2, \ldots, 0,$

where $u_t = h_t(x_t)$, $x_{t+1} = f_t(x_t)$ solve the equations

(1.13)
$$\frac{\partial r_t}{\partial u_t}(x_t, u_t) + \frac{\partial g_t}{\partial u_t} \left\{ \frac{\partial r_{t+1}}{\partial x_{t+1}} + \frac{\partial g_{t+1}}{\partial x_{t+1}} \left[\frac{\partial r_{t+2}}{\partial x_{t+2}} + \frac{\partial g_{t+2}}{\partial x_{t+2}} \right. \right.$$

$$\left. \left. \cdot \left(\frac{\partial r_{t+3}}{\partial x_{t+3}} + \frac{\partial g_{t+3}}{\partial x_{t+3}} \left\{ \ldots + \frac{\partial g_T}{\partial x_T} [W_0'(x_{T+1})] \right\} \right) \right] \right\} = 0,$$

and $x_{s+1} = g_s(x_s, u_s)$ for $s = t, t + 1, \ldots, T$, given that $u_{s+1} = h_{s+1}(x_{s+1})$ for $s = t, t + 1, \ldots, T - 1$.

1.3 Bellman's Equations

The equations of system (1.13) have interpretations as the marginal conditions from the following sequence of problems. Define the value function for a one-period problem $W_1(x_T)$ by

(1.14) $W_1(x_T) = \max_{u_T} \{ r_T(x_T, u_T) + W_0(x_{T+1}) \},$

subject to $x_{T+1} = g_T(x_T, u_T)$, with x_T given. We form the Lagrangian for this problem, and the first-order conditions can be expressed, after the Lagrange multiplier has been eliminated, as

(1.15) $\dfrac{\partial r_T}{\partial u_T}(x_T, u_T) + \dfrac{\partial g_T(x_T, u_T)}{\partial u_T} W_0'(x_{T+1}) = 0,$

which precisely matches the marginal condition for u_T in (1.8). Equation (1.15) and the transition law $x_{T+1} = g_T(x_T, u_T)$ are to be solved jointly for $u_T = h_T(x_T)$. Now imagine substituting the solution $u_T = h_T(x_T)$ of (1.15) and (1.8d) into (1.14) to get

(1.16) $W_1(x_T) = r_T[x_T, h_T(x_T)] + W_0(g_T[x_T, h_T(x_T)])$.

Formally, differentiating (1.16) gives

$$W_1'(x_T) = \left(\frac{\partial r_T}{\partial x_T} + \frac{\partial g_T}{\partial x_T} W_0'\right) + \frac{\partial h_T}{\partial x_T}\left[\frac{\partial r_T}{\partial u_T} + \frac{\partial g_T}{\partial u_T} W_0'(x_{T+1})\right],$$

where all functions dated T are evaluated at $[x_T, h_T(x_T)]$ and which by virtue of (1.15) becomes

(1.17) $W_1'(x_T) = \dfrac{\partial r_T}{\partial x_T} [x_T, h_T(x_T)]$

$$+ \frac{\partial g_T}{\partial x_T} [x_T, h_T(x_T)] W_0'(g_T[x_T, h_T(x_T)]).$$

Because we have not shown that $\partial h_T/\partial x_T$ exists, this argument is informal or heuristic and should be regarded as only a way of remembering the correct answer. Correct arguments are given by Benveniste and Scheinkman (1979) and Lucas (1977).

Now define the value function for the two-period problem $W_2(x_{T-1})$ as

(1.18) $W_2(x_{T-1}) = \max\limits_{u_{T-1}}\{r_{T-1}(x_{T-1}, u_{T-1}) + W_1(x_T)\}$,

subject to $x_T = g_{T-1}(x_{T-1}, u_{T-1})$, with x_{T-1} given. If we proceed as with the problem defined by (1.14), the first-order condition for the problem on the right side of (1.18) can be expressed as

$$\frac{\partial r_{T-1}}{\partial u_{T-1}} (x_{T-1}, u_{T-1}) + \frac{\partial g_{T-1}(x_{T-1}, u_{T-1})}{\partial u_{T-1}} W_1'(x_T) = 0.$$

If we use formula (1.17) for $W_1'(x_T)$, this equation becomes

(1.19) $\dfrac{\partial r_{T-1}}{\partial u_{T-1}} (x_{T-1}, u_{T-1}) + \dfrac{\partial g_{T-1}(x_{T-1}, u_{T-1})}{\partial u_{T-1}}$

$$\cdot\left(\frac{\partial r_T}{\partial x_T} [x_T, h_T(x_T)] + \frac{\partial g_T}{\partial x_T} [x_T, h_T(x_T)] W_0'(g_T[x_T, h_T(x_T)])\right) = 0.$$

This equation and the transition law $x_T = g_{T-1}(x_{T-1}, u_{T-1})$ are to be solved jointly for $u_{T-1} = h_{T-1}(x_{T-1})$, $x_T = f_{T-1}(x_{T-1})$. Again proceeding as above, we can obtain

(1.20) $W_2'(x_{T-1}) = \dfrac{\partial r_{T-1}}{\partial x_{T-1}} [x_{T-1}, h_{T-1}(x_{T-1})]$

$$+ \frac{\partial g_{T-1}}{\partial x_{T-1}} W_1'(g_{T-1}[x_{T-1}, h_{T-1}(x_{T-1})]),$$

or, using (1.17),

$$W_2'(x_{T-1}) = \frac{\partial r_{T-1}}{\partial x_{T-1}} [x_{T-1}, h_{T-1}(x_{T-1})]$$

$$+ \frac{\partial g_{T-1}}{\partial x_{T-1}} [x_{T-1}, h_{T-1}(x_{T-1})]$$

$$\cdot \left\{ \frac{\partial r_T}{\partial x_T} [x_T, h_T(x_T)] \right.$$

$$\left. + \frac{\partial g_T}{\partial x_T} [x_T, h_T(x_T)] \ W_0'[f_T(x_T)] \right\},$$

where x_T is evaluated at $x_T = f_{T-1}(x_{T-1}) = g_{T-1}[x_{T-1}, h_{T-1}(x_{T-1})]$. Notice that Equation (1.19) is precisely the version of the marginal condition in (1.8) for u_{T-1}.

The pattern for the recursion is now set. We iterate on the following functional equation in the value functions

$$(1.21) \qquad W_{j+1}(x_{T-j}) = \max_{u_{T-j}} \{ r_{T-j}(x_{T-j}, u_{T-j}) + W_j(x_{T-j+1}) \},$$

subject to $x_{T-j+1} = g_{T-j}(x_{T-j}, u_{T-j})$, x_{T-j} given. The functional equation (1.21) is a version of Bellman's equation — named after Richard Bellman (1957). The idea is to proceed recursively and to work backward, first solving the one-period problem with $j + 1 = 1$, deducing $W_1(x_T)$, then solving the two-period problem with $j + 1 = 2$, deducing the two-period value function $W_2(x_{T-1})$. The process is repeated until we obtain the $(T + 1)$-period value function $W_{T+1}(x_0)$. This procedure gives the optimal value of the problem as a function of the initial state x_0. Along the way we have calculated the optimal feedback rules $u_{T-j} = h_{T-j}(x_{T-j}), j = 0, 1, \ldots, T$. The preceding argument suggests that this backward recursion generates the same marginal conditions as the original problem (1.8). Indeed, the backward recursion technique always solves the original problem if a solution exists.

The derivative of the value functions obeys the recursion

$$W_{j+1}'(x_{T-j}) = \frac{\partial r_{T-j}}{\partial x_{T-j}} [x_{T-j}, h_{T-j}(x_{T-j})]$$

$$+ \frac{\partial g_{T-j}}{\partial x_{T-j}} W_j'(g_{T-j}[x_{T-j}, h_{T-j}(x_{T-j})]).$$

Comparing this equation with (1.7b) and (1.7c), we find that $W_j'(x_{T+1-j}) = \lambda_{T-j}$. The Lagrange multipliers λ_{T-j} in (1.6) thus give the marginal value of the state variables for the j-period problem.

The following observations supply another perspective on the recursive nature of our problem. Let us simply define the $(T + 1)$-period value function $W_{T+1}(x_0)$ by

(1.22) $\quad W_{T+1}(x_0) = \max_{u_0, u_1, \dots, u_T} \{r_0(x_0, u_0) + r_1(x_1, u_1) + \dots + r_T(x_T, u_T)$

$$+ W_0(x_{T+1})\},$$

where the maximization is understood to be subject to $x_{t+1} = g_t(x_t, u_t)$, $t = 0, \dots, T$, and x_0 given. Notice that the objective function and constraints (transition equations) have been specialized to have the key property that controls dated t influence states x_{s+1} and returns $r_s(x_s, u_s)$ for $s \geq t$ but not earlier. This key property gives the problem its recursive structure. In particular, the property makes it legitimate to cascade the maximization operator and to write (1.22) as

(1.23) $\quad W_{T+1}(x_0) = \max_{u_0}\{r_0(x_0, u_0) + \max_{u_1}\{r_1(x_1, u_1) + \max_{u_2}\{r_2(x_2, u_2)$

$$+ \dots + \max_{u_T}\{r_T(x_T, u_T) + W_0(x_{T+1})\} \dots \}\}\},$$

where the maximization over u_t is understood to be subject to $x_{t+1} = g_t(x_t, u_t)$ with x_t given. Equation (1.23) indicates that the original large optimization problem on the right side of (1.22) can be broken up into $(T + 1)$ smaller problems. First, the problem in the innermost brackets is solved, the optimizer being $u_T = h_T(x_T)$ and the optimized value being $W_1(x_T)$. Then the problem in the second innermost brackets is solved for $u_{T-1} = h_{T-1}(x_{T-1})$ with optimized value $W_2(x_{T-1})$. This process of proceeding from the problems in the innermost brackets outward is equivalent to iterating on Bellman's functional equation (1.21).

The preceding argument implies that the optimal policies $u_t = h_t(x_t)$, $t = 0, \dots, T$ have a self-enforcing character in the following sense. Consider the "remainder" of the objective function at some time $s > 0$, namely,

(1.24) $\quad \max_{u_s, u_{s+1}, \dots, u_T} \{r_s(x_s, u_s) + \dots + r_T(x_T, u_T) + W_0(x_{T+1})\},$

subject to $x_{t+1} = g_t(x_t, u_t)$, $t = s, \dots, T$, with x_s given. Then the solution of the maximum problem (1.24) is simply to use the remaining functions $u_s = h_s(x_s)$, $s = t, \dots, T$ that were computed for the original problem. Furthermore, the maximized value of (1.24) is $W_{T-s+1}(x_s)$. Thus as time advances, there is no incentive to depart from the original plan. This self-enforcing character of optimal policies is known as **Bellman's principle of optimality**. Optimal policies that have this property are said to be time consistent. This property is special, is a consequence of the recursive character of the problem (1.4)–(1.5) and will not characterize the solutions of more general problems.

It is a feature of the solution to problem (1.4)–(1.5) that in general a different policy function $u_t = h_t(x_t)$, mapping the state at t into the control at t, is to be used at each date $t = 0, \ldots, T$. This is a consequence of two features of the problem: the fact that the horizon T is finite and the fact that the functions $r_t(x_t, u_t)$ and $g_t(x_t, u_t)$ have been permitted to depend on time in arbitrary ways. For many practical applications it is inconvenient that the policy function varies over time. One would like to discover contexts in which the same policy function is used for each period t. In the interests of achieving this objective, we now specialize problem (1.4)–(1.5) with the aim of generating conditions under which the policy functions h_j converge as $j \to -\infty$. We assume that

(1.25) $r_t(x_t, u_t) = \beta^t r(x_t, u_t), \qquad 0 < \beta < 1$
$g_t(x_t, u_t) = g(x_t, u_t).$

With this specification, Bellman's equation (1.21) becomes

$$W_{j+1}(x_{T-j}) = \max_{u_{T-j}}\{\beta^{T-j} r(x_{T-j}, u_{T-j}) + W_j(x_{T-j+1})\}.$$

Multiplying both sides by β^{j-T} gives

(1.25′) $\beta^{j-T} W_{j+1}(x_{T-j}) = \max_{u_{T-j}}\{r(x_{T-j}, u_{T-j}) + \beta \cdot \beta^{j-1-T} W_j(x_{T-j+1})\}.$

Now define the current value function

$$V_{j+1}(x_{T-j}) = \beta^{j-T} W_{j+1}(x_{T-j}).$$

Notice that for $j = T$, we have $V_{T+1}(x_0) = W_{T+1}(x_0)$. Also notice that the current value function can be directly defined as

$$V_{j+1}(x_{T-j}) = \max_{u_{T-j}, u_{T-j+1}, \ldots, u_T} \{r(x_{T-j}, u_{T-j}) + \beta r(x_{T-j+1}, u_{T-j+1})$$
$$+ \ldots + \beta^j r(x_T, u_T) + \beta^{j+1} V_0(x_{T+1})\}.$$

In terms of the current value function, (1.25′) asserts that Bellman's equation becomes

(1.26) $V_{j+1}(x_{T-j}) = \max_{u_{T-j}}\{r(x_{T-j}, u_{T-j}) + \beta V_j(x_{T-j+1})\},$

subject to $x_{T-j+1} = g(x_{T-j}, u_{T-j})$ and x_{T-j} given. More compactly, we can write (1.26) as

(1.27) $V_{j+1}(x) = \max_u\{r(x, u) + \beta V_j(\check{x})\},$

subject to $\tilde{x} = g(x, u)$, x given, where the tilde denotes next-period values. Under particular conditions, iterations on (1.27) starting from any bounded and continuous initial V_0 converge as $j \to \infty$. See Bertsekas (1976, chap. 6) or Lucas, Prescott, and Stokey (forthcoming). The argument used to prove this claim is outlined in Section A.8. In this case the limit function $V = \lim_{j \to \infty} V_j$ satisfies the following version of Bellman's equation:

$$(1.28) \qquad V(x) = \max_u \{r(x, u) + \beta V(\tilde{x})\},$$

where the maximization is subject to $\tilde{x} = g(x, u)$, with x given. The limiting value function V that solves (1.28) turns out to be the optimal value function for the infinite horizon problem

$$(1.29) \qquad V(x_0) = \max_{\{u_s\}_{s=0}^\infty} \sum_{t=0}^\infty \beta^t r(x_t, u_t),$$

where the maximization is subject to $x_{t+1} = g(x_t, u_t)$, with x_0 given. Problem (1.29) is a version of a discounted dynamic programming problem. Under various particular regularity conditions,[1] it turns out that (1) the functional equation (1.28) has a unique strictly concave solution; (2) this solution is approached in the limit as $j \to \infty$ by iterations on (1.26) starting from any bounded and continuous initial V_0; (3) there is a unique and time-invariant optimal policy of the form $u_t = h(x_t)$, where h is chosen to maximize the right side of (1.28); (4) off corners, the limiting value function V is differentiable with

$$(1.30) \qquad V'(x) = \frac{\partial r}{\partial x} [x, h(x)] + \beta \frac{\partial g}{\partial x} [x, h(x)] \, V'(g[x, h(x)]).$$

This is a version of the formula of Benveniste and Scheinkman (1979). It is a great convenience of the specialization (1.25) of the objective function and transition functions, and also a convenience of the specification of an infinite horizon, that they imply a time-invariant policy function $u_t = h(x_t)$, for it is a routine practice in economics to seek setups in which agents use time-invariant decision rules. (Ample econometric considerations recommend or require such setups.)

The preceding results provide two methods for solving the functional

---

1. Alternative sets of regularity conditions work. One set of sufficient conditions is (1) r is concave and bounded, (2) the constraint set generated by g is convex and compact, that is, the set of $\{x_{t+1}, x_t, u_t : x_{t+1} \leq g(x_t, u_t)\}$ for admissible u_t is convex and compact. See Lucas (1977), and Bertsekas (1976) for further details of convergence results. See Benveniste and Scheinkman (1979) and Lucas (1977) for the results on differentiability of the value function. A proof of the uniform convergence of iterations on (1.27) is contained in Section A.7 of the Appendix.

equation (1.28). The first method is constructive and simply involves iterating on (1.26), starting from $V_0 = 0$, until V_j has converged. The second method involves guessing a solution V and verifying that it is a solution to (1.28). The second method relies on the uniqueness of the solution to (1.28), but because it also relies on luck in making a good guess, it is not generally available. In the examples below, the guess-and-verify method is often used. The reader should, however, be alerted to the fact that the objective functions and constraints of these problems have been especially rigged so that the method will work. Essentially there are only two classes of specifications of preferences and constraints for which the method will work, namely, variants of specifications with linear constraints and quadratic preferences or Cobb-Douglas constraints and logarithmic preferences.

In many problems, there is no unique way of defining states and controls, and several alternative definitions lead to the same solution of the problem. Sometimes the states and controls can be defined in such a way that x_t does not appear in the transition equation, so that $\partial g_t / \partial x_t \equiv 0$. In this case, the system (1.8a)–(1.8b) simplifies to

$$\frac{\partial r_t}{\partial u_t}(x_t, u_t) + \frac{\partial g_t}{\partial u_t}(u_t) \cdot \frac{\partial r_{t+1}(x_{t+1}, u_{t+1})}{\partial x_{t+1}} = 0, \qquad x_{t+1} = g_t(u_t).$$

The first equation is a version of what is called an Euler equation. Under circumstances in which the second equation can be inverted to yield u_t as a function of x_{t+1}, using the second equation to eliminate u_t from the first equation produces a second-order difference equation in x_t.

Most of the dynamic programming problems that we solve in this book are discounted dynamic programming problems.

1.4 Nonstochastic Examples

We now consider several examples of single-agent optimization problems that can be solved using dynamic programming.

Saving under Certainty

Consider the problem of a consumer in a nonrandom environment who seeks to maximize $\sum_{t=0}^{\infty} \beta^t u(c_t)$, $0 < \beta < 1$, subject to $A_{t+1} = R_t(A_t + y_t - c_t)$, A_0 given, where y_t, $t = 0, 1, \ldots$, is a known sequence of exponential order less than $1/\beta$ and R_t, $t = 0, 1, \ldots$, is a known and given sequence of one-period gross rates of return on nonlabor wealth. Here c_t is consumption, A_t is nonlabor wealth at the beginning of time t, and y_t is labor income at t. Labor income is assumed to be beyond the control of the agent. For concreteness let y_t equal λy_{t-1}, and say that $R_t = R > 0$ for all t, assuming that $R > \lambda > 0$. To rule out a strategy of infinite consumption supported by unbounded borrowing, we also impose the restriction that, for $t \geq 0$,

$$(1.31) \qquad c_t + \sum_{j=1}^{\infty} \left(\prod_{k=0}^{j-1} R_{t+k}^{-1} \right) c_{t+j} = y_t + \sum_{j=1}^{\infty} \left(\prod_{k=0}^{j-1} R_{t+k}^{-1} \right) y_{t+j} + A_t.$$

We define the state of the system as (A_t, y_t, R_{t-1}) and define the control at t, u_t, as $R_t^{-1} A_{t+1} = A_t + y_t - c_t$. Evidently the control u_t is gross savings. The transition equation for A_t becomes $A_{t+1} = R_t u_t$, which does not involve the state at t. The function $r_t(x_t, u_t)$ becomes $\beta^t u(A_t + y_t - R_t^{-1} A_{t+1}) = \beta^t u(A_t + y_t - u_t)$. Bellman's equation becomes

$$v(A_t, y_t, R_{t-1}) = \max_{u_t} \{ u(A_t + y_t - u_t) + \beta v(u_t R_t, y_{t+1}, R_t) \},$$

where $u_t = R_t^{-1} A_{t+1}$, $y_{t+1} = \lambda y_t$, $R_t = R$. Benveniste and Scheinkman's formula (1.30) gives $\partial v(A_t, y_t, R_{t-1})/\partial A_t = u'(c_t)$. The Euler equation for u_t then becomes

$$-\beta^t u'(A_t + y_t - R_t^{-1} A_{t+1})$$
$$+\beta^{t+1} R_t u'(A_{t+1} + y_{t+1} - R_{t+1}^{-1} A_{t+2}) = 0$$

or

$$(1.32) \qquad -u'(c_t) + \beta R_t u'(c_{t+1}) = 0.$$

We seek a consumption plan that satisfies (1.32) and the "isoperimetric condition" (1.31).

As an example, suppose that $u(c_t) = \ln c_t$. Then (1.32) requires that

$$c_{t+j} = \beta^j \left(\prod_{k=0}^{j-1} R_{t+k} \right) c_t.$$

Substituting this into the left side of (1.31) gives $(1 - \beta)^{-1} c_t$. Therefore (1.31) and (1.32) imply that

$$(1.33) \qquad c_t = (1 - \beta) \left[y_t + \sum_{j=1}^{\infty} \left(\prod_{k=0}^{j-1} R_{t+k} \right) y_{t+j} + A_t \right],$$

so that the agent always consumes a constant fraction of his or her total human and nonhuman wealth. Equation (1.33) is valid for any sequences $\{R_t\}_{t=0}^{\infty}$, $\{y_t\}_{t=0}^{\infty}$ such that the right side converges.

To specialize (1.33) to the case in which $y_t = \lambda y_{t-1}$ and $R_t = R$, write out (1.33) as

$$c_t = (1 - \beta)(A_t + y_t + R_t^{-1} y_{t+1} + R_t^{-1} R_{t+1}^{-1} y_{t+2} + \ldots).$$

Repeatedly substituting $R_{t+1}^{-1} = R^{-1}$ and $y_{t+1} = \lambda y_t$ into the above equation gives

$$c_t = (1 - \beta)(A_t + y_t + R^{-1}\lambda y_t + R^{-2}\lambda^2 y_t + \ldots)$$

or $\quad c_t = (1 - \beta)\left[A_t + y_t\left(\frac{1}{1 - \lambda R^{-1}}\right)\right],$

where we require that $\lambda R^{-1} < 1$. That is, income is assumed to grow at a rate less than the interest rate. In the decision rule stated above consumption varies directly with current income y_t, inversely with the currently observed interest rate R, and directly with the rate of growth of income λ.

Optimal Growth

A consumer aims to maximize

$$\sum_{t=0}^{\infty} \beta^t u(c_t), \qquad 0 < \beta < 1$$

subject to $\quad c_t + k_{t+1} = f(k_t), \qquad k_0 > 0$ given, $\qquad c_t \geq 0,$

where $u'(0) = +\infty$, $u' > 0$, $u'' < 0$, $f'(0) = +\infty$, $f'(\infty) = 0$, $f' > 0$, and $f'' < 0$. Here c_t is consumption and k_t is the stock of capital. This is a version of the problem that was studied by T. C. Koopmans (1963) and David Cass (1965).

Let the state be defined as k_t and the control as k_{t+1}. Bellman's equation is then

$$v(k_t) = \max_{k_{t+1}}\{u[f(k_t) - k_{t+1}] + \beta v(k_{t+1})\}.$$

The first-order condition is

(1.34) $\quad -u'[f(k_t) - k_{t+1}] + \beta v'(k_{t+1}) = 0.$

Benveniste and Scheinkman's equation (1.30) implies that $v(k_t)$ is differentiable with

(1.35) $\quad v'(k_t) = u'[f(k_t) - k_{t+1}]f'(k_t),$

where k_{t+1} is evaluated at the optimum $k_{t+1} = h(k_t)$.

Because $u(\cdot)$ and $f(\cdot)$ are strictly concave, it follows that $v(k)$ is strictly concave. From this inference it follows that the optimal policy function, the solution $k_{t+1} = h(k_t)$ of (1.34), is a nondecreasing function of k_t.[2]

There is a maximum capital stock that can be sustained as a stationary equilibrium, namely that which would eventually emerge if c_t were to be zero for all t. If c_t were zero for all t, k_t would evolve according to the difference equation $k_{t+1} = f(k_t)$. Because $f'(0) = +\infty$, $f'' < 0$, and because $f'(\infty) = 0$, the equation $\bar{k} = f(\bar{k})$ has a unique positive solution. Evidently $k_{t+1} = f(k_t)$ converges to $\bar{k}$ as $t \to \infty$. [To verify this point, plot $f(k_t)$ against a $45°$ line.]

Let the system begin with $k_0 \in (0, \bar{k}]$. Then for $t \geq 1$, k_t must evidently remain in the bounded interval $[0, \bar{k}]$. Because the optimal policy function $h(k_t) = k_{t+1}$ is nondecreasing in k_t, it can be shown that $k_0, k_1, k_2, \ldots$, is a monotone, bounded sequence. On the one hand, suppose that $k_1 > k_0$. Then because $h(\cdot)$ is nondecreasing, we have $k_2 = h(k_1) \geq h(k_0) = k_1, k_3 = h(k_2) \geq h(k_1) = k_2$, and so on. On the other hand, suppose that $k_1 < k_0$. Then $k_2 = h(k_1) \leq h(k_0) = k_1$, $k_3 = h(k_2) \leq h(k_1) = k_2$, and so on. It follows that k_t is a monotone, bounded sequence. Inasmuch as monotone, bounded sequences converge, it follows that k_t converges to a limit point $k_\infty(k_0)$ as $t \to \infty$.

The preceding convergence argument leaves open the possibility that the limit point $k_\infty(k_0)$ depends on the starting point k_0. It does not do so, however, as the following argument verifies. Let k_∞ be a limit point. At the limit point, (1.34) and (1.35) hold, and $k_{t+1} = k_t = k_\infty$. The implication is that $\beta f'(k_\infty) = 1$, an equation that determines a unique optimal stationary value k_∞. Note that the "gross rate of return" $f'(k_\infty) = \beta^{-1}$ in the stationary state and is independent of the specifics of the current-period utility function and the production function. Note also that the optimal stationary capital stock depends on $f(\cdot)$ and β but not on $u(\cdot)$.

We now specialize this example by following Brock and Mirman (1972) and considering the particular functional forms $u(c) = \ln c$ and $f(k) = Ak^\alpha$, $A > 0, 0 < \alpha < 1$. We will use the guess-and-verify method for this problem. The guess may not seem an obvious one. The inspiration for the guess can be

---

2. From (1.35), we have that $v'(k)$ is continuous. This follows from the continuity of $h(k)$, $f(k)$, and $f'(k)$. For two levels k_i of k, $i = 1, 2$, consider the first-order condition $u'[f(k_i) - h(k_i)] = \beta V'[h(k_i)]$. Assume that $k_1 \geq k_2$ and that $h(k_1) < h(k_2)$. By strict concavity of $v(\cdot)$ and continuity of $v'(\cdot)$, it follows that (1) for all $h(k_i)$, $v'[h(k_i)]$ is well defined, and (2) $h(k_1) < h(k_2)$ implies $v'[h(k_1)] > v'[h(k_2)]$. Therefore, $u'[f(k_1) - h(k_1)] > u'[f(k_2) - h(k_2)]$. By strict concavity of u, the preceding inequality holds if and only if $f(k_1) - h(k_1) < f(k_2) - h(k_2)$, or equivalently, $0 < h(k_2) - h(k_1) < f(k_2) - f(k_1) \leq 0$. This is a contradiction produced by the assumption that for $k_1 \geq k_2$, $h(k_1) < h(k_2)$. Therefore $h(k)$ is nondecreasing in k. (The argument in this note was constructed by Rodolfo Manuelli.)

understood by working Exercise 1.1 at the end of the chapter. For this example we make the guess

(1.36) $v(k) = E + F \ln k,$

where E and F are undetermined coefficients. For this guess, the first-order necessary condition (1.34) implies the following formula for the optimal policy $\tilde{k} = h(k)$, where $\tilde{k}$ is next period's value and k is this period's value of the capital stock:

(1.37) $\tilde{k} = \dfrac{\beta F}{1 + \beta F} Ak^{\alpha}.$

Substituting (1.37) into the right side of (1.35) gives

(1.38) $v'(k) = (1 + \beta F)\alpha k^{-1}.$

Differentiating (1.36) gives

(1.39) $v'(k) = Fk^{-1}.$

Equating (1.38) and (1.39) permits one to solve for F, $F = \alpha/(1 - \alpha\beta)$. Substituting this expression for F back into (1.36) and (1.37) gives

(1.40) $v(k) = E + \dfrac{\alpha}{1 - \alpha\beta} \ln k$

$\qquad\quad \tilde{k} = A\beta\alpha k^{\alpha}.$

The fact that expressions (1.38) and (1.39) for $v'(k)$ have identical functional forms both verifies the original guess (1.36) and permits one to solve for the undetermined coefficient F. An alternative procedure for verifying the guess involves substituting (1.37) into Bellman's functional equation and equating the result to the right side of (1.36). Solving the resulting equation for E and F again gives $F = \alpha/(1 - \alpha\beta)$ and now gives

$$E = (1 - \beta)^{-1} \left[\ln A(1 - \alpha\beta) + \frac{\beta\alpha}{1 - \alpha\beta} \ln A\beta\alpha \right].$$

In Exercise 1.1, the reader is asked to construct the same solution (1.37) to the functional equation, using the method of iterating on Bellman's equation (1.26) starting from $v_0(k) = 0$. For this purpose it is useful to note that the term $F = \alpha/(1 - \alpha\beta)$ that appears in (1.40) can be interpreted as a geometric sum $\alpha[1 + \alpha\beta + (\alpha\beta)^2 + \ldots]$.

Equation (1.40) shows that the optimal policy is to have capital move according to the difference equation $k_{t+1} = A\beta\alpha k_t^{\alpha}$, or $\ln k_{t+1} =$

In $A\beta\alpha + \alpha \ln k_t$. Because $\alpha < 1$, we know that k_t converges as $t \to \infty$ for any positive initial value k_0. The stationary point is given by the solution of $k_\infty = A\beta\alpha k_\infty^\alpha$, or $k_\infty^{\alpha-1} = (A\beta\alpha)^{-1}$. Notice that this example obeys the general conclusion established above that k_∞ is determined from the solution of $\beta f'(k_\infty) = 1$.

1.5 The Optimal Linear Regulator Problem

We now consider a special class of dynamic programming problems in which the return functions r_t are quadratic and the transition functions g_t are linear. This specification leads to the widely used optimal linear regulator problem. We consider the special case in which the return functions r_t and transition functions g_t are both time invariant. The problem is to maximize over choice of $\{u_t\}_{t=0}^\infty$ the criterion

$$(1.41) \qquad \sum_{t=0}^{\infty} \{x_t'Rx_t + u_t'Qu_t\},$$

subject to $x_{t+1} = Ax_t + Bu_t$, x_0 given. Here x_t is an $(n \times 1)$ vector of state variables, u_t is a $(k \times 1)$ vector of controls, R is a negative semidefinite symmetric matrix, Q is a negative definite symmetric matrix, A is an $(n \times n)$ matrix, and B is an $(n \times k)$ matrix. We guess that the value function is quadratic, $V(x) = x'Px$, where P is a negative semidefinite symmetric matrix.

Using the transition law to eliminate next period's state, Bellman's equation becomes

$$(1.42) \qquad x'Px = \max_u \{x'Rx + u'Qu + (Ax + Bu)'P(Ax + Bu)\}.$$

The first-order necessary condition for the maximum problem on the right side of (1.42) is

$$(1.43) \qquad (Q + B'PB)u = -B'PAx,$$

which implies the feedback rule for u:

$$(1.44) \qquad u = -(Q + B'PB)^{-1}B'PAx$$

or

$$(1.45) \qquad u = -Fx,$$

where $F = (Q + B'PB)^{-1}B'PA$. Substituting the optimizer (1.45) into the right side of (1.42) and rearranging gives

(1.46) $P = R + A'PA - A'PB(Q + B'PB)^{-1}B'PA.$

Equation (1.46) is called the algebraic matrix Riccati equation.

Under particular conditions, Equation (1.46) has a unique negative semi-definite solution, which is approached in the limit as $j \to \infty$ by iterations on the matrix Riccati difference equation:[3]

(1.47) $P_{j+1} = R + A'P_jA - A'P_jB(Q + B'P_jB)^{-1}B'P_jA,$

starting from $P_0 = 0$. Equation (1.47) is derived much like (1.46) except that one starts from the iterative version of Bellman's equation (1.26) rather than from the asymptotic version (1.28).

A modified version of problem (1.41) is the discounted optimal linear regulator problem, to maximize

(1.48) $\displaystyle\sum_{t=0}^{\infty} \beta^t\{x_t'Rx_t + u_t'Qu_t\}, \qquad 0 < \beta < 1,$

subject to $x_{t+1} = Ax_t + Bu_t$, x_0 given. For this problem Bellman's recursive equation (1.26) implies the following matrix Riccati difference equation modified for discounting:

(1.49) $P_{j+1} = R + \beta A'P_jA - \beta^2 A'P_jB(Q + \beta B'P_jB)^{-1}B'P_jA.$

The algebraic matrix Riccati equation is modified correspondingly. The value function for the infinite horizon problem is simply $V(x_0) = x_0'Px_0$, where P is the limiting value of P_j resulting from iterations on (1.49) starting from $P_0 = 0$. The optimal policy is $u_t = -Fx_t$, where $F = \beta(Q + \beta B'PB)^{-1}B'PA$.

Upon substituting the optimal control $u_t = -Fx_t$ into the law of motion $x_{t+1} = Ax_t + Bu_t$, we obtain the optimal "closed-loop system" $x_{t+1} = (A - BF)x_t$. This difference equation governs the evolution of x_t under the optimal control. The system is said to be stable if $\lim_{t\to\infty} x_t = 0$ starting from any initial $x_0 \in R^n$. Assume that the eigenvalues of $(A - BF)$ are distinct, and use the eigenvalue decomposition $(A - BF) = C\Lambda C^{-1}$ where the columns of C are the eigenvectors of $(A - BF)$ and Λ is a diagonal matrix of eigenvalues of $(A - BF)$. Write the above equation as $x_{t+1} = C\Lambda C^{-1}x_t$. The solution of this difference equation for $t > 0$ is readily verified by repeated substitution to be $x_t = C\Lambda^t C^{-1}x_0$. Evidently, the system is stable for all

---

3. If the eigenvalues of A are bounded in modulus below unity, this result obtains, but much weaker conditions also suffice. See Bertsekas (1976, chap. 4) and Sargent (1981).

$x_0 \in R^n$ if and only if the eigenvalue of $(A - BF)$ of maximum absolute value is strictly less than unity in absolute value. When this condition is met, $(A - BF)$ is said to be a "stable matrix."

A literature is devoted to characterizing the conditions on A, B, R, and Q under which the optimal closed-loop system matrix $(A - BF)$ is stable. These results are described in detail in Sargent (1981) and may be briefly described here for the undiscounted case $\beta = 1$. Heuristically, the conditions on A, B, R, and Q that are required for stability are as follows. First, A and B must be such that it is *possible* to pick a control law $u_t = -Fx_t$ that drives x_t to zero eventually, starting from any $x_0 \in R^n$ ["the pair (A, B) must be stabilizable"]. Second, the matrix R must be such that the controller *wants* to drive x_t to zero as $t \to \infty$. Notice from (1.41) that, if R is strictly negative definite, the controller will want to drive x_t to zero, because $x_t' R x_t < 0$ for $x_t \neq 0$. If x_t does not approach zero, then the objective function is $-\infty$. When R is not strictly negative definite, however, the possibility emerges that the planner does not care whether some components of x_t fail to go to zero as $t \to \infty$. To attain stability of $(A - BF)$, it is necessary both for the planner to dislike it that some components of x_t threaten not to go to zero in the absence of countervailing control actions and for (A, B) to be such that the controller has the ability to drive those components to zero as $t \to \infty$ by an appropriate choice of F.

These conditions are discussed under the subjects of controllability, stabilizability, reconstructability, and detectability in the literature on linear optimal control. (For continuous-time linear systems, these concepts are described by Kwakernaak and Sivan 1972; for discrete-time systems, see Sargent 1981.) These conditions subsume and generalize the transversality conditions used in the discrete-time calculus of variations (see Sargent 1986). That is, the case when $(A - BF)$ is stable corresponds to the situation in which it is optimal to solve "stable roots backward and unstable roots forward." See Sargent (1986, chap. 9). Hansen and Sargent (1981) describe the relationship between Euler equation methods and dynamic programming for a class of linear optimal control systems. Also see Chow (1981).

The conditions under which $(A - BF)$ is stable are also the conditions under which x_t converges to a unique stationary distribution in the stochastic version of the linear regulator problem (see Section 1.8).

1.6 Stochastic Control Problems

We now consider a modification of problem (1.29) to permit uncertainty of particular kinds. We modify the transition equation and consider the problem, to maximize

(1.50) $E_0 \sum_{t=0}^{\infty} \beta^t r(x_t, u_t), \qquad 0 < \beta < 1,$

subject to

(1.51) $x_{t+1} = g(x_t, u_t, \epsilon_{t+1}),$

x_0 known and given at $t = 0$, where ϵ_t is a sequence of independently and identically distributed random variables with cumulative probability distribution function prob$\{\epsilon_t \leq e\} = F(e)$ for all t; $E_t(y)$ denotes the mathematical expectation of a random variable y, given information known at t. At time t, x_t is assumed to be known, but $x_{t+j}, j \geq 1$ is not known at t. That is, ϵ_{t+1} is realized at $(t + 1)$, after u_t has been decided at t. In problem (1.50)–(1.51), uncertainty is injected by assuming that x_t follows a random difference equation.

Problem (1.50–1.51) continues to have a recursive structure, stemming jointly from the additive separability of the objective function (1.50) in pairs (x_t, u_t) and from the difference equation characterization of the transition law (1.51). In particular, controls dated t affect returns $r(x_s, u_s)$ for $s \geq t$ but not earlier. This feature implies that dynamic programming methods remain appropriate.

The problem is to maximize (1.50) subject to (1.51) by choice of a "policy" or "contingency plan" $u_t = h(x_t)$. The version of Bellman's functional equation corresponding to (1.28) becomes

(1.52) $V(x) = \max_u \{r(x, u) + \beta E[V[g(x, u, \epsilon)]|x]\},$

where $E\{V[g(x, u, \epsilon)]|x\} = \int V[g(x, u, \epsilon)]dF(\epsilon)$ and where $V(x)$ is the optimal value of the problem starting from x at $t = 0$. The solution $V(x)$ of (1.52) can be found by iterating on

(1.53) $V_{j+1}(x) = \max_u \{r(x, u) + \beta E[V_j[g(x, u, \epsilon)]|x]\},$

starting from any bounded continuous initial V_0. Under various particular regularity conditions, there obtain versions of the same four properties listed in Section 1.3. See Lucas, Prescott, and Stokey (forthcoming) or the framework presented in the Appendix.

The first-order necessary condition for the problem on the right side of (1.52) is

$$\frac{\partial r(x, u)}{\partial u} + \beta E\left[\frac{\partial g}{\partial u}(x, u, \epsilon)V'(g(x, u, \epsilon))|x\right] = 0,$$

which we obtained simply by differentiating the right side of (1.52), passing the differentiation operation under the E (an integration) operator. Off corners, the value function satisfies

$$V'(x) = \frac{\partial r}{\partial x} [x, h(x)] + \beta E \left\{ \frac{\partial g}{\partial x} [x, h(x), \epsilon] V'(g[x, h(x), \epsilon]) | x \right\}.$$

In the special case in which $\partial g / \partial x \equiv 0$, the formula for $V'(x)$ becomes

$$V'(x) = \frac{\partial r}{\partial x} [x, h(x)].$$

Substituting this formula into the first-order necessary condition for the problem gives the stochastic Euler equation

$$\frac{\partial r}{\partial u} (x, u) + \beta E \left[\frac{\partial g}{\partial u} (x, u, \epsilon) \frac{\partial r}{\partial x} (\tilde{x}, \tilde{u}) | x \right] = 0,$$

where tildes over x and u denote next-period values.

1.7 Examples of Stochastic Control Problems

We now give several examples of stochastic dynamic programming problems.

Consumption with a Random Return

A consumer seeks to maximize

$$E_0 \sum_{t=0}^{\infty} \beta^t u(c_t), \qquad 0 < \beta < 1,$$

subject to $A_{t+1} = R_t(A_t - c_t), t \geq 0, A_0$ given, where $u'(c) > 0, u''(c) < 0$, and where A_t is assets at the beginning of period t, c_t is consumption at t, and R_t is the gross rate of return on assets between periods t and $(t + 1)$. We assume that R_t becomes known at the beginning of period $(t + 1)$, after a decision about consumption at t, c_t, must be made. Assume that R_t is governed by a first-order Markov process, with transitions governed by $\text{prob}\{R_t \leq R' | R_{t-1} = R\} = F(R', R)$. When time t decisions must be made, the consumer knows A_t and $R_{t-1}, R_{t-2}, \ldots$. To rule out perpetual borrowing at the rate of return R_t, we impose the requirement that A_t must satisfy $\lim_{t \to \infty} E_0 \beta^t A_t = 0$.

For this problem we define the state as (A_t, R_{t-1}) and the control $\hat{u}_t$ as $(A_t - c_t)$. The transition equation for A_t is then given by $A_{t+1} = R_t(A_t - c_t) = R_t \hat{u}_t$, whereas the transition equation for R is implicitly defined by $F(R', R)$. Let $v(A_t, R_{t-1})$ be the value of the problem for a consumer with initial assets A_t when the last observed rate of return is R_{t-1}. Then Bellman's functional equation is

$$v(A_t, R_{t-1}) = \max_{\hat{u}_t}\{u(A_t - \hat{u}_t) + \beta E_t v(\hat{u}_t R_t, R_t)\}.$$

The first-order necessary condition for the problem on the right is

$$-u'(c_t) + \beta E_t v_1(\hat{u}_t R_t, R_t)R_t = 0.$$

Applying the Benveniste-Scheinkman formula to evaluate $v_1(A_t, R_{t-1})$ gives

$$v_1(A_t, R_{t-1}) = u'(c_t).$$

Using this formula in the first-order necessary condition gives the Euler equation

(1.54) $u'(c_t) = \beta E_t u'(c_{t+1})R_t.$

A solution of the agent's optimization problem is a saving policy function $u_t = h(A_t, R_{t-1})$, which implies a consumption policy function $c_t = c(A_t, R_{t-1}) \equiv A_t - h(A_t, R_{t-1})$. This policy function must satisfy the Euler equation (1.54) and must imply that the boundary condition on assets $\lim_{t \to \infty} E_0 \beta^t A_t = 0$ is satisfied. Substituting the function $c(A_t, R_{t-1})$ into the Euler equation and using the transition equation gives

(1.55) $u'[c(A_t, R_{t-1})] = \beta E_t u'[c(R_t[A_t - c(A_t, R_{t-1})], R_t)]R_t.$

This is a functional equation in the optimal policy function $c(A_t, R_{t-1})$.

To take a specific example, let $u(c)$ equal $\ln c$ and let R_t be an independently and identically distributed random process such that $1 \le ER_t < 1/\beta^2$. We guess that the optimal policy takes the form $c_t = \gamma A_t$, where γ is a constant to be determined. Substituting this guess into (1.54) gives

$$\frac{1}{\gamma A_t} = \beta E \frac{R_t}{\gamma R_t(A_t - \gamma A_t)},$$

where E is now the unconditional expectation operator. Solving for γ gives $\gamma = 1 - \beta$. The optimal policy is of the form $c_t = (1 - \beta)A_t$. It can be verified that this policy satisfies the boundary condition that we have imposed on asset accumulation. The optimal policy is to consume a constant fraction of wealth, $0 < \gamma < 1$, where $\gamma = 1 - \beta$.

Under the optimal policy, assets evolve according to $A_{t+1} = R_t(1 - \gamma)A_t$, which implies that

$$A_t = (1 - \gamma)^t \prod_{j=0}^{t-1} R_j A_0, \qquad t \ge 1.$$

Consequently, we have that

$$c_t = \gamma(1 - \gamma)^t \prod_{j=0}^{t-1} R_j A_0, \qquad t \geq 1, \qquad c_0 = \gamma A_0.$$

The optimal value of $E_0 \sum_{t=0}^{\infty} \beta^t \ln c_t$ is then given by

$$\ln \gamma A_0 + E_0 \sum_{t=1}^{\infty} \beta^t \ln \left[\gamma(1 - \gamma)^t \prod_{j=0}^{t-1} R_j A_0 \right].$$

Because R_j is independently and identically distributed, evaluating this expression gives

$$v(A_0, R_{-1}) = \frac{1}{1 - \beta} \ln \gamma + \ln (1 - \gamma) \sum_{t=0}^{\infty} \beta^t t$$
$$+ \sum_{t=0}^{\infty} \beta^t t E \ln R + \frac{1}{1 - \beta} \ln A_0,$$

where $E \ln R$ is the expectation of $\ln R_t$ for all t. Still, $\sum_{t=0}^{\infty} t\beta^t = \beta/(1 - \beta)^2$ (see Sargent 1979, Eq. 21, p. 88). Therefore the value function can be written

$$v(A_0, R_{-1}) = \frac{1}{1 - \beta} \ln \gamma + \ln (1 - \gamma) \frac{\beta}{(1 - \beta)^2} + \frac{\beta}{(1 - \beta)^2} E \ln R$$
$$+ \frac{1}{1 - \beta} \ln A_0.$$

The value depends directly on the mean of the logarithm of the rate of return but is independent of the realization of the rate of return at the beginning of the current period. This last property is special and depends on the assumption that R_t is distributed independently and identically over time.

Dynamic Portfolio Theory

This example generalizes the preceding one to the case in which a consumer can allocate his or her assets among a set of n assets, where the ith asset bears gross rate of return R_{it} at time t. Here R_{it} is assumed to be a positive random variable that is bounded from above with probability 1. The consumer maximizes $E_0 \sum_{t=0}^{\infty} \beta^t u(c_t)$ by choosing contingency plans for s_{it} for $i = 1, \ldots, n$ and $t \geq 0$, subject to

$$c_t + \sum_{i=1}^{n} s_{it} = A_t, \qquad t \geq 0$$
$$A_{t+1} = \sum_{i=1}^{n} s_{it} R_{it}, \qquad t \geq 0, \qquad A_0 \text{ given}$$
$$\lim_{t \to \infty} E_0 \beta^t A_t = 0.$$

Here s_{it} is the amount of asset i purchased in period t, and c_t is consumption at t. At time t, A_t and R_{it-1}, $i = 1, \ldots, n$ are observed, but R_{it}, $i = 1, \ldots, n$ is not observed until the beginning of period $(t + 1)$. We assume that R_{it} is governed by a Markov process, with transition probabilities given by $\text{prob}\{R_t \leq R' | R_{t-1} = R\} = F(R', R)$, where $R_t = (R_{1t}, \ldots, R_{nt})$ and R' and R are both n-dimensional vectors. Shortly we will specialize the setup to the case in which R_t and R_{t-1} are independently distributed for all t.

We define the state for this problem as (A_t, R_{t-1}), whereas the control is now the vector $(s_{1t}, \ldots, s_{nt})$. Bellman's functional equation is

$$v(A_t, R_{t-1}) = \max_{s_{1t}, \ldots, s_{nt}} \left\{ u(A_t - \sum_{i=1}^{n} s_{it}) + \beta E_t v \left(\sum_{i=1}^{n} s_{it} R_{it}, R_t \right) \right\}.$$

The first-order necessary conditions for the problem on the right are

$$u' \left(A_t - \sum_{i=1}^{n} s_{it} \right) = \beta E_t R_{it} v_1 \left(\sum_{k=1}^{n} s_{kt} R_{kt}, R_t \right), \qquad i = 1, \ldots, n.$$

The Benveniste-Scheinkman formula implies that $v_1 = u'(A_t - \sum_{i=1}^{n} s_{it})$. Substituting this equation into the above first-order conditions gives

$$u' \left(A_t - \sum_{i=1}^{n} s_{it} \right) = \beta E_t R_{it} u' \left(\sum_{k=1}^{n} R_{kt} s_{kt} - \sum_{j=1}^{n} s_{jt+1} \right),$$
$$i = 1, \ldots, n.$$

We now want to solve for optimal policy functions $s_{it} = s_i(A_t, R_{t-1})$. Substituting the policy functions into the preceding Euler equation gives

$$(1.56) \quad u' \left[A_t - \sum_{i=1}^{n} s_i(A_t, R_{t-1}) \right]$$
$$= \beta E_t R_{it} u' \left\{ \sum_{k=1}^{n} R_{kt} s_k(A_t, R_{t-1}) - \sum_{j=1}^{n} s_j \left[\sum_{k=1}^{n} R_{kt} s_k(A_t, R_{t-1}), R_t \right] \right\},$$
$$i = 1, \ldots, n.$$

This is a set of n functional equations in the n unknown functions $s_i(A_t, R_{t-1})$, $i = 1, \ldots, n$.

We now consider the special case in which R_{it}, $i = 1, \ldots, n$, is distributed independently and identically both over time *and* across i. Furthermore, we suppose that $u(c) = [1/(1 - \alpha)]c^{1-\alpha}$, where $0 < \alpha < 1$, so that $u'(c) = c^{-\alpha}$. For this case we make the guess that $s_{it} = kA_t$, $i = 1, \ldots, n$, where k is a constant to be determined. Note that we are guessing that k is independent of i, a guess inspired by the independence and identity of the distribution of the R_{it} over time and across i. Substituting this guess into

(1.56), using $u'(c) = c^{-\alpha}$ and rearranging, gives

$$k^\alpha = \beta E_t \frac{R_{it}}{\left(\sum_{j=1}^{n} R_{jt}\right)^\alpha}, \qquad i = 1, \ldots, n.$$

Because R_{it} is independently and identically distributed, the above equation can hold for all $i = 1, \ldots, n$. This result verifies our guess and gives an equation that can be solved for k. (Notice how this example conforms to the preceding one.)

In the present example the household allocates the same constant fraction of wealth to each asset in each period. This result depends on the independence of the R_{it} over time and the independence and identity of the distribution across assets i. We now explore the implications of relaxing the assumption of identical distributions across i while retaining independence across time and assets. Under these new assumptions we guess that the optimal policies will be of the form $s_{it} = k_i A_t$. Substituting this guess into the Euler equation gives

$$u'\left[A_t\left(1 - \sum_{i=1}^{n} k_i\right)\right] = \beta E_t R_{it} u'\left[\sum_{h=1}^{n} k_h R_{ht} A_t\left(1 - \sum_{j=1}^{n} k_j\right)\right],$$
$$i = 1, \ldots, n.$$

Further specializing this example, we take $u(c) = \ln c$. Substituting $u'(c) = c^{-1}$ into the above equations and rearranging gives

$$1 = \beta E_t \frac{R_{it}}{\sum_{j=1}^{n} k_j R_{jt}}, \qquad i = 1, \ldots, n.$$

This is a system of n equations in the n unknowns $k_1, \ldots, k_n$. For example, when $n = 2$, we have the two equations

$$1 = \beta E_t[k_1 + (k_2 R_{2t}/R_{1t})]^{-1}$$
$$1 = \beta E_t[(k_1 R_{1t}/R_{2t}) + k_2]^{-1},$$

which are to be solved for k_1 and k_2.

Stochastic Optimal Growth
We consider the stochastic growth example of Brock and Mirman (1972), to maximize

$$E_0 \sum_{t=0}^{\infty} \beta^t \ln c_t, \qquad 0 < \beta < 1,$$

subject to $c_t + k_{t+1} = Ak_t^\alpha \theta_t$, $0 < \alpha < 1$, where $\ln \theta_t$ is an independently and identically distributed random variable with normal distribution with mean zero and variance σ^2. (The stochastic optimal growth model is a workhorse in the literatures on capital asset pricing and business fluctuations; see Brock 1982 and Kydland and Prescott 1982.) A planner is supposed to know (k_t, θ_t) at time t but not to know future values of θ. We define the state of the system as (k_t, θ_t). Bellman's equation becomes

$$(1.57) \qquad V(k_t, \theta_t) = \max_{k_{t+1}} \{\ln(Ak_t^\alpha \theta_t - k_{t+1}) + \beta E[V(k_{t+1}, \theta_{t+1}) | k_t, \theta_t]\}.$$

The reader is invited to verify the guess that the solution of (1.56) is of the form $V(k, \theta) = E + F \ln k + G \ln \theta$, where E, F, and G are undetermined coefficients, and that the optimal policy rule is $k_{t+1} = A\alpha\beta k_t^\alpha \theta_t$.

1.8 The Stochastic Linear Optimal Regulator Problem

We consider the discounted stochastic linear optimal regulator problem, to maximize

$$(1.58) \qquad E_0 \sum_{t=0}^{\infty} \beta^t \{x_t' R x_t + u_t' Q u_t\}, \qquad 0 < \beta < 1,$$

subject to x_0 given, and the law of motion

$$(1.59) \qquad x_{t+1} = Ax_t + Bu_t + \epsilon_{t+1}, \qquad t \geq 0,$$

where ϵ_{t+1} is an $(n \times 1)$ vector of random variables that is independently and identically distributed through time and obeys the normal distribution with mean vector zero and contemporaneous covariance matrix

$$(1.60) \qquad E\epsilon_t \epsilon_t' = \Sigma$$

(See Kwakernaak and Sivan 1972 for an extensive study of the continuous-time version of this problem; also see Chow 1981.) The matrixes R, Q, A, and B obey the assumption described in Section 1.5 above.

For this problem the value function turns out to be

$$(1.61) \qquad v(x) = x'Px + d,$$

where P is the unique negative semidefinite solution of the discounted algebraic matrix Riccati equation corresponding to (1.49), which is the limit of iterations on (1.49) starting from $P_0 = 0$, and where d is given by

$$(1.62) \qquad d = \beta(1 - \beta)^{-1} \mathrm{tr} P \Sigma$$

where "tr" denotes the trace of a matrix. Furthermore, the optimal policy continues to be given by $u_t = -Fx_t$, where

(1.63) $F = \beta(Q + \beta B'P'B)^{-1}B'PA.$

A notable feature of this solution is that the feedback rule (1.63) is identical with the rule for the corresponding nonstochastic linear optimal regulator problem.

To prove the preceding assertions, we substitute the guess (1.61) into Bellman's equation to obtain

$$v(x) = \max_u\{x^TRx + u^TQu + \beta E[(Ax + Bu + \epsilon)^T$$
$$\cdot P(Ax + Bu + \epsilon)] + \beta d\},$$

where ϵ is the realization of ϵ_{t+1} when $x_t = x$ and where $E\epsilon|x = 0$. (Both prime ['] and superscript T denote transposition.) The above equation implies

$$v(x) = \max_u\{x^TRx + u^TQu + \beta E(x^TA^TPAx + x^TAPBu$$
$$+ x^TA^TP\epsilon + u^TB^TPAx + u^TB^TPBu + u^TB^TP\epsilon$$
$$+ \epsilon^TPAx + \epsilon^TPBu + \epsilon^TP\epsilon) + \beta d\}.$$

Evaluating the expectations inside the braces and using $E\epsilon|x = 0$ gives

$$v(x) = \max_u\{x^TRx + u^TQu + \beta 2x^TA^TPBu + x^TA^TPAx$$
$$+ \beta u^TB^TPBu + \beta E\epsilon^TP\epsilon\} + \beta d.$$

The first-order condition for u is

$$(Q + \beta B^TPB)u = -\beta B^TPAx,$$

which implies (1.63). Using $E\epsilon^TP\epsilon = \text{tr}E\epsilon^TP\epsilon = \text{tr}PE\epsilon\epsilon^T = \text{tr}P\Sigma$, substituting (1.63) into the preceding expression for $v(x)$, and using (1.61) gives

$$P = R + \beta A'PA - \beta^2A'PB(Q + \beta B'PB)^{-1}B'PA,$$
and $d = \beta(1 - \beta)^{-1}\text{tr}P\Sigma.$

This step concludes the demonstration of the claims about the optimal value function and the optimal decision rule.

It is a remarkable feature of this solution that, although through d the objective function (1.60) depends on Σ, the covariance matrix of the "noises" ϵ, the optimal decision rule $u_t = -Fx_t$ is independent of Σ. This is the message of (1.63) and the discounted algebraic Riccati equation for P, which are identical with the formulas derived earlier under certainty. In other words, when expressed in the feedback form $u_t = h(x_t)$, the optimal policy function that solves this problem is independent of the noise statistics of the problem. This feature is called the "certainty equivalence principle" by economists. This is a special property of the optimal linear regulator problem and is due to the quadratic nature of the objective function and the linear nature of the transition equation. Certainty equivalence does not characterize stochastic control problems generally.

For the stochastic optimal linear regulator, substituting the optimal control $u_t = -Fx_t$ into the transition equation gives the stochastic optimal closed-loop system $x_{t+1} = (A - BF)x_t + \epsilon_{t+1}$. Under the condition that $(A - BF)$ is a stable matrix (that is, one whose eigenvalue of maximum absolute value is less than unity in absolute value), the system converges as $t \rightarrow \infty$ to a unique stationary probability distribution. The spectral density of the stationary distribution is given by

$$S_x(\omega) = [I - (A - BF)e^{-i\omega}]^{-1} \Sigma [I - (A - BF)^T e^{+i\omega}]^{-1},$$
$$\omega \epsilon [-\pi, \pi].$$

Here $S_x(\omega)$ is the Fourier transform of the covariogram of x_t,

$$S_x(\omega) = \sum_{\tau=-\infty}^{\infty} C_x(\tau)e^{-i\omega\tau},$$

where $C_x(\tau) = Ex_t x_{t-\tau}$. The covariances $C_x(\tau)$ can be recovered from $S_x(\omega)$ by the inversion formula

$$C_x(\tau) = (1/2\pi) \int_{-\pi}^{\pi} S_x(\omega)e^{+i\omega\tau} d\omega.$$

Spectral densities for continuous-time systems are discussed by Kwakernaak and Sivan (1982). For an elementary discussion of discrete-time systems, see Sargent (1986). Also see Sargent (1986, chap. 11) for definitions of the spectral density function and methods of evaluating the above integral.

The preceding discussion shows how the stochastic optimal linear regulator provides a complete description of the theoretical second moments of the stationary distribution of the controlled process x_t. The mapping from (A, B, R, Q) to these theoretical moments that is implicitly described by the above equations is the foundation of econometric methods designed to estimate a wide class of linear rational expectations models (see Hansen and Sargent 1980, 1981). Briefly, these methods use the following procedures for matching observations with theory. A sample of observations for some elements of x_t, $t = 1, \ldots, T$, is assumed to be available. All possible sample second moments of the observations are calculated. How well the theory matches the observations is measured by choosing a metric that gives the distance between the sample moments and the theoretical moments associated with a given (A, B, R, Q). The metric is chosen not arbitrarily but in order to deliver good statistical properties of the estimates of (A, B, Q, R), consistency and asymptotic efficiency. Then A, B, Q, and R are estimated by choosing them to minimize the metric. For discussions of a good metric, see Hansen and Sargent (1980, 1982). The theory is "tested" by measuring how far the observations deviate from the theory, A, B, Q, and R being set at their best values.

As a simple example of a stochastic linear regulator problem, consider a monopolist who seeks to maximize

$$E_0 \sum_{t=0}^{\infty} \beta^t[P_t Y_t - J_t K_t - (d/2)(K_{t+1} - K_t)^2], \qquad 0 < \beta < 1$$

subject to $\quad P_t = A_0 - A_1 Y_t + \theta_t, \qquad A_0, A_1 > 0$
$\qquad\qquad\qquad Y_t = fK_t \qquad\qquad\qquad f > 0$
$\qquad\qquad\qquad J_{t+1} = \lambda J_t + \epsilon_{Jt}, \qquad\qquad |\lambda| < 1/\sqrt{\beta}$
$\qquad\qquad\qquad \theta_{t+1} = \mu\theta_t + \epsilon_{\theta t}, \qquad\qquad |\mu| < 1/\sqrt{\beta},$

K_0 given, J_t, θ_t, and K_t known at time t. Here P_t is output price, Y_t is output, J_t is the rental rate on capital, and θ_t is a random shock to demand, whereas ϵ_{Jt} and $\epsilon_{\theta t}$ are white noises. The maximization is over a stochastic process for K_{t+1} as a linear function of (K_t, J_t, θ_t).

To map this problem into the stochastic linear regulator problem, we define the state x_t as the vector $(K_t, J_t, u_t, 1)'$, whereas the control u_t is simply $K_{t+1} - K_t$. Then take A, B, Q, and R to be

$$A = \begin{bmatrix} 1 & 0 & 0 & 0 \\ 0 & \lambda & 0 & 0 \\ 0 & 0 & \mu & 0 \\ 0 & 0 & 0 & 1 \end{bmatrix}, \quad B = \begin{bmatrix} 1 \\ 0 \\ 0 \\ 0 \end{bmatrix}$$

$$R = \begin{bmatrix} -A_1 f^2 & -1/2 & f/2 & A_0 f/2 \\ -1/2 & 0 & 0 & 0 \\ f/2 & 0 & 0 & 0 \\ A_0 f/2 & 0 & 0 & 0 \end{bmatrix}, \quad Q = -d/2, \quad \epsilon_t = \begin{bmatrix} 0 \\ e_{Jt} \\ \epsilon_{\theta t} \\ 0 \end{bmatrix}$$

The optimal feedback law is an investment schedule of the form $u_t = -Fx_t$ or $(K_{t+1} - K_t) = -F(K_t, J_t, \theta_t, 1)'$.

Problems of the kind exhibited in this example can be formulated as stochastic discrete-time calculus-of-variations problems and can be solved as linear difference equations (see Sargent 1986). The methods involve two steps: (1) factoring the characteristic polynomial associated with the nonstochastic version of the problem in order to obtain the feedback and feedforward parts of the solution; and (2) utilizing the Wiener-Kolmogorov linear least-squares forecasting formula in order to express the feedforward part in terms of information available at the decision date. Notice that the linear regulator problem in effect accomplishes both optimization and prediction — and does so simultaneously via iterations on the matrix Riccati difference equation.

In Exercises 1.6 and 1.7, the reader is asked to take two problems with very large state spaces and to map them into linear regulator problems. These exercises are designed to show the chief advantage of the linear regulator framework: the tractability it retains even in the face of state spaces of very large dimension.

1.9 Dynamic Programming and Lucas's Critique

Recall the following version of the time-invariant, discounted stochastic control problem treated in Section 1.6, namely, to choose a strategy for u_t that maximizes

$$E_0 \sum_{t=0}^{\infty} \beta^t r(x_t, u_t), \qquad 0 < \beta < 1,$$

subject to $x_{t+1} = g(x_t, u_t, \epsilon_{t+1})$, $t \geq 0$, where ϵ_{t+1} is a sequence of independently and identically distributed random variables. We have seen that the solution is a time-invariant policy function $u_t = h(x_t)$ that satisfies the functional equation

$$(1.64) \qquad v(x_t) = r[x_t, h(x_t)] + \beta E(v(g[x_t, h(x_t), \epsilon_{t+1}])|x_t).$$

In general, the optimal policy $h(x_t)$ that solves the functional equation (1.64) depends on the return function $r(x_t, u_t)$, on the transition function $g(x_t, u_t, \epsilon_{t+1})$, on the probability distribution of ϵ_{t+1}, and on β. In particular, even with preferences [that is, β and $r(x_t, u_t)$] fixed, the optimal decision rule $u_t = h(x_t)$ depends on the law of motion $g(x_t, u_t, \epsilon_{t+1})$. The implication is that, in dynamic decision problems, it is in general impossible to find a single decision rule $h(x_t)$ that will be invariant with respect to variations in the laws of motion $g(x_t, u_t, \epsilon_{t+1})$. This principle is illustrated in a variety of ways in the examples that we have considered above.

Robert E. Lucas (1976) criticized a range of econometric policy evaluation procedures because they used models that assumed private agents' decision rules to be invariant with respect to the laws of motion that they faced. Those models took as structural (that is, as invariant under interventions) such private agents' decision rules as consumption functions, investment schedules, portfolio balance schedules, and labor supply schedules. The models were then routinely subjected to hypothetical policy experiments that changed the stochastic processes (or laws of motion, g) of such variables as income flows, tax rates, wage rates, prices, and interest rates, variables that entered private agents' constraints and decision rules. Those hypothetical experiments violated the principle that an optimal decision rule $h(x_t)$ is a function of the law of motion $g(x_t, u_t, \epsilon_{t+1})$.

Lucas's criticism was a particularly telling one because it embraced two of the fundamental ideas that underlay the enterprise of building large-scale Keynesian econometric models. First, there was the idea that for policy experiments it was important to isolate relationships that were structural, that is, invariant with respect to the class of interventions to be studied. Lucas observed that dynamic optimization theory ultimately implied that the key structural equations in Keynesian macroeconometric models, such as the consumption, investment, and portfolio balance schedule, should not be regarded as structural. Second, there was the idea that it was useful to derive the private agents' decision rules from the hypothesis of optimizing behavior in a dynamic context, an idea reflected with increasing sophistication by many works within the Keynesian tradition.

1.10 Dynamic Games and the Time Inconsistency Phenomenon

We now briefly describe the structure of a two-player dynamic, or "differential," game with no randomness. (A more general treatment of the issues described here is to be found in Hansen, Epple, and Roberds 1985; also see Basar and Olsder 1982.) The transition equation of the system is assumed to be

$$(1.65) \qquad x_{t+1} = g(u_{1t}, u_{2t}),$$

where x_t is again the state vector, u_{1t} is the control vector of the first player, and u_{2t} is the control vector of the second player. Player i has an objective described by

$$(1.66) \qquad \sum_{t=0}^{T} \beta^t r_i(x_t, u_{1t}, u_{2t}) + \beta^{T+1} V_{0i}(x_{T+1}), \qquad 0 < \beta < 1, \qquad i = 1, 2,$$

where $r_i(x_t, u_{1t}, u_{2t})$ is the return function of the ith player. Player i is assumed to maximize (1.66) subject to (1.65) with x_0 given and also subject to some particular assumption about player j's choice of $\{u_{jt}\}$ or about player j's way of choosing it. Alternative particular assumptions about how player i

imagines player j to choose u_{jt} determine the equilibrium concept of the game.

We first describe a particular version of a Nash equilibrium. Assume that player 1 takes player 2's actions $\{u_{2s}\}_{s=0}^{T}$ as given and as beyond player 1's control and that player 2 takes the symmetrical view with respect to player 1's actions. Then player 1's actions solve the following version of the system (1.8) of Euler equations and transition equations

(1.67a) $\quad \dfrac{\partial r_1}{\partial u_{1t}}(x_t, u_{1t}, u_{2t}) + \beta \dfrac{\partial g}{\partial u_{1t}}(u_{1t}, u_{2t})\dfrac{\partial r_1}{\partial x_{t+1}}(x_{t+1}, u_{1t+1}, u_{2t+1}) = 0,$

$\qquad t = 0, 1, \ldots , T - 1$

(1.67b) $\quad x_{t+1} = g(u_{1t}, u_{2t}), \qquad t = 0, \ldots , T,$

subject to x_0 given and $\{u_{2s}\}_{s=0}^{T}$ known, and the terminal condition

(1.67c) $\quad \beta^T \dfrac{\partial r_1}{\partial u_{1T}}(x_T, u_{1T}, u_{2T}) + \beta^{T+1} \dfrac{\partial g}{\partial u_{1T}}(u_{1T}, u_{2T})\dfrac{\partial V_{01}}{\partial x_{T+1}}(u_{T+1}) = 0.$

Analogously, player 2's actions solve

(1.68a) $\quad \dfrac{\partial r_2}{\partial u_{2t}}(x_t, u_{1t}, u_{2t}) + \beta \dfrac{\partial g}{\partial u_{2t}}(u_{1t}, u_{2t})\dfrac{\partial r_2}{\partial x_{t+1}}(x_{t+1}, u_{1t+1}, u_{2t+1}) = 0,$

$\qquad t = 0, \ldots , T - 1$

(1.68b) $\quad x_{t+1} = g(u_{1t}, u_{2t}), \qquad t = 0, 1, \ldots , T,$

subject to x_0 given and $\{u_{1s}\}_{s=0}^{T}$ known, and the terminal condition

(1.68c) $\quad \beta^T \dfrac{\partial r_2}{\partial u_{2T}}(x_T, u_{1T}, u_{2T}) + \beta^{T+1} \dfrac{\partial g}{\partial u_{2T}}(u_{1T}, u_{2T})\dfrac{\partial V_{02}}{\partial x_{T+1}}(x_{T+1}) = 0.$

In a Nash equilibrium, Equations (1.67a), (1.67b), (1.67c), (1.68a), and (1.68c) are solved jointly for $\{x_{t+1}, u_{1t}, u_{2t}\}$, $t = 0, 1, \ldots , T$.

We note two features of this equilibrium concept. First, each player's problem continues to be a recursive one, because under the assumption that the other player's actions are given, u_{it} affects returns $r_i(x_s, u_{1s}, u_{2s})$ dated t and later but not earlier. Thus each player's problem satisfies Bellman's principle of optimality. Second, we note that the entire system formed by (1.67a), (1.67b), (1.68a), and the terminal conditions is itself block recursive and can be solved by working backward, starting from date T. Thus the Nash equilibrium itself can be computed by recursive methods.

We now turn to a particular dominant-player game. We continue to assume that player 1 regards player 2's actions as given and beyond player 1's control. Player 2, however, is now assumed to understand that his controls influence agent 1's simply by virtue of the fact that agent 1's actions solve the Euler equation (1.67a), taking u_{2s} as given. Let us represent (1.67a), (1.67c) in the implicit form

(1.69) $\phi(x_t, x_{t+1}, u_{1t}, u_{1t+1}, u_{2t}, u_{2t+1}) = 0,$ $t = 0, 1, \ldots, T - 1$

$$\frac{\partial r_1}{\partial u_{1T}} (x_T, u_{1T}, u_{2T}) + \beta \frac{\partial g}{\partial u_{1T}} (u_{1T}, u_{2T}) \frac{\partial V_{01}}{\partial x_{T+1}} (x_{T+1}) = 0.$$

The decisions u_{1s} of the follower agent 1 are determined by (1.69) and by the relevant terminal condition, given x_0 and the actions u_{2s} of the leader. The leader is imagined to choose $\{u_{2s}, u_{1s}, s \geq 0\}$ to maximize (1.66) with $i = 2$, subject to both (1.65) and (1.69). We can represent the leader's problem as being to choose $u_{20}, \ldots, u_{2T}, u_{10}, \ldots, u_{1T}$, to maximize the Lagrangian

(1.70) $$L = \sum_{t=0}^{T} \beta^t r_2(x_t, u_{1t}, u_{2t}) + \beta^{T+1} V_{02}(x_{T+1})$$

$$+ \sum_{t=0}^{T} \beta^t \lambda_t'[g(u_{1t}, u_{2t}) - x_{t+1}]$$

$$+ \sum_{t=0}^{T-1} \beta^t \mu_t'[\phi(x_t, x_{t+1}, u_{1t}, u_{1t+1}, u_{2t}, u_{2t+1})]$$

$$+ \theta' \left[\frac{\partial r_1}{\partial u_{1T}} (x_T, u_{1T}, u_{2T}) + \beta \frac{\partial g}{\partial u_{1T}} (u_{1T}, u_{2T}) \frac{\partial V_{01}}{\partial x_{T+1}} (x_{T+1}) \right],$$

where $\lambda_t, t = 0, \ldots, T; \mu_t, t = 0, \ldots, T - 1$; and θ are each vectors of Lagrange multipliers. The maximization is performed with x_0 taken as given. The first-order necessary condition for the maximization of (1.70) with respect to u_{2t} is

(1.71) $$\beta \frac{\partial r_2(x_t, u_{1t}, u_{2t})}{\partial u_{2t}} + \beta \frac{\partial g(u_{1t}, u_{2t})}{\partial u_{2t}} \lambda_t$$

$$+ \beta \frac{\partial \phi}{\partial u_{2t}} (x_t, x_{t+1}, u_{1t}, u_{1t+1}, u_{2t}, u_{2t+1})\mu_t$$

$$+ \frac{\partial \phi}{\partial u_{2t}} (x_{t-1}, x_t, u_{1t-1}, u_{1t}, u_{2t-1}, u_{2t})\mu_{t-1} = 0,$$

$$t = 0, 1, \ldots, T - 1.$$

The reader is invited to obtain the remainder of the first-order necessary conditions and to analyze the resulting system of difference equations for determining $\{x_t, u_{1t}, u_{2t}\}$ via the solution of the dominant player's maximum problem. In addition, the reader is asked to verify that this system of equations is simultaneous and not block recursive (make a table for the system analogous to Table 1.1). This feature of the system and the nature of its cause can readily be seen by comparing (1.71) with (1.68a). In (1.71) the effects of u_{2t} for $t \geq 1$ on values of u_{1s} for $s < t$ and on *past* values of x_s and $r_2(x_s, u_{1s}, u_{2s})$ for $s < t$ are taken into account. Because the follower agent 1's actions at $s < t$ depend on u_{2t}, the leader's problem fails to be recursive. Accordingly, Bellman's principle of optimality may fail to characterize the leader's problem. The failure of the dominant player's problem to satisfy the principle of optimality is often called the time inconsistency of optimal plans.[4] Consequently the optimal plan is not generally self-enforcing in the sense described in Section 1.3 above.

Dynamic games occur in a variety of contexts in dynamic macroeconomics, industrial organization, and public finance. Early examples in macroeconomics were given by Kydland and Prescott (1977) and by Calvo (1978).

The following is a version of Calvo's (1978) example of a system in which private agents' responses to the government tax strategy confront the government with a nonrecursive problem in choosing a tax strategy. This example departs in some details from the preceding framework but exhibits the same essential nonrecursivity of the dominant player's (the government's) problem. The economy is one in which a representative private agent chooses c_t and m_{t+1} sequences to maximize

$$(1.72) \qquad \sum_{t=0}^{\infty} \beta^t u(c_t, m_{t+1}/p_t), \qquad 0 < \beta < 1,$$

subject to

$$(1.73) \qquad c_t + \tau_t + m_{t+1}/p_t = y(\tau_t) + m_t/p_t, \qquad m_0 > 0 \text{ given,}$$

where $u(c_t, m_{t+1}/p_t) = \ln c_t + \gamma \ln(m_{t+1}/p_t), \gamma > 0$. Here c_t is consumption of a single nonstorable good at time t, m_{t+1} is currency carried over from time t to $(t + 1)$, and p_t is the price level at time t. The government imposes a distorting tax (or subsidy) of τ_t at time t. Following Calvo, we represent the distortion by simply positing that output at t is given by a diminishing function of τ_t, $y(\tau_t)$ where $y' < 0$. The private agent maximizes (1.72) by choosing sequences c_t, m_{t+1}, where $t \geq 0$, taking as given the sequences τ_t, p_t.

---

4. For a solution to fail to satisfy the principle of optimality, it seems to be sufficient that there exist no way of reformulating the problem (say, by redefining variables) so that it becomes recursive. Some problems appear not to be recursive when written in one way but can be transformed into equivalent recursive ones.

The government seeks to maximize the utility of the representative agent (1.72), subject to the constraints

(1.74) $c_t + g_t = y(\tau_t)$

(1.75) $g_t = \tau_t + (m_{t+1} - m_t)/p_t,$

where $g_t \geq 0$, $t \geq 0$, is an exogenously given sequence of government purchases. Equation (1.74) is the economy's resource constraint, whereas (1.75) is the government's budget constraint. The government takes $\{g_t, t \geq 0\}$ as given and chooses sequences of $\{m_{t+1}, \tau_t, t \geq 0\}$ to maximize (1.72). In performing this maximization, the government is assumed to take as given that the economy is in equilibrium and that private agents are solving their optimum problem. Technically, this is an example of a "team" dynamic game, because the government and the private agent share the same objective function. Private agents are assumed to regard $\{p_t, \tau_t\}_{t=0}^{\infty}$ as given sequences.

An "equilibrium" is defined as a collection of sequences for $(m_{t+1}, \tau_t, p_t, c_t)$ that solve the optimum problems of both the private agent and the government.

It can be verified that a private agent's problem is a recursive one. If we let $y(\tau) + m/p$ be the state at t, Bellman's equation for this problem can be expressed as

$$v[y(\tau) + m/p] = \max_{c,m'}\{u(c, m'/p) + \beta v[y(\tau') + m'/p']\},$$

$$c + \tau + m'/p \leq y(\tau) + m/p.$$

By our usual methods the Euler equation for this problem can be rearranged to imply the difference equation

(1.76) $\dfrac{1}{c_t p_t} = \beta \dfrac{1}{c_{t+1} p_{t+1}} + \dfrac{\gamma}{m_{t+1}}.$

We now use (1.76) and the equilibrium condition $[c_t = y(\tau_t) - g_t]$ to solve for p_t as a function of the (m_{t+1}, τ_t) process chosen by the government. Substituting the equilibrium condition into (1.76), regarding (1.76) as determining p_t as a function of the m_{t+j} sequence, and solving the difference equation (1.76) forward produce

(1.77) $1/p_t = \gamma[y(\tau_t) - g_t] \displaystyle\sum_{j=0}^{\infty} \beta^j \dfrac{1}{m_{t+j+1}}.$

Equation (1.77) gives the equilibrium price level as a function of the sequences (τ_t, m_{t+1}) chosen by the government to finance the exogenously given g_t expenditure sequence. Equation (1.77) embodies the results of the Cagan effect (see Cagan 1956) by means of which expectations of future settings of the currency stock influence the current price level.

We now consider the government's problem, which is to maximize (1.72) subject to (1.74), (1.75), and (1.77) by choosing sequences for (τ_t, m_{t+1}). In maximizing subject to (1.77), the government is taking into account the fact that private agents behave in a way that makes the current price level a function of future m_{t+j}. If we substitute (1.74) and (1.77) into (1.72), the government's problem can be formulated as being the maximization of

$$(1.78) \qquad \sum_{t=0}^{\infty} \beta^t u \left(y(\tau_t) - g_t, \, \gamma m_{t+1}[y(\tau_t) - g_t] \sum_{j=0}^{\infty} \beta^j \frac{1}{m_{t+j+1}} \right),$$

subject to

$$(1.79) \qquad g_t = \tau_t + (m_{t+1} - m_t)/p_t,$$

by choosing sequences for τ_t and m_{t+1}, $t \geq 0$. This problem is evidently not a recursive one, because future values of the control m_{t+j+1} influence the government's return $u(c_t, m_{t+1}/p_t)$ at date t. The reason is that private agents respond to the government's choice of an m_{t+1+j} sequence by making the current price level respond to future settings of m_{t+1}.[5]

A consequence of the failure of the government's problem to be recursive is that the government's problem cannot be solved sequentially using the method of dynamic programming. As a result, the government's optimal plan will lack the self-enforcing character of dynamic programming solutions described above. In particular, if the government were imagined to reopen its planning process and to consider optimizing the "remainder" of (1.72) namely $\sum_{t=s}^{\infty} \beta^t u(c_t, m_{t+1}/p_t)$, $s > 0$, by choosing $\{m_{t+1}, \tau_t \text{ for } t \geq s\}$ subject to (1.74), (1.75), and (1.77), then in general the government would want to depart from the original plan for $(m_{t+1}, \tau_t, t \geq 0)$. This incentive would emerge because the government would want to neglect the effect of m_{t+1} for $t > s$ on p_v for $0 \leq v < s$ in setting m_{t+1} for $t > s$, an effect that was taken into account in the original plan for $\{m_{t+1}, \tau_t, t \geq 0\}$. This lack of a self-enforcement incentive is known as the time inconsistency problem.[6]

5. Hansen, Epple, and Roberds (1985) explicitly calculate a solution of the dominant player's problem for a class of linear-quadratic games. Their method is applied to a simple optimal taxation example in Sargent (1986). In these setups dynamic inconsistency of the optimal policy for the dominant player is evident from the time-varying form of its decision rule.

6. Lucas and Stokey (1983) study two versions of an optimal taxation problem. In their model without currency, they show that there exists a plan for restructuring the government debt each period that, if followed, renders the optimal tax plan time consistent. This finding can be regarded as providing a decentralization scheme between a tax authority and a debt-management authority that is capable of supporting an optimal plan in a self-enforcing way.

The time inconsistency phenomenon that is illustrated in Calvo (1978) also surfaces in a wide variety of other dynamic optimal taxation examples.

1.11 Conclusions

Recursive dynamic optimization is a main tool of macroeconomic modeling today. In this chapter most of the examples have been models of single agents (Section 1.10 on dynamic games is the exception). In the next three chapters, models will be constructed in which dynamic programming is used to compute and study dynamic general equilibrium models. In these models the single agent who is solving the problem is a fictitious social planner. Solving the planner's problem will be the instrument for computing sequences of equilibrium prices and quantities.

The reader is urged to tackle the exercises below. They provide the practice required for comfort with the notions of states and controls and for recognition of problems whose structure obeys the special conditions required to apply dynamic programming.

Exercises

Exercise 1.1. **Brock-Mirman (1972)**

Consider the Brock-Mirman problem of maximizing

$$\sum_{t=0}^{\infty} \beta^t \ln c_t, \qquad 0 < \beta < 1,$$

subject to $c_t + k_{t+1} \le Ak_t^\alpha, 0 < \alpha < 1, k_0$ given. Let $v(k)$ be the optimal value function. Use recursions on Bellman's equation (1.27), starting from $v_0(k) \equiv 0$ to show that

$$v(k) = (1 - \beta)^{-1}\left[\ln A(1 - \alpha\beta) + \frac{\alpha\beta}{1 - \alpha\beta} \ln A\beta\alpha \right] + \frac{\alpha}{1 - \alpha\beta} \ln k.$$

Exercise 1.2. **Howard Policy-Improvement Algorithm**

Consider the Brock-Mirman problem: to maximize

$$E_0 \sum_{t=0}^{\infty} \beta^t \ln c_t,$$

subject to $c_t + k_{t+1} \le Ak_t^\alpha\theta_t$, k_0 given, $A > 0$, $1 > \alpha > 0$, where $\{\theta_t\}$ is an i.i.d. sequence with $\ln \theta_t$ distributed according to a normal distribution with mean zero and variance σ^2.

Consider the following algorithm. Guess at a policy of the form $k_{t+1} =$

$h_0(Ak_t^\alpha \theta_t)$ for any constant $h_0 \in (0, 1)$. Then form

$$J_0(k_0, \theta_0) = E_0 \sum_{t=0}^{\infty} \beta^t \ln(Ak_t^\alpha \theta_t - h_0 Ak_t^\alpha \theta_t).$$

Next choose a new policy h_1 by maximizing

$$\ln(Ak^\alpha \theta - k') + \beta E J_0(k', \theta'),$$

where $k' = h_1 Ak^\alpha \theta$. Then form

$$J_1(k_0, \theta_0) = E_0 \sum_{t=0}^{\infty} \beta^t \ln(Ak_t^\alpha \theta_t - h_1 Ak_t^\alpha \theta_t).$$

Continue iterating on this scheme until successive h_j have converged.

Show that, for the present example, this algorithm converges to the optimal policy function in one step.

Exercise 1.3. Levhari and Srinivasan (1969)

Assume that

$$u(c) = \frac{1}{1 - \alpha} c^{1-\alpha}, \qquad \alpha > 0.$$

Assume that R_t is independently and identically distributed and is such that $ER_t^{1-\alpha} < 1/\beta$. Consider the problem

$$\max E \sum_{t=0}^{\infty} \beta^t u(c_t), \qquad 0 < \beta < 1,$$

subject to $A_{t+1} \le R_t(A_t - c_t)$, $A_0 > 0$ given. It is assumed that c_t must be chosen before R_t is observed. Show that the optimal policy function takes the form $c_t = \lambda A_t$, and give an explicit formula for λ.

Hint. Consider a value function of the general form $v(A) = BA^{1-\alpha}$, for some constant B.

Exercise 1.4 Habit Persistence: 1

Consider the problem of choosing a consumption sequence c_t to maximize

$$\sum_{t=0}^{\infty} \beta^t (\ln c_t + \gamma \ln c_{t-1}), \qquad 0 < \beta < 1, \qquad \gamma > 0,$$

subject to $\quad c_t + k_{t+1} \le Ak_t^\alpha,$
$\qquad\qquad A > 0,$
$\qquad\qquad 0 < \alpha < 1,$
$\qquad\qquad k_0 > 0, \quad \text{and} \quad c_{-1} \text{ given}.$

Here c_t is consumption at t, and k_t is capital stock at the beginning of period t. The current utility function $\ln c_t + \gamma \ln c_{t-1}$ is designed to represent habit persistence in consumption.

a. Let $v(k_0, c_{-1})$ be the value of $\sum_{t=0}^{\infty} \beta^t(\ln c_t + \gamma \ln c_{t-1})$ for a consumer who begins time 0 with capital stock k_0 and lagged consumption c_{-1} and behaves optimally. Formulate Bellman's functional equation in $v(k, c_{-1})$.

b. Prove that the solution of Bellman's equation is of the form $v(k, c_{-1}) = E + F \ln k + G \ln c_{-1}$ and that the optimal policy is of the form $\ln k_{t+1} = I + H \ln k_t$, where E, F, G, H, and I are constants. Give explicit formulas for the constants E, F, G, H, and I in terms of the parameters A, β, α, and γ.

Exercise 1.5 Habit Persistence: 2

Consider the more general version of the preceding problem, to maximize

$$\sum_{t=0}^{\infty} \beta^t u(c_t, c_{t-1}), \qquad 0 < \beta < 1,$$

subject to $c_t + k_{t+1} \leq f(k_t)$, $k_0 > 0$, c_{-1} given, where $u(c_t, c_{t-1})$ is twice continuously differentiable, bounded, increasing in both c_t and c_{t-1}, and concave in (c_t, c_{t-1}), and where $f'(0) = +\infty$, $f' > 0$, $f'' < 0$.

a. Formulate Bellman's functional equation for this problem.

b. Argue that in general, the optimal consumption plan is to set c_t as a function of both k_t and c_{t-1}. What features of the example in the preceding problem combine to make the optimal consumption plan expressible as a function of k_t alone?

Exercise 1.6. Lucas and Prescott (1971) and Kydland and Prescott (1982) Meet a Linear Regulator

Consider a linear quadratic version of a Lucas and Prescott (1971) model that has been modified to incorporate a rich time-to-build structure, à la Kydland and Prescott (1982). We first describe the model in terms of lag operators and then show how it can be mapped into a linear regulator problem.

The equilibrium of the model is supposed to solve the following problem:

(1)
$$\max E_0 \sum_{t=0}^{\infty} \beta^t \{(A_0 - A_1 Y_t + v_t)Y_t - J_t i_t - [d(L)K_t][g(L)K_t]\},$$

$$1 > \beta > 0, \qquad A_0 > 0, \qquad A_1 > 0,$$

subject to

(2)
$$Y_t = a(L)K_t$$
$$K_{t+1} = (1 - \sigma)K_t + z_t^0, \qquad 0 < \sigma < 1,$$
$$z_t^l = z_{t-1}^{l+1}, \qquad l = 0, 1, \ldots, S - 1$$
$$\alpha(L)J_t = \epsilon_{Jt}$$
$$\xi(L)v_t = \epsilon_{vt}$$
$$i_t = \sum_{j=0}^{S-1} \tau_j z_t^j$$

where

(3)
$$a(L) = a_0 + a_1 L + \ldots + a_N L^N$$
$$d(L) = d_0 + d_1 L + \ldots + d_N L^N$$
$$g(L) = g_0 + g_1 L + \ldots + g_N L^N$$
$$\alpha(L) = 1 - \alpha_1 L - \ldots - \alpha_p L^p$$
$$\xi(L) = 1 - \xi_1 L - \ldots - \xi_q L^q,$$

where N, M, R, p, and q are all nonnegative and finite. In (2), ϵ_{Jt} and ϵ_{ut} are fundamental white noises for J_t and u_t, respectively. At time t, variables dated t and earlier are observed.

In (1), Y_t denotes output, c_t is investment expenditures, J_t is the price of new capital goods, K_t is the stock of capital, and v_t is a random process disturbing demand. The technology potentially incorporates two sorts of time-to-build delays. First, output Y_t is a distributed lag, $a(L)K_t$, of the capital stock K_t that is in place. As a result, given the capital stock, the one factor of production, it requires time to produce output. Second, time elapses between the moment when investment decisions z_t^s are made at time t and the moment when the machines can be used as capital, z_{t+s}^0, at time $(t + s)$; z_t^j is interpreted as the number of machines in stage j available at time t. Only machines in stage 0 can increase the capital stock.

One interpretation of the parameters τ_j is that they represent the fraction of the total cost of a machine that is incurred when it is in stage j. Total expenditures in this concept, $\sum_{j=0}^{S-1} \tau_j z_t^j$, therefore correspond to investment at time j. It is also possible to think of the parameters τ_j as representing payments to another firm that "builds" the machines. In this sense they can reflect financing arrangements. The firm or industry also faces generalized costs of factor adjustment, which are represented by the cost term $[d(L)K_t][g(L)K_t]$.

This problem can be interpreted in a variety of ways. First, it can be interpreted as the solution of a monopoly problem, where the demand curve facing the monopolist is $p_t = A_0 - A_1 Y_t + v_t$, where p_t is the output price.

Second, it can be interpreted as the solution of a rational expectations competitive equilibrium where the demand curve is $p_t = A_0 - 2A_1 Y_t + v_t$. Third, it can be interpreted as the outcome of a particular kind of Nash equilibrium (see Hansen, Epple, and Roberds 1985).

a. Show how this general problem can be mapped into the structure of the optimal linear regulator problem. Specify the vector of states and controls and the matrixes R, Q, A, and B.

b. Display the solution in feedback form, and show the difference equation that governs the state under the optimal rule.

Exercise 1.7. Interrelated Factor Demand

For another illustration of a problem that can readily be mapped into the linear regulator framework, consider the interrelated factor demand problem, to maximize

$$-E \sum_{t=0}^{\infty} \beta^t \{ y_t^T F y_t + [G(L)y_t]^T [H(L)y_t] + J_t^T y_t \}$$

where $\quad y_t = \begin{pmatrix} y_{1t} \\ y_{2t} \end{pmatrix}, \quad J_t = \begin{pmatrix} J_{1t} \\ J_{2t} \end{pmatrix},$

F is positive semidefinite; $G(L) = G_0 + G_1 L + \ldots + G_m L^m$, $H(L) = H_0 + H_1 L + \ldots + H_m L^m$, where G_j and H_j are each (2×2) matrixes. It is assumed that $G_0^T H_0$ is positive definite.

Here J_t denotes a (2×1) vector of factor costs, y_t denotes a (2×1) vector of factors of production, and $[G(L)y_t]^T H(L)y_t$ denotes generalized costs of adjustment. The maximization is subject to a Markov law for J of the form $J_{t+1} = \alpha_1 J_t + \ldots + \alpha_{p+1} J_{t-p} + \epsilon_{t+1}$, where ϵ_{t+1} is a (2×1) vector white noise. At time 0, y_{t-j-1} and J_{t-j}, $j \geq 0$, are taken as given.

a. Specify this problem as a linear regulator by defining the states and controls x_t, u_t as well as the matrixes A, B, Q, and R.

Hint. It is easier to map the problem into the following more general version of the linear regulator problem.

$$\max E \sum_{t=0}^{\infty} \beta^t \left\{ (x_t^T, u_t^T) \begin{bmatrix} \overline{R} & \overline{W} \\ \overline{W}^T & \overline{Q} \end{bmatrix} \begin{pmatrix} x_t \\ u_t \end{pmatrix} \right\},$$

subject to $x_{t+1} = \overline{A} x_t + \overline{B} u_t + \epsilon_{t+1}$.

The following well-known argument indicates that there is no loss of generality — when Q is nonsingular — in restricting ourselves to the case in which $W = 0$. Simply note that the previous problem is equivalent to the following

$$\max E \sum_{t=0}^{\infty} \beta^t \{x_t^T(\overline{R} - \overline{W}\overline{Q}^{-1}\overline{W}^T)x_t + v_t^T\overline{Q}v_t\},$$

subject to $x_{t+1} = (\overline{A} - \overline{B}\overline{Q}^{-1}\overline{W}^T)x_t + \overline{B}v_t + \epsilon_{t+1}$, where $v_t = \overline{Q}^{-1}\overline{W}^Tx_t$ $+ u_t$. Therefore, defining R, Q, A, and B by

$$R = \overline{R} - \overline{W}\overline{Q}^{-1}\overline{W}^T$$
$$Q = \overline{Q}$$
$$A = \overline{A} - \overline{B}\overline{Q}^{-1}\overline{W}^T$$
$$B = \overline{B}$$

gives us the standard version of the problem.

Exercise 1.8. Two-Sector Growth Models

a. Consider the following two-sector model of optimal growth. A social planner seeks to maximize the utility of the representative agent given by $\sum_{t=0}^{\infty}\beta^t u(c_t, l_t)$, where c_t is consumption of good 1 at t, whereas l_t is leisure at t.

Sector 1 produces consumption goods using capital, k_{1t}, and labor, n_{1t}, according to the production function $c_t \le f_1(k_{1t}, n_{1t})$. Sector 2 produces the capital good according to the production function $k_{t+1} \le f_2(k_{2t}, n_{2t})$. Total employment, $n_t = n_{1t} + n_{2t}$, and leisure, l_t, is constrained by the endowment of time, $\bar{l}$, and satisfies $l_t + n_t \le \bar{l}$. The sum of the amounts of capital used in each sector cannot exceed the initial capital in the economy, that is, $k_{1t} + k_{2t} \le k_t$, $k_0 > 0$ given. Formulate this problem as a dynamic programming problem. Display the functional equation that the value function satisfies, and clearly specify the state and control variables.

b. Consider another economy that is similar to the previous one except for the fact that capital is sector specific. The economy starts period t with given amounts of capital k_{1t} and k_{2t} that must be used in sectors 1 and 2, respectively. During this period the capital-good sector produces capital that is specific to each sector according to the transformation curve $g(k_{1t+1}, k_{2t+1}) \le f_2(k_{2t}, n_{2t})$. Display the Bellman's equation associated with the planner's problem. Specify which variables you choose as states and which as controls.

Exercise 1.9. Learning to Enjoy Spare Time

A worker's instantaneous utility, $u(\cdot)$, depends on the amount of market-produced goods consumed, c_{1t}, and also on the amount of home-produced goods, c_{2t} (for example, entertainment, leisure). In order to acquire market-produced goods, the worker must allocate some amount of time, l_{1t}, to market activities that pay a salary of w_t, measured in terms of consumption good. The worker takes wages as given and beyond the worker's control. There is no borrowing or lending. It is known that the market wage evolves according to the law of motion $w_{t+1} = h(w_t)$.

The quantity of home-produced goods depends on the stock of "expertise" that the worker has at the beginning of the period, which we label a_t. This stock of "expertise" depreciates at the rate δ and can be increased by allocating time to nonmarket activities. To summarize the problem, the individual agent maximizes

$$\sum_{t=0}^{\infty} \beta^t u(c_{1t}, c_{2t}), \qquad 0 < \beta < 1,$$

subject to $\quad c_{1t} \leq w_t l_{1t}$ [budget constraint]

$\qquad\qquad c_{2t} \leq f(a_t)$ [production function of the home-produced good]

$\qquad\qquad a_{t+1} \leq (1 - \delta)a_t + l_{2t}$ [law of motion of the stock of expertise]

$\qquad\qquad l_{1t} + l_{2t} \leq \bar{l}$ [restriction on the uses of time]

$\qquad\qquad w_{t+1} = h(w_t)$ [law of motion for the wage rate]

$\qquad\qquad a_0 > 0$ [given].

It is assumed that $u(\cdot)$ and $f(\cdot)$ are bounded and continuous. Formulate this problem as a dynamic programming problem.

Exercise 1.10. **Investment with Adjustment Costs**

A firm maximizes present value of cash flow, with future earnings discounted at the rate β. Income at time t is given by sales, $p_t \cdot q_t$, where p_t is the price of good, and q_t is the quantity produced. The firm behaves competitively and therefore takes prices as given. It knows that prices evolve according to a law of motion given by $p_{t+1} = f(p_t)$.

Total or gross production depends on the amounts of capital, k_t, and labor, n_t, and on the square of the difference between current ratio of sales to investment, x_t, and the previous-period ratio. This last feature captures the notion that changes in the ratio of sales to investment require some reallocation of resources within the firm and consequently reduce the level of efficiency. It is assumed that the wage rate is constant and equal to w. Capital depreciates at the rate δ. The firm's problem is

$$\max \sum_{t=0}^{\infty} \beta^t \{p_t q_t - w n_t\}, \qquad 0 < \beta < 1,$$

subject to $q_t + x_t \leq g\left[k_t, n_t, \left(\dfrac{q_t}{x_t} - \dfrac{q_{t-1}}{x_{t-1}}\right)^2\right]$

$k_{t+1} \leq (1 - \delta)k_t + x_t, \qquad 0 < \delta < 1$

$p_{t+1} = f(p_t)$

$k_0 > 0, \quad \dfrac{q_{-1}}{x_{-1}} > 0 \quad$ given.

We assume that $g(\,\cdot\,)$ is bounded, increasing in the first two arguments and decreasing in the third. Formulate the firm's problem recursively, that is, formulate Bellman's functional equation for this problem. Identify the state and the controls, and indicate the laws of motion of the state variables.

Exercise 1.11. Investment with Signal Extraction

Consider a firm that maximizes expected present value of dividends. It is assumed that the price of the good produced by the firm is constant and equal to one. Production requires the use of a single input: capital that is firm specific. Total production, $f(k_t)$, is divided between sales, q_t, and investment, x_t. Revenue from sales is taxed at the rate τ_t. At time t, τ_t is known, as is z_t—a variable that is related to τ_{t+1} by the function $\tau_{t+1} = g(z_t, \epsilon_{t+1})$, where ϵ_{t+1} is an i.i.d. random variable that is not observed at t but whose distribution is known to the firm. Notice that, given z_t, the function g induces a conditional distribution of τ_{t+1} that we denote $F(\tau_{t+1}, z_t)$. The stochastic process $\{z_t\}$ is Markov with transition function $H(z', z) \equiv \text{prob}\{z_{t+1} \leq z' | z_t = z\}$. The capital stock depreciates at the rate τ. The problem faced by the firm is

$$\max E_0 \sum_{t=0}^{\infty} \beta^t(1 - \tau_t)q_t, \qquad 0 < \beta < 1,$$

subject to $q_t + x_t \leq f(k_t)$

$k_{t+1} \leq (1 - \delta)k_t + x_t, \qquad k_0 \text{ given}, \qquad 0 < \delta < 1.$

It is assumed that $f(k)$ is increasing, concave, and bounded.

Formulate the firm's problem as a dynamic programming problem (that is, display Bellman's equation).

References and Suggested Readings

Basar, Tamer, and Geert Jan Olsder. 1982. *Dynamic Noncooperative Game Theory.* New York: Academic Press.

Bellman, Richard. 1957. *Dynamic Programming.* Princeton, N.J.: Princeton University Press.

Bellman, Richard, and Stuart E. Dreyfus. 1962. *Applied Dynamic Programming.* Princeton, N.J.: Princeton University Press.

Benveniste, Lawrence, and Jose Scheinkman. 1979. On the differentiability of the value function in dynamic models of economics. *Econometrica* 47(3): 727–732.

Bertsekas, Dimitri. 1976. *Dynamic Programming and Stochastic Control.* New York: Academic Press. (Esp. chaps. 2, 6.)

Bertsekas, Dimitri, and Steven E. Shreve. 1978. *Stochastic Optimal Control: The Discrete Time Case.* New York: Academic Press.

Brock, William A. 1982. Asset prices in a production economy. In *The Economics of Information and Uncertainty,* ed. J. J. McCall, pp. 1–43. Chicago: University of Chicago Press.

Brock, William A., and Leonard Mirman. 1972. Optimal economic growth and uncertainty: the discounted case. *Journal of Economic Theory* 4(3):479–513.

Cagan, Phillip. 1956. The monetary dynamics of hyperinflation. In *Studies in the Quantity Theory of Money,* ed. Milton Friedman, pp. 25–117. Chicago: University of Chicago Press.

Calvo, Guillermo A. 1978. On the time consistency of optimal policy in a monetary economy. *Econometrica* 46(6):1411–1428.

Cass, David. 1965. Optimum growth in an aggregative model of capital accumulation. *Review of Economic Studies* 32(3):233–240.

Chow, Gregory. 1981. *Econometric Analysis by Control Methods.* New York: Wiley, 1981.

Hansen, Lars P., Dennis Epple, and Will Roberds. 1985. Linear-quadratic duopoly models of resource depletion. In *Energy, Foresight, and Strategy,* ed. Thomas J. Sargent, pp. 101–142. Washington, D.C.: Resources for the Future.

Hansen, Lars P., and Thomas J. Sargent. 1980. Formulating and estimating dynamic linear rational expectations models. *Journal of Economic Dynamics and Control* 2(1):7–46.

——— 1981. Linear rational expectations models for dynamically interrelated variables. In *Rational Expectations and Econometric Practice,* ed. R. E. Lucas, Jr., and T. J. Sargent, pp. 127–156. Minneapolis: University of Minnesota Press.

——— 1982. Instrumental variables procedures for estimating linear rational expectations models. *Journal of Monetary Economics* 9(3):263–296.

Koopmans, T. C. 1963. On the concept of optimal economic growth. Cowles Foundation Discussion Paper. Yale University, New Haven.

Kwakernaak, Huibert, and Raphael Sivan. 1972. *Linear Optimal Control Systems.* New York: Wiley, 1972.

Kydland, Finn E., and Edward C. Prescott. 1977. Rules rather than discretion: the inconsistency of optimal plans. *Journal of Political Economy* 85(3):473–491.

——— 1982. Time to build and aggregate fluctuations. *Econometrica* 50(6):1345–1371.

Levhari, D., and T. N. Srinivasan. 1969. Optimal savings under uncertainty. *Review of Economic Studies* 36(2):153–163.

Lucas, Robert E., Jr. 1976. Econometric policy evaluation: a critique. In *The Phillips Curve and Labor Markets,* ed. K. Brunner and A. H. Meltzer, pp. 19–46. Amsterdam: North-Holland, 1976.

——— 1977. Class notes on dynamic programming. University of Chicago. Unpublished.

——— 1978. Asset prices in an exchange economy. *Econometrica* 46(6):1426–1445.

Lucas, Robert E., Jr., and Edward C. Prescott. 1971. Investment under uncertainty. *Econometrica* 39(5):659–681.

Lucas, Robert E., Jr., Edward C. Prescott, and Nancy L. Stokey. *Recursive Methods for Economic Dynamics.* Forthcoming.

Lucas, Robert E., Jr., and Nancy Stokey. 1983. Optimal monetary and fiscal policy in an economy without capital. *Journal of Monetary Economics* 12(1):55–94.

Sargent, Thomas J. 1981. Lecture notes on filtering, control, and rational expectations. University of Minnesota, Minneapolis. Unpublished.

——— 1979. *Macroeconomic Theory.* New York: Academic Press.

——— 1986. *Macroeconomic Theory.* 2nd ed. New York: Academic Press.

2 | Search

This chapter applies dynamic programming in contexts in which there is a choice between only two actions, as distinguished from the situations studied in the previous chapter, in which the control was typically permitted to take on a continuum of values. The two actions are whether to accept or reject a take-it-or-leave-it offer. In particular, we shall study a variety of search problems, including several contexts in which a buyer or seller is confronted with a probability distribution of prices or characteristics of a job or good from which additional offers can be drawn at a fixed cost per offer. Given the worker's perception of the probability distribution of offers, the worker must devise a strategy for deciding how many offers to solicit before deciding to accept one.

The theory of search was pioneered by Stigler and McCall. It is interesting to macroeconomists because it provides a tool for studying the phenomenon of seemingly unemployed resources. We observe unemployed workers and pieces of capital and variations over time in aggregates of these variables. To explain these observations, search theory puts sellers of labor or capital in a setting in which they rationally *choose* to reject available offers and to remain unemployed in return for the opportunity to wait for better prospective offers in the future. We want to use the theory to study how workers' choices would respond to variations in the rate of unemployment compensation, the perceived riskiness of wage distributions, the quality of information about jobs, and the "technology" for sampling the wage distribution.

The present chapter aims to provide an introduction to the techniques used in the search literature and a sampling of search models. The chapter is also intended to offer further practice in applying the technique of dynamic programming.

2.1 Nonnegative Random Variables

Let us begin with some characteristics of nonnegative random variables that possess first moments. We consider a random variable p with a cumulative probability distribution function $F(P)$ defined by $\text{prob}\{p \le P\} = F(P)$. We assume that $F(0) = 0$, that is, that p is nonnegative. We also have the conditions that $F(\infty) = 1$ and that F, a nondecreasing function, is continuous from the right. Later we shall add the assumption that there is an upper bound $B < \infty$ such that $F(B) = 1$, so that p is bounded with probability 1.

The mean of p, Ep, is defined by

(2.1) $$Ep = \int_0^\infty p \, dF(p).$$

Saying that $u = 1 - F(p)$, $v = p$, and using the integration-by-parts formula

$$\int_a^b u \, dv = uv \Big|_a^b - \int_a^b v \, du,$$

we verify that

$$\int_0^\infty [1 - F(p)] \, dp = \int_0^\infty p \, dF(p).$$

Thus we have the following important alternative formula for the mean of a nonnegative random variable:

(2.2) $$Ep = \int_0^\infty [1 - F(p)] \, dp.$$

Now consider two independent random variables p_1 and p_2 drawn from the distribution F. Consider the event $\{(p_1 > p) \cap (p_2 > p)\}$, which by the independence assumption has probability $[1 - F(p)]^2$. The event $\{(p_1 > p) \cap (p_2 > p)\}$ is equivalent to the event $\{\min(p_1, p_2) > p\}$, where "min" denotes the minimum. Therefore, if we use formula (2.2), the random variable $\min(p_1, p_2)$ has mean

(2.3) $$E \min(p_1, p_2) = \int_0^\infty [1 - F(p)]^2 \, dp.$$

Similarly, if $p_1, p_2, \ldots, p_n$ are n independent random variables drawn from F, we have that $\text{prob}\{\min(p_1, p_2, \ldots, p_n) > p\} = [1 - F(p)]^n$ and that

(2.4) $M_n \equiv E \min(p_1, p_2, \ldots, p_n) = \int_0^\infty [1 - F(p)]^n \, dp,$

where M_n is defined as the expected value of the minimum of $p_1, \ldots, p_n$.

2.2 Stigler's Model of Search

Using formula (2.4), we can display George Stigler's (1961) model of searching for the lowest price p drawn from known distribution $F(p)$. Stigler imagines that, at a constant cost of c per offer or draw, an agent can solicit additional offers. The agent's problem is to specify the number of offers, n, to solicit in advance of searching. The number of offers, n, is required to be a positive integer. Stigler models the agent as selecting the number of offers to minimize the expected minimum price plus the total costs of search:

$$M_n + nc = \int_0^\infty [1 - F(p)]^n \, dp + nc.$$

Define the decrease in the expected minimum price of searching an nth time, $n \geq 2$, as

$$G_n = M_{n-1} - M_n = \int_0^\infty [1 - F(p)]^{n-1} \, dp - \int_0^\infty [1 - F(p)]^n \, dp$$

or

(2.5) $G_n = \int_0^\infty [1 - F(p)]^{n-1} F(p) \, dp.$

From (2.5) we have that $G_n > 0$, that G_n is a decreasing function of n, and that $\lim_{n \to \infty} G_n = 0$. The rule derived by Stigler is to set n so that $G_n \geq c > G_{n+1}$, so that the cost of search is less than the decrease in the expected minimum price resulting from the nth search but exceeds the decrease in the expected minimum price resulting from search $(n + 1)$. According to this model, n is a function of c and of F. An increase in c causes n to decrease. (A "mean-preserving increase in spread" in the sense to be defined below, can be shown to imply that n increases, given c.)

Stigler's model has been criticized because it attributes to the agent the objective of minimizing over the number of searches, n, the expected minimum price over n searches plus the total costs of search. That objective is distinct from and presumably less sensible than that of devising a strategy to minimize the expected value of the random variable "price plus total costs of search." These two objectives are evidently not equivalent. The second one corresponds to searching for the lowest price. The limitation of the former objective can be seen from the fact that it leads to a decision rule that is not *sequential*. Imagine that, on the very first draw, an agent is fortunate enough to draw the minimum price, that is, the price p for which $F(p) = 0$. It is pointless to search further, yet the objective function posited by Stigler and the decision rule derived under it require the agent to search n times. Presumably the minimization of the alternative objective of expected price plus total search costs will involve a *sequential* strategy that inspects each draw and, depending on its value, determines whether or not to continue the search.

2.3 Sequential Search for the Lowest Price

We first solve a version of the problem in which there is *no recall* of past offers. The agent searches by selecting independent drawings from the distribution F, at a cost of c per drawing. The agent can accept the offer currently in hand or can reject it without possibility of recall and then sample once again. Consider the problem of an agent who has offer s in hand. Let the function $v(s)$ be the minimum expected price plus the additional search costs of an agent who has offer s in hand and who behaves optimally. The agent can take either of two actions: (1) accept the offer s and terminate the search or (2) reject the offer, bear an additional search cost c, and draw a new price s'. For this problem, Bellman's equation is then

$$(2.6) \qquad v(s) = \min\{s, c + \int v(s') \, dF(s')\}.$$

A graph of $v(s)$ appears in Figure 2.1. Because $c + \int v(s') \, dF(s')$ is simply a positive constant, the graph of $v(s)$ must be as it is depicted in Figure 2.1. Evidently there exists a critical number $\bar{s} = c + \int_0^\infty v(s') \, dF(s')$ such that

$$(2.7) \qquad v(s) = \begin{cases} s & \text{for } s \le \bar{s} \\ \bar{s} = c + \displaystyle\int_0^\infty v(s') \, dF(s') & \text{for } s \ge \bar{s}. \end{cases}$$

Evidently the optimal strategy is to reject offers $s \ge \bar{s}$ and to accept offers $s \le \bar{s}$. The optimal strategy is thus to set a *reservation price* $\bar{s}$.

To characterize $\bar{s}$ in terms of F and c, use (2.7) to write

$$\bar{s} = c + \int_0^\infty v(s') \, dF(s')$$

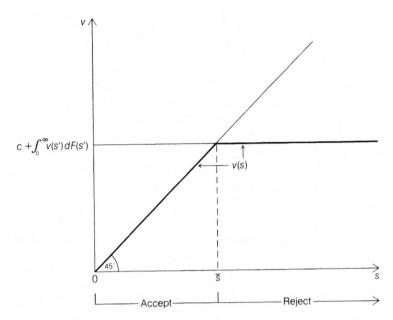

Figure 2.1. The function $v(s) = \min\{s, c + \int_0^\infty v(s')dF(s')\}$. The critical number $\bar{s}$ satisfies $\bar{s} = c + \int_0^\infty v(s')dF(s')$. The optimal strategy is to accept $s \le \bar{s}$.

or $\qquad \bar{s} = c + \displaystyle\int_0^{\bar{s}} s\,dF(s) + \bar{s}\int_{\bar{s}}^\infty dF(s)$

or $\qquad \bar{s}\displaystyle\int_0^{\bar{s}} dF(s) + \bar{s}\int_{\bar{s}}^\infty dF(s) = c + \int_0^{\bar{s}} s\,dF(s) + \bar{s}\int_{\bar{s}}^\infty dF(s).$

Rearranging the above equation gives the characterization

(2.8) $\qquad \displaystyle\int_0^{\bar{s}} (\bar{s} - s)\,dF(s) = c.$

Now define $u = (\bar{s} - s)$, $dv = dF(s)$, and use the integration-by-parts formula $\int u\,dv = uv - \int v\,du$ to get $\int_0^{\bar{s}} (\bar{s} - s)\,dF(s) = \int_0^{\bar{s}} F(s)\,ds$. Substituting this equation into (2.8) gives the useful characterization

(2.9) $\qquad \displaystyle\int_0^{\bar{s}} F(s)\,ds = c.$

Define the function

(2.10) $\qquad g(s) = \displaystyle\int_0^s F(p)\,dp.$

This function has the characteristics that $g(0) = 0$, $g(s) \geq 0$, $g'(s) = F(s) > 0$, and $g''(s) = F'(s) > 0$ for $s > 0$. Thus we can depict the determination of the optimal reservation price $\bar{s}$ as in Figure 2.2.

We now consider search with recall. The agent sequentially makes independent drawings from distribution F at a cost of c per draw. After each drawing, the agent can accept it or any previous drawing or else can elect to continue the search by making an additional drawing at a cost c. We now let s denote the best offer that the agent has received thus far. We define $J(s)$ as the minimum expected price plus additional search costs of an agent who has best price offer s in hand and who behaves optimally. The agent can accept the offer s, in which case $J(s) = s$. Alternatively, the agent can elect to reject s at this time while retaining the option to recall it and sample once more at a cost c. The value of taking this alternative is $c + J(s) \int_s^\infty dF(s') + \int_0^s J(s') \, dF(s')$, the second term reflecting the event that $s' > s$ and the third term reflecting the event $s' < s$. Thus Bellman's equation becomes

$$(2.11) \quad J(s) = \min\{s, c + J(s) \int_s^\infty dF(s') + \int_0^s J(s') \, dF(s')\}.$$

It is natural to conjecture that the solution of the problem with recall is identical to the solution of the problem without recall. This conjecture is motivated by the form of the optimal rule for the problem without recall, in

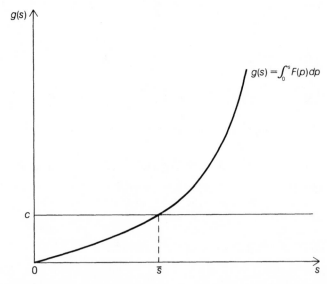

Figure 2.2. The optimal reservation price $\bar{s}$, given the cost per draw c and the distribution $F(p)$.

which the agent accepts the first offer less than $\bar{s}$ that comes along, a form of rule in which the agent seems not to be constrained by the inability to recall past offers. Thus we guess that the functional equation (2.11) has the solution

$$(2.12) \qquad J(s) = \begin{cases} s & \text{for } s \leq \bar{s} \\ \bar{s} & \text{for } s \geq \bar{s}, \end{cases}$$

where $\bar{s}$ satisfies $\bar{s} = c + \int_0^{\bar{s}} s\, dF(s) + \bar{s} \int_{\bar{s}}^{\infty} dF(s)$, the same condition that was implied by (2.7). It is straightforward to verify that this guess is correct and that consequently the optimal policy is to set a reservation price $\bar{s}$ that again satisfies (2.9) and to accept the first offer that comes along that is less than $\bar{s}$.

Under the guess (2.12), for $s \geq \bar{s}$, (2.11) becomes

$$J(s) = \min\{s, c + \bar{s} \int_{\bar{s}}^{\infty} dF(s') + \int_0^{\bar{s}} s'\, dF(s')\}$$

or $\qquad J(s) = \min\{s, \bar{s}\} = \bar{s}$,

which verifies the guess for $s \geq \bar{s}$. For $s \leq \bar{s}$, (2.11) becomes

$$J(s) = \min\{s, c + s \int_s^{\infty} dF(s') + \int_0^{s} s'\, dF(s')\}.$$

Define the term $c + s \int_s^{\infty} dF(s') + \int_0^{s} s'\, dF(s') \equiv \phi(s)$. Note that $\phi(\bar{s}) \equiv \bar{s}$, which implies that $J(\bar{s}) = \bar{s}$, as required. It remains to establish that for $s < \bar{s}$, $J(s) = s$. This point can be established if we can show that $\phi(s) > s$ for $s < \bar{s}$, which follows from the facts that $\phi(\bar{s}) = \bar{s}$ and that, by Leibniz's rule, $\phi'(s) = \int_s^{\infty} dF(s) < 1$.

Thus we have verified that our guess about $J(s)$ solves the functional equation. It is known that functional equations of the form of (2.11) have a unique solution. See the Appendix for a method of proof.

2.4 Mean-Preserving Spreads

Rothschild and Stiglitz have introduced the notion of mean-preserving spreads as a convenient way of characterizing the riskiness of two distributions with the same mean. Consider a class of distributions with the same mean. We index this class by a parameter r belonging to some set R. For the rth distribution we denote $\text{prob}\{p \leq P\} = F(P, r)$. We assume that there is a single finite B such that $F(B, r) = 1$ for all r in R and continue to assume as above that $F(0, r) = 0$ for all r in R, so that we are considering a class of distributions R for nonnegative, bounded random variables.

From (2.2) above, we now have that $Ep = \int_0^B [1 - F(s, r)] \, ds$, or

(2.13) $Ep = B - \displaystyle\int_0^B F(s, r) \, ds.$

Therefore, two distributions with the same value of $\int_0^B F(s, r) \, ds$ have identical means. We write this as the identical means condition:

(i) $\displaystyle\int_0^B [F(\theta, r_1) - F(\theta, r_2)] \, d\theta = 0$

Two distributions r_1, r_2 are said to satisfy the single-crossing property if (ii) there exists a $\hat{\theta}$ with $0 < \hat{\theta} < B$ such that

(ii) $F(\theta, r_2) - F(\theta, r_1) \leq 0 \, (\geq 0)$ when $\theta \geq (\leq) \, \hat{\theta}.$

Figure 2.3 illustrates the single-crossing property. If two distributions r_1 and r_2 satisfy (i) and (ii), we can regard distribution r_2 as having been obtained from r_1 by a process that shifts probability toward the tails of the distribution while keeping the mean constant.

Properties (i) and (ii) imply (iii), the following property:

(iii) $\displaystyle\int_0^y [F(\theta, r_2) - F(\theta, r_1)] \, d\theta \geq 0,$ $0 \leq y \leq B.$

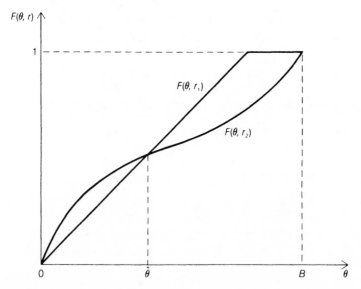

Figure 2.3. Two distributions, r_1 and r_2, that satisfy the single-crossing property.

Rothschild and Stiglitz regard properties (i) and (iii) as defining the concept of a "mean-preserving increase in spread." In particular, a distribution indexed by r_2 is said to have been obtained from a distribution indexed by r_1 by a mean-preserving increase in spread if the two distributions satisfy (i) and (iii).[1]

For infinitesimal changes in r, Diamond and Stiglitz use the differential versions of (i) and (iii) to rank distributions with the same mean in order of riskiness. An increase in r is said to represent a mean-preserving increase in risk if

$$\text{(iv)} \quad \int_0^B F_r(\theta, r) \, d\theta = 0$$

$$\text{(v)} \quad \int_0^y F_r(\theta, r) \, d\theta \geq 0, \qquad 0 \leq y \leq B,$$

where $F_r(\theta, r) = \partial F(\theta, r)/\partial r$.

2.5 Increases in Risk and the Reservation Price

From Equation (2.9) or Figure 2.2, together with condition (iii) or (v), it immediately follows that a mean-preserving increase in spread causes the reservation price $\bar{s}$ to decrease. In other words, with a given mean, the appropriate response to a riskier distribution is to become choosier and to hold out for a lower price.

Given the mean, the buyer is better off with a riskier price distribution. The reason is that the frequency of both relatively high and relatively low prices increases when the price distribution becomes riskier. The buyer is "censoring" the price distribution by means of a reservation price strategy. Under such a decision rule, given the mean, a riskier price distribution is more desirable because it gives a censored price distribution with a lower mean net of search costs.

2.6 Intertemporal Job Search

We now consider an unemployed worker who is searching for a job in real time under the following circumstances. Each period the worker draws one

---

1. Rothschild and Stiglitz (1970, 1971) use (i) and (iii) to characterize mean-preserving spreads rather than (i) and (ii) because (i) and (ii) fail to possess transitivity. That is, if $F(\theta, r_2)$ is obtained from $F(\theta, r_1)$ via a mean-preserving spread in the sense that the term has in (i) and (ii), and $F(\theta, r_3)$ is obtained from $F(\theta, r_2)$ via a mean-preserving spread in the sense of (i) and (ii), it does not follow that $F(\theta, r_3)$ satisfies the single crossing property (ii) vis-à-vis distribution $F(\theta, r_1)$. A definition based on (i) and (iii), however, does provide a transitive ordering, which is a desirable feature for a definition designed to order distributions according to their riskiness.

offer w from the same wage distribution $F(W) = \text{prob}\{w \leq W\}$, with $F(0) = 0$, $F(B) = 1$ for $B < \infty$. The worker has the option of rejecting the offer, in which case he or she receives c this period in unemployment compensation and waits until next period to draw another offer from F; alternatively, the worker can accept the offer to work at w, in which case he or she receives a wage of w per period forever. Neither quitting nor firing is permitted.

Let y_t be the worker's income in period t. We have that $y_t = c$ if the worker is unemployed and that $y_t = w$ if the worker has accepted an offer to work at wage w. The unemployed worker devises a strategy to maximize $E \sum_{t=0}^{\infty} \beta^t y_t$ where $0 < \beta < 1$ is a discount factor.

Let $v(w)$ be the expected value of $\sum_{t=0}^{\infty} \beta^t y_t$ for a worker who has offer w in hand, who is deciding whether to accept or to reject it, and who behaves optimally. We assume no recall, for convenience. Bellman's functional equation becomes

$$(2.14) \qquad v(w) = \max \left\{ \frac{w}{1 - \beta}, c + \beta \int v(w') \, dF(w') \right\},$$

where the maximization is over the two actions, (1) accept the wage offer w and work forever at wage w or (2) reject the offer, receive c this period, and draw a new offer w' from distribution F next period. Figure 2.4 graphs the functional equation (2.14) and reveals that its solution will be of the form

$$(2.15) \qquad v(w) = \begin{cases} \dfrac{\bar{w}}{1 - \beta} = c + \beta \displaystyle\int_0^{\infty} v(w') \, dF(w') & \text{if } w \leq \bar{w} \\[3mm] \dfrac{w}{1 - \beta} & \text{if } w \geq \bar{w}. \end{cases}$$

Using (2.15), we can convert the functional equation (2.14) into an ordinary equation in the reservation wage $\bar{w}$. Evaluating $v(\bar{w})$ and using (2.15), we have

$$\frac{\bar{w}}{1 - \beta} = c + \beta \int_0^{\bar{w}} \frac{\bar{w}}{1 - \beta} \, dF(w') + \beta \int_{\bar{w}}^{\infty} \frac{w'}{1 - \beta} \, dF(w')$$

or

$$\frac{\bar{w}}{1 - \beta} \int_0^{\bar{w}} dF(w') + \frac{\bar{w}}{1 - \beta} \int_{\bar{w}}^{\infty} dF(w')$$

$$= c + \beta \int_0^{\bar{w}} \frac{\bar{w}}{1 - \beta} \, dF(w') + \beta \int_{\bar{w}}^{\infty} \frac{w'}{1 - \beta} \, dF(w')$$

or

$$\bar{w} \int_0^{\bar{w}} dF(w') - c = \frac{1}{1 - \beta} \int_{\bar{w}}^{\infty} (\beta w' - \bar{w}) \, dF(w').$$

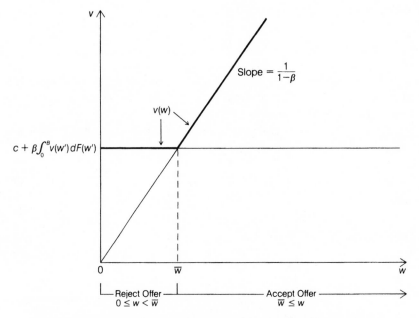

Figure 2.4. The function $v(w) = \max\{w/(1 - \beta), c + \beta\int_0^B v(w')dF(w')\}$. The reservation wage $\overline{w} = (1 - \beta)[c + \beta\int_0^B v(w')dF(w')]$.

Adding $\overline{w}\int_{\overline{w}}^\infty dF(w')$ to both sides gives

$$(2.16) \qquad (\overline{w} - c) = \frac{\beta}{1 - \beta}\int_{\overline{w}}^\infty (w' - \overline{w})\, dF(w').$$

Equation (2.16) is often used to characterize the determination of the reservation wage $\overline{w}$. The left side is the cost of searching one more time when an offer $\overline{w}$ is in hand. The right side is the expected benefit of searching one more time in terms of the expected present value associated with drawing $w' > \overline{w}$. Equation (2.16) instructs the agent to set $\overline{w}$ so that the cost of searching one more time equals the benefit.

Let us define the function on the right side of (2.16) as

$$(2.17) \qquad h(w) = \frac{\beta}{1 - \beta}\int_w^\infty (w' - w)\, dF(w').$$

Notice that $h(0) = \beta/(1 - \beta)\, Ew$, that $h(\infty) = 0$, and that $h(w)$ is differentiable, with derivative given by

$$h'(w) = -\frac{\beta}{1 - \beta}[1 - F(w)] < 0.$$

We also have

$$h''(w) = + \frac{\beta}{1 - \beta} F'(w) > 0,$$

so that $h(w)$ is convex to the origin. Figure 2.5 graphs $h(w)$ against $(w - c)$, and indicates how $\overline{w}$ is determined. From Figure 2.5 it is apparent that an increase in c leads to an increase in $\overline{w}$.

To get an alternative characterization of the condition determining $\overline{w}$, we return to (2.16) and express it as

$$\overline{w} - c = \frac{\beta}{1 - \beta} \int_{\overline{w}}^{\infty} (w' - \overline{w}) \, dF(w') + \frac{\beta}{1 - \beta} \int_{0}^{\overline{w}} (w' - \overline{w}) \, dF(w')$$

$$- \frac{\beta}{1 - \beta} \int_{0}^{\overline{w}} (w' - \overline{w}) \, dF(w')$$

$$= \frac{\beta}{1 - \beta} Ew - \frac{\beta}{1 - \beta} \overline{w} - \frac{\beta}{1 - \beta} \int_{0}^{\overline{w}} (w' - \overline{w}) \, dF(w')$$

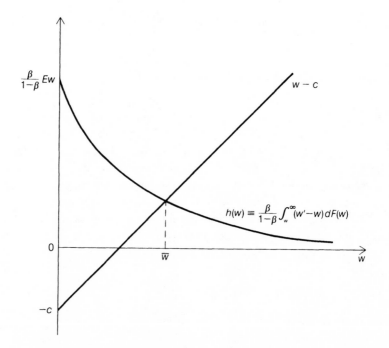

Figure 2.5. The reservation wage, $\overline{w}$, that satisfies $\overline{w} - c = [\beta/(1 - \beta)] \int_{\overline{w}}^{\infty} (w' - \overline{w}) dF(w') \equiv h(\overline{w})$.

or $\qquad \overline{w} - (1 - \beta)c = \beta Ew - \beta \int_0^{\overline{w}} (w' - \overline{w}) \, dF(w').$

Applying integration by parts to the last integral on the right side and re-arranging, we have

(2.18) $\qquad \overline{w} - c = \beta(Ew - c) + \beta \int_0^{\overline{w}} F(w') \, dw'.$

Equation (2.18) can be expressed alternatively as $\overline{w} - c = \beta(Ew - c) + \beta g(\overline{w})$, where $g(s)$ is the function defined by (2.10). Recall that $g'(s) = F(s)$, which is between zero and one, and that $g''(s) = F'(s) > 0$. In Figure 2.6 we graph the determination of $\overline{w}$, using Equation (2.18). Figure 2.6 can be used to establish two propositions about $\overline{w}$. First, given F, $\overline{w}$ increases when the rate of unemployment compensation c increases. Second, given c, a mean-preserving increase in risk causes $\overline{w}$ to increase. This second proposition follows directly from Figure 2.6 and the characterization (iii) or (v) of a mean-preserving increase in risk. From the definition of g in (2.10) and the

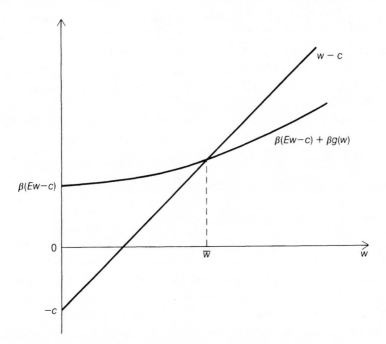

Figure 2.6. The reservation wage, $\overline{w}$, that satisfies $\overline{w} - c = \beta(Ew - c) + \beta\int_0^{\overline{w}} F(w')dw' \equiv \beta(Ew - c) + \beta g(\overline{w}).$

characterization (iii) or (v), a mean-preserving spread causes an upward shift in $\beta(Ew - c) + \beta g(w)$.

2.7 Waiting Times

It is straightforward to derive the probability distribution of the waiting time until a job offer is accepted. Let N be the random variable "length of time until a successful offer is encountered," with the understanding that $N = 1$ if the first job offer is accepted. Let $\lambda = \int_0^{\bar{w}} dF(w')$ be the probability that a job offer is rejected. Then we have that $\text{prob}\{N = 1\} = (1 - \lambda)$. The event that $N = 2$ is the event that the first draw is less than $\bar{w}$, which occurs with probability λ, and that the second draw is greater than $\bar{w}$, which occurs with probability $(1 - \lambda)$. By virtue of the independence of successive draws, we have $\text{prob}\{N = 2\} = (1 - \lambda)\lambda$. More generally, $\text{prob}\{N = j\} = (1 - \lambda)\lambda^{j-1}$, so the waiting time is geometrically distributed. The mean waiting time is defined as

$$\sum_{j=1}^{\infty} j \cdot \text{prob}\{N = j\} = \sum_{j=1}^{\infty} j(1 - \lambda)\lambda^{j-1}.$$

Using the algebra of z transforms, we say that $h(z) = \sum_{j=0}^{\infty} h_j z^j$ and note that $h'(z) = \sum_{j=1}^{\infty} j h_j z^{j-1}$ and $h'(1) = \sum_{j=1}^{\infty} j h_j$. (For an introduction to z transforms, see Gabel and Roberts 1973.) The z transform of the sequence $(1 - \lambda)\lambda^{j-1}$ is given by $\sum_{j=1}^{\infty} (1 - \lambda)\lambda^{j-1} z^j = (1 - \lambda)z/(1 - \lambda z)$. Evaluating $h'(z)$ at $z = 1$ gives, after some simplification, $h'(1) = 1/(1 - \lambda)$. Therefore we have that the mean waiting time is given by $(1 - \lambda) \sum_{j=1}^{\infty} j\lambda^{j-1} = 1/(1 - \lambda)$. As a result, the mean waiting time to a successful job offer equals the reciprocal of the probability of an accepted offer on a single trial.

EXERCISE. Prove that, given F, the mean waiting time increases with increases in the rate of unemployment compensation, c.

2.8 Firing

We now briefly consider a modification of the job search model in which each period after the first period on the job the worker faces probability $1 > \alpha > 0$ of being fired. The probability α of being fired next period is assumed to be independent of tenure. The worker continues to sample wage offers from a time-invariant and known probability distribution F and to receive unemployment compensation in the amount c. The worker receives a time-invariant wage w on a job until he or she is fired.

We let $v(w)$ be the expected present value of income of a previously unemployed worker who has offer w in hand and who behaves optimally. If she rejects the offer, she receives c in unemployment compensation this period and next period draws a new offer w', whose value to her now is $\beta \int v(w') \, dF(w')$. If she rejects the offer, $v(w) = c + \beta \int v(w') \, dF(w')$. If she accepts the offer, she receives w this period, with probability α that she is fired and must draw again next period receiving $\beta \int v(w') \, dF(w')$ and with probability $(1 - \alpha)$ that she is not fired, in which event she receives $\beta v(w)$. Therefore, if she accepts the offer $v(w) = w + \beta \alpha \int v(w') \, dF(w') + \beta(1 - \alpha)v(w)$. Thus Bellman's functional equation becomes

$$v(w) = \max\{w + \beta \alpha Ev + \beta(1 - \alpha)v(w), \; c + \beta Ev\},$$

where $Ev = \int v(w') \, dF(w')$. This equation has a solution of the form[2]

$$v(w) = \begin{cases} \dfrac{w + \beta \alpha Ev}{1 - \beta(1 - \alpha)}, & w \geq \overline{w} \\ c + \beta Ev, & w \leq \overline{w}, \end{cases}$$

where $\overline{w}$ solves $\quad \dfrac{\overline{w} + \beta Ev}{1 - \beta(1 - \alpha)} = c + \beta Ev.$

The optimal policy is of the reservation wage form. The reservation wage $\overline{w}$ will not be characterized here as a function of c, F, and α; instead the reader is invited to do so by pursuing the implications of the above formula.

2.9 Jovanovic's Matching Model

The preceding models invite questions about how we envision the determination of the wage distribution F. Given F, we have seen that the worker sets a reservation wage $\overline{w}$ and refuses all offers less than $\overline{w}$. If homogeneous firms were facing a homogeneous population of workers all of whom used such a decision rule, no wages less than $\overline{w}$ would ever be recorded. Furthermore, it would seem to be in the interest of each firm simply to offer the reservation wage $\overline{w}$ and never to make an offer exceeding it. These considerations reveal a force that would tend to make the wage distribution collapse to a trivial one concentrated at $\overline{w}$. This situation, however, would invalidate the assumptions under which the reservation wage policy was derived. It is thus a serious challenge to imagine an equilibrium context in which there survive both a distribution of wage or price offers and optimal search activity by individual

---

2. That it takes this form can be established by guessing that $v(w)$ is nondecreasing in w. This guess implies the equation in the text for $v(w)$, which is nondecreasing in w. This argument verifies that $v(w)$ is nondecreasing, given the uniqueness of the solution of Bellman's equation.

agents in the face of that distribution. A number of attempts have been made to meet this challenge.

One interesting effort stems from matching models, in which the main idea is to reinterpret w not as a wage but instead, more broadly, as a parameter characterizing the entire quality of a match occurring between a pair of agents. The parameter w is regarded as a summary measure of the productivities or utilities jointly generated by the activities of the match. We can consider pairs consisting of a firm and a worker, a man and a woman, a house and an owner, or a person and a hobby. The idea is to analyze the way in which matches form and maybe also dissolve by viewing both parties to the match as being drawn from populations that are statistically homogeneous to an outside observer, even though the match is idiosyncratic from the perspective of the parties to the match.

Jovanovic has used a model of this kind supplemented by a hypothesis that both sides of the match behave optimally but only gradually learn about the quality of the match. Jovanovic was motivated by a desire to explain three features of labor market data: (1) on average, wages rise with tenure on the job, (2) quits are negatively correlated with tenure (that is, a quit has a higher probability of occurring earlier in tenure than later), and (3) the probability of a subsequent quit is negatively correlated with the current wage rate. Jovanovic's insight was that each of these empirical regularities could be interpreted as reflecting the operation of a matching process with gradual learning about match quality. We consider a simplified version of Jovanovic's model of matching. (Prescott and Townsend 1980 describe a discrete-time version of Jovanovic's model, which has been simplified here.) A market has two sides that could be variously interpreted as consisting of firms and workers, or men and women, or owners and renters, or lakes and fishermen. Following Jovanovic, we shall adopt the firm-worker interpretation here. An unmatched worker and a firm form a pair and jointly draw a random match parameter θ from a probability distribution with cumulative distribution function $\text{prob}\{\theta \leq X\} = F(X)$. Here the match parameter reflects the marginal productivity of the worker in the match. In the first period, before the worker decides whether to work at this match or to wait and independently to draw a new match next period from the same distribution F, the worker and the firm both observe only $(\theta + \zeta)$, where ζ is a random noise that is uncorrelated with θ. Thus in the first period, the worker-firm pair receives only a noisy observation on θ. This situation corresponds to that when both sides of the market form only an error-ridden impression of the quality of the match at first. On the basis of this noisy observation, the firm, which is imagined to operate competitively under

constant returns to scale, offers to pay the worker the conditional expectation of θ, given $(\theta + \zeta)$, for the first period, with the understanding that in
subsequent periods it will pay the worker the expected value of θ, depending
on whatever additional information both sides of the match receive. Given
this policy of the firm, the worker decides whether to accept the match and to
work this period for $E[\theta|(\theta + \zeta)]$ or to refuse the offer and draw a new match
parameter θ' and noisy observation on it, $(\theta' + \zeta')$, next period. If the worker
decides to accept the offer in the first period, then in the second period both
the firm and the worker are assumed to observe the true value of θ. This
situation corresponds to that in which both sides learn about each other and
about the quality of the match. In the second period the firm offers to pay the
worker θ then and forever more. The worker next decides whether to accept
this offer or to quit, to be unemployed this period, and to draw a new match
parameter and a noisy observation on it next period.

We can conveniently think of this process as having three stages. Stage 1 is
the "predraw" stage, in which a previously unemployed worker has yet to
draw the one match parameter and the noisy observation on it that he is
entitled to draw after being unemployed the previous period. We let Q
denote the expected present value of wages, before drawing, of a worker who
was unemployed last period and who behaves optimally. The second stage of
the process occurs after the worker has drawn a match parameter θ, has
received the noisy observation of $(\theta + \zeta)$ on it, and has received the firm's
wage offer of $E[\theta|(\theta + \zeta)]$ for this period. At this stage, the worker decides
whether to accept this wage for this period and the prospect of receiving θ in
all subsequent periods. The third stage occurs in the next period, when the
worker and firm discover the true value of θ and the worker must decide
whether to work at θ this period and in all subsequent periods that he
remains at this job (match).

We now add some more specific assumptions about the probability distri-
bution of θ and ζ. We assume that θ and ζ are independently distributed
random variables. Both are normally distributed, θ being normal, with mean
μ and variance σ_0^2, and ζ being normal, with mean 0 and variance 1. Thus we
write

(2.19) $\theta \sim N(\mu, \sigma_0^2), \quad \zeta \sim N(0, 1).$

In the first period, after drawing a θ, the worker and firm both observe the
noise-ridden version of θ, $x = \theta + \zeta$. Both worker and firm are interested in
making inferences about θ, given the observation $(\theta + \zeta)$. They are assumed
to use Bayes's law, and to calculate the "posterior" probability distribution
of θ, that is, the probability distribution of θ conditional on $(\theta + \zeta)$. The

probability distribution of θ, given $\theta + \zeta = x$, is known to be normal, with mean m_1 and variance σ_1^2 given by[3]

(2.20) $$m_1 = \mu + \frac{\sigma_0^2}{\sigma_0^2 + 1}(x - \mu)$$

$$\sigma_1^2 = \frac{\sigma_0^2}{\sigma_0^2 + 1}.$$

After drawing θ and observing $x = \theta + \zeta$ the first period, the firm is assumed to offer the worker a wage of $m_1 = E[\theta|(\theta + \zeta)]$ the first period and a promise to pay θ for the second period and thereafter. (Jovanovic proved that this would be an equilibrium decision rule for the firm under competitive conditions.) The worker has the choice of accepting or rejecting the offer.

From (2.20) and the property that the random variable $x - \mu = \theta + \zeta - \mu$ is normal, with mean zero and variance $(\sigma_0^2 + 1)$, it follows that m_1 is itself normally distributed, with mean μ and variance $\sigma_0^4/(\sigma_0^2 + 1)$:

(2.21) $$m_1 \sim N\left(\mu, \frac{\sigma_0^4}{\sigma_0^2 + 1}\right).$$

Note that $\sigma_0^4/(\sigma_0^2 + 1) = \sigma_0^2/(1/\sigma_0^2 + 1) < \sigma_0^2$, so that m_1 has the same mean but a smaller variance than θ.

The worker seeks to maximize the expected present value of wages. We now proceed to solve the worker's problem by working backward. At stage 3, the worker knows θ and is confronted by the firm with an offer to work this period and forever more at a wage of θ. We let $J(\theta)$ be the expected present value of wages of a worker at stage 3 who has a known match θ in hand and who behaves optimally. The worker who accepts the match this period receives θ this period and faces the same choice at the same θ next period. (The worker can quit next period, though it will turn out that the worker who does not quit this period never will.) Therefore, if the worker accepts the match, the value of match θ is given by $\theta + \beta J(\theta)$, where β is the discount factor. The worker who rejects the match must be unemployed this period and must draw a new match next period. The expected present value of wages of a worker who was unemployed last period and who behaves optimally is Q. Therefore, Bellman's functional equation is $J(\theta) = \max\{\theta + \beta J(\theta), \beta Q\}$. This equation is graphed in Figure 2.7 and evidently has the

3. These formulas can be derived as applications of the recursive projection technique described in Sargent (1979, chap. 10). In the special case in which random variables are jointly normally distributed, linear least-squares projections equal conditional expectations.

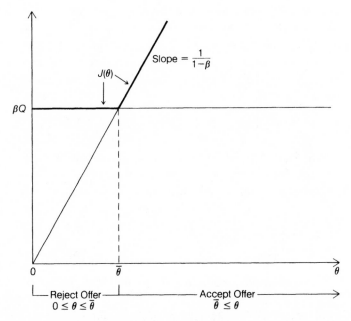

Figure 2.7. The function $J(\theta) = \max\{\theta + \beta J(\theta), \beta Q\}$. The reservation wage in stage 3, $\bar{\theta}$, satisfies $\bar{\theta}/(1 - \beta) = \beta Q$.

solution

$$(2.22) \qquad J(\theta) = \begin{cases} \theta + \beta J(\theta) = \dfrac{\theta}{1 - \beta} & \text{for } \theta \geq \bar{\theta} \\ \beta Q & \text{for } \theta \leq \bar{\theta}. \end{cases}$$

The optimal policy is a reservation wage policy: accept offers $\theta \geq \bar{\theta}$, and reject offers $\theta \leq \bar{\theta}$, where θ satisfies

$$(2.23) \qquad \frac{\bar{\theta}}{1 - \beta} = \beta Q.$$

We now turn to the worker's decision in stage 2, given the decision rule in stage 3. In stage 2, the worker is confronted with a current wage offer $m_1 = E[\theta|(\theta + \zeta)]$ and a conditional probability distribution function that we write as $\text{prob}\{\theta \leq s|\theta + \zeta\} = F(s|m_1, \sigma_1^2)$. (Because the distribution is normal, it can be characterized by the two parameters m_1, σ_1^2.) We let $V(m_1)$ be the expected present value of wages of a worker at the second stage who has offer m_1 in hand and who behaves optimally. The worker who rejects the offer is unemployed this period and draws a new match parameter next period. The expected present value of this option is βQ. The worker who accepts the offer receives a wage of m_1 this period and a probability distribution of wages of $F(\theta'|m_1, \sigma_1^2)$ for next period. The expected present value of this option is $m_1 + \beta \int J(\theta') \, dF \, (\theta'|m_1 \, \sigma_1^2)$. Bellman's functional equation for the second stage therefore becomes

$$(2.24) \qquad V(m_1) = \max \left\{ (m_1 + \beta \int J(\theta') \, dF \, (\theta'|m_1, \sigma_1^2), \beta Q \right\}.$$

Note that both m_1 and $\beta \int J(\theta') \, dF \, (\theta'|m_1, \sigma_1^2)$ are increasing in m_1, whereas βQ is a constant. For this reason a reservation wage policy will be an optimal one. The functional equation evidently has the solution

$$(2.25) \qquad V(m_1) = \begin{cases} m_1 + \beta \int J(\theta') \, dF \, (\theta'|m_1, \sigma_1^2) & \text{for } m_1 \geq \overline{m}_1 \\ \beta Q & \text{for } m_1 \leq \overline{m}_1. \end{cases}$$

If we use (2.25), an implicit equation for the reservation wage $\overline{m}_1$ is then

$$(2.26) \qquad V(\overline{m}_1) = \overline{m}_1 + \beta \int J(\theta') \, dF \, (\theta'|\overline{m}_1, \sigma_1^2) = \beta Q.$$

Using (2.26) and (2.22), we shall show that $\overline{m}_1 < \overline{\theta}$, so that the worker becomes choosier over time with the firm. This force makes wages rise with tenure.

Using (2.22) and (2.23) repeatedly in (2.26), we obtain

$$\overline{m}_1 + \beta \frac{\overline{\theta}}{1 - \beta} \int_0^{\overline{\theta}} dF \, (\theta'|\overline{m}_1, \sigma_1^2) + \frac{\beta}{1 - \beta} \int_{\overline{\theta}}^\infty \theta' \, dF \, (\theta'|\overline{m}_1, \sigma_1^2)$$

$$= \frac{\overline{\theta}}{1 - \beta} = \frac{\overline{\theta}}{1 - \beta} \int_0^{\overline{\theta}} dF \, (\theta'|\overline{m}_1, \sigma_1^2)$$

$$+ \frac{\overline{\theta}}{1 - \beta} \int_{\overline{\theta}}^\infty dF \, (\theta'|\overline{m}_1, \sigma_1^2).$$

Rearranging this equation, we get

$$(2.27) \qquad \overline{\theta} \int_0^{\overline{\theta}} dF \, (\theta'|\overline{m}_1, \sigma_1^2) - \overline{m}_1 = \frac{1}{1 - \beta} \int_{\overline{\theta}}^\infty (\beta \theta' - \overline{\theta}) \, dF \, (\theta'|\overline{m}_1, \sigma_1^2).$$

Now note the identity

$$(2.28) \qquad \overline{\theta} = - \frac{\beta}{1 - \beta} \int_0^{\overline{\theta}} \overline{\theta} \, dF - \frac{\beta}{1 - \beta} \int_{\overline{\theta}}^\infty \overline{\theta} \, dF$$

$$+ \frac{1}{1-\beta} \int_0^{\bar{\theta}} \bar{\theta} \, dF + \frac{1}{1-\beta} \int_{\bar{\theta}}^{\infty} \bar{\theta} \, dF,$$

where dF is understood as $dF(\theta'|\bar{m}_1, \sigma_1^2)$. Adding (2.28) to (2.27) gives

$$(2.29) \qquad \bar{\theta} - \bar{m}_1 = \frac{\beta}{1-\beta} \int_{\bar{\theta}}^{\infty} (\theta' - \bar{\theta}) \, dF(\theta'|\bar{m}_1, \sigma_1^2).$$

The right side of (2.29) is positive. The left side is therefore also positive, so that we have established that

$$(2.30) \qquad \bar{\theta} > \bar{m}_1.$$

Equation (2.29) resembles Equation (2.16), which we encountered above, and has a related interpretation. Given $\bar{\theta}$ and $\bar{m}_1$, the right side is the expected benefit of a match $\bar{m}_1$, namely the expected present value of the match in the event that the match parameter eventually turns out to exceed the reservation match $\bar{\theta}$ so that the match endures. The left side is the one-period cost of temporarily staying in a match paying less than the eventual reservation match value $\bar{\theta}$: having remained unemployed for a period in order to have the privilege of drawing the match parameter θ, the worker has made an investment to acquire this opportunity and must make a similar investment to acquire a new one. Having only the noisy observation of $(\theta + \zeta)$ on θ, the worker is willing to stay in matches m_1 with $\bar{m}_1 < m_1 < \bar{\theta}$ because it is worthwhile to speculate that the match is really better than it seems now and will seem next period.

Now turning briefly to stage 1, we have defined Q as the predraw expected present value of wages of a worker who was unemployed last period and who is about to draw a match parameter and a noisy observation on it. Evidently Q is given by

$$(2.31) \qquad Q = \int V(m_1) \, dG\left(m_1|\mu, \frac{\sigma_0^4}{1+\sigma_0^2}\right),$$

where $G[m_1|\mu_1, \sigma_0^4/(1+\sigma_0^2)]$ is the normal distribution with mean μ and variance $\sigma_0^4/(1+\sigma_0^2)$, which, as we saw above, is the distribution of m_1.

Collecting some of the equations, we see that the worker's optimal policy is determined by

$$(2.22) \qquad J(\theta) = \begin{cases} \theta + \beta J(\theta) = \dfrac{\theta}{1-\beta} & \text{for } \theta \geq \bar{\theta} \\[2ex] \beta Q & \text{for } \theta \leq \bar{\theta} \end{cases}$$

$$(2.25) \qquad V(m_1) = \begin{cases} m_1 + \beta \int J(\theta') \, dF\,(\theta'|m_1, \sigma_0^2) & \text{for } m_1 \geq \overline{m}_1 \\ \beta Q & \text{for } m_1 \leq \overline{m}_1 \end{cases}$$

$$(2.29) \qquad \overline{\theta} - \overline{m}_1 = \frac{\beta}{1 - \beta} \int_{\overline{\theta}}^{\infty} (\theta' - \overline{\theta}) \, dF\,(\theta'|\overline{m}_1, \sigma_1^2)$$

$$(2.31) \qquad Q = \int V(m_1) \, dG\left(m_1|\mu, \frac{\sigma_0^4}{1 + \sigma_0^2}\right).$$

To analyze formally the existence and uniqueness of a solution to these equations, one would proceed as follows. Use (2.22), (2.25), and (2.31) to write a single functional equation in V,

$$V(m_1) = \max \left\{ m_1 + \beta \int \max \left[\frac{\theta}{1 - \beta}, \beta \int V(m_1') \, dG \right. \right.$$
$$\left. \cdot \left(m_1'|\mu, \frac{\sigma_0^4}{1 + \sigma_0^2} \right) \right] dF\,(\theta|m_1, \sigma_1^2), \beta \int V(m_1') \, dG$$
$$\left. \cdot \left(m_1'|\mu, \frac{\sigma_0^4}{1 + \sigma_0^2} \right) \right\}.$$

The expression on the right defines an operator, T, mapping continuous functions V into continuous functions TV. The functional equation above can be expressed $V = TV$. The operator T can be directly verified to satisfy the following two properties: (1) it is monotone, that is, $v(m) \geq z(m)$ for all m implies $(Tv)(m) \geq (Tz)(m)$ for all m; (2) for all positive constants c, $T(v + c) \leq Tv + \beta c$. These are the conditions that Blackwell used to show that an equation $Tv = v$ has a unique continuous solution. See the Appendix.

We now proceed to calculate probabilities and expectations of some interesting events and variables. The probability that a previously unemployed worker accepts an offer is given by

$$\text{prob}\{m_1 \geq \overline{m}_1\} = \int_{\overline{m}_1}^{\infty} dG\,[m_1|\mu, \sigma_0^4/(1 + \sigma_0^2)].$$

The probability that a previously unemployed worker accepts an offer and then quits the second period is given by

$$\text{prob}\{(\theta \le \bar{\theta}) \cap (m_1 \ge \overline{m}_1)\} = \int_{\overline{m}_1}^{\infty} \int_{-\infty}^{\bar{\theta}} dF\,(\theta|m_1,\sigma_1^2)$$
$$\cdot dG\,[m_1|\mu,\sigma_0^4/(1+\sigma_0^2)].$$

The probability that a previously unemployed worker accepts an offer the first period and also elects not to quit the second period is given by

$$\text{prob}\{(\theta \ge \bar{\theta}) \cap (m_1 \ge \overline{m})\} = \int_{\overline{m}_1}^{\infty} \int_{\theta}^{\infty} dF\,(\theta|m_1,\sigma_1^2)\,dG\,(m_1|\mu,\sigma_m^2),$$

where $\sigma_m^2 = \sigma_0^4/(1+\sigma_0^2)$.

The mean wage of those employed the first period is given by

$$(2.32) \qquad \overline{w}_1 = \frac{\displaystyle\int_{\overline{m}_1}^{\infty} m_1\,dG\,(m_1|\mu,\sigma_m^2)}{\displaystyle\int_{\overline{m}_1}^{\infty} dG\,(m_1|\mu,\sigma_m^2)},$$

whereas the mean wage of those workers who are in the second period of tenure is given by

$$(2.33) \qquad \overline{w}_2 = \frac{\displaystyle\int_{\overline{m}_1}^{\infty} \int_{\theta}^{\infty} \theta\,dF\,(\theta|m_1,\sigma_1^2)\,dG\,(m_1|\mu,\sigma_m^2)}{\displaystyle\int_{\overline{m}_1}^{\infty} \int_{\theta}^{\infty} dF\,(\theta|m_1,\sigma_1^2)\,dG\,(m_1|\mu,\sigma_m^2)}.$$

We shall now prove that $\overline{w}_2 > \overline{w}_1$, so that wages rise with tenure. (The following argument is entirely due to Lars Hansen.)

We begin by evaluating (2.32), using the following formula from Johnson and Kotz (1971) for $E(x|x > \underline{x})$ where x is distributed $N(\mu, \sigma^2)$:

$$(2.34) \qquad E(x|x > \underline{x}) = \mu + \frac{\sigma\phi\left(\dfrac{\mu - \underline{x}}{\sigma}\right)}{\Phi\left(\dfrac{\mu - \underline{x}}{\sigma}\right)},$$

where ϕ is the standardized normal density, and Φ is the standardized normal cumulative distribution function. Applying this formula to (2.32), we get

$$\overline{w}_1 = \mu + \sigma_m \frac{\phi\left(\dfrac{\mu - \overline{m}_1}{\sigma_m}\right)}{\Phi\left(\dfrac{\mu - \overline{m}_1}{\sigma_m}\right)},$$

where $\sigma_m^2 = \sigma_0^4/(1 + \sigma_0^2)$. Use (2.34) to get

$$(2.35) \quad \int_{\overline{\theta}}^{\infty} \theta \, dF\,(\theta|m_1, \sigma_1^2) = m_1 \Phi\left(\frac{m_1 - \overline{\theta}}{\sigma_1}\right) + \phi\left(\frac{m_1 - \overline{\theta}}{\sigma_1}\right)\sigma_1$$

$$> m_1 \Phi\left(\frac{m_1 - \overline{\theta}}{\sigma_1}\right).$$

Also note that

$$\int_{\overline{\theta}}^{\infty} dF\,(\theta|m_1, \sigma_1^2) = 1 - \Phi\left(\frac{\overline{\theta} - m_1}{\sigma_1}\right) = \Phi\left(\frac{m_1 - \overline{\theta}}{\sigma_1}\right),$$

where the last equality follows from the symmetry of the normal density about its mean. Using (2.35) and the last equation, we have from (2.33) that

$$\overline{w}_2 = \frac{\displaystyle\int_{\overline{m}_1}^{\infty} \int_{\overline{\theta}}^{\infty} \theta \, dF\,(\theta|m_1, \sigma) \, dG\,(m_1|\mu, \sigma_m^2)}{\displaystyle\int_{\overline{m}_1}^{\infty} \Phi\left(\frac{m_1 - \overline{\theta}}{\sigma_1}\right) dG\,(m_1|\mu, \sigma_m^2)}$$

$$> \frac{\displaystyle\int_{\overline{m}_1}^{\infty} m_1 \, \Phi\left(\frac{m_1 - \overline{\theta}}{\sigma_1}\right) dG\,(m_1|\mu, \sigma_m^2)}{\displaystyle\int_{\overline{m}_1}^{\infty} \Phi\left(\frac{m_1 - \overline{\theta}}{\sigma_1}\right) dG\,(m_1|\mu, \sigma_m^2)} \equiv \tilde{w}_2.$$

Because $\overline{w}_2 > \tilde{w}_2$, if we can show that $\tilde{w}_2 > \overline{w}_1$, we will have shown that $\overline{w}_2 > \overline{w}_1$, as desired.

Define the density

$$(2.36) \quad \tilde{g}_2(m_1) = \begin{cases} \dfrac{\Phi\left(\dfrac{m_1 - \overline{\theta}}{\sigma_1}\right) g(m_1|\mu, \sigma_m^2)}{K_2}, & m_1 \geq \overline{m}_1 \\[4mm] 0, & m_1 < \overline{m}_1, \end{cases}$$

where $K_2 = \int_{\overline{m}_1}^{\infty} \Phi[(m_1 - \overline{\theta})/\sigma_1] \, dG\,(m_1|\mu, \sigma_m^2)$ and where $g(m_1|\mu, \sigma_m^2)$ is the normal density corresponding to the normal cumulative distribution function $G(m_1|\mu, \sigma_m^2)$. Let $\tilde{G}_2$ be the distribution function corresponding to $\tilde{g}_2$. Define the density

(2.37) $\qquad g_1(m_1) = \begin{cases} \dfrac{g(m_1|\mu, \sigma_m^2)}{K_1}, & m_1 \geq \overline{m}_1 \\ 0, & m_1 < \overline{m}_1, \end{cases}$

where $K_1 = \int_{\overline{m}_1}^{\infty} dG\,(m_1|\mu, \sigma_m^2)$. Let G_1 be the distribution function corresponding to g_1. Then evidently

(2.38) $\qquad \overline{w}_1 = \int_{\overline{m}_1}^{\infty} m_1\, dG_1\,(m_1) = \overline{m}_1 + \int_{\overline{m}_1}^{\infty} [1 - G_1(m_1)]\, dm_1$

(2.39) $\qquad \tilde{w}_2 = \int_{\overline{m}_1}^{\infty} m_1\, d\tilde{G}_2\,(m_1) = \overline{m}_1 + \int_{\overline{m}_1}^{\infty} [1 - \tilde{G}_2(m_1)]\, dm,$

where the second equalities follow from integration by parts.

Now using (2.36) and (2.37), we have that

(2.40) $\qquad \tilde{g}_2(m_1) = \dfrac{K_1}{K_2} \Phi\left(\dfrac{m_1 - \overline{\theta}}{\sigma_1}\right) g_1(m_1).$

Because Φ is a monotonically increasing function of m_1, given that $\overline{\theta} > -\infty$, and because both $\tilde{g}_2$ and g_1 are probability densities, it follows that there is an m_1^* such that

(2.41) $\qquad \tilde{g}_2(m_1) \gtreqless g_1(m_1) \qquad$ for $m_1 \gtreqless m_1^*$,

so that the densities have a single crossing, as illustrated in Figure 2.8. Therefore $\tilde{G}_2(m_1) < G(m_1)$ for $m_1 > \overline{m}_1$, and $1 - \tilde{G}_2(m_1) > 1 - G(m_1)$ for $m_1 > \overline{m}_1$. It then follows from (2.38) and (2.39) that $\tilde{w}_2 > \overline{w}_1$. Because $\overline{w}_2 > \tilde{w}_2$, it also follows that $\overline{w}_2 > \overline{w}_1$. Therefore mean wages rise with tenure. Notice that this argument works for any $\overline{\theta} > -\infty$ and does not require that $\overline{m}_1 < \overline{\theta}$.

The model thus implies that "wages rise with tenure," both in the sense that mean wages rise with tenure and in the sense that $\overline{\theta} > \overline{m}_1$, which asserts that the lower bound on second-period wages exceeds the lower bound on first-period wages. That wages rise with tenure was observation (a) that Jovanovic sought to explain.

Jovanovic's model also explains observation (b), that quits are negatively correlated with tenure. The model implies that quits occur between the first and second periods of tenure. Having decided to stay for two periods, the worker never quits.

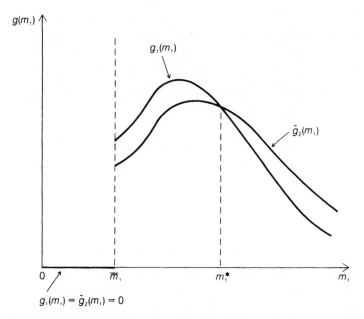

Figure 2.8. Probability densities $g_1(m_1)$ and $\tilde{g}_2(m_1)$ that have a single crossing point m_1^*.

The model also accounts for observation (c), namely that the probability of a subsequent quit is negatively correlated with the current wage rate. The probability of a subsequent quit is given by

$$\text{prob}\{\theta' < \bar{\theta}|m_1\} = \int_{-\infty}^{\bar{\theta}} dF\,(\theta'|m_1, \sigma_1^2),$$

which is evidently negatively correlated with m_1, the first-period wage. Thus the model explains each observation that Jovanovic sought to interpret. In the version of the model that we have studied, a worker eventually becomes permanently matched with probability 1. If we were studying a population of such workers of fixed size, all workers would eventually be absorbed into the state of being permanently matched. To provide a mechanism for replenishing the stock of unmatched workers, one could combine the Jovanovic model of Section 2.9 with the "firing" model of Section 2.8. By letting matches θ "go bad" with probability λ each period, one could presumably modify Jovanovic's model to get the implication that, with a fixed population of workers, a fraction would remain unmatched each period because of the dissolution of previously acceptable matches.

One could enrich the model above, as Jovanovic did, by assuming that the firm and worker never directly observe θ. Instead, for each period i that the match endures, they acquire an additional noisy observation $x_i = \theta + \zeta_i$, upon θ, where ζ_i is independently drawn from a normal distribution with mean 0 and variance 1. At each stage of tenure j, the firm best estimates θ by $m_j = E(\theta | \theta + \zeta_1, \theta + \zeta_2, \ldots, \theta + \zeta_j)$. Using the recursive projection formula or, equivalently, Bayes's law, it can be shown that m_j can be computed recursively via

$$m_j = \frac{h_{j-1}}{h_{j-1} + 1} m_{j-1} + \frac{1}{h_{j-1} + 1} (\theta + \zeta_j)$$

$$h_j = h_{j-1} + 1,$$

where $h_j \equiv 1/\sigma_j^2$, where σ_j is the conditional variance of m_j around μ. In this model there is a sequence of reservation wages $\overline{m}_j$ that rise monotonically with tenure j. Jovanovic analyzed a continuous-time version of this model.

Jovanovic's work is one outstanding example of an extension to the basic McCall model that has yielded valuable insights about labor market phenomena. A variety of other extensions have been proposed, some of which are described in the exercises and in the references.

2.10 Conclusions

The situations analyzed in this chapter are ones in which a currently unemployed worker rationally chooses to refuse an offer to work, preferring to remain unemployed today in exchange for better prospects tomorrow. The worker is "voluntarily unemployed" in one sense, having chosen to reject the current draw from the distribution of offers. In this model, the activity of unemployment is an investment incurred to improve the situation faced in the future. A theory in which unemployment is voluntary has the advantage of permitting an analysis of the forces impinging on the choice to remain unemployed. Thus we can study the response of the worker's decision rule to changes in the distribution of offers, the rate of unemployment compensation, the number of offers per period, and so on.

This chapter has aimed to provide an introduction to some of the methods used in search theory but has not sought to provide a comprehensive survey of the recent literature. There has recently been much creative research in this area. Especially noteworthy are recent models of equilibrium search, in which setups are devised for which the distribution of offers is endogenously determined. Versions of equilibrium search models have been constructed by Peter Diamond (1981), Mortensen (1982), Lucas and Prescott (1974), and Watanabe (1984). (Also see the papers by Albrecht and Axell 1984 and Reinganum 1979.)

In the work of Diamond (1981) and Mortensen (1982), the distribution of offers received by a given individual is a function of effort that the individual and other searchers devote to search activity. There is thus an externality in the technology for generating offers. In a Nash or competitive equilibrium, each searcher neglects the effects that his search effort has on the constraints faced by other searchers, generating a suboptimal equilibrium. In setups like Diamond's or Mortensen's, there is potential scope for other mechanisms to improve outcomes vis-à-vis the Nash or competitive outcome. Employment agencies, for example, can potentially improve matters, as can tax-subsidy schemes for search activity. A benefit of the explicit model of voluntary unemployment associated with search models is that such alternative mechanisms can be studied in a context in which individual agents purposefully adjust their search behavior in response to the mechanism that is in place.

In the models of Lucas and Prescott (1974) and Watanabe (1984), an equilibrium framework is devised for studying search activity over the business cycle. These models utilize the "island model" of Phelps (1970) to motivate an interpretation of a nontrivial offer distribution in terms of spatial separation and costly movement over space. Watanabe (1984) imposes a "statistical index structure" on the productivity shocks at each location, so that productivity in a given location is the sum of a serially correlated location-specific shock and an orthogonal economywide shock. Workers see only the current productivity in their own location. This stochastic structure confronts workers with a signal extraction problem that creates an equilibrium business cycle in the sense of serially correlated movements in the aggregate unemployment rate. Randall Wright (forthcoming) has used a version of a closely related setup to interpret U.S. time series on the aggregate unemployment rate.

Although this book will not pursue search theory further, two ideas associated with search theory will recur in later chapters that deal with monetary theory. First, in monetary theory as well as in search theory, physical separation in time and space plays a key role. In particular, setups will eventually be described in which spatial separation and patterns of movement of agents create a role for government-issued currency. Second, the discussion will focus on alternative monetary theories, including some in which government-issued currency is voluntarily held and others in which it is involuntarily held. The analytical advantages associated with a theory of voluntary unemployment will also recommend theories with voluntarily held currency.

Exercises

Exercise 2.1. **Being Unemployed with Only a Chance of an Offer**

An unemployed worker samples wage offers on the following terms. Each period, with probability ϕ, $1 > \phi > 0$, she receives no offer (we may regard this as a wage offer of zero forever). With probability $(1 - \phi)$ she receives an offer to work for w forever, where w is drawn from a cumulative distribution function $F(w)$. Successive drawings across periods are independently and identically distributed. The worker chooses a strategy to maximize

$$E \sum_{t=0}^{\infty} \beta^t y_t, \quad \text{where } 0 < \beta < 1,$$

$y_t = w$ if the worker is employed, and $y_t = c$ if the worker is unemployed. Here c is unemployment compensation, and w is the wage at which the worker is employed. Assume that, having once accepted a job offer at wage w, the worker stays in the job forever.

Let $v(w)$ be the expected value of $\sum_{t=0}^{\infty} \beta^t y_t$ for an unemployed worker who has offer w in hand and who behaves optimally. Write Bellman's functional equation for the worker's problem.

Exercise 2.2. **Two Offers per Period**

Consider an unemployed worker who each period can draw *two* independently and identically distributed wage offers from the cumulative probability distribution function $F(w)$. The worker will work forever at the same wage after having once accepted an offer. In the event of unemployment during a period, the worker receives unemployment compensation c. The worker derives a decision rule to maximize $E \sum_{t=0}^{\infty} \beta^t y_t$, where $y_t = w$ or $y_t = c$, depending on whether she is employed or unemployed. Let $v(w)$ be the value of $E \sum_{t=0}^{\infty} \beta^t y_t$ for a currently unemployed worker who has best offer w in hand.

a. Formulate Bellman's equation for the worker's problem.

b. Prove that the worker's reservation wage is *higher* than it would be had the worker faced the same c and been drawing only *one* offer from the same distribution $F(w)$ each period.

Exercise 2.3. **A Random Number of Offers per Period**

An unemployed worker is confronted with a random number, n, of job offers each period. With probability π_n, the worker receives n offers in a given period, where $\pi_n \geq 0$ for $n \geq 1$, and $\sum_{n=1}^{N} \pi_n = 1$ for $N < +\infty$. Each offer is drawn independently from the same distribution $F(w)$. Assume that the number of offers n is independently distributed across time. The worker works forever at wage w after having accepted a job and receives unemployment compensation of c during each period of unemployment. He chooses a strategy to maximize $E \sum_{t=0}^{\infty} \beta^t y_t$, where $y_t = c$ if he is unemployed, $y_t = w$ if he is employed.

Let $v(w)$ be the value of the objective function of an unemployed worker who has best offer w in hand and who proceeds optimally. Formulate Bellman's equation for this worker.

Exercise 2.4. Cyclical Fluctuations in Number of Job Offers

Modify Exercise 2.3 as follows. Let the number of job offers n follow a Markov process, with

$$\text{prob\{number of offers next period} = m|\text{number of offers this}$$
$$\text{period} = n\} = \pi_{mn}, \qquad m = 1, \ldots, N, \qquad n = 1, \ldots, N$$
$$\sum_{m=1}^{N} \pi_{mn} = 1 \qquad \text{for } n = 1, \ldots, N.$$

Here $[\pi_{mn}]$ is a "stochastic matrix" generating a Markov chain. Keep all other features of the problem as in Exercise 2.3. The worker gets n offers per period, where n is now generated by a Markov chain so that the number of offers is possibly correlated over time.

a. Let $v(w, n)$ be the value of $E \sum_{t=0}^{\infty} \beta^t y_t$ for an unemployed worker who has received n offers this period, the best of which is w. Formulate Bellman's equation for the worker's problem.

b. Show that the optimal policy is to set a reservation wage $\bar{w}(n)$ that depends on the number of offers received this period.

Exercise 2.5. Choosing the Number of Offers

An unemployed worker must choose the number of offers n to solicit. At a cost of $k(n)$ the worker receives n offers this period. Here $k(n + 1) > k(n)$ for $n \geq 1$. The number of offers n must be chosen in advance at the beginning of the period and cannot be revised during the period. The worker wants to maximize $E \sum_{t=0}^{\infty} \beta^t y_t$. Here y_t consists of w each period she is employed but not searching, $[w - k(n)]$ the first period she is employed but searches for n offers, and $[c - k(n)]$ each period she is unemployed but solicits and rejects n offers. The offers are each independently drawn from $F(w)$. The worker who accepts an offer works forever at wage w.

Let Q be the value of the problem for an unemployed worker who has not yet chosen the number of offers to solicit. Formulate Bellman's equation for this worker.

Exercise 2.6. **Mortensen Externality**

Two parties to a match (say, worker and firm) jointly draw a match parameter θ from a c.d.f. $F(\theta)$. Once matched, they stay matched forever, each one deriving a benefit of θ per period from the match. Each unmatched pair of agents can influence the number of offers received in a period in the following way. The worker receives n offers per period, with $n = f(c_1 + c_2)$, where c_1 is the resources the worker devotes to searching and c_2 is the resources the typical firm devotes to searching. Symmetrically, the representative firm receives n offers per period where $n = f(c_1 + c_2)$. (We shall define the situation so that firms and workers have the same reservation θ so that there is never unrequited love.) Both c_1 and c_2 must be chosen at the beginning of the period, prior to searching during the period. Firms and workers have the same preferences, given by the expected present value of the match parameter θ, net of search costs. The discount factor β is the same for worker and firm.

a. Consider a Nash equilibrium in which party i chooses c_i, taking c_j, $j \neq i$, as given. Let Q_i be the value for an unmatched agent of type i before the level of c_i has been chosen. Formulate Bellman's equation for agents of types 1 and 2.

b. Consider the social planning problem of choosing c_1 and c_2 sequentially so as to maximize the criterion of λ times the utility of agent 1 plus $(1 - \lambda)$ times the utility of agent 2, $0 < \lambda < 1$. Let $Q(\lambda)$ be the value for this problem for two unmatched agents before c_1 and c_2 have been chosen. Formulate Bellman's equation for this problem.

c. Comparing the results in (a) and (b), argue that, in the Nash equilibrium, the optimal amount of resources has not been devoted to search.

Exercise 2.7. **Variable Labor Supply**

An unemployed worker receives each period a wage offer w drawn from the distribution $F(w)$. The worker has to choose whether to accept the job — and therefore to work forever — or to search for another offer and collect c in unemployment compensation. The worker who decides to accept the job must choose the number of hours to work in each period. The worker chooses a strategy to maximize

$$E \sum_{t=0}^{\infty} \beta^t u(y_t, l_t), \qquad \text{where } 0 < \beta < 1,$$

and $y_t = c$ if the worker is unemployed, and $y_t = w(1 - l_t)$ if the worker is employed and works $(1 - l_t)$ hours; l_t is leisure with $0 \le l_t \le 1$.

Analyze the worker's problem. Argue that the optimal strategy has the reservation wage property. Show that the number of hours worked is the same in every period.

Exercise 2.8. Wage Growth Rate and the Reservation Wage

An unemployed worker receives each period an offer to work for wage w_t forever, where $w_t = w$ in the first period and $w_t = \phi^t w$ after t periods in the job. Assume $\phi > 1$, that is, wages increase with tenure. The initial wage offer is drawn from a distribution $F(w)$ that is constant over time (entry-level wages are stationary); successive drawings across periods are independently and identically distributed.

The worker's objective function is to maximize

$$E \sum_{t=0}^{\infty} \beta^t y_t, \qquad \text{where } 0 < \beta < 1,$$

and $y_t = w_t$ if the worker is employed and $y_t = c$ if the worker is unemployed, where c is unemployment compensation. Let $v(w)$ be the optimal value of the objective function for an unemployed worker who has offer w in hand. Write Bellman's equation for this problem. Argue that, if two economies differ only in the growth rate of wages of employed workers, say $\phi_1 > \phi_2$, the economy with the higher growth rate has the smaller reservation wage.

Note. Assume that $\phi_i \beta < 1$, $i = 1, 2$.

Exercise 2.9. Search with a Finite Horizon

Consider a worker who lives two periods. In each period the worker, if unemployed, receives an offer of lifetime work at wage w, where w is drawn from a distribution F. Wage offers are identically and independently distributed over time. The worker's objective is to maximize $E\{y_1 + \beta y_2\}$, where $y_t = w$ if the worker is employed and is equal to c—unemployment compensation—if the worker is not employed.

Analyze the worker's optimal decision rule. In particular, establish that the optimal strategy is to choose a reservation wage in each period and to accept any offer with a wage at least as high as the reservation wage and to reject offers below that level. Show that the reservation wage decreases over time.

Exercise 2.10. Finite Horizon and Mean-Preserving Spread

Consider a worker who draws every period a job offer to work forever at wage w. Successive offers are independently and identically distributed drawings from a distribution $F_i(w)$, $i = 1, 2$. Assume that F_1 has been obtained from F_2 by a mean-preserving spread (see Section 2.4). The worker's objective is to maximize

$$E \sum_{t=0}^{T} \beta^t y_t, \qquad 0 < \beta < 1,$$

where $y_t = w$ if the worker has accepted employment at wage w and is zero otherwise. Assume that both distributions, F_1 and F_2, share a common upper bound, B.

a. Show that the reservation wages of workers drawing from F_1 and F_2 coincide at $t = T$ and $t = T - 1$.

b. Argue that for $t \le T - 2$ the reservation wage of the workers that sample wage offers from the distribution F_1 is higher than the reservation wage of the workers that sample from F_2.

c. Now introduce unemployment compensation: the worker who is unemployed collects c dollars. Prove that the result in (a) no longer holds, that is, the reservation wage of the workers that sample from F_1 is higher than the one corresponding to workers that sample from F_2 for $t = T - 1$.

Exercise 2.11. **Pissarides' Analysis of Taxation and Variable Search Intensity**

An unemployed worker receives each period a zero offer (or no offer) with probability $[1 - \pi(e)]$. With probability $\pi(e)$ the worker draws an offer w from the distribution F. Here e stands for effort — a measure of search intensity — and $\pi(e)$ is increasing in e. A worker who accepts a job offer can be fired with probability $\alpha, 0 < \alpha < 1$. The worker chooses a strategy, that is, whether to accept an offer or not and how much effort to put into search when unemployed, to maximize

$$E \sum_{t=0}^{\infty} \beta^t y_t, \qquad 0 < \beta < 1,$$

where $y_t = w$ if the worker is employed with wage w and $y_t = 1 - e + z$ if the worker spends e units of leisure searching and does not accept a job. Here z is unemployment compensation. For the worker who searched and accepted a job, $y_t = w - e - T(w)$; that is, in the first period the wage is net of search costs. Throughout, $T(w)$ is the amount paid in taxes when the worker is employed. We assume that $w - T(w)$ is increasing in w. Assume that $w - T(w) = 0$ for $w = 0$, that, if $e = 0$, $\pi(e) = 0$ — that is, the worker gets no offers — and that $\pi'(e) > 0$, $\pi''(e) < 0$.

a. Analyze the worker's problem. Establish that the optimal strategy is to choose a reservation wage. Display the condition that describes the optimal choice of e, and show that the reservation wage is independent of e.

b. Assume that $T(w) = t(w - a)$ where $0 < t < 1$ and $a > 0$. Show that an increase in a decreases the reservation wage and increases the level of effort, increasing the probability of accepting employment.

c. Show under what conditions a change in t has the opposite effect.

Exercise 2.12. **Search and Nonhuman Wealth**

An unemployed worker receives every period an offer to work forever at wage w, where w is drawn from the distribution $F(w)$. Offers are independently and identically distributed. Every agent has another source of income, which we denote ϵ_t, and that may be regarded as nonhuman wealth. In every period all agents get a realization of ϵ_t, which is independently and identically distributed over time, with distribution function $G(\epsilon)$. We also assume that w_t and ϵ_t are independent. The objective of a worker is to maximize

$$E \sum_{t=0}^{\infty} \beta^t y_t, \qquad 0 < \beta < 1,$$

where $y_t = w + \phi \epsilon_t$ if the worker has accepted a job that pays w, and $y_t = c + \epsilon_t$ if the worker remains unemployed. We assume that $0 < \phi < 1$ to reflect the fact that an employed worker has less time to engage in the collection of nonhuman wealth. Assume $1 > \text{prob}\{w \geq c + (1 - \phi)\epsilon\} > 0$.

Analyze the worker's problem. Write down Bellman's equation and show that the reservation wage increases with the level of nonhuman wealth.

Exercise 2.13. **Search and Asset Accumulation**

A worker receives, when unemployed, an offer to work forever at wage w, where w is drawn from the distribution $F(w)$. Wage offers are identically and independently distributed over time. The worker maximizes

$$E \sum_{t=0}^{\infty} \beta^t u(c_t, l_t), \qquad 0 < \beta < 1,$$

where c_t is consumption and l_t is leisure. Assume R_t is i.i.d. with distribution $H(R)$. The budget constraint is given by

$$a_{t+1} \leq R_t(a_t + w_t n_t - c_t)$$

and $l_t + n_t \leq 1$ if the worker has a job that pays w_t. If the worker is unemployed, the budget constraint is $a_{t+1} \leq R_t(a_t + z - c_t)$ and $l_t = 1$. Here z is unemployment compensation. It is assumed that $u(\cdot)$ is bounded and that a_t, the worker's asset position, cannot be negative. This corresponds to a no borrowing assumption. Write down Bellman's equation for this problem.

References and Suggested Readings

Albrecht, James, and Bo Axell. 1984. An equilibrium model of search unemployment. *Journal of Political Economy* 92(5):824–840.

Bertsekas, Dimitri. 1976. *Dynamic Programming and Stochastic Control.* New York: Academic Press.

Blackwell, David. 1965. Discounted dynamic programming. *Annals of Mathematical Statistics* 36(1):226–235.

Diamond, Peter A. 1981. Mobility costs, frictional unemployment, and efficiency. *Journal of Political Economy* 89(4):798–812.

Diamond, Peter A., and Joseph Stiglitz. 1974. Increases in risk and in risk aversion. *Journal of Economic Theory* 8(3):337–360.

Gabel, R. A., and R. A. Roberts. 1973. *Signals and Linear Systems.* New York: Wiley.

Johnson, Norman, and Samuel Kotz. 1971. *Continuous Univariate Distributions.* New York: Wiley.

Jovanovic, Boyan. 1979. Job matching and the theory of turnover. *Journal of Political Economy* 87(5):972–990.

Lippman, Steven A., and John J. McCall. 1976. The economics of job search: a survey. *Economic Inquiry* 14(3):347–368.

Lucas, Robert E., Jr., and Edward C. Prescott. 1974. Equilibrium search and unemployment. *Journal of Economic Theory* 7(2):188–209.

McCall, John J. 1970. Economics of information and job search. *Quarterly Journal of Economics* 84(1):113–126.

Mortensen, Dale T. 1982. The matching process as a noncooperative bargaining game. In *The Economics of Information and Uncertainty,* ed. John J. McCall, pp. 233–258. Chicago: University of Chicago Press for the National Bureau of Economic Research.

Phelps, Edmund S. 1970. Introduction to *Microeconomic Foundations of Employment and Inflation Theory.* New York: Norton.

Pissarides, Christopher A. 1983. Efficiency aspects of the financing of unemployment insurance and other government expenditures. *Review of Economic Studies* 50(1):57–69.

Prescott, Edward C., and Robert M. Townsend. 1980. Equilibrium under uncertainty: multiagent statistical decision theory. In *Bayesian Analysis in Econometrics and Statistics,* ed. Arnold Zellner, pp. 169–194. Amsterdam: North-Holland.

Reinganum, Jennifer F. 1979. A simple equilibrium model of price dispersion. *Journal of Political Economy* 87(4):851–858.

Rothschild, Michael, and Joseph Stiglitz. 1970. Increasing risk I: a definition. *Journal of Economic Theory* 2(3):225–243.

—— 1971. Increasing risk II: its economic consequences. *Journal of Economic Theory* 3(1):66–84.

Sargent, Thomas J. 1979. *Macroeconomic Theory.* New York: Academic Press.

Stigler, George. 1961. The economics of information. *Journal of Political Economy* 69(3):213–225.

Watanabe, Shinichi. 1984. Search unemployment, the business cycle, and stochastic growth. Ph.D. diss., University of Minnesota.

Wright, Randall. Job search and cyclical unemployment. *Journal of Political Economy.* Forthcoming.

3 | Asset Prices and Consumption

This chapter applies recursive structures to which dynamic programming is applicable in order to construct theories of consumption and asset prices. Versions of these theories underlie the best recent empirical work in this area. Although the theories all use recursive structures, they differ in that some explicitly describe complete general economic equilibria and others are best regarded as partial analyses. Thus our first two examples, Hall's random walk theory of consumption and the random walk theory of stock prices, both emerge from studying marginal conditions for the consumer's problem and from imposing restrictions directly upon them. As we shall see, it is possible to describe simple general equilibrium setups that deliver these restrictions.

All of our models envision a representative consumer in some version of the following setting. The consumer maximizes

$$(3.1) \quad E_0 \sum_{t=0}^{\infty} \beta^t u(c_t), \quad 0 < \beta < 1,$$

subject to

$$(3.2) \quad A_{t+1} = R_t(A_t + y_t - c_t),$$

with A_0 given. Here c_t is consumption of an agent at time t, y_t is the agent's "labor income," A_t is the amount of a single earning asset valued in units of the consumption good, held at the beginning of period t, and R_t is the real gross rate of return on the asset between dates t and $(t + 1)$, measured in units of time $(t + 1)$ consumption good per time t consumption good. In general we shall imagine that $\{R_t\}$ is a random process and that R_t becomes known to the agent only at the beginning of period $(t + 1)$. We also assume that $\{y_t\}$ is an uncontrollable random process, with additional properties to be specified as needed below. At the beginning of period t, when c_t is chosen, we assume that the agent knows at least values of R, dated $(t - 1)$ and earlier, as well as values of y, dated t and earlier. In (3.1), E_t denotes the mathematical expectation conditional on information known at the beginning of time t. If A_t is negative, it indicates that the agent is borrowing. We shall eventually assume a limit on the amount of borrowing that can be done.

We further assume that, in (3.1), $u(\cdot)$ is concave, strictly increasing, and twice continuously differentiable. Because we have assumed that labor income y_t is uncontrollable by the agent and evolves according to a stochastic process that the agent cannot affect, the model does not incorporate simultaneous determination of consumption and labor supply.

This problem is a version of problem (1.50)–(1.51) of Chapter 1, as the reader may verify by defining the state at t as A_t and current and past y, letting $(1/R_t)A_{t+1}$ be the control and R_t the random shock. The Euler equation associated with control $(1/R_t)A_{t+1}$ is readily verified to be

$$(3.3) \qquad u'(c_t) = E_t \beta R_t u'(c_{t+1}), \qquad t = 0, 1, \ldots$$

Special cases of the Euler equation (3.3) provide the basis for several theories, which will now be summarized.

3.1 Hall's Random Walk Theory of Consumption

First, suppose that R_t is a constant and risk-free rate of return, so that $R_t = R > 1$, for all t, with certainty. Then (3.3) implies that

$$(3.4) \qquad E_t u'(c_{t+1}) = (\beta R)^{-1} u'(c_t),$$

which is Robert Hall's (1978) result that the marginal utility of consumption follows a univariate first-order Markov process and that no other variables in the information set help to predict (to Granger cause) $u'(c_{t+1})$, once lagged $u'(c_t)$ has been included.[1]

---

1. See Granger (1969) for his definition of causality. A random process z_t is said *not* to cause a random process x_t if $E(x_{t+1}|x_t, x_{t-1}, \ldots, z_t, z_{t-1}, \ldots) = E(x_{t+1}|x_t, x_{t-1}, \ldots)$. The absence of Granger causality can be tested in several ways. A direct way is to compute the two regressions mentioned in the preceding definition and test for their equality. An alternative way is to test the one-sidedness of the distributed lag of z_t on $\{x_s\}_{s=-\infty}^{\infty}$ described by Sims (1972).

As an example, with the constant relative risk aversion utility function $u(c_t) = c_t^{\gamma}/\gamma$, (3.4) becomes

$$E_t c_{t+1}^{\gamma-1} = (\beta R)^{-1} c_t^{\gamma-1}.$$

Using aggregate data, Hall tested implication (3.4) for the special case of quadratic utility by testing for the absence of Granger causality from other variables to c_t.

3.2 The Random Walk Theory of Stock Prices

A second special case of (3.3) is the random walk theory of stock prices. Here we interpret the asset as a share of an enterprise that sells for price p_t measured in consumption goods at period t per share during period t and pays nonnegative random dividends of d_t consumption goods to the owner of the share at the beginning of t. We assume that d_t is governed by a Markov process, with time-invariant transition density $f(d', d)$ where $\text{prob}\{d_{t+1} \le d' | d_t = d\} = \int_0^{d'} f(s, d) ds$. Letting s_t denote the number of shares owned by the consumer at the beginning of t, and letting $(p_t + d_t)s_t = A_t$ in (3.2), we have that (3.2) can be represented as

$$(3.5) \qquad (p_{t+1} + d_{t+1})s_{t+1} = \frac{p_{t+1} + d_{t+1}}{p_t} [(p_t + d_t)s_t + y_t - c_t].$$

The gross yield on shares is $R_t = (p_{t+1} + d_{t+1})/p_t$. Substituting $(p_{t+1} + d_{t+1})/p_t = R_t$ into (3.3) gives

$$1 = \beta E_t \left(\frac{p_{t+1} + d_{t+1}}{p_t} \right) \frac{u'(c_{t+1})}{u'(c_t)}.$$

For any two random variables x, y, we have the formula $E_t xy = E_t x E_t y + \text{cov}_t(x, y)$, where $\text{cov}_t(x, y) \equiv E_t(x - E_t x)(y - E_t y)$. [This formula defines the conditional covariance $\text{cov}_t(x, y)$.] Applying this formula in the above equation to evaluate

$$E_t \left(\frac{p_{t+1} + d_{t+1}}{p_t} \right) \frac{u'(c_{t+1})}{u'(c_t)}$$

gives

$$(3.6) \qquad 1 = \beta E_t \left(\frac{p_{t+1} + d_{t+1}}{p_t} \right) E_t \frac{u'(c_{t+1})}{u'(c_t)}$$
$$+ \beta \, \text{cov}_t \left[\frac{u'(c_{t+1})}{u'(c_t)}, \frac{p_{t+1} + d_{t+1}}{p_t} \right].$$

To obtain the random walk theory of stock prices, it is necessary to assume, first, that $E_t u'(c_{t+1})/u'(c_t)$ is a constant and, second that

$$\text{cov}_t \left[\frac{u'(c_{t+1})}{u'(c_t)}, \frac{p_{t+1} + d_{t+1}}{p_t} \right] = 0.$$

For convenience, suppose that $E_t u'(c_{t+1})/u'(c_t) = 1$ and that

$$\text{cov}_t \left[\frac{u'(c_{t+1})}{u'(c_t)}, \frac{p_{t+1} + d_{t+1}}{p_t} \right] = 0.$$

For this statement to be true, it is sufficient that $u(c_t)$ is linear in c_t, so that $u'(c_t)$ is independent of c_t. In this case, Equation (3.6) implies that

(3.7) $E_t(p_{t+1} + d_{t+1}) = \beta^{-1} p_t.$

Equation (3.7) states that, when the share price is adjusted for dividends and discounting, it follows a first-order univariate Markov process and that no other variables Granger cause the share price. These implications have been tested extensively in the literature on efficient markets.[2] We also note that the stochastic difference equation (3.7) has the class of solutions (see the Appendix)

(3.8) $p_t = \sum_{j=1}^{\infty} \beta^j E_t d_{t+j} + \gamma_t \left(\frac{1}{\beta} \right)^t,$

where γ_t is any random process that obeys $E_t \gamma_{t+1} = \gamma_t$ (that is, γ_t is a "martingale"). If we set $\gamma_t = 0$, Equation (3.8) becomes a commonly used formula linking share prices with expected future dividends. Shiller (1981) studies some of the empirical implications of this formula.

3.3 Lucas's Model of Asset Prices

The previous two special applications of (3.3) do not spell out complete general equilibrium setups and so leave open the exact way in which the economy is imagined to fit together, say, to yield the constant gross interest rate assumed in Hall's example. The next example, Lucas's asset-pricing model, does use general equilibrium reasoning in an essential way.[3] Lucas imagines an economy consisting of a large number of identical agents solving

2. For a survey of this literature, see Fama (1976a). An important early theoretical contribution to the literature was Samuelson (1965). An important early empirical application to the term structure of interest rates was by Roll (1970).
3. See Lucas (1978). Also see the important early work by Stephen LeRoy (1973). Breeden (1979) was an early work on the consumption-based capital-asset-pricing model.

problem (3.1)–(3.2), in which $y_t = 0$ for all t. The only durable good in the economy is a set of "trees," which are for convenience equal in number to the number of people in the economy. Each period, each tree yields fruit or dividends in the amount d_t to its owner at the beginning of period t. The fruit is nonstorable, but the tree is perfectly durable. Each agent starts life at time zero with one tree and with its initial dividend of the consumption good, fruit. We let p_t be the price of a tree in period t, measured in units of consumption goods per tree. We again have (3.3), with $R_t = (p_{t+1} + d_{t+1})/p_t$, or

$$(3.9) \qquad E_t \beta \frac{u'(c_{t+1})}{u'(c_t)} \left(\frac{p_{t+1} + d_{t+1}}{p_t} \right) = 1.$$

In this economy, however, we must have that in equilibrium, $c_t = d_t$, because all consumers are identical and $u(\cdot)$ is strictly increasing, and there is only one source of goods, this period's dividends. Substituting $c_t = d_t$ into (3.9) and rearranging, we have

$$(3.10) \qquad p_t = E_t \beta \frac{u'(d_{t+1})}{u'(d_t)} (p_{t+1} + d_{t+1}).$$

Using recursions on (3.10) and the law of iterated expectations, we find that a solution of (3.10) is

$$p_t = E_t \sum_{j=1}^{\infty} \beta^j \left\{ \prod_{s=0}^{j-1} \frac{u'(d_{t+s+1})}{u'(d_{t+s})} \right\} d_{t+j}$$

or

$$(3.11) \qquad p_t = E_t \sum_{j=1}^{\infty} \beta^j \frac{u'(d_{t+j})}{u'(d_t)} d_{t+j},$$

which is a generalization of (3.8) in which the share price is an expected discounted stream of dividends but with time-varying and stochastic discount rates.

Let us study the special case of (3.11) that emerges when $u(c_t) = \ln c_t$. Then (3.11) becomes

$$(3.12) \qquad p_t = E_t \sum_{j=1}^{\infty} \beta^j d_t$$

or

$$(3.13) \qquad p_t = \frac{\beta}{1 - \beta} d_t.$$

Equation (3.13) is an example of an asset-pricing function, which maps the state of the economy at t, d_t, into the price of a capital asset at t.

In more general versions of Lucas's model, the asset-pricing function is a key object in terms of which the equilibrium of the model is defined. In order to make the conditional expectation in (3.9) well defined, it is necessary to impute to the representative agent a view about the law of motion over time of d_t and p_t. The specification of an actual law of motion for d_t, which agents are supposed to know, and a perceived pricing function that maps the history of d_t into p_t implies that a law of motion for p_t has been perceived. Given that E_t in (3.10) is calculated using the perceived pricing function, Equation (3.10) maps the perceived pricing function into an actual pricing function. The notion of a rational expectations equilibrium is that the actual pricing function equals the perceived pricing function. We will now more formally study the nature of the mapping from perceived to actual pricing functions that is induced by (3.10).

We reconsider the economy in Lucas's model, being careful to specify the distributions with respect to which E_t in (3.9) is taken. All agents are identical with respect to both preferences and endowments. We can therefore work with a representative agent. There is one tree per agent. Each tree produces the same dividend d_t at t. The dividend d_t is assumed to be governed by a Markov process with a time-invariant transition probability distribution function given by $\text{prob}\{d_{t+1} \le x' | d_t = x\} = F(x', x)$. The conditional expectations in (3.9) will eventually be defined with respect to this transition probability.

The competitive equilibrium consumption allocation of this economy can readily be computed once we have noted that the economy can be treated as autarkic. Because preferences and endowment patterns are the same across all individuals, there can be no gains from trade. Each household maximizes $E_0 \sum_{t=0}^{\infty} \beta^t u(c_t)$ subject to $c_t \le d_t$. Evidently the solution is to set c_t equal to d_t.

We permit the existence of a competitive market in trees.[4] Ownership of a tree at the beginning of period t entitles the owner to receive the dividend in period t and to have the right to sell the tree at price p_t in period t. If we let s_t be the number of trees owned at the beginning of period t, the consumer's consumption at t is constrained by

$$(3.14) \qquad c_t + p_t s_{t+1} \le (p_t + d_t) s_t.$$

---

4. The rest of the section follows Lucas (1978) closely.

We confront the household with the problem of maximizing

(3.15) $E_0 \sum_{t=0}^{\infty} \beta^t u(c_t),$

subject to (3.14). In order for this problem to be well posed, we must posit a law of motion for the stock price p_t. This step is necessary so that the constraints of the problem will be fully spelled out and so that the conditional expectation in (3.15) will be well defined. By way of specifying this law of motion, we posit a pricing function

(3.16) $p_t = h(x_t),$

where h is a continuous, bounded function defined on the domain of the current state x_t, where in Lucas's model the state x_t equals current dividends d_t. Together with the transition law $F(x', x)$ for dividends, (3.16) defines the perceived law of motion for tree prices.

Let $v(s[h(x) + x])$ be the optimal value for problem (3.14), (3.15), (3.16), when the individual initially owns s trees, when the current dividend equals x, and when the current price of trees is $h(x)$. Bellman's equation is

$$v(s[h(x) + x]) = \max_{s'} \{u([h(x) + x]s - h(x)s')$$

$$+ \beta \int v([h(x') + x']s') \, dF(x', x)\},$$

where we have substituted for consumption from $c = (p + x)s - s'p$ and for p from $p = h(x)$. Here a prime denotes next-period values. The first-order necessary condition associated with this problem is

$$h(x)u'([h(x) + x]s - h(x)s')$$

$$= \beta \int [h(x') + x']v'([h(x') + x']s') \, dF(x', x)$$

Benveniste and Scheinkman's formula implies that $v'([h(x) + x]s) = u'(c)$. Using this and $c(x) = [h(x) + x]s - h(x)s'$ in the first-order condition, we have

$$h(x)u'[c(x)] = \beta \int [h(x') + x']u'[c(x')] \, dF(x', x)$$

or

(3.17) $w(x) = \beta \int w(x') \, dF(x', x) + \beta \int x'u'[c(x')] \, dF(x', x),$

where we have defined $w(x)$ as

$$w(x) = h(x)u'[c(x)].$$

Now, in equilibrium, $s = s' = 1$, there being one tree per person, and $c(x) = [h(x) + x]s - h(x)s' = x$. Substituting these into (3.17) gives

(3.18) $w(x) = \beta \int w(x') \, dF(x', x) + \beta \int x'u'(x') \, dF(x', x).$

Equation (3.18) is a functional equation in the unknown function $w(x) = h(x)u'(x)$. Because $u(x)$ is known, once $w(x)$ has been determined, $h(x)$ can be computed as $h(x) = w(x)/u'(x)$. We seek to solve the functional equation (3.18) for $w(x)$.

Lucas assumed that $u(0) = 0$ and that $u(c)$ is concave and bounded by B where $0 < B < +\infty$. The implication is that $xu'(x)$ is also bounded by B. To show that it is, note the inequalities $0 = u(0) \le u(c) + u'(c)(-c) \le B - cu'(c)$ (from the definition of concavity). These inequalities imply that $cu'(c) \le B$. It follows that

$$g(x) \equiv \beta \int x'u(x') \, dF(x', x) \le \beta B.$$

The function $g(x)$ is also continuous. The functional equation (3.18) can thus be written as

(3.19) $w(x) = \beta \int w(x') \, dF(x', x) + g(x).$

Because $g(x)$ is a continuous and bounded function, it can be proved that the functional equation (3.19) has a unique continuous and bounded solution. (See the Appendix for a proof.) Furthermore, the solution of the functional equation is approached by iterations on $w^j(x)$ defined by

(3.20) $w^{j+1}(x) = \beta \int w^j(x') \, dF(x', x) + g(x),$

starting from any initial continuous and bounded function $w^0(x)$. Once the limiting function $w(x)$ is known, the pricing function $h(x)$ can be calculated as $w(x)/u'(x)$.

Let us write Equation (3.20) as

(3.21) $h^{j+1}(x)u'(x) = \beta \int h^j(x')u'(x') \, dF(x', x) + g(x).$

Equation (3.21) can be regarded as mapping a perceived pricing function $h^j(x)$ into an actual pricing function $h^{j+1}(x)$. A rational expectations equilibrium is a fixed point of this mapping from perceived pricing functions to actual pricing functions.

We have already calculated one example of an equilibrium pricing function in (3.13). The following section will describe another example using a discrete-state version of the model that was suggested by Mehra and Prescott (1985).

3.4 Mehra and Prescott's Finite-State Version of Lucas's Model

Mehra and Prescott (1985) consider a discrete-state space version of Lucas's one-kind-of-tree model. Let dividends assume the n possible distinct values $[\sigma_1, \sigma_2, \ldots, \sigma_n]$. Let dividends evolve through time according to a Markov chain, with

$$\text{prob}\{d_{t+1} = \sigma_l | d_t = \sigma_k\} = P_{kl} > 0.$$

The $(n \times n)$ matrix P with element P_{kl} is called a stochastic matrix. The matrix satisfies $\Sigma_{l=1}^n P_{kl} = 1$ for each k. Express Equation (3.10) of Lucas's model as

(3.22) $p_t u'(d_t) = \beta E_t p_{t+1} u'(d_{t+1}) + \beta E_t d_{t+1} u'(d_{t+1}).$

Express the price at t as a function of the state σ_k at t, $p_t = p(\sigma_k)$. Define $p_t u'(d_t) = p(\sigma_k)u'(\sigma_k) \equiv w_k, k = 1, \ldots, n$. Also define $\gamma_k = \beta E_t d_{t+1} u'(d_{t+1}) = \beta \Sigma_{l=1}^n \sigma_l u'(\sigma_l) P_{kl}$. Then Equation (3.22) can be expressed as

$$p(\sigma_k)u'(\sigma_k) = \beta \sum_{l=1}^n p(\sigma_l)u'(\sigma_l)P_{kl} + \beta \sum_{l=1}^n \sigma_l u'(\sigma_l)P_{kl}$$

or $$w_k = \gamma_k + \beta \sum_{l=1}^n P_{kl} w_l,$$

or in matrix terms, $w = \gamma + \beta P w$, where w and γ are column vectors. The equation can be represented as $(I - \beta P)w = \gamma$. This equation has a unique solution given by[5]

---

5. Uniqueness follows by the fact that, because P is a nonnegative matrix with row sums all equaling unity, the eigenvalue of maximum modulus P has modulus unity. The maximum eigenvalue of βP then has modulus β. (This point follows from Frobenius's theorem.) The implication is that $(I - \beta P)^{-1}$ exists and that the expansion $I + \beta P + \beta^2 P^2 + \ldots$ converges and equals $(I - \beta P)^{-1}$.

(3.23) $w = (I - \beta P)^{-1} \gamma.$

The price of the asset in state σ_k—call it p_k—can then be found from $p_k = w_k / [u'(\sigma_k)]$. Notice that (3.23) can be represented as

(3.24) $w = (I + \beta P + \beta^2 P^2 + \ldots) \gamma$

or $p(\sigma_k) = p_k = \sum_l (I + \beta P + \beta^2 P^2 + \ldots)_{kl} \dfrac{\gamma_l}{u'(\sigma_k)},$

where $(I + \beta P + \beta^2 P^2 + \ldots)_{kl}$ is the (k, l) element of the matrix $(I + \beta P + \beta^2 P^2 + \ldots)$. We ask the reader to interpret this formula.

3.5 Asset Pricing More Generally

Lucas's model exhibits the features shared by a variety of (representative-agent) capital asset–pricing models. (See Brock 1982 and Altug 1985, for example.) These all use versions of stochastic optimal growth models to generate optimal stochastic processes for consumption that can be reinterpreted as equilibrium consumption processes for a dynamic stochastic competitive economy with the same preferences and technology. The equilibrium consumption process is then used in conjunction with some version of the Euler equation (3.3) to compute the price (or shadow price) of an asset under analysis.

More precisely, such asset-pricing models can be constructed by the following steps:

1. Describe the preferences, technology, and endowments of a dynamic economy, then solve for the equilibrium intertemporal consumption allocation. In models in which the competitive equilibrium consumption allocation equals that of some fictitious social planning problem, it is often easiest simply to solve this social planning problem.
2. Imagine setting up a competitive market in some particular asset that represents a specific claim on future consumption goods. Permitting private agents to buy and sell whatever amounts they want at equilibrium asset prices, solve a representative agent's optimum problem. In particular, derive the Euler equation analogous to (3.3) for this asset.
3. Set the consumption that appears in the Euler equation derived in (2) equal to the equilibrium consumption that was derived in (1). This procedure will give the asset price at t as a function of the state of the economy at t.

The Term Structure of Interest Rates

Pertinent theories have been developed by several writers.[6] The economy is identical to the one assumed by Lucas. In particular, there is a single representative agent with preferences $E_0 \sum_{t=0}^{\infty} \beta^t u(c_t)$. Each period, $(d_t > 0)$ units of the consumption good become available per capita. The dividends d_t evolve according to a Markov process, with transition probabilities given by $\text{prob}\{d_{t+1} \leq x' | d_t = x\} = F(x', x)$. The social planning problem is to maximize $E_0 \sum_{t=0}^{\infty} \beta^t u(c_t)$ subject to $c_t \leq d_t$. Evidently the solution of this problem is $c_t = d_t$ for all t. We now suppose that there are markets in one- and two-period perfectly safe loans, which bear gross rates of return R_{1t} and R_{2t}, respectively. At the beginning of t, the returns R_{1t} and R_{2t} are known with certainty and are risk free from the viewpoint of the agents. That is, at t, R_{1t}^{-1} is the price of a perfectly sure claim to one unit of consumption at time $(t + 1)$, and R_{2t}^{-1} is the price of a perfectly sure claim to one unit of consumption at time $(t + 2)$. Both of these prices are denominated in units of time t consumption goods. If we proceed with step (2), the representative agent solves the problem of maximizing

$$E_0 \sum_{t=0}^{\infty} \beta^t u(c_t),$$

subject to the condition that

$$c_t + L_{1t} + L_{2t} \leq d_t + L_{1t-1} R_{1t-1} + L_{2t-2} R_{2t-2},$$

where L_{jt} is the amount lent for j periods at time t. We could solve this problem by using dynamic programming. Here, however, just for variety's sake, we choose to solve the problem by forming the Lagrangian

$$J = E_0 \sum_{t=0}^{\infty} \beta^t [u(c_t) + \lambda_t (d_t + L_{1t-1} R_{1t-1}$$
$$+ L_{2t-2} R_{2t-2} - c_t - L_{1t} - L_{2t})],$$

where $\{\lambda_t\}$ is a sequence of random Lagrange multipliers. Assuming that this problem has a solution with finite value of the objective function, we have among the first-order necessary conditions,

$$[u'(c_t) - \lambda_t] = 0$$
$$-\lambda_t + \beta E_t \lambda_{t+1} R_{1t} = 0$$
$$-\lambda_t + \beta^2 E_t \lambda_{t+2} R_{2t} = 0.$$

---

6. Dynamic asset-pricing theories for the term structure of interest rates are developed by Cox, Ingersoll, and Ross (1985a, b) and by LeRoy (1983).

Substituting the first into each of the second and third conditions gives

$$(3.25) \qquad E_t\left[\beta\frac{u'(c_{t+1})}{u'(c_t)}R_{1t}\right]=1$$

$$(3.26) \qquad E_t\left[\beta^2\frac{u'(c_{t+2})}{u'(c_t)}R_{2t}\right]=1$$

If we recall that R_{1t} and R_{2t} are known with certainty at the beginning of t, Equations (3.25) and (3.26) imply

$$R_{1t}^{-1}=E_t\beta\frac{u'(c_{t+1})}{u'(c_t)}$$

$$R_{2t}^{-1}=E_t\beta^2\frac{u'(c_{t+2})}{u'(c_t)}.$$

(Here we are using the property of conditional expectations that, for any variable x_t included in the information set conditioning the expectation at t, $E_t z x_t = x_t E_t z$ for any random variable z.) To complete the model, we perform step (3) and set d_t equal to c_t in (3.25) and (3.26). As an example, let us take $u(c) = \ln c$ and set d_t equal to c_t, in which case Equations (3.25)–(3.26) imply that

$$R_{1t}^{-1}=\beta E_t(d_t/d_{t+1})$$
$$R_{2t}^{-1}=\beta^2 E_t(d_t/d_{t+2}).$$

Let us further specialize things by assuming that dividends follow the stochastic process

$$d_{t+1}=\rho d_t\theta_{t+1},\qquad \rho>0,$$

where θ_{t+1} is a sequence of independently and identically distributed random variables that are positive with probability 1. Then the two equations above imply that

$$(3.27) \qquad R_{1t}^{-1}=\frac{\beta}{\rho}\left[E\left(\frac{1}{\theta}\right)\right]$$

$$R_{2t}^{-1}=\left(\frac{\beta}{\rho}\right)^2\left[E\left(\frac{1}{\theta}\right)\right]^2,$$

where we are using the independence over time of θ_t. The level of interest rates rises with the term to maturity if $\rho/[\beta E(\theta^{-1})]>1$ and falls if $\rho/[\beta E(\theta^{-1})]<1$.

Let us write Equation (3.25) as

$$\beta \frac{u'(c_{t+1})}{u'(c_t)} R_{1t} = 1 + \zeta_{1t+1},$$

where $E_t \zeta_{1t+1}$ is the least-squares residual that by construction satisfies $E_t \zeta_{1t+1} = 0$. That is, we are using (3.25) and the definition of the "projection equation"

$$\beta \frac{u'(c_{t+1})}{u'(c_t)} R_{1t} = E_t \beta \frac{u'(c_{t+1})}{u'(c_t)} R_{1t} + \zeta_{1t+1}.$$

Because R_{1t} is known at time t, this equation leads to

(3.28) $$\beta \frac{u'(c_{t+1})}{u'(c_t)} = R_{1t}^{-1} + R_{1t}^{-1} \zeta_{1t+1}.$$

The variable ζ_{1t+1} is the least-squares one-step-ahead forecast error involved in predicting $R_{1t}\beta u'(c_{t+1})/u'(c_t)$ from information dated t and earlier. Because R_{2t} is known at time t, (3.26) can be written

(3.29) $$R_{2t}^{-1} = E_t \left[\beta \frac{u'(c_{t+1})}{u'(c_t)} \beta \frac{u'(c_{t+2})}{u'(c_{t+1})} \right].$$

Substituting (3.28) into (3.29) gives

$$R_{2t}^{-1} = E_t[(R_{1t}^{-1} + R_{1t}^{-1}\zeta_{1t+1})(R_{1t+1}^{-1} + R_{1t+1}^{-1}\zeta_{1t+2})]$$
$$= R_{1t}^{-1} E_t(R_{1t+1}^{-1} + R_{1t+1}^{-1}\zeta_{1t+1} + R_{1t+1}^{-1}\zeta_{1t+1}\zeta_{1t+2}$$
$$+ R_{1t+1}^{-1}\zeta_{1t+2}).$$

(3.30) $$R_{2t}^{-1} = R_{1t}^{-1}[E_t R_{1t+1}^{-1} + \text{cov}_t(R_{1t+1}^{-1}, \zeta_{1t+1})]$$
$$+ R_{1t}^{-1} E_t R_{1t+1}^{-1}\zeta_{1t+1}\zeta_{1t+2} + R_{1t}^{-1} E_t R_{1t+1}^{-1}\zeta_{1t+2}$$

Now, for the last two terms we apply the law of iterated expectations, which states that $E_t E_{t+1}(\cdot) = E_t(\cdot)$. We obtain

$$E_t R_{1t+1}^{-1}\zeta_{1t+1}\zeta_{1t+2} = E_t E_{t+1} R_{1t+1}^{-1}\zeta_{1t+1}\zeta_{1t+2}$$
$$= E_t R_{1t+1}^{-1} E_{t+1}\zeta_{1t+1}\zeta_{1t+2} = 0$$

and $$E_t R_{1t+1}^{-1}\zeta_{1t+2} = E_t E_{t+1} R_{1t+1}^{-1}\zeta_{1t+2}$$
$$= E_t R_{1t+1}^{-1} E_{t+1}\zeta_{1t+2} = 0.$$

Substituting these two equalities into (3.30) gives

(3.31) $$R_{2t}^{-1} = R_{1t}^{-1}[E_t R_{1t+1}^{-1} + \text{cov}_t(R_{1t+1}^{-1}, \zeta_{1t+1})],$$

where

$$\zeta_{1t+1} = \beta \frac{u'(c_{t+1})}{u'(c_t)} R_{1t} - 1.$$

Equation (3.31) is a generalized version of the pure expectations theory of the term structure of interest rates, adjusted for the risk premium $\text{cov}_t(R_{1t+1}^{-1}, \zeta_{1t+1})$. The pure expectations theory hypothesizes that $R_{2t}^{-1} = R_{1t}^{-1} E_t R_{1t+1}^{-1}$. Formula (3.31) implies that the pure expectations theory holds only in special cases. One special case occurs when utility is linear in consumption, so that $u'(c_{t+1})/u'(c_t) = 1$. In this case, R_{1t}, given by (3.25), is a constant, equal to β^{-1}, and $\text{cov}_t(R_{1t+1}^{-1}, \zeta_{1t+1}) = 0$. A second special case occurs when there is no uncertainty, so that $\zeta_{1t+1} \equiv 0$, in which case $\text{cov}_t(R_{1t+1}^{-1}, \zeta_{1t+1}) = 0$.

Another way to obtain a version of (3.31) is to use (3.25) and (3.26) to represent R_{2t}^{-1} as

$$R_{2t}^{-1} = E_t \beta \frac{u'(c_{t+1})}{u'(c_t)} \beta \frac{u'(c_{t+2})}{u'(c_{t+1})}.$$

Using the law of iterated expectations we obtain

$$R_{2t}^{-1} = E_t E_{t+1} \beta \frac{u'(c_{t+1})}{u'(c_t)} \beta \frac{u'(c_{t+2})}{u'(c_{t+1})}$$

$$= E_t \beta \frac{u'(c_{t+1})}{u'(c_t)} E_{t+1} \beta \frac{u'(c_{t+2})}{u'(c_{t+1})}$$

$$= E_t \beta \frac{u'(c_{t+1})}{u'(c_t)} R_{1t+1}^{-1}.$$

When we use the definition of conditional covariance, the equality becomes

$$R_{2t}^{-1} = E_t \frac{\beta u'(c_{t+1})}{u'(c_t)} E_t R_{1t+1}^{-1} + \text{cov}_t \left[\beta \frac{u'(c_{t+1})}{u'(c_t)}, R_{1t+1}^{-1} \right].$$

When we use (3.25), this becomes

$$(3.31') \qquad R_{2t}^{-1} = R_{1t}^{-1} E_t R_{1t+1}^{-1} + \text{cov}_t \left[\beta \frac{u'(c_{t+1})}{u'(c_t)}, R_{1t+1}^{-1} \right].$$

This is a restatement of (3.31) and is again a generalized version of the expectations theory of the term structure of interest rates.

An n-Tree Version of Lucas's Model

We now suppose that there are n kinds of trees, or "stocks," each person in the economy initially being endowed with one of each kind of tree. At the beginning of period t, the owner of one ith kind of tree receives a "dividend" of d_{it} units of consumption good. As before, the consumption good is non-storable, whereas trees last forever. Where $\bar{d}_t$ is the n-dimensional vector $(d_{1t}, d_{2t}, \ldots, d_{nt})$, we assume that $\bar{d}_t$ is a nonnegative Markov process with transition density $h(\bar{d}', \bar{d})$. Our task is to construct a theory of the prices of different kinds of trees.

We say that $d_t = \sum_{i=1}^{n} d_{it}$. As our first step, we calculate the solution of the planning problem, which is $c_t = d_t$. Next, we imagine a market in "shares of stock" or titles to trees, letting s_{it} be the number of trees or shares of the ith kind owned by the representative agent at the beginning of period t. The representative consumer is imagined to maximize

$$E_0 \sum_{t=0}^{\infty} \beta^t u(c_t),$$

subject to the constraint

$$\sum_{i=1}^{n} p_{it} s_{it+1} = \sum_{i=1}^{n} (p_{it} + d_{it}) s_{it} - c_t.$$

We ask the reader to formulate this as a dynamic programming problem and to derive and analyze Bellman's functional equation. The Euler equation for the ith stock can be represented as

$$p_{it} = \beta E_t \left[\frac{u'(c_{t+1})}{u'(c_t)} (p_{it+1} + d_{it+1}) \right].$$

Substituting equilibrium consumption $c_t = d_t$ gives

(3.32) $$p_{it} = \beta E_t \left[\frac{u'(d_{t+1})}{u'(d_t)} (p_{it+1} + d_{it+1}) \right].$$

We shall now restrict (3.32) further by specializing preferences and technology. First, we shall assume that $u(c) = \ln c$, which implies that (3.32) becomes

(3.33) $$p_{it} = \beta E_t \left[\frac{d_t}{d_{t+1}} (p_{it+1} + d_{it+1}) \right].$$

We now proceed to derive a collection of equilibrium pricing functions. We shall use the method of guessing and verifying. We assume time-varying, possibly stochastic price functions of the linear form

(3.34) $p_{it} = \phi_{it} d_t,$ $i = 1, \ldots, n.$

[Notice that, at this point, (3.34) is vacuous, because ϕ_{it} can always be chosen to make (3.34) true. The following argument, however, will restrict ϕ_{it}.] Substituting (3.34) into both sides of (3.33) gives

$$\phi_{it} d_t = \beta E_t \phi_{it+1} d_t + \beta E_t \left(\frac{d_{it+1}}{d_{t+1}} \right) d_t,$$

which implies

(3.35) $\phi_{it} = \beta E_t \phi_{it+1} + \beta E_t \left(\dfrac{d_{it+1}}{d_{t+1}} \right).$

Iterating on (3.35) implies that

(3.36) $\phi_{it} = \displaystyle\sum_{j=1}^{\infty} \beta^j E_t \left(\frac{d_{it+j}}{d_{t+j}} \right).$

Equation (3.36) gives the pricing function in terms of the conditional distribution of the $\{d_{it}, d_t\}$ stochastic process. Notice that, in the special case that $n = 1$, (3.36) collapses to $p_t = (\beta/(1 - \beta))d_t$, which agrees with (3.13).

As an application of (3.36), take the special case in which $n = 2$,

(3.37) $d_{1t} = (1/2)(1 - \epsilon_t)d_t,$

and

(3.38) $d_{2t} = (1/2)(1 + \epsilon_t)d_t.$

Assume that ϵ_t is a random variable whose distribution is concentrated in the interval between zero and one and that ϵ_t also obeys a Markov process for which $E_t \epsilon_{t+j} = \rho^j \epsilon_t$, $|\rho| < 1$. Equation (3.37) implies that $d_{1t}/d_t = (1/2)(1 - \epsilon_t)$ and consequently that $E_t d_{1t+j}/d_{t+j} = (1/2)(1 - \rho^j \epsilon_t)$. By implication,

(3.39) $\phi_{1t} = \dfrac{1}{2} \left(\dfrac{\beta}{1 - \beta} - \dfrac{\beta \rho \epsilon_t}{1 - \beta \rho} \right)$

$\phi_{2t} = \dfrac{1}{2} \left(\dfrac{\beta}{1 - \beta} + \dfrac{\beta \rho \epsilon_t}{1 - \beta \rho} \right).$

Note that we could have specified the state of the economy as the pair (d_t, ϵ_t), in which case a pair of time-invariant but quadratic asset-pricing functions would have worked. We would of course find the same functions that we found above.

Lucas (1978) and Brock (1982) provide proofs that, in similar models, the asset-pricing functions are unique. A one-asset version of the proof strategy is described in Section 3.3 above and in the Appendix. This uniqueness argument, which derives from the study of an iterative process like that induced by (3.35), gives us some peace of mind when we use the guess-and-verify method.

Contingent Claim Markets

Following the construction of Lucas (1982), we now use optimal stochastic growth models to price claims to virtually all imaginable assets all at once. We do so by first pricing all one-step-ahead state-contingent securities. Later we will show how to derive all j-step-ahead state-contingent securities prices as functions of the prices of one-step-ahead state-contingent securities. To start, let the state of the economy in this period be x. The state of the economy in Lucas's model includes the current dividend d_t and all information available at t that helps predict future dividends. Let the state of the economy evolve according to a Markov process described by density $f(x', x)$ defined by

$$\text{prob}\{x_{t+1} \le x' | x_t = x\} = \int_{-\infty}^{x'} f(u, x) \, du \equiv F(x', x).$$

We imagine that there is a pricing function or "pricing kernel" with the following property. In period t, if the economy is in state x_t, one can purchase or sell a claim to one unit of a period $(t + 1)$ consumption good contingent on the event that x_{t+1} belongs to a set A in period $(t + 1)$, at a price in terms of time t consumption of

$$\int_{x_{t+1} \in A} q(x_{t+1}, x_t) \, dx_{t+1}.$$

Letting $A = \Omega \equiv$ the entire space of possible x, for example, one finds that the time t price of a perfectly certain claim on period $(t + 1)$ consumption is

$$\int_{x_{t+1} \in \Omega} q(x_{t+1}, x_t) \, dx_{t+1},$$

which was earlier defined as $1/R_{1t}$.

We imagine that there are competitive markets in all such one-period contingent claims. We shall imagine that agents in Lucas's one-kind-of-tree economy are confronted with an opportunity to trade such one-period-ahead state-contingent commodities. The representative household now faces the problem of maximizing

$$E_0 \sum_{t=0}^{\infty} \beta^t u(c_t),$$

subject to the sequence of constraints

$$c_t + p_t s_{t+1} + \int q(x_{t+1}, x_t) y(x_{t+1}) \, dx_{t+1} \leq (p_t + d_t) s_t + y(x_t).$$

Here $y(x_{t+1})$ is the net amount of the date $(t + 1)$ good, contingent on the assumption by the state of the economy at $(t + 1)$ of the value x_{t+1}, which the consumer purchases at time t. The consumer pays $q(x_{t+1}, x_t)$ for one unit of consumption good in state x_{t+1}, given that this period's state is x_t. The agent starts period t with $(p_t + d_t)s_t$ time t worth of goods from owning trees, and $y(x_t)$ from last period's purchase (or sale if the figure is negative) of one-period contingent commodities.

As we know from the results of Section 3.3, for this model it is possible to express the share price p_t as a function of the state of the economy, and we use $p_t = p(x_t)$. We also express dividends as a function of the state of the economy, $d_t = d(x_t)$. Using these functions, Bellman's equation for the optimization problem above is

$$v[(p + d)s + y(x), x]$$

$$= \max_{c, s', y(x')} \left\{ u(c) + \beta \int v[(p' + d')s' + y(x'), x'] f(x', x) \, dx' \right\},$$

where the maximization is subject to

$$(p + d)s + y(x) - c - ps' - \int q(x', x) y(x') \, dx' \geq 0.$$

Here primes denote next-period values, whereas the absence of primes denotes this-period values; s' denotes the beginning of next period's holding of trees, whereas $y(x')$ denotes purchases of one-period-ahead contingent claims. The variables p', d' are next period's price of trees and dividends. Here p and d are understood to denote functions $p(x)$ and $d(x)$; p' and d' are understood to denote $p(x')$ and $d(x')$. The *state* variables are $[(p + d)s + y(x), x]$, the first denoting this period's wealth of the individual agent and the second indicating the overall position of the economy. The *controls* are the scalars c, s', and the *function* $y(x')$. Note that next period's state can be expressed solely as a function of the controls and random variables exogenous to the agent, namely, $(p' + d')s' + y(x')$. This observation will be pertinent when we apply Benveniste and Scheinkman's formula for the derivative of the value function.

To solve the constrained-maximization problem on the right side of the functional equation, we form the Lagrangian

$$J = u(c) + \beta \int v[(p' + d')s' + y(x'), x']f(x', x) \, dx'$$
$$+ \lambda \left[(p + d)s + y - c - ps' - \int q(x', x)y(x') \, dx' \right],$$

where λ is a nonnegative multiplier.

Consider the piece of the Lagrangian involving integration over x':

$$\beta \int v([p(x') + d(x')]s' + y(x'), x')f(x', x) \, dx'$$
$$- \lambda \int q(x', x)y(x') \, dx'$$
$$\equiv \int G[y(x'), \dot{y}(x'), x', s'; q(x', x), f(x', x)] \, dx',$$

where $\dot{y}(x') \equiv (d/dx')y(x')$. The preceding equality defines the function G. The problem is to find the extremum of $\int G \, dx'$ by choice of a *function* $y(x')$ mapping the domain of x' into the real line, and a scalar s'. This is a classical calculus-of-variations problem. The Euler equations associated with an extremum of $\int G \, dx'$ with respect to the function $y(x')$ and the scalar s' are, respectively,

$$G_y - \frac{d}{dx'}G_{\dot{y}} = 0 \qquad \text{for all } x'$$
$$\int G_{s'} \, dx' = 0,$$

where G_y, $G_{\dot{y}}$, $G_{s'}$, G_s, are the derivatives of G with respect to y, $\dot{y}$, and s', respectively. For the above definition of G, we have $G_y = \beta v_1 f(x', x) - \lambda q(x', x)$, $G_{\dot{y}} = 0$, $G_{s'} = \beta v_1 f(x', x)(p' + d')$. Using these expressions in the Euler equations and the definition of G above gives the first-order conditions. With respect to c, s', and $y(x')$, these are, respectively,

$$u'(c) = \lambda$$

$$\beta \int (p' + d')v_1[(p' + d')s' + y(x'), x']f(x', x)\, dx' = p\lambda$$

$$\beta v_1[(p' + d')s' + y(x'), x']f(x', x) = \lambda q(x', x).$$

Here v_1 denotes the partial derivative of v with respect to its first argument. Using the Benveniste-Scheinkman formula for the derivative of the value function, we have $v_1[(p + d)s + y(x), x] = u'(c)$. Substituting this equation into the third necessary condition and using the first necessary condition to eliminate λ, we have the formula

(3.40) $$q(x', x) = \beta \frac{u'[c(x')]}{u'[c(x)]} f(x', x)$$

for contingent claims prices. Thus we have completed step (2) of our general program for building models of asset prices, equation (3.40) being an Euler equation.

To complete the characterization of $q(x', x)$, we follow step (3) of our program and say that $c = d = x$, where x is now both the level of dividends and the state in Lucas's tree model:

(3.41) $$q(x', x) = \beta \frac{u'(x')}{u'(x)} f(x', x).$$

Equation (3.41) is our formula for the equilibrium asset-pricing kernel.

The kernel $q(x', x)$ can be used to find the price at t of any risky one-period claim whose realized return at $(t + 1)$ is a function of the realization of x_{t+1}. Let $w(x')$ be any function of x'. Then the price at t of a claim that pays off the state-contingent amount $w(x_{t+1})$ at $(t + 1)$ when the state at $(t + 1)$ is x_{t+1} is to be priced according to

(3.42) $$\int w(x')q(x', x)\, dx' = \int w(x')\beta \frac{u'(x')}{u'(x)} f(x', x)\, dx'.$$

Suppose for example, that $w(x') = 1$ for all x' in the sample space of realizations of x'. The function $w(x') = 1$ is the payoff function for a sure claim on one unit of consumption next period. Formula (3.42) becomes

$$\beta \int \frac{u'(x')}{u'(x)} f(x', x)\, dx'.$$

Notice that this equals $(1/R_{1t})$, the price at t of a sure claim on time $(t + 1)$ consumption, which we computed earlier.

As a second example, let us price an asset with payoff function $w(x') = 1$ if $x' \leq \bar{x}$, 0 if $x' > \bar{x}$. The price of such a claim is

$$\beta \int_{x' \leq \bar{x}} \frac{u'(x')}{u'(x)} f(x', x) \, dx'.$$

Arbitrage Asset-Pricing Formulas

The theory of Lucas's that we have been studying imposes restrictions on asset prices, consumption, and "production" that come from several sources, namely, (1) the technology by which "trees" produce "dividends"; (2) the structure of preferences; (3) the distribution of endowments and preferences across agents; and (4) an arbitrage condition that is imposed in the course of computing equilibrium prices and requires that asset prices be such that no sure opportunities for unbounded profits exist. Arbitrage asset-pricing theories characterize the restrictions across asset prices that stem from assuming only (4), also assuming that utility is strictly increasing in consumption, which would hold in *any* equilibrium, regardless of the other assumptions about (1), (2), and (3).[7] Arbitrage asset-pricing theories are formed by exhausting the implications of the notion that, in equilibrium, asset prices must be such that individuals' budget sets remain bounded. Such theories are formed by arguments involving manipulation only of agents' constraint sets.

Let $q^{(j)}(x^j, x)$ be the price at t when the state of the economy is x for a unit of the consumption good in period $(t + j)$, contingent on the state's being x^j at time $(t + j)$. Thus $q^{(j)}(x^j, x)$ is the pricing kernel for j-step-ahead contingent claims. Let $y^{(j)}(x^j, x)$ be the amount of such claims purchased at time t when the economy is in state x. Let an agent's initial wealth denominated in units of the good at t be θ, and let the agent's wealth next period be θ'. As above, let $p(x)$ be the price of a share of trees entitling the owner to a proportionate share in the future stream of dividends. Let s' be the number of such shares purchased during the current period. Let the trees give dividends of $\xi_t = \xi(x_t)$. The agent's budget constraint is then

$$c + p(x)s' + \sum_{j=1}^{\infty} \int q^{(j)}(x^j, x) y^{(j)}(x^j, x) \, dx^j \leq \theta.$$

7. Arbitrage pricing theory was introduced by Stephen Ross (1976). Ross presented the theory in a different setup from the one used here, but the main idea is the same. Ross posited a particular statistical process for asset returns, then derived the restrictions on the process that are implied by the hypothesis that there exist no arbitrage possibilities.

Next period's wealth is given by

$$\theta'(x') = s'[p(x') + \xi'] + y^{(1)}(x', x)$$
$$+ \sum_{j=2}^{\infty} \int q^{(j-1)}(x^j, x') y^{(j)}(x^j, x) \, dx^j.$$

Multiplying the second equation by $q^{(1)}(x', x)$, integrating with respect to x', and using the result to eliminate $\int q^{(1)}(x', x) y^{(1)}(x', x) \, dx'$ from the first equation, we have

A

$$c + s' \overbrace{\left\{ p(x) - \int [p(x') + \xi'] q^{(1)}(x', x) \, dx' \right\}}$$

B

$$+ \sum_{j=2}^{\infty} \int \overbrace{\left[q^{(j)}(x^j, x) - \int q^{(j-1)}(x^j, x') q^{(1)}(x', x) \, dx' \right]}$$
$$\cdot y^{(j)}(x^j, x) \, dx^j + \int \theta'(x') q^{(1)}(x', x) \, dx' \le \theta.$$

We suppose that s' and $y^{(j)}(x^j, x)$ can take on any values the agent chooses. Unless the terms A and B multiplying s and $y^{(j)}(x^j, x)$ are zero [almost everywhere zero in the case of $y^{(j)}(x^j, x)$], the individual can obtain unbounded consumption and wealth [$\int \theta'(x') q^{(1)}(x', x) \, dx'$] while still satisfying the budget constraint. This situation is not feasible. Therefore, those terms must be zero, so that we have:

(3.43) $$c + \int \theta'(x') q^{(1)}(x', x) \, dx' \le \theta$$

$$p(x) = \int [p(x') + \xi'] q^{(1)}(x', x) \, dx'$$

$$q^{(j)}(x^j, x) = \int q^{(j-1)}(x^j, x') q^{(1)}(x', x) \, dx', \quad j \ge 2.$$

Equation (3.43) provides a recursive way of calculating prices of j-period contingent claims once one-period claims have been priced.

The two preceding equations give some restrictions across asset prices that are independent of preferences and the distribution of agents with respect to preferences and endowments. The role of Lucas's assumption that all agents are identical in their preferences and initial endowments is to create a framework in which the initial pricing kernel $q^{(1)}(x', x)$ can readily be calculated. Then the remaining kernels can be calculated recursively. Using Equation (3.40), we have, for example,[8]

$$q^{(2)}(x', x) = \beta^2 \int \frac{u'[c(x')]}{u'[c(x)]} f(x', u)f(u, x) \, du.$$

Crop Insurance

We shall now use the contingent claims prices to construct a model of crop insurance in the Lucas one-tree model. We consider a version of the Lucas one-kind-of-tree model in which dividends follow a first-order Markov law with transition density $f(x', x)$, where x is now dividends. We let $q_\alpha(x)$ be the price in current consumption goods of a claim on one unit of consumption next period, contingent on the event that next period's dividends fall below α. We think of the asset being priced as "crop insurance," a claim to consumption when next period's crops fall short of α per tree.

From the preceding section, we have

(3.44) $\qquad q_\alpha(x) = \beta \int_0^\alpha \frac{u'(x')}{u'(x)} f(x', x) \, dx';$

we are now letting x' be dividends. Upon noting that

$$\int_0^\alpha u'(x') f(x', x) \, dx' = \text{prob}\{x_{t+1} \leq \alpha | x_t = x\}$$

$$\cdot E\{u'(x_{t+1}) | x_{t+1} \leq \alpha, x_t = x\},$$

we can represent the preceding equation as

(3.45) $\qquad q_\alpha(x) = \dfrac{\beta}{u'(x_t)} \text{prob}\{x_{t+1} \leq \alpha | x_t = x\}$

$$\cdot E\{u'(x_{t+1}) | x_{t+1} \leq \alpha, x_t = x\}.$$

Notice that, in the special case of risk neutrality [$u'(x) = $ constant], Equation (3.45) collapses to

$$q_\alpha(x) = \beta \, \text{prob}\{x_{t+1} \leq \alpha | x_t = x\},$$

which is an intuitively plausible formula for the risk-neutral case. When $u'' < 0$ and $x_t \geq \alpha$, Equation (3.45) implies that $q_\alpha(x) > \beta \, \text{prob}\{x_{t+1} \leq$

---

8. Recall that the two-step-ahead transition function $f^{(2)}(x', x)$ obeys $f^{(2)}(x', x) = \int f(x', u)f(u, x) \, du$, where $\text{prob}\{x_{t+2} \leq x' | x_t = x\} = \int_{-\infty}^{x'} f^{(2)}(u, x) \, du$.

$\alpha|x_t = x\}$ [because then $E\{u'(x_{t+1})|x_{t+1} \le \alpha, x_t = x\} > u'(x_t)$ for $x_t \ge \alpha$]. In other words, when the representative consumer is risk averse ($u'' < 0$), and when $x \ge \alpha$, the price of crop insurance $q_\alpha(x)$ exceeds the "actuarily fair" price of β prob$\{x_{t+1} \le \alpha|x_t = x\}$.

Another way to represent (3.44) that is perhaps more convenient for purposes of empirical testing is

$$(3.46) \qquad 1 = \frac{\beta}{u'(x_t)} E[u'(x_{t+1})R_{\alpha t}]|x_t$$

$$\text{where} \quad R_{\alpha t} = \begin{cases} 0 & \text{if } x_{t+1} > \alpha \\ 1/q_\alpha(x_t) & \text{if } x_{t+1} \le \alpha. \end{cases}$$

3.6 The Modigliani-Miller Theorem

Let us consider a two-kind-of-tree version of Lucas's model. Each kind of tree yields dividends (bears fruit) according to a Markov process. We say that $d_t = d_{1t} + d_{2t}$, where d_{it} is dividends of the ith kind of tree and d_t is total dividends. The state of the economy $x_t = (d_{1t}, d_{2t})$. We assume that x_t follows a Markov process described by the transition density $f(x', x)$.

Suppose that the first kind of tree lives forever, throwing off the nonnegative dividend stream $\{d_{1t}\}$. As for the second kind of tree, we assume the following special structure of dividends in order to represent the idea of bankruptcy simply. The dividend stream of type 2 trees is governed by a two-state Markov process. Dividends take either the value $\sigma_1 > 0$ or the value $\sigma_2 = 0$. Furthermore, once dividends have assumed the value zero, they remain zero forevermore (that is, the tree has died). This specification can be represented by stating that $\{d_{2t}\}$ follows a two-state Markov chain with transition matrix

$$P = \begin{bmatrix} p_{11} & (1 - p_{11}) \\ 0 & 1 \end{bmatrix}, \qquad 0 < p_{11} < 1,$$

where $p_{ij} = $ prob$\{d_{t+1} = \sigma_j | d_t = \sigma_i\}$. Thus p_{11} is the probability that a living tree of type 2 will be alive next period.

Now imagine that trees represent firms of types 1 and 2. Firms of type i each own only one tree of type i. Consider a firm of type 2. Suppose that it issues bonds and equities, which represent packages of state-contingent claims of the following particular kinds. It issues a number b of bonds that pay off r per bond per period in periods when $rb \le d_{2t+j}$ and d_{2t+j}/b when $d_{2t+j} < rb$. Here r is a constant "coupon rate." The other security is an equity that promises to pay $(d_{2t+j} - rb)$ in periods when $d_{2t+j} > rb$ and zero when

$d_{2t+j} \leq rb$. The total value of the second kind of firm's bonds, B_{2t}, at time t is given by

$$(3.47) \qquad B_{2t} = \sum_{j=1}^{\infty} \int_{d_{2t+j} \geq rb} rbq^{(j)}(x_{t+j}, x_t) \, dx_{t+j}$$

$$+ \sum_{j=1}^{\infty} \int_{d_{2t+j} < rb} d_{2t+j}q^{(j)}(x_{t+j}, x_t) \, dx_{t+j}.$$

The total value of the firm's equities, S_{2t}, at time t is

$$(3.48) \qquad S_{2t} = \sum_{j=1}^{\infty} \int_{d_{2t+j} > rb} (d_{2t+j} - rb)q^{(j)}(x_{t+j}, x_t) \, dx_{t+j}.$$

Adding (3.47) and (3.48), we find that the total value of the firm is

$$(3.49) \qquad B_{2t} + S_{2t} = \sum_{j=1}^{\infty} \int d_{2t+j}q^{(j)}(x_{t+j}, x_t) \, dx_{t+j},$$

where d_{2t+j} is understood as a function of x_{t+j}. Equation (3.49) exhibits the Modigliani-Miller proposition that the value of the firm, that is, the total value of the firm's bonds and equities, is independent of the number of bonds b outstanding. Total value of the firm is also independent of the coupon rate r.[9]

For our example, it is reasonable to imagine that $rb < \sigma_1$, so that the firm issues a small enough number of bonds and sets a small enough coupon r to enable it to pay the promised interest as long as the tree is alive. Once dividends drop to zero, however, they remain at zero forever. The firm is then bankrupt, its total value dropping to zero and remaining there forevermore.

3.7 Government Debt and the Ricardian Proposition

We now use a version of Lucas's one-kind-of-tree model to exposit the Ricardian proposition that tax financing and bond financing of a given stream of government expenditures are equivalent.[10] This proposition may

9. See Modigliani and Miller (1958). The present treatment follows Hirshleifer (1966) and Stiglitz (1969).

10. An article by Robert Barro (1974) promoted strong interest in the Ricardian proposition. Barro described the proposition in a context distinct from the present one but closely related to it. Barro used an overlapping-generations model but assumed altruistic agents who cared about their descendants. Restricting preferences to ensure an operative bequest motive, Barro described an overlapping-generations structure that is equivalent with a model with an infinitely lived representative agent.

usefully be viewed as an application of the Modigliani-Miller theorem to government finance and obtains under circumstances in which the government is essentially like a firm in the constraints that it confronts with respect to its financing decisions.

We now add to Lucas's model a government that spends current output according to a nonnegative stochastic process $\{g_t\}$ that satisfies $g_t < d_t$ for all t. The variable g_t denotes per capita government expenditures at t. For analytical convenience we assume that g_t is thrown away, giving no utility to private agents. The government finances its expenditures by a stream of lump-sum per capita taxes $\{\tau_t\}$, a stream that we assume is a stochastic process expressible as a function of x_t at time t, and by issuing one-period debt that is permitted to be state contingent. Letting x_t be the state of the economy at t, the government's budget constraint is

$$(3.50) \qquad g_t = \tau_t + \int q(x_{t+1}, x_t) b(x_{t+1}) \, dx_{t+1} - b(x_t),$$

where $b(x_{t+1})$ is the amount of $(t + 1)$ goods that the government promises at t to deliver, provided the economy is in state x_{t+1} at $(t + 1)$, and where $q(x_{t+1}, x_t)$ is the current price of one-period-ahead goods at time t, provided the next period's state is x_{t+1}. If the government decides to issue only one-period risk free debt, for example, we have $b(x_{t+1}) = b_{t+1}$ for all x_{t+1}, so that

$$\int q(x_{t+1}, x_t) b(x_{t+1}) \, dx_{t+1} = b_{t+1} \int q(x_{t+1}, x_t) \, dx_{t+1}$$

$$= b_{t+1} / R_{1t}.$$

Equation (3.50) then becomes

$$(3.51) \qquad g_t = \tau_t + b_{t+1} / R_{1t} - b_t.$$

Equation (3.51) is a standard form of the government's budget constraint under conditions of certainty.

We assume that d_t is given by a Markov process with transition density $f(d_{t+1}, d_t)$. We further assume that g_t, d_t are jointly described by a Markov process with transition density $h(g_{t+1}, d_{t+1}; g_t, d_t)$, where

$$\text{prob}\{d_{t+1} \le d', g_{t+1} \le g' | g_t = g, d_t = d\}$$

$$= \int_0^{d'} \int_0^{g'} h(z, s; g, d) \, ds \, dz.$$

The state of the economy is now $(g_t, d_t) \equiv x_t$.

If we write the budget constraint (3.50) in the form

$$b(x_t) = \tau_t(x_t) - g_t(x_t) + \int q(x_{t+1}, x_t)b(x_{t+1}) \, dx_{t+1},$$

and iterate upon it to eliminate future $b(x_{t+j})$, we eventually find that[11]

$$(3.52) \qquad b(x_t) = \tau_t - g_t + \sum_{j=1}^{\infty} \int_{x_{t+j}} [\tau_{t+j}(x_{t+j})$$
$$- g_{t+j}(x_{t+j})] q^{(j)}(x_{t+j}, x_t) \, dx_{t+j},$$

where $q^{(j)}(x_{t+j}, x_t)$ are the j-step-ahead contingent claims prices defined in Equation (3.43). Equation (3.52) states that the value of government debt maturing at time t equals the present value of the stream of government surpluses. If all government debt is perfectly safe, (3.52) simplifies to

$$b_t = \tau_t - g_t + \sum_{j=1}^{\infty} (\tau_{t+j} - g_{t+j}) R_{jt}^{-1}$$

$$\text{where} \quad R_{jt}^{-1} = \int_{x_{t+j}} q^{(j)}(x_{t+j}, x_t) \, dx_{t+j}.$$

We can now apply the three steps outlined above to construct equilibrium prices. The social planning problem for this economy is to maximize $E_0 \sum_{t=0}^{\infty} \beta^t u(c_t)$ subject to $c_t \leq d_t - g_t$, whose solution is $c_t = d_t - g_t$. Proceeding as we did in earlier sections, equilibrium state-contingent prices are described by

$$(3.53) \qquad q(x_{t+1}, x_t) = \beta \frac{u'(d_{t+1} - g_{t+1})}{u'(d_t - g_t)} \cdot h(d_{t+1}, g_{t+1} | d_t, g_t).$$

Equilibrium rates on perfectly safe j-period bonds, for example, are given by

$$(3.54) \qquad R_{jt}^{-1} = \beta^j E_t \frac{u'(d_{t+j} - g_{t+j})}{u'(d_t - g_t)}.$$

For this economy, the following Ricardian proposition holds: the equilibrium consumption stream and state-contingent prices depend only on the stochastic process for output d_t and government expenditure g_t. In particular, consumption and state-contingent prices are both independent of the stochastic process τ_t for taxes. In this model, the choices of the time pattern of

---

11. Repeated substitution, exchange of orders of integration, and use of the definition (3.43) of (j)-step-ahead contingent claim pricing functions are the steps used in deriving (3.52) from the preceding equation.

taxes and government bond issues have no effect on any "relevant" equilibrium price or quantity. (Some asset prices may be affected, however; see Exercise 3.1.) The reason is that, as indicated by Equation (3.50) or (3.52), larger deficits $(g_t - \tau_t)$, accompanied by larger values of government debt $b(x_t)$, now signal future government surpluses. The agents in this model accumulate these government bond holdings and expect to use their proceeds to pay off the very future taxes whose prospects support the value of the bonds. Notice also that, given the stochastic process for (g_t, d_t), the way in which the government finances its deficits (or invests its surpluses) is irrelevant. Thus it does not matter whether it borrows using short-term, long-term, safe, or risky instruments. This irrelevance of financing is an application of the Modigliani-Miller theorem. Equation (3.52) may be interpreted as stating that the present value of the government is independent of such financing decisions.

3.8 Remarks on Testing and Estimation

All of the theories that we have described in this chapter have implications characterized by some version of the following equation:

$$(3.55) \qquad 1 = \beta^j E\left[\frac{u'(c_{t+j})}{u'(c_t)} R_{j,t}^i \big| x_t\right], \qquad i = 1, \ldots, n,$$

where x_t is the state of the economy at t, j is the horizon of the payoff of the asset in question, c_t is consumption at t, and $R_{j,t}^i$ is the j-period realized return from t to $(t + j)$ of the ith asset in question. Here j is the maturity of the ith asset. In (3.55), $E(\cdot | x_t)$ is the mathematical expectation operator conditioned on x_t. It is possible to show that $E\{y|x\} = 1$ implies $\hat{E}\{y|x\} = 1$, where $\hat{E}$ is the linear least-squares projection operator. Thus (3.55) implies

$$(3.56) \qquad 1 = \beta^j \hat{E}\left[\frac{u'(c_{t+j})}{u'(c_t)} R_{j,t}^i \big| x_t\right].$$

Suppose that time-series data are available on $x_{1t} \subset x_t$, c_t, $R_{j,t}^i$ for $t = 1, \ldots, T$, $i = 1, \ldots, m$, where for each asset i there is a corresponding horizon j. Here x_{1t} is a subset of the information that agents are imagined to see at time t and that is included in the state of the economy at time t. Suppose also that one adopts a parametric form of the utility function, such as $u(c) = (c^\gamma - 1)/\gamma$, $\gamma \le 1$. For the true value of γ, Equation (3.56) then predicts that a linear regression of $u'(c_{t+j})R_{j,t}^i/u'(c_t)$ against c_t, x_{1t} and a constant will have coefficient $1/\beta^j$ on the constant term and zero coefficients on all other variables c_t, x_{1t}. Standard statistical hypothesis tests can be applied to test this implication of the theory. When γ is not known, this procedure can be modified slightly to permit estimating γ while simultaneously testing the theory. It is then necessary to reestimate the linear equation (3.56) repeatedly for different assumed values of γ, selecting as the estimate of γ the value of γ that gives the best fit. This procedure is a version of nonlinear least squares. The risk aversion parameter γ is often estimated this way in practice.

The same procedure could be applied to each different asset i to get n distinct estimates of β and γ. The theory predicts that the same estimates of β and γ should emerge for each asset. This restrictive and powerful implication of the theory can be tested empirically. Hansen and Singleton (1982) describe the statistical theory required to implement such procedures and also provide some sample applications. Versions of this test have been applied to testing theories of consumption by Hall (1978) and Hansen and Singleton (1982), theories of the term structure of interest rates by Fama (1976b), and stock prices by Hansen and Singleton (1983). The variance bounds tests used by Shiller (1981) and by LeRoy and Porter (1981) also test some of the implications of a special case of (3.55) or (3.56). The same procedures could be used to test theories of insurance prices.

3.9 Conclusions

This chapter has repeatedly illustrated a method for computing equilibrium asset prices. The method is first to compute a competitive equilibrium consumption allocation. Next, some consumer is identified who is at an interior solution with respect to holdings of a particular asset, so that the Euler equation associated with that asset holds with equality for this consumer. Finally, the consumer's Euler equation is evaluated at that consumer's equilibrium consumption, giving a set of restrictions between the asset price and the determinants of the process for the equilibrium consumption allocation assigned to this particular consumer.

We have used this method in the context of a model of a representative, infinitely lived agent. The method is more generally applicable, however, and also works in the context of models with agents who have heterogeneous preferences and endowments. The method is applicable, for example, in the context of overlapping-generations models, though here it is more difficult to apply.[12] One advantage of the model in the present chapter is that it is easy

12. See Gregory Huffman (1984) and Pamela Labadie (1986). In overlapping-generations models, the old are on corners with respect to asset purchases. One needs to use only the Euler equation of the young to deduce asset-pricing implications.

to calculate the equilibrium consumption allocation of an agent who is "off corners" with respect to potential asset purchases.[13]

The model with government purchases, described in Section 3.7, will form the basis for the next two chapters. We saw in Section 3.7 that, given the process $\{g_t\}_{t=0}^{\infty}$ for government purchases, it is immaterial how the government finances its expenditures. All feasible tax-borrowing plans yield the same present value of taxes and the same equilibrium consumption allocation and asset prices. The portfolio, term structure, and risk structure of government debt are irrelevant. In this model, government debt is valued just like private assets, namely, according to the value of the state-contingent stream of claims to subsequent consumption to which the government-supplied asset represents a claim.

The next two chapters examine two ways in which the model of Section 3.7 can be modified to incorporate a government-supplied currency that is inconvertible into current or future consumption goods but is valued nevertheless. Unlike the government debt described in Section 3.7, an inconvertible currency commits the government to no future payoffs. [In terms of the notation of Section 3.5, $w(x') \equiv 0$ for an inconvertible currency.] There is thus no reason for such an asset to be valued in the context of the model of Section 3.7. The next chapter pursues this matter and then considers how the model of Section 3.7 might be modified so that an inconvertible currency has positive value in equilibrium. Modification is required if we desire a theory of the price level for a system with an inconvertible currency.

Exercises

Exercise 3.1. Taxation and Stock Prices
Consider a version of Lucas's one-tree model along the lines of the discussion in Section 3.3, with $u(c) = \ln c$. Let d_t follow a Markov process with prob$\{d_{t+j} \le d'|d_t = d\} = \int_0^{d'} f(s, d)\, ds$. Let a government spend or "throw away" g_t per capita in period t, where $0 \le g_t < d_t$. Let g_t be given by $g_t = d_t \epsilon_t$, where ϵ_t is a Markov process with prob$\{\epsilon_{t+1} \le \epsilon'|\epsilon_t = \epsilon\} = \int_0^{\epsilon'} k(s, \epsilon)\, ds$. Assume that the only assets traded are titles to trees or shares.

a. Assume that all government expenditures are financed by a lump-sum head tax of τ_t per worker at time t. This tax is independent of the property owned by the representative consumer. Calculate the equilibrium price function for shares (that is, titles to trees).

13. Eichenbaum, Hansen, and Richard (1984) and Eichenbaum and Hansen (1985) use a framework in which there is some heterogeneity across agents but in which a representative agent construct still describes the aggregate data.

b. Now assume that there is an income tax on dividends. In particular, at time t, dividends are taxed at the rate of τ_t/d_t, so that τ_t units of time t good are collected on dividends.

1. Assume the balanced budget rule $g_t = \tau_t$. Calculate the equilibrium price function for titles to trees.
2. Assume the taxing rule $\tau_t = g_t + b(1 - 1/R_{1t})$, where $b > 0$ is a permanent level of borrowing. Now calculate the equilibrium price function of titles to trees.

In what sense are your results consistent with the claim that (state-contingent) prices are independent of the tax strategy, given a stochastic process for per capita government expenditures?

Exercise 3.2. **Contingent Claims Prices in a Brock-Mirman Economy**
Consider the stochastic growth model: maximize $E_0 \sum_{t=0}^{\infty} \beta^t \ln c_t$, subject to $c_t + k_{t+1} \leq Ak_t^\alpha \theta_t$, $A > 0$, $0 < \alpha < 1$, k_0 given, where θ is an independently and identically distributed positive random variable with density $f(\theta_t)$. At time t the planner knows $\{\theta_{t-j}, k_{t-j}, j = 0, 1, \ldots\}$.
a. Show that the optimizing consumption and capital accumulation plans are

$$c_t = (1 - \alpha\beta)k_t^\alpha \theta_t$$
$$k_{t+1} = \alpha\beta Ak_t^\alpha \theta_t.$$

b. Show that, for a competitive economy with these preferences and technology, the contingent claims prices can be expressed as

$$q[(\theta_{t+1}, k_{t+1}), (\theta_t, k_t)] = \frac{\beta}{(\alpha\beta A)^\alpha} k_t^{\alpha(1-\alpha)} \theta_t^{1-\alpha} \theta_{t+1}^{-1} f(\theta_{t+1}),$$

where the state of the economy is defined as $(\theta_t, k_t) \equiv x_t$. Show that

$$q^{(2)}[(\theta_{t+2}, k_{t+2}), (\theta_t, k_t)]$$
$$= \beta^2 \frac{1}{(\beta\alpha A)^{(\alpha+\alpha^2)}} k_t^{\alpha(1-\alpha^2)} \theta_t^{(1-\alpha^2)} \frac{f(\theta_{t+2})}{\theta_{t+2}} E\left(\frac{1}{\theta_{t+1}^\alpha}\right).$$

c. Show that, in a competitive economy with these preferences and technology, the interest rates on sure one-period and two-period loans are given by

$$1/R_{1t} = \frac{\beta}{(\alpha\beta A)^\alpha} k_t^{\alpha(1-\alpha)} \theta_t^{1-\alpha} E(\theta_{t+1}^{-1})$$

$$1/R_{2t} = \frac{\beta^2}{(\beta\alpha A)^{(\alpha+\alpha^2)}} k_t^{\alpha(1-\alpha^2)} \theta_t^{1-\alpha^2} E\left(\frac{1}{\theta_{t+1}^\alpha}\right) E\left(\frac{1}{\theta_{t+2}}\right).$$

Exercise 3.3. Trees (Stocks) in the Utility Function

Consider the following version of Lucas's tree economy. There are two kinds of trees. The first kind is ugly and gives no direct utility in itself but yields a stream of fruit $\{d_{1t}\}$, where d_{1t} is a positive random process obeying a first-order Markov process. The fruit is nonstorable and gives utility. The second kind of tree is beautiful and so yields utility in itself. This tree also yields a stream of the same kind of fruit $\{d_{2t}\}$, where it happens that $d_{2t} \equiv d_{1t} \equiv (1/2)d_t$ for all t, so that the physical yields of the two kinds of trees are equal. There is one of each kind of tree for each of the N individuals in the economy. Trees last forever, but the fruit is not storable. Trees are the only source of fruit.

Each of the N individuals in the economy has preferences described by

$$E_0 \sum_{t=0}^{\infty} \beta^t u(c_t, s_{2t}),$$

where $u(c_t, s_{2t}) = \ln c_t + \gamma \ln s_{2t}$, $\gamma \geq 0$, where c_t is consumption of fruit in period t and s_{2t} is the stock of beautiful trees owned at the beginning of period t. The owner of a tree of either kind i at the beginning of a period receives the fruit d_{it} produced by the tree during that period.

Let p_{it} be the price of a tree of type i ($i = 1, 2$) during period t. Let R_{it} be the gross rate of return on trees of type i held from t to $(t + 1)$. Consider a rational expectations competitive equilibrium of this economy with markets in stocks of each kind of tree.

a. Find pricing functions mapping the state of the economy at t into p_{1t} and p_{2t} (give precise formulas).

b. Prove that, if $\gamma > 0$, then $R_{1t} > R_{2t}$ for all t (that is, beautiful trees are dominated in rate of return).

Exercise 3.4. Government Debt in the Utility Function

Take the model of Section 3.7, but replace preferences with the alternative

$$E_0 \sum_{t=0}^{\infty} \beta^t u(c_t, b_{gt+1}/R_{gt}),$$

where $u_{12} \neq 0$. Is the rate of return in private securities independent of the government financing decision?

Exercise 3.5. Tobin's q

Consider a version of Lucas's one-kind-of-tree model in which "fruit" is storable with no physical depreciation. Letting k_t be the amount of fruit stored per representative agent from time $(t - 1)$ to time t, the social planning problem is: maximize $E_0 \sum_{t=0}^{\infty} \beta^t u(c_t)$, subject to $c_t + k_{t+1} \leq (d_t + k_t)$

and $k_{t+1} \geq 0$ for all $(t + 1)$. Notice that only nonegative amounts of fruit can be stored. Assume that dividends follow a Markov process with transition $f(d', d)$. The social planner chooses sequences $\{c_t, k_{t+1}\}$.

a. Let $v(k + d, d)$ be the value function for the social planning problem. Show that the marginal conditions for the social planning problem imply that

$$\beta \int v_1(k' + d', d')f(d', d)\, dd' \leq u'(c),$$

with equality if $k' > 0$.

b. Now imagine a competitive equilibrium with markets in trees and stocks of capital (stores of fruit). The representative consumer faces the problem of maximizing $E_0 \sum_{t=0}^{\infty} \beta^t u(c_t)$, subject to

$$c_t + p_{kt} k_{t+1} + p_t s_{t+1} \leq s_t(p_t + d_t) + k_t$$
$$k_{t+1} \geq 0,$$

where p_{kt} is the price of capital, p_t the price of trees, s_t number of trees held at the beginning of time t, and k_t the number of units of fruit held over from time $(t - 1)$. Show that in equilibrium the prices of trees and capital obey the conditions

$$p_t = \beta E_t \left[\frac{u'(c_{t+1})}{u'(c_t)} (p_{t+1} + d_{t+1}) \right]$$

$$p_{kt} \geq \beta E_t \left[\frac{u'(c_{t+1})}{u'(c_t)} \right], \quad = \quad \text{if } k_{t+1} > 0.$$

c. Show that, in this model, given the pair (d_t, k_t), investment $(k_{t+1} - k_t)$ is positively correlated with Tobin's q, that is, p_k, which is the price of the existing stock of capital relative to the cost of newly produced goods (fruit).

Exercise 3.6. **A Generalization of Logarithmic Preferences**

Consider an economy with a single representative consumer who maximizes

$$E \sum_{t=0}^{\infty} \beta^t u(c_t), \quad 0 < \beta < 1, \quad \text{where}$$
$$u(c_t) = \ln(c_t + \alpha), \quad \alpha \neq 0.$$

The sole source of the single good is an everlasting tree that produces d_t units of the consumption good in period t. At the beginning of time 0, each consumer owns one such tree. The dividend process d_t is Markov, with

$$\text{prob}\{d_{t+1} \leq d' | d_t = d\} = F(d', d).$$

Assume that the conditional density $f(d', d)$ of F exists. There are competitive markets in titles to trees and in state-contingent claims. Let p_t be the price at t of a title to all *future* dividends from the tree.

a. Prove that equilibrium price p_t satisfies

$$p_t = (d_t + \alpha) \sum_{j=1}^{\infty} \beta^j E_t \left(\frac{d_{t+j}}{d_{t+j} + \alpha} \right).$$

b. Find a formula for the risk-free one-period interest rate R_{1t}. Prove that, in the special case in which $\{d_t\}$ is independently and identically distributed, R_{1t} is given by $R_{1t}^{-1} = \beta k(d_t + \alpha)$, where k is a constant. Give a formula for k.

c. Find a formula for the risk-free two-period interest rate R_{2t}. Prove that, in the special case in which d_t is independently and identically distributed, R_{2t} is given by $R_{2t}^{-1} = \beta^2 k(d_t + \alpha)$, where k is the same constant that you found in part b.

Exercise 3.7. Arbitrage Pricing

At t when $x_t = x$, an asset A promises to pay off $w(x')$ when $x_{t+1} = x'$. The price of this asset at t, p_{At}, is given by the function $p_{At} = g(x_t)$. Construct an argument to show that, unless $g(x) = \int w(x')q(x', x)\, dx'$, there exist arbitrage opportunities.

Exercise 3.8. Modigliani-Miller

An agent L lives in a Lucas tree economy with a very large number of other agents. The one-step-ahead equilibrium pricing kernel in this economy is $q(x', x)$. At time t, the agent L is given a gift of a lottery ticket that has a nonnegative function $w(x')$ written on it. The lottery ticket entitles its owner to receive $w(x')$ units of consumption good at time $(t + 1)$ contingent on $(x_{t+1} = x')$.

Agent L decides to sell claims to parts of her lottery ticket in order to increase her consumption of time t goods. She proceeds as follows. She plans to sell B units of bonds bearing coupon rate R, a fixed number. Each bond will pay off at $(t + 1)$ as follows:

> payoff per bond if $w(x') \geq RB$: R
> payoff per bond if $w(x') \leq RB$: $w(x')/B$.

In addition to selling bonds, agent L sells equities in the amount of S shares. Each unit of equities promises to pay off as follows:

> payoff per share if $w(x') \geq RB$: $[w(x') - RB]/S$
> payoff per share if $w(x') \leq RB$: 0.

The agent chooses the coupon rate R and numbers of bonds and shares, B and S, to maximize the value of the lottery ticket. If we let $p_B(t)$ be the price of the bonds and $p_s(t)$ the price of the shares, the value of the lottery ticket in time t goods is $p_B(t)B + p_s(t)S$.

a. Use an arbitrage argument to find formulas for $p_B(t)$ and $p_s(t)$ in terms of $q(x', x)$.

b. Find the value of the lottery ticket $p_B(t)B + p_s(t)S$ as a function of B, S, R, $w(x')$, and $q(x', x)$.

c. What values of R, B, and S does agent L choose?

Exercise 3.9. **Arbitrage Pricing and the Term Structure of Interest Rates**
Let R_{2t} be the two-period sure rate of interest. Construct an arbitrage argument to show that

$$R_{2t}^{-1} = \int q^{(2)}(x_{t+2}, x_t) \, dx_{t+2}.$$

Exercise 3.10. **Pricing One-Period Options**
Consider a one-tree, one-good Lucas tree model. Preferences of the representative agent are

$$E_0 \sum_{t=0}^{\infty} \beta^t u(c_t), \qquad 0 < \beta < 1,$$

where $u(c_t) = \ln c_t$. Each tree gives off a nonstorable "fruit" or dividend x_t where x_t is a nonnegative random variable governed by a Markov process with stationary one-step transition density $f(x', x)$. We assume that, for any x', $\partial F(x', x)/\partial x < 0$. The sign is implied by positive serial correlation of x_t. The economy starts off with each household owning one tree.

a. Derive the equilibrium pricing function, mapping x_t into the price of trees p_t.

b. Derive a formula for the equilibrium kernel $q(x', x)$ for pricing one-step-ahead contingent claims.

c. Consider an "option" that entitles the current owner to exercise the right to buy, but only if the owner chooses to do so, one tree one period into the future at the fixed price $\bar{p}$. The price $\bar{p}$ is known at t, whereas the option to buy is exercised at $(t + 1)$. Let $\sigma(x_t)$ be the function that prices this option at time t. Find a formula for the pricing function $\sigma(x_t)$ in terms of the parameters describing preferences and endowments.

d. Show that, if there are two options at prices $\bar{p}_1$ and $\bar{p}_2$, and $\bar{p}_1 > \bar{p}_2$, then $\sigma(x_t, \bar{p}_1) < \sigma(x_t, \bar{p}_2)$. Prove that the covariance between share prices and option prices is positive.

e. Consider two economies that are identical except for the discount factor β. Show that, in the economy with a higher degree of patience (that is, higher β), the price of trees is higher, and the one-period-ahead risk-free interest rate is lower for each x.

Exercise 3.11. **Pricing n-Period Options**

Consider a pure exchange economy where the representative agent has preferences over stochastic processes for consumption given by

$$E\left[\sum_{t=0}^{\infty} \beta^t u(c_t)\right], \qquad 0 < \beta < 1,$$

where we assume that u is continuously differentiable and strictly concave. Let the state of the economy be given by the stochastic process $\{x_t\}$. We assume that x_t is a Markov process with density $f(x', x)$ and is such that for every continuous function $h(x)$ the function $y(x) = \int h(x')f(x', x)\, dx'$ is a continuous function of x. We also assume that x_t has compact support (that is, the state space is compact) and that the equilibrium level of consumption, $c(x)$, is a continuous function of the state. Let the price of a stock be given by $p_t = p(x_t)$, where $p(\cdot)$ is assumed continuous. Let $w^n(x, \bar{p})$ be the value of an option to buy, ex-dividend, one share at price $\bar{p}$ either in the current period or in one of the following n periods. The holder of this option is free not to exercise it.

a. Show how to compute $w^n(\cdot)$ as a function of $w^{n-1}(\cdot)$. In particular, show explicitly how to compute $w^1(\cdot)$. Argue that, for any pair $(x, \bar{p})$, $w^n(x, \bar{p}) \geq w^{n-1}(x, \bar{p}) \geq \ldots \geq w^1(x, \bar{p})$.

Hint. It may be helpful to price options as "bundles" of commodities and to use the prices of contingent claims $q(x', x)$.

b. Display the functional equation whose solution is $w^\infty(x, \bar{p})$: the price of an option that can be exercised at any time.

c. (Optional.) Establish that there is only one solution $w^\infty(\cdot)$ and also show that

$$w^\infty(x, \bar{p}) = \lim_{n \to \infty} w^n(x, \bar{p}).$$

d. Suppose we know that, in the next n periods, the stock will not pay dividends. Let $z^n(x, \bar{p})$ be the value of an option to buy one share at price $\bar{p}$, n periods ahead. Notice that, although $w^n(\cdot)$ is the price of a contract that allows the owner to exercise the option in any of the following n periods, $z^n(\cdot)$ does so only in the nth period; that is, $z^n(\cdot)$ is a more constrained contract. Show, however, that, for such a dividendless stock, $z^n(x, \bar{p}) = w^n(x, \bar{p})$, provided that the risk-free interest rate, $R(x)$, is greater than one for almost all x—in other words, show that the option will never be exercised until the last period.

References and Suggested Readings

Altug, Sumru. 1985. Time to build and equilibrium pricing. University of Minnesota, Minneapolis.

Barro, Robert J. 1974. Are government bonds net wealth? *Journal of Political Economy* 82(6):1095–1117.

Benveniste, Lawrence, and José Scheinkman. 1979. On the differentiability of the value function in dynamic models of economics. *Econometrica* 47(3):727–732.

Breeden, Douglas T. 1979. An intertemporal asset pricing model with stochastic consumption and investment opportunities. *Journal of Financial Economics* 7(3):265–296.

Brock, William A. 1982. Asset prices in a production economy. In *The Economics of Information and Uncertainty*, ed. J. J. McCall, pp. 1–43. Chicago: University of Chicago Press.

Brock, William A., and Leonard Mirman. 1972. Optimal economic growth and uncertainty: the discounted case. *Journal of Economic Theory* 4(3):479–513.

Cox, John C., Jonathan E. Ingersoll, Jr., and Stephen A. Ross. 1985a. An intertemporal general equilibrium model of asset prices. *Econometrica* 53(2):363–384.

——— 1985b. A theory of the term structure of interest rates. *Econometrica* 53(2):385–408.

Eichenbaum, Martin, and Lars P. Hansen. 1985. Estimating models with intertemporal substitution using aggregate time series data. Carnegie-Mellon University, Pittsburgh, Pa.

Eichenbaum, Martin, Lars P. Hansen, and S. F. Richard. 1984. The dynamic equilibrium pricing of durable consumption goods. Carnegie Mellon University, Pittsburgh, Pa.

Fama, Eugene F. 1976a. *Foundations of Finance: Portfolio Decisions and Securities Prices.* New York: Basic Books.

——— 1976b. Inflation uncertainty and expected returns on treasury bills. *Journal of Political Economy* 84(3):427–448.

Granger, C. W. J. 1969. Investigating causal relations by econometric models and cross-spectral methods. *Econometrica* 37(3):424–438.

Grossman, Sanford J., and Robert J. Shiller. 1981. The determinants of the variability of stock market prices. *American Economic Review* 71(2):222–227.

Hall, Robert E. 1978. Stochastic implications of the life cycle-permanent income hypothesis: theory and evidence. *Journal of Political Economy* 86(6):971–988. (Reprinted in *Rational Expectations and Econometric Practice*, ed. Thomas J. Sargent and Robert E. Lucas, Jr., pp. 501–520. Minneapolis: University of Minnesota Press, 1981.)

Hansen, Lars P., and Kenneth J. Singleton. 1982. Generalized instrumental variables estimation of nonlinear rational expectations models. *Econometrica* 50(5):1269–1286.

——— 1983. Stochastic consumption, risk aversion, and the temporal behavior of asset returns. *Journal of Political Economy* 91(2):249–265.

Hirshleifer, Jack. 1966. Investment decision under uncertainty: applications of the state preference approach. *Quarterly Journal of Economics* 80(2):252–277.

Huffman, Gregory. 1984. The representative agent, overlapping generations, and asset pricing. Working Paper 8405. University of Western Ontario, Department of Economics. London.

Kihlstrom, Richard E., and Leonard J. Mirman. 1974. Risk aversion with many commodities. *Journal of Economic Theory* 8:361–388.

Labadie, Pamela. 1986. Comparative dynamics and risk premia in an overlapping generations model. *Review of Economic Studies* 53(1):139–152.

LeRoy, Stephen F. 1973. Risk aversion and the Martingale property of stock prices. *International Economic Review* 14(2):436–446.

——— 1982. Risk-aversion and the term structure of interest rates. *Economics Letters* 10(3–4):355–361. (Correction in *Economics Letters* [1983] 12(3–4):339–340.)

LeRoy, Stephen F., and Richard D. Porter. 1981. The present-value relation: tests based on implied variance bounds. *Econometrica* 49(3):555–574.

Lucas, Robert E., Jr. 1978. Asset prices in an exchange economy. *Econometrica* 46(6):1426–1445.

——— 1982. Interest rates and currency prices in a two-country world. *Journal of Monetary Economics* 10(3):335–359.

Mehra, Rajnish, and Edward C. Prescott. 1985. The equity premium: a puzzle. *Journal of Monetary Economics* 15(2):145–162.

Modigliani, F., and M. H. Miller. 1958. The cost of capital, corporation finance, and the theory of investment. *American Economic Review* 48(3):261–297.

Roll, Richard. 1970. *The Behavior of Interest Rates: An Application of the Efficient Market Model to U.S. Treasury Bills.* New York: Basic Books.

Ross, Stephen A. 1976. The arbitrage theory of capital asset pricing. *Journal of Economic Theory* 13(3): 341–360.

Samuelson, Paul A. 1965. Proof that properly anticipated prices fluctuate randomly. *Industrial Management Review* 6(1):41–49.

Sargent, Thomas J. 1979. *Macroeconomic Theory.* New York: Academic Press.

Sargent, Thomas J. 1980. Tobin's q and the rate of investment in general equilibrium. In *On the State of Macroeconomics,* Carnegie-Rochester Conference Series 12, ed. K. Brunner and A. Meltzer, pp. 107–154. Amsterdam: North-Holland.

Shiller, Robert J. 1981. Do stock prices move too much to be justified by subsequent changes in dividends? *American Economic Review* 71(3): 421–436.

Sims, Christopher A. 1972. Money, income, and causality. *American Economic Review* 62(4):540–552.

Stiglitz, Joseph E. 1969. A reexamination of the Modigliani-Miller theorem. *American Economic Review* 59(5):784–793.

Monetary Economics and Government Finance | II

4 | Currency in the Utility Function

This chapter introduces some issues in monetary theory, focusing on difficulties in creating a model in which an inconvertible government currency has value and describing the nature of these difficulties by using the Lucas tree model to price an inconvertible government currency. In equilibrium, an inconvertible currency is valueless; this result generally obtains in Arrow-Debreu models.

The chapter also describes one way of altering the specification of the model economy so that a positive value is assigned to an inconvertible currency (namely, by altering preferences so that the real value of currency enters the current-period utility function). The model is used to illustrate some ideas in monetary economics.

4.1 The Price of Inconvertible Government Currency in Lucas's Tree Model

Let us consider a version of Lucas's tree model in which the government attempts to place an unbacked inconvertible currency into existence at time $t = 0$, using it to finance government purchases at $t = 0$. The government puts M units per capita of unbacked paper called dollars into circulation. The value of this paper is w_t, measured in goods at t per dollar. Thus w_t is the reciprocal of the price level at t. The government sets lump-sum taxes $\tau_t = 0$ for all $t \geq 0$. As for government purchases, the government selects

(4.1) $$g_0 = Mw_0$$
$$g_t = 0, \quad t \geq 1.$$

Notice from (4.1) that g_0 depends on the equilibrium value of w_0. In particular, if $w_0 = 0$, the government purchases no goods at $t = 0$.

As before, we assume that the only source of the nonstorable consumption good is trees. At time t each tree yields x_t units of the consumption good. We assume that $x_t \geq x > 0$, so that x_t is uniformly bounded away from zero from below. We assume that there is no uncertainty, so that $\{x_t\}_{t=0}^{\infty}$ is a known sequence. There is one tree per consumer. Each consumer starts off owning one tree at time $t = 0$.

We now use the steps of our asset-pricing method to determine both the price of trees p_t and the value of currency w_t, $t \geq 0$. If we take g_t and w_t as given to the social planner and use (4.1), the solution of the social planning problem is $c_0 = x_0 - Mw_0$, $c_t = x_t$, $t \geq 1$.

We now study the representative consumer's problem when confronted with a given nonnegative sequence for w_t, $t \geq 0$. The consumer maximizes

$$(4.2) \qquad \sum_{t=0}^{\infty} \beta^t u(c_t),$$

subject to

$$(4.3) \qquad c_t + s_{t+1} p_t + w_t m_{t+1} \leq s_t(p_t + x_t) + w_t m_t, \qquad t \geq 0,$$
$$m_0 = 0, \qquad s_0 = 1.$$

Here c_t is consumption at t, p_t is the price of trees, s_t is the number of trees owned at the beginning of period t, w_t is the value of currency at t, and m_t is the amount of currency owned at the beginning of period t. The maximization of (4.2) is over sequences for (c_t, m_{t+1}, s_{t+1}) for $t \geq 0$ and is subject to $m_{t+1} \geq 0$, $m_0 = 0$, $s_0 = 1$. The Lagrangian associated with this problem is

$$L = \sum_{t=0}^{\infty} \beta^t \{u(c_t) + \lambda_t[s_t(p_t + x_t) + w_t m_t - c_t - s_{t+1} p_t - w_t m_{t+1}]\},$$

where $\{\lambda_t\}$ is a sequence of nonnegative multipliers. Assuming an interior solution for c_t implies that $\lambda_t = u'(c_t)$. The first-order conditions for s_{t+1} and m_{t+1} then are

$$(4.4) \qquad \beta \frac{u'(c_{t+1})}{u'(c_t)} \left(\frac{p_{t+1} + x_{t+1}}{p_t} \right) = 1$$

$$(4.5) \qquad \beta \frac{u'(c_{t+1})}{u'(c_t)} w_{t+1} \leq w_t, \qquad = \text{ if } m_{t+1} > 0.$$

The last pair of inequalities can be expressed as

$$(4.6) \qquad m_{t+1} w_t \left[1 - \beta \frac{u'(c_{t+1})}{u'(c_t)} \frac{w_{t+1}}{w_t} \right] = 0.$$

Defining R_t as the risk-free one-period gross interest rate, we have $(p_{t+1} + x_{t+1})/p_t = R_t$. This equation together with (4.4) gives the standard formula

(4.7) $\qquad \beta \dfrac{u'(c_{t+1})}{u'(c_t)} R_t = 1.$

Substituting the equilibrium allocations $c_0 = x_0 - Mw_0$, $c_t = x_t$, $t \geq 1$, into the above equation gives

(4.8) $\qquad \beta \dfrac{u'(x_1)}{u'(x_0 - Mw_0)} = 1/R_0$

$\qquad\qquad \beta \dfrac{u'(x_{t+1})}{u'(x_t)} = 1/R_t, \qquad$ for $t \geq 1.$

From (4.7), Equation (4.6) can evidently be represented as

(4.9) $\qquad m_{t+1} w_t \left(1 - R_t^{-1} \dfrac{w_{t+1}}{w_t}\right) = 0, \qquad t \geq 0.$

There is one more equilibrium condition, namely that the demand for currency to hold between t and $(t + 1)$, m_{t+1}, must equal the supply M. Saying that $m_{t+1} = M$ in (4.9) gives

(4.10) $\qquad Mw_t \left(1 - R_t^{-1} \dfrac{w_{t+1}}{w_t}\right) = 0, \qquad t \geq 0.$

We now seek a solution of (4.10) and (4.7) or (4.8) in which $w_t > 0$ for all $t \geq 0$. Evidently, if $w_t > 0$, we require

$\qquad\qquad 1 - R_t^{-1} \dfrac{w_{t+1}}{w_t} = 0$

or $\qquad w_{t+1} = R_t w_t, \qquad t \geq 0.$

Solving this difference equation gives

$\qquad\qquad w_t = \left(\prod_{j=0}^{t-1} R_j\right) w_0.$

Using (4.8) in the above equation gives

(4.11) $\qquad w_t = \beta^{-t} \dfrac{u'(x_0 - Mw_0)}{u'(x_t)} w_0.$

Because we have assumed that $x_t \geq x > 0$, it follows that $u'(x_t) \leq u'(x) < +\infty$. Therefore, $u'(x_0 - Mw_0)/u'(x_t)$ is a bounded sequence for any w_0 satisfying $0 \leq Mw_0 \leq x_0$. If $w_0 > 0$, and $0 < Mw_0 \leq x_0$ ($g_0 = Mw_0 \leq x_0$ is a requirement of feasibility), Equation (4.11) implies that w_t grows without bound as $t \rightarrow \infty$. If w_t were to grow without bound, however, the budget constraint (4.3) implies that the consumer's initial wealth at t, $s_t(p_t + x_t) + w_t m_t = (p_t + x_t) + w_t M$ would be growing without bound. If this were so, then $c_t = x_t$ for $t \geq 1$ would not be an optimal consumption plan for a consumer facing the given prices for (p_t, w_t), $t \geq 0$. It would not be optimal because it would be feasible to consume more in some periods without reducing consumption in any other periods. Therefore such a path for w_t cannot be an equilibrium, and we cannot have $w_0 > 0$. Instead, we must have $w_0 = 0$, $w_t = 0$ for $t \geq 1$. Notice that if $w_t = 0$ whenever $t \geq 0$, the consumer's first-order condition for m_{t+1} is satisfied wherever $t \geq 0$.

In summary, a unique equilibrium for this model has $w_t = 0$ whenever $t \geq 0$ and $g_t = 0$ whenever $t \geq 0$. An unbacked currency is valueless in this economy. In this economy, assets are valued according to the value of the stream of consumption that they support. An unbacked or inconvertible currency promises to pay off nothing in the future. We have seen that introducing an asset with such a payoff stream into Lucas's tree model leaves the equilibrium interest rates unaltered and causes the asset to receive zero value.

It is significant that the zero value assigned to an inconvertible currency in this economy coexists with two other features of the economy. One feature is that there is a unique competitive equilibrium consumption allocation in this economy and that it is Pareto optimal. A second feature is that this is a high-interest-rate economy in the sense that

$$\prod_{j=0}^{t-1} R_j = \beta^{-t} \frac{u'(x_0)}{u'(x_t)}$$

is diverging to $+\infty$ as $t \rightarrow \infty$. Furthermore, if the currency is to be voluntarily held, it must bear the equilibrium rate of interest. The high interest rate that currency must bear for it to be valued prevents it from being valued, as the preceding argument stresses.

Models that permit an unbacked currency to be valued are typically constructed by assuming an economy that departs from one or both of these two features. All models of unbacked currency adopt some device to lower the rate of return that currency must bear in order to be demanded. Currency-in-the-utility-function models and cash-in-advance models employ devices that drive the rate of return on currency below the rate of return on assets with comparable risk characteristics. Currency-in-the-utility-function models usually also eliminate the optimality of competitive equilibria. Overlapping-generations models and Bewley-Townsend models alter the specification of endowments, preferences, and technologies so that the uniqueness and optimality of competitive equilibrium no longer necessarily obtain, and room is thereby created for an inconvertible currency to be valued.

4.2 Issues and Models in Monetary Economics

We shall eventually study several models of economies with valued fiat currency: models with currency in the utility function, cash-in-advance models, Bewley-Townsend models with loan market failures, and overlapping-generations models.[1] Each of these models deviates from the Arrow-Debreu model in an essential way, a necessity because there is no room for valued unbacked currency within the Arrow-Debreu model. With the possible exception of currency-in-the-utility-function models, each of these models supposes an environment in which decentralized trading occurs in contrast to the centralized trading of the Arrow-Debreu model. The different models of fiat currency differ significantly in the ways in which they deviate from the Arrow-Debreu structure. In models with currency in the utility function, preferences are altered vis-à-vis an Arrow-Debreu model by the inclusion of the stock of a particular asset — usually government-issued currency — directly in the utility function. In cash-in-advance models, the market structure and households' constraints are altered vis-à-vis an Arrow-Debreu model in that at least some goods can be purchased only with currency accumulated in advance of shopping. This constraint is motivated, more or less implicitly, by an appeal to locational decentralization. In models of the Bewley-Townsend type, the endowment and location patterns are altered vis-à-vis the Arrow-Debreu model in a way that hampers loan markets enough to leave a consumption-smoothing role for an unbacked currency. Finally, in the overlapping-generations model, agents are arranged intertemporally in a way that prevents markets in private loans and insurance alone from supporting a Pareto-optimal allocation, thereby leaving a potential social role for an unbacked currency.

We study these models to increase our understanding of a variety of phenomena and government policy choices involving currency and its substitutes. The things that we want such models to help us understand include money-price correlations, free banking versus government regulation of banks, inferior rates of return on government-supplied currencies, interna-

---

1. See, for example, Sidrauski (1967), Fischer (1983), and LeRoy (1984a, 1984b); Lucas (1980, 1982); Bewley (1980) and Townsend (1980); Sargent and Wallace (1982).

tional exchange rate determination, effects of government open-market operations, and coordination of monetary and fiscal policies.

1. *Money-price correlations.* We want to interpret time-series and cross-country correlations between aggregate stocks of various categories of liabilities, on the one hand, and price levels and international exchange rates, on the other hand. From the standpoint of understanding correlations between price level and money, what are the appropriate categories of evidences of indebtedness to include in the aggregate defined as "money"? Should the demand for privately issued bank notes, checking accounts, money market funds, foreign currencies and securities, and other evidences of private and public credit be modeled in the same way as that for government currency?

Sargent and Wallace (1982) build a model in which the answer to this question depends on the set of legal restrictions governing entry into banking. Under free banking, a wide aggregate, being the sum of government currency ("outside money") and intermediated private indebtedness ("inside money") is best correlated with the price level. Under a quantity theory restriction that gives the government a monopoly in issuing small-denomination notes (it can be interpreted as a 100 percent reserves regime) high-powered money is best correlated with the price level.

2. *Free banking versus government regulations of banks.* Should the government monopolize the issue of currency, or should there be free entry into the business of creating small-denomination risk-free evidences of indebtedness? What principles ought to guide the design and administration of a system for government regulation of banks and other intermediaries that issue liabilities in competition with government currency? Is the goal of price-level stability sufficient to guide and rationalize regulation of those intermediaries? Sargent and Wallace (1982) deal with these issues within the context of an overlapping-generations model. Stanley Fischer (1983) studies them with a currency-in-the-utility-function model.

3. *Inferior rates of return on government-supplied currencies.* What forces explain the widely observed and persistent rate-of-return dominance that other assets (for example, large-denomination government securities and private securities) exhibit over currency? How do we explain the variation over time in the extent of this dominance, that is, the time-series fluctuations in nominal rates of interest? (Models of the Fisher effect on nominal interest rates offer one explanation.) Neil Wallace (1983) describes these issues.

4. *International exchange rate determination.* What determines international exchange rates on country-specific currencies? What explains the number of currencies that are issued throughout the world (with a few exceptions, one currency per country)? Is there a role for currency controls and capital controls in managing a country's currency?

5. *Effect of government open-market operations.* What are the effects of open-market operations in domestic and foreign currencies? What aspects of the economic structure impart effectiveness to open-market operations?

6. *Coordination of monetary and fiscal policies.* What are the intertemporal dimensions of the coordination problem faced by the monetary and fiscal authorities? How much control can a central bank have over the value of its currency? This issue was studied by Sargent and Wallace (1981).

Because they have different structures of preferences, endowments, and technologies, models differ in their perspective on these issues. Currency-in-the-utility-function and cash-in-advance models each have implications about issues 1, 3, 4, and 5 that stem relatively directly from the definition of the class of assets that the analyst decides to include in the cash-in-advance constraint or in the utility function. Typically this definition determines the class of assets best correlated with the price level. This definition also determines a class of assets that is dominated in rate of return by those assets not in the utility function or not qualifying for the cash-in-advance constraint. For multiple-country, multiple-currency versions of these models, the exchange rate is influenced intimately by the details of the specification of the cash-in-advance restriction or the utility function for currency-in-the-utility-function models. Altering these features of the models directly alters the implications for exchange rate determination. Central bank exchanges of other assets for assets in the utility function or for assets that satisfy the cash-in-advance constraint influence equilibrium rates of return and price levels. As for issue 2, the matter is largely decided at the point at which the analyst specifies the class of liabilities entering the utility function or satisfying the cash-in-advance constraint. If private agents do not have access to the technology for issuing these liabilities, which is the usual assumption, then there is no need to prohibit private agents from issuing such liabilities. If private agents do have access to such technologies, then the money-in-the-utility-function or cash-in-advance models must be regarded as relying on a set of implicit legal restrictions that prohibit private agents from exploiting the arbitrage profits that exist in these models and that only the central bank is permitted to exploit. These arbitrage opportunities are symptomized by the domination of government-issued currency in rate of return.

Overlapping-generations and Bewley-Townsend models both provide quite a different perspective on these issues from that offered by currency-in-the-utility-function and cash-in-advance models. In overlapping-generations models, endowment and preference patterns exist in which fiat currency coexists with and bears the same return as risk-free private indebtedness. Private indebtedness and fiat currency compete for a place in private portfolios solely on the basis of rate of return. In overlapping-generations models without legal restrictions, currency, if it is valued, is not dominated in rate of return. The consequence is that disturbances to excess demands for private securities impinge on the equilibrium value of government currency. As a result, the price level–money correlations may be strongest for wide aggregates of currency and inside indebtedness. Then, too, the goal of price-level stability is well served by the adoption of legal restrictions that prevent private intermediaries from issuing liabilities that compete well with government-supplied currency; see Sargent and Wallace (1982). The extensive substitutability of private securities for government securities limits the government's ability to collect seignorage via an inflation tax and means that rates of return on all private securities are in general influenced by government attempts to extract seignorage. Again, this substitutability can justify legal regulations designed to protect a government's currency from competition and to facilitate collection of an inflation tax. At a positive level, the hypothesis that legal restrictions force people to hold government-supplied currency has been used to account for the observed patterns of positive and time-varying nominal interest rates; see Wallace (1983).

The hypothesis of legal restrictions has also been invoked to explain exchange rate determination in the context of overlapping-generations models. In these models without legal restrictions on asset trading, it has been found that equilibrium international exchange rates are indeterminate. In these models, legal restrictions can play the role of making demands for country-specific currencies well defined and can give different countries scope to impose different inflation tax rates. In the overlapping-generations model without legal restrictions, countries must coordinate their monetary and fiscal policies, because each government is able to impose an inflation tax on the residents of all countries. The forces for coordination are less evident in cash-in-advance and currency-in-the-utility-function models, shutting down at the point in the analysis when the utility functions or cash-in-advance constraints are specified.

4.3 Government Debt in the Utility Function

We begin our discussion of models with currency in the utility function by studying a model in which government one-period debt is in the utility function. We begin in this way in order to stress the formal equivalence between government debt and currency in these models and the rate-of-return dominance that characterizes the equilibrium.

We now consider a one-tree version of Lucas's model, in which a government purchases g_t goods per capita in period t. We assume that g_t gives rise to no utility and that $0 \le g_t < d_t$ for all t. We assume that (g_t, d_t) is governed by a first-order Markov process. The government finances its expenditures g_t by a combination of lump-sum taxes τ_t per capita in period t and by borrowing in the amount b_{gt+1}/R_{gt} per capita in sure one-period loans at t. The government's budget constraint in per capita terms is

$$(4.12) \qquad g_t = \tau_t + b_{gt+1}/R_{gt} - b_{gt},$$

where R_{gt} is the gross rate of return on one-period government loans from time t to $(t + 1)$ and b_{gt} is the amount per capita that the government owes in maturing one-period loans at time t. We let R_t denote the one-period gross interest rate on one-period private securities.

All agents are identically endowed initially with one tree, each of which yields dividend stream $\{d_t\}$. Individuals have common preferences described by

$$(4.13) \qquad E_0 \sum_{t=0}^{\infty} \beta^t [\ln c_t + \gamma \ln(b_{gt+1}/R_{gt})], \qquad 0 < \beta < 1,$$

where $\gamma \ge 0$. When $\gamma > 0$, government debt enters the utility function directly. Private securities do not enter the utility function directly but only indirectly, via the stream of consumption that they support. This specification of preferences implies that, at equal risk-free rates of return, individuals prefer to hold government debt rather than private debt.

The representative consumer's budget constraint at t is

$$c_t + \tau_t + \frac{b_{gt+1}}{R_{gt}} + \frac{b_{t+1}}{R_t} + s_{t+1} a_t \le b_{gt} + b_t + s_t(a_t + d_t),$$

where b_{t+1} is the quantity of risk-free private loans maturing at $(t + 1)$ purchased at t, denominated in time $(t + 1)$ goods; R_t is the gross interest rate on perfectly sure one-period private securities; s_{t+1} is the number of trees owned at the end of period t; a_t is the price of trees at t; and d_t is dividends on trees at t.

We assume that the government runs its fiscal policy so that $b_{gt+1} > 0$ for all $t \ge 0$. Proceeding as in Chapter 3 with our three steps to study equilibrium asset prices and returns, we find, from the Euler equations for private securities and government securities, respectively, that

$$(4.14) \qquad 1 = E_t \beta R_t \frac{c_t}{c_{t+1}}$$

$$(4.15) \qquad 1 = E_t \beta R_{gt} \frac{c_t}{c_{t+1}} + \gamma E_t R_{gt} \frac{c_t}{b_{gt+1}},$$

where in equilibrium $c_t = d_t - g_t$. Because R_t and R_{gt} are known at time t, Equations (4.14) and (4.15) imply that

$$(4.16) \qquad R_{gt}^{-1} = R_t^{-1} + \gamma E_t \frac{c_t}{b_{gt+1}}.$$

Thus if $\gamma > 0$, $R_{gt} < R_t$ for all realizations of $c_t = d_t - g_t$. In this case, risk-free private debt dominates government debt in rate of return. Note that the rate of return on risk-free private debt obeys $R_t^{-1} = \beta E_t\{(d_t - g_t)/(d_{t+1} - g_{t+1})\}$. Therefore R_t^{-1} is independent of the quantity of government bonds b_{gt+1}. (The independence of the rate of return on private securities from the government's financing decision in this model is special and depends on our having assumed that utility is separable in consumption and government debt.) Equation (4.16) shows, however, that when $\gamma > 0$, R_{gt} varies directly with the quantity of government bonds. As b_{gt+1} grows without limit, R_{gt} approaches R_t from below.

This model incorporates a limiting version of the view toward government debt described by Tobin (1961, 1963). Government-supplied liabilities, including currency and other forms of government debt, are assumed to be very good or perfect substitutes for one another but are more attractive than are private securities. In the limit, government debt and government currency are taken to be perfect substitutes for one another, whereas private securities are imperfect substitutes for government securities. Tobin described the implications of such assumptions for the effectiveness of government open-market operations. (See Chapter 8 for descendants of Tobin's analysis.) Tobin intended to contrast such assumptions with the alternative ones incorporated in many standard macroeconomic models, which Tobin attributed to Keynes: namely, that private securities and government interest-bearing securities are perfect substitutes for one another but that both are imperfect substitutes for government-supplied currency. Let us now modify the preceding model to accommodate this view.

4.4 Government Currency in the Utility Function

As a start, the model of the preceding section can be reinterpreted in the following way. Let m_{t+1} be the amount of government-issued, non-interest-bearing currency called dollars held by a representative agent from period t to $(t + 1)$. Let p_t be the price level, measured in dollars per time t good. Then dollars yield a gross rate of return from t to $(t + 1)$ of p_t/p_{t+1}. We can then reinterpret the preceding model as being one in which all government debt takes the form of dollars and in which real balances of dollars are in the utility function. We simply set $m_{t+1}/p_t = b_{gt+1}/R_{gt}$, $b_{gt} = m_t/p_t$, and $R_{gt} = p_t/p_{t+1}$. With this interpretation, the government budget constraint becomes

(4.17) $\qquad g_t = \tau_t + \dfrac{m_{t+1}}{p_t} - \dfrac{m_t}{p_t}.$

Preferences of the representative agent become

(4.18) $\qquad E_0 \displaystyle\sum_{t=0}^{\infty} \beta^t[\ln c_t + \gamma \ln(m_{t+1}/p_t)].$

The budget constraint of the representative agent is

$$c_t + \tau_t + \frac{m_{t+1}}{p_t} + \frac{b_{t+1}}{R_t} + s_{t+1}a_t \le \frac{m_t}{p_t} + b_t + s_t(a_t + d_t).$$

Equation (4.15) becomes

$$1 = \beta E_t \frac{p_t}{p_{t+1}} \frac{c_t}{c_{t+1}} + \gamma E_t \frac{p_t}{p_{t+1}} \frac{c_t p_{t+1}}{m_{t+1}}$$

or

(4.19) $\qquad 1/p_t = \beta E_t \dfrac{c_t}{c_{t+1}} \, 1/p_{t+1} + \gamma E_t \dfrac{c_t}{m_{t+1}}.$

The stochastic difference equation (4.19) has solution

(4.20) $\qquad 1/p_t = \gamma c_t \displaystyle\sum_{j=0}^{\infty} \beta^j E_t \frac{1}{m_{t+j+1}},$

which expresses p_t^{-1} as a geometric sum of expected future values of m_t^{-1}.

Equations (4.19) and (4.20) can be used to describe a version of the Fisher equation relating the nominal interest rate to the rate of inflation. Begin by noting that in this model the kernel for pricing one-step-ahead real state-contingent claims is given by $q(x', x) = \beta(c/c')f(x', x)$, where the state $x = (d, g)$ and where $c = d - g$. Let the sure nominal interest rate factor be denoted $\phi(x_t)$, which is the price in dollars at t of a sure claim on one dollar at time $(t + 1)$. Evidently, we have

$$\phi(x_t) = \beta E_t \frac{c_t}{c_{t+1}} \frac{p_t}{p_{t+1}}.$$

Equation (4.19) asserts

$$1 = \phi(x_t) + \gamma E_t \frac{p_t c_t}{m_{t+1}}.$$

Note that, if $\gamma = 0$, the above equation asserts that $1 = \phi(x_t)$ if an equilibrium exists. In other words, when currency is not in the utility function, the net nominal interest must equal zero. We saw in Section 4.1, however, that no equilibrium with valued unbacked currency exists when $\gamma = 0$.

Because $p_t c_t / m_{t+1}$ is known at time t, we can write the preceding equation as

(4.21) $$\phi(x_t) = 1 - \gamma \frac{p_t c_t}{m_{t+1}}.$$

To derive a version of Fisher's equation, suppose that the currency process takes the deterministic form:

$$\frac{1}{m_t} = \lambda^t \frac{1}{m_0} \quad \text{for } t \geq 1,$$

where $|\beta\lambda| < 1$. Here λ^{-1} is the gross growth rate of currency. Under this circumstance, Equation (4.20) becomes

$$\frac{m_{t+1}}{p_t c_t} = \frac{\gamma}{1 - \lambda\beta}.$$

Substituting this expression for $m_{t+1}/p_t c_t$ in (4.21) and solving for $\phi(x_t)$ gives $\phi(x_t) = \lambda\beta$. This equation states that the nominal interest rate factor (the reciprocal of the gross nominal interest rate) varies directly with λ, the rate of growth of the reciprocal of currency. Under the special policy of a constant growth rate for currency for all future periods, the above equation shows that an increase in the rate of growth of currency causes a proportional increase in the gross nominal interest rate. The reciprocal of the gross inflation rate under this special policy obeys

$$\frac{p_t}{p_{t+1}} = \lambda \frac{c_{t+1}}{c_t}.$$

The preceding two equations qualify as a version of Fisher's theory of the relation between nominal interest rates and the rate of inflation.

We now briefly consider the special case of (4.19) in which $\{d_t - g_t\}$ is a perfectly forecastable series, so that conditional expectations equal subsequently realized values. Then (4.19) can be expressed as

(4.19') $$\frac{m_{t+1}}{p_t} = \frac{\gamma c_t}{1 - (p_t/p_{t+1})R_t^{-1}},$$

where $R_t^{-1} = \beta c_t / c_{t+1}$. This equation is a version of a demand schedule for currency. Because $p_t/p_{t+1} = R_{gt}$, and we know that $0 < R_{gt}R_t^{-1} < 1$, the demand for real balances defined by this equation is nonnegative. The demand for currency approaches satiation only when $R_{gt}R_t^{-1}$ approaches unity.

4.5 Seignorage and the Optimum Quantity of Currency

We now introduce another interpretation of the preceding model. We suppose that, in addition to issuing currency, the government borrows in the market for private loans. The government's loans in the private market do not enter private agents' utility function. Only currency enters the utility function. The government's budget constraint is now

$$(4.22) \qquad g_t = \tau_t + \frac{m_{t+1}}{p_t} - \frac{m_t}{p_t} + \frac{b_{t+1}}{R_t} - b_t,$$

where b_t is now government one-period interest-bearing loans due at time t. This equation can also be expressed as

$$(4.23) \qquad D_t = \frac{m_{t+1}}{p_{t+1}} \frac{p_{t+1}}{p_t} - \frac{m_t}{p_t} + \frac{b_{t+1}}{R_t} - b_t,$$

where $D_t = g_t - \tau_t$ is the per capita government deficit when we exclude from expenditures the interest payment on the government debt. That is, D_t is the net-of-interest government deficit per capita.

Let us study the special case in which $c_t = d_t - g_t = \bar{c}$, a constant for all t. Then we have that $R_t = \beta^{-1}$ for all t, and (4.23) can be expressed as

$$(4.24) \qquad D_t - \beta b_{t+1} + b_t = \frac{m_{t+1}}{p_t} - \frac{m_t}{p_{t-1}} \frac{p_{t-1}}{p_t}.$$

For the purposes of discussing several issues in monetary economics, it will suffice to focus on alternative stationary states. Suppose that $D_t - \beta b_{t+1} + b_t = D + (1 - \beta)b$, a constant for all t. We want to study the stationary solutions that arise when $D_t - \beta b_{t+1} + b_t = D + (1 - \beta)b$, $m_{t+1}/p_t = \bar{m}$, and $p_t/p_{t+1} = R_m$ for all t in (4.24). This substitution yields

$$(4.25) \qquad D + (1 - \beta)b = \bar{m}(1 - R_m).$$

Substituting steady-state values into the demand schedule for money (4.21) and substituting the result into (4.25), we have

$$(4.26) \qquad D + (1 - \beta)b = \gamma c \frac{(1 - R_m)}{1 - R_m \beta}, \qquad 0 \le R_m < \beta^{-1}.$$

Figure 4.1 plots the right side of (4.26), which gives the stationary value of real seignorage per capita that is collected when a gross yield on currency of R_m is sustained. Because $\beta^{-1} > R_m \geq 0$, we see that supremum of feasible stationary values of seignorage is γc. It is not feasible to attain this supremum, because attaining it requires that $R_m = 0$ and that "infinite inflation" be sustained. At the other extreme, as $R_m \to \beta^{-1}$ from below, stationary per capita real balances grow without bound. Figure 4.1 and Equation (4.26), together with the demand function (4.19'), show that, in order to increase stationary real balances, the government must decrease $D + (1 - \beta)b$. There is no finite value of $D + (1 - \beta)b$ that satiates the economy with holdings of currency. This feature is a consequence of the specification of preferences (4.18) and would be altered if (4.18) were changed to specify that the marginal utility of (m_{t+1}/p_t) becomes zero for m_{t+1}/p_t greater than some finite amount.

Equation (4.26) or Figure 4.1 can be used to illustrate some ideas in monetary theory. One is the classical doctrine that, in order to support a stable price level ($R_m = 1$), it is necessary and sufficient that the government budget be in balance in the sense that the current value of government

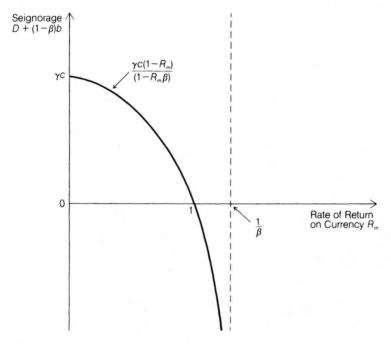

Figure 4.1. The seignorage raised, $D + (1 - \beta)b = \gamma c(1 - R_m)/(1 - R_m\beta)$, for the rate of return on currency $0 \leq R_m \leq \beta^{-1}$.

interest-bearing indebtedness equal the present value of the net-of-interest government surplus. If $R_m = 1$ in (4.26), then $b = -D/(1 - \beta)$. This equation states that the value of government debt equals the present value of the prospective government net-of-interest surpluses.

Another doctrine is the "unpleasant monetarist arithmetic" of Sargent and Wallace (1981). Equation (4.26) states that, for a given stationary value of the net-of-interest government deficit D, the higher the stationary value of interest-bearing government debt b, the lower the rate of return on currency, that is, the higher the inflation rate. This is the foundation of Sargent and Wallace's result that, given $D > 0$, a monetary authority cannot forever forestall inflation by open-market operations that sell interest-bearing bonds to the public. Furthermore, the larger the stationary stock of interest-bearing debt b that is bequeathed to the future, the larger the inflation rate must eventually become. Such "unpleasant arithmetic" is discussed further in Chapters 5 and 7.

We now briefly turn to consider another special case of the system formed by (4.21) and (4.22). In (4.22), we now set $g_t = 0$, $b_t = 0$ for all t. Then (4.22) becomes

$$(4.27) \qquad -\tau_t = \frac{m_{t+1}}{p_t} - \frac{m_t}{p_{t-1}} \frac{p_{t-1}}{p_t}.$$

We wish to find tax-currency creation policies that support an equilibrium in which

$$(4.28) \qquad p_{t+1} = \rho \frac{c_t}{c_{t+1}} p_t$$

when a constant $\rho > \beta$. Substituting (4.28) and $R_t^{-1} = \beta c_t/c_{t+1}$ into (4.21) gives

$$(4.29) \qquad \frac{m_{t+1}}{p_t} = \frac{\gamma c_t}{1 - \beta/\rho}.$$

Substituting (4.29) and (4.28) into (4.27) gives

$$(4.30) \qquad \tau_t = \frac{\gamma(1 - \rho)}{\rho - \beta} c_t.$$

From (4.29) and (4.30), we note that it is not possible to satiate the system with currency holdings, as can be seen by noting that if $\rho \downarrow \beta$ in (4.29) and (4.30), then

$$\lim_{\rho \downarrow \beta}(m_{t+1}/p_t) = +\infty, \quad \text{and} \quad \lim_{\rho \downarrow \beta} \tau_t = +\infty.$$

It is not feasible (or meaningful) to send people a lump-sum tax bill reading "+∞." Therefore, in this economy, there exists no attainable finite "optimal quantity of money" in the sense in which Milton Friedman (1969) uses the term. As explained above, this situation reflects the specification of preferences in (4.18).

At the other extreme, (4.28), (4.29), and (4.30) show that the supremum of seignorage over classes of policies satisfying (4.29) is equal to

$$\gamma c_t = -\lim_{\rho \to \infty} \frac{\gamma(1-\rho)}{(\rho - \beta)} c_t.$$

This limit cannot be attained, however, as (4.28) makes clear.

4.6 A Neutrality Proposition

We consider the following slight generalization of the model of the previous two sections. We suppose that private agents have preferences that can be represented by the function

$$(4.31) \qquad E_0 \sum_{t=0}^{\infty} \beta^t u(c_t, m_{t+1}/p_t), \qquad 0 < \beta < 1,$$

where $u(c_t, m_{t+1}/p_t)$ is increasing in c_t and m_{t+1}/p_t, twice continuously differentiable and concave. The representative private agent's budget constraint can be represented as

$$c_t + \int q(x_{t+1}, x_t) b_{t+1}^d(x_{t+1}) dx_{t+1} + m_{t+1}/p_t$$
$$\leq d_t - \tau_t + b_t^d(x_t) + m_t/p_t,$$

where $b_{t+1}^d(x_{t+1})$ is the amount of maturing one-period claims to time $(t+1)$ goods in state x_{t+1} held by the representative private agent; $q(x_{t+1}, x_t)$ is the one-step-ahead kernel for pricing all private claims as well as interest-bearing government claims; and τ_t is lump-sum taxes at t. The technology continues as above, as does the stochastic process for government expenditures. The government budget constraint is now

$$(4.32) \qquad g_t = \tau_t + \frac{m_{t+1} - m_t}{p_t} + \int q(x_{t+1}, x_t) b_{t+1}(x_{t+1}) dx_{t+1} - b_t(x_t).$$

Here $b_{t+1}(x_{t+1})$ is the quantity of one-period state-contingent debt issued by the government at t. Equation (4.32) implies the present value form of the government budget constraint

(4.33) $\int q(x_{t+1}, x_t)b_{t+1}(x_{t+1})dx_{t+1}$

$$= \sum_{j=1}^{\infty} \int q^{(j)}(x_{t+j}, x_t)\left(\tau_{t+j} + \frac{m_{t+j+1} - m_{t+j}}{p_{t+j}} - g_{t+j}\right) dx_{t+j}.$$

This equation states that the value of one-period debt issued at t equals the present value of the future government surpluses (net of interest), where seignorage revenues are included in government revenue. The price level p_t is permitted to be a function of the state of the economy at t, x_t, which now includes (d_t, g_t) and any variables influencing prospective rates of money creation.

As before, we have that $D_t = g_t - \tau_t$. As in Section 4.5, we have assumed that government-issued currency is in the utility function (4.31), whereas interest-bearing state-contingent government debt $b_{t+1}(x_{t+1})$ is not in the utility function.

Given stochastic processes for d_t and g_t, an equilibrium of this model is defined as a collection of stochastic processes m_0, $b_0(x_0)$ and $[c_t, m_{t+1}/p_t, b_{t+1}(x_{t+1}), p_t, \tau_t, t \geq 0]$, and a pricing function $q(x_{t+1}, x_t)$ such that

1. $c_t = d_t - g_t$.
2. The government budget constraint (4.32) is satisfied for all $t \geq 0$.
3. Given $q(x_{t+1}, x_t)$, the processes $c_t, m_{t+1}/p_t$, maximize (4.31) subject to the consumer's budget constraint.

For this model, the marginal conditions for the consumer, which are the basis for the asset-pricing formulas, are

(4.34) $q(x', x) = \beta \dfrac{u_1[c',(m/p)']}{u_1[c, (m/p)]} f(x', x)$

$u_1[c, (m/p)] = u_2(c, m/p) + \beta \int \dfrac{p}{p'} u_1[c', (m/p)']f(x', x)dx',$

where (m/p) denotes the current value of m_{t+1}/p_t and $(m/p)'$ denotes the value one period ahead; p is understood to be expressed as a function of the state of the economy x. Here $f(x', x)$ is the transition density for the state x, which is assumed to be Markov.

Equations (4.34) indicate that in general the prices of all assets will depend on those elements of the model that influence the equilibrium quantity of (m_{t+1}/p_t), $t \geq 0$. In particular, the first equation of (4.34) collapses to our previous versions of the formula for the one-period-ahead pricing kernel only in special cases, as when $u(\cdot, \cdot)$ is separable.

We now state a proposition that delineates some circumstances in which an open-market operation at time $t = 0$ is neutral.

PROPOSITION. *Suppose that an initial equilibrium exists, and denote it* $\{[\bar{c}_t, \overline{m}_{t+1}/\bar{p}_t, \bar{b}_{t+1}(x_{t+1}), \bar{p}_t, \bar{\tau}_t, t \geq 0], \bar{q}(x_{t+1}, x_t)\}$ *and* $\bar{b}_0(x_0), \overline{m}_0$. *Hold the stochastic process* (g_t, d_t) *fixed. Then there exists another equilibrium, denoted by carets, such that* $\hat{m}_0 = \overline{m}_0, \hat{\tau}_0, = \bar{\tau}_0, \hat{b}_0(x_0) = \bar{b}_0(x_0)$, *which can be constructed as follows. Relative to the equilibrium bearing macrons, regard the government as conducting an open-market purchase of securities that satisfies the equation*

(4.35)
$$\frac{\hat{m}_1 - \overline{m}_0}{\hat{p}_0} + \int \bar{q}^{(1)}(x_1, x_0)\hat{b}_1(x_1)dx_1$$
$$= \frac{\overline{m}_1 - \overline{m}_0}{\bar{p}_0} + \int \bar{q}^{(1)}(x_1, x_0)\bar{b}_1(x_1)dx_1.$$

Suppose that the government alters future state-contingent tax collections to offset the altered value of its interest-bearing debt:

(4.36)
$$\int q(x_1, x_0)[\bar{b}_1(x_1) - \hat{b}(x_1)]\, dx_1 = \sum_{j=1}^{\infty} \bar{q}^{(j)}(x_j, x_0)[\bar{\tau}_j(x_j) - \hat{\tau}_j(x_j)]dx_j.$$

Then the equilibrium bearing carets satisfies the equations $\hat{c}_t = \bar{c}_t, \hat{q}(x_{t+1}, x_t) = \bar{q}(x_{t+1}, x_t), \overline{m}_{t+1}/\bar{p}_t = \hat{m}_{t+1}/\hat{p}_t$, *for* $t \geq 0$. *The initial price level changes according to*

$$\left(1 - \frac{\bar{p}_0}{\hat{p}_0}\right)\frac{\overline{m}_0}{\bar{p}_0} = \int \bar{q}^{(1)}(x_1, x_0)[\bar{b}_1(x_1) - \hat{b}_1(x_1)]dx_1.$$

Subsequent state-contingent government borrowings in the caret-bearing equilibrium can be found by using (4.36) and (4.33). This statement completes the proposition.

To prove the proposition, one simply proceeds by verifying that the suggested caret-bearing equilibrium satisfies the government budget constraint (4.32) at $t = 0$, (4.33), and the asset-pricing formulas implied by (4.34). Essentially, all agents' budget sets are unaltered between the macron- and the caret-bearing equilibria. Note that seignorage collected at time 0, $(m_1 - m_0)/p_0$, differs across the two equilibria. In the experiment of this proposition, the alteration in seignorage collected at $t = 0$ is just offset by alterations in lump-sum state-contingent taxes τ_t collected for $t \geq 1$.

This proposition gives circumstances and a definition of an open-market operation under which an increase in the currency stock at $t = 0$ accomplished via an open-market operation is "neutral," leaving the consumption stream and the stream of real interest rates unaltered while bringing about a change in the price level proportional to the change in the stock of currency. Notice that $\overline{m}_{t+1}/\overline{p}_t = \hat{m}_{t+1}/\hat{p}_t$ for $t \geq 0$, a "quantity theory of money" result. One of the key conditions used to obtain the result is condition (4.36), which states that, when bonds are purchased from the public by the government $[\overline{b}_1(x_1) < \hat{b}_1(x_1)]$, the present value of future taxes is reduced by just the amount of the difference in costs of servicing this debt. This adjustment in taxes means that the government budget constraint (4.33) will remain in balance, with the same present value of seignorage collected for periods $t \geq 1$,

$$\left[\sum_{j=1}^{\infty} \int q^{(j)}(x_j, x_0) \left(\frac{m_{j+1} - m_j}{p_j} \right) dx_j \right],$$

as in the initial equilibrium. A change in the price-level path proportional to the change in the initial money supply at $t = 0$ leaves the present value of future seignorage unaltered and also leaves the asset-pricing formulas based on (4.34) satisfied at the initial equilibrium value of $\overline{q}^{(1)}(x_{t+1}, x_t)$.

Such an open-market operation has precisely the same effect on the equilibrium as an increase in the money supply at time 0 accomplished via a lump-sum transfer (a reduction in τ_0). Notice that the budget constraint at zero, namely,

$$g_0 = \tau_0 - \frac{m_1 - m_0}{p_0} + \int q(x_1, x_0) b_1(x_1) dx_1 - b_0(x_0),$$

remains satisfied at initial equilibrium values of $b_1(x_1)$, g_0, $b_0(x_0)$ as long as $\tau_0 - (m_1 - m_0)/p_0$ is held constant. It is straightforward to show that variations in m_1 brought about in this way are neutral. We ask the reader to demonstrate this point formally, once again using (4.33) and (4.34).

The proposition described in this section is of some interest because it depicts open-market operations as having effects like "helicopter drops" (that is, like once-and-for-all increases in money brought about by transfers), or pure changes in monetary units.

The results of this proposition depend sensitively on the fact that the alteration in currency occurs at $t = 0$. In general, such a neutrality proposition cannot be stated for anticipated future open-market operations that occur for $t \geq 1$. The reason is that, in response to anticipated future money supply changes, current rates of return must change in order to satisfy (4.34).

4.7 Conclusions

If an inconvertible currency is added to the model of Chapter 3, it turns out to be worthless. Adding an unbacked currency does nothing to change the equilibrium asset-pricing kernel. The unchanged asset-pricing kernel assigns zero value to an inconvertible currency, which is after all a promise to pay zero consumption goods in the future.

There are several ways of building a model that assigns positive value to an inconvertible currency. One way is to alter the specification of the economy (the preferences, endowment, technology, and location pattern) in such a way that introduction of an inconvertible currency would alter the equilibrium pricing kernel. This approach is taken in the Bewley-Townsend model of Chapter 6 and the overlapping-generations model of Chapter 7. An alternative approach is to alter the specification of the economy so that one asset — inconvertible currency — has a source of value over and above the value of the subsequent consumption stream that it can support. This approach is taken by currency-in-the-utility-function models and cash-in-advance models. In currency-in-the-utility-function models, an inconvertible currency is valued even though other assets dominate it in rate of return. The model imputes to agents an extra motive for holding the inconvertible currency apart from its value in supporting subsequent consumption. This feature is modeled by entering real balances of currency as an argument in the utility function.

When government-issued currency is dominated in rate of return in equilibrium, unexploited arbitrage profits are available to those agents who are entitled to issue government currency or perfect substitutes for it. These unexploited arbitrage profits are coincident with the presence of effects on the price level and rates of return of government open-market exchanges of currency for other assets. Sargent and Wallace (1983) describe the relationship between the existence of unexploited arbitrage profits in government-issued securities and the conditions for relevance of central bank open-market operations. The potential arbitrage profits associated with issuing currencylike assets can also be interpreted as reflecting an incentive to establish banks that issue private currency (bank notes) that has the same return stream and physical attributes as government-issued currency. The model must be regarded as incorporating effects of some force inhibiting private agents from exploiting these arbitrage opportunities (for example, legal restrictions against private bank notes or an absolute refusal on the part of private agents to regard private bank notes as comparable to government currency notes).

In currency-in-the-utility-function models, much is decided at the stage in the analysis where we specify the list of assets that qualify for direct appearance in the utility function. When we rule out private bank notes as components of the currency stock, for example, we insulate the model of Section 4.4 against forces that, if unlocked, would cause it to collapse to the model of Section 4.1. As another example, consider the ways in which we might extend the currency-in-the-utility-function model to study two or more countries, each of which issues its own inconvertible currency. How are we to specify the argument involving currency in the utility function? One possibility would be to enter total real balances of domestic and foreign currencies in the utility function of a resident of each country. This specification would lead to pervasive indeterminacy of the exchange rate along the lines that we see occurring in the models of Chapters 5 and 7. See Sargent (1983) for details of this argument. Alternatively, we could specify that residents of each country derive utility only from holding real balances in the form of currency issued by the domestic government. Mexican residents have real balances only of pesos in their utility function, whereas U.S. residents have real balances only in dollars in their utility function. This specification leads to determinate demands for country-specific currencies and determinate country-specific price levels and international exchange rates. In particular a version of the "monetary theory of the exchange rate" emerges. In such models, forces like those leading to "dollarization" are ruled out in specifying the utility function.

References and Suggested Readings

Bewley, Truman. 1980. The optimum quantity of money. In *Models of Monetary Economies,* ed. J. H. Kareken and N. Wallace, pp. 169–210. Minneapolis: Federal Reserve Bank of Minneapolis.

Fischer, Stanley. 1983. A framework for monetary and banking analysis. *Economic Journal* 93(supp. March):1–16.

Fisher, Irving. [1907]1930. *The Theory of Interest.* London: Macmillan.

Friedman, Milton. 1969. *The Optimum Quantity of Money and Other Essays.* Chicago: Aldine.

LeRoy, Stephen. 1984a. Nominal prices and interest rates in general equilibrium: money shocks. *Journal of Business* 57(2):177–195.

——— 1984b. Nominal prices and interest rates in general equilibrium: endowment shocks. *Journal of Business* 57(2):197–213.

Lucas, Robert E. 1980. Equilibrium in a pure currency economy. *Economic Inquiry* 18(2):203–220. (Reprinted in *Models of Monetary Economies,* ed. J. H. Kareken and N. Wallace, pp. 131–145. Minneapolis: Federal Reserve Bank of Minneapolis, 1980.)

———— 1982. Interest rates and currency prices in a two-country world. *Journal of Monetary Economics* 10(3):335–360.

Sargent, Thomas J. 1983. Comment on G. Ortiz's "Dollarization in Mexico: Causes and Consequences." In *Financial Policies and the World Capital Market,* ed. P. Aspe-Armella, R. Dornbusch, and M. Obstfeld, pp. 95–106. Chicago: University of Chicago Press, for the National Bureau of Economic Research.

Sargent, Thomas J., and Neil Wallace. 1981. Some unpleasant monetarist arithmetic. Federal Reserve Bank of Minneapolis *Quarterly Review* 5(3):1–17.

———— 1982. The real bills doctrine vs. the quantity theory: a reconsideration. *Journal of Political Economy* 90(6):1212–1236.

———— 1983. A model of commodity money. *Journal of Monetary Economics* 12(1):163–187.

Sidrauski, Miguel. 1967. Rational choice and patterns of growth in a monetary economy. *American Economic Review* 57(2):534–544.

Tobin, James. 1961. Money, capital, and other stores of value. *American Economic Review* 51(2):26–37.

———— 1963. An essay on the principles of debt management. In *Fiscal and Debt Management Policies,* ed. William Fellner et al., pp. 141–215. Englewood Cliffs, N.J.: Prentice-Hall. (Reprinted in James Tobin, *Essays in Economics,* 2 vols., vol. 1, pp. 378–455. Amsterdam: North-Holland, 1971.)

Townsend, Robert. 1980. Models of money with spatially separated agents. In *Models of Monetary Economies,* ed. J. H. Kareken and N. Wallace, pp. 265–303. Minneapolis: Federal Reserve Bank of Minneapolis.

Wallace, Neil. 1983. A legal restrictions theory of the demand for "money" and the role of monetary policy. Federal Reserve Bank of Minneapolis *Quarterly Review* 7(1):1–7.

5 | Cash-in-Advance Models

This chapter describes several versions of Lucas's cash-in-advance model (1980, 1982).[1] A valued government-issued unbacked currency is added to the Lucas tree model of Chapter 3. The source of currency's value is a set of restrictions on the pattern of exchanges that requires goods to be purchased with government-issued currency that must be acquired prior to purchasing goods. As we saw in the previous chapter, some deviations from the structure of Lucas's tree model are required if an unbacked currency is to be valued. The construction of the cash-in-advance model is guided by a concern with finding deviations from the Lucas tree model that are *minimal* in the sense that they leave equilibrium consumption allocations and real rates of interest identical to those of the Lucas tree model. The aim is to create a model in which the real economy remains separate from forces determining purely nominal variables. This goal is to be accomplished in a context like that of Lucas's tree model, in which a rich array of state-contingent prices is calculable, so that a version of classical monetary theory consistent with a modern intertemporal capital–asset–pricing model is constructed.

As we shall see, the cash-in-advance model may be used to describe a variety of doctrines and issues in monetary theory. We shall study the following matters: (1) the relation between real and nominal interest rates, for which Lucas's model recovers a version of Irving Fisher's theory; (2) "neu-

---

1. The cash-in-advance model embodies a version of the constraint on transactions recommended by Clower (1967).

trality" propositions, including irrelevance propositions for government open-market exchanges of indexed government debt for nominal government debt and for government choices of debt issues or taxation as ways of financing government expenditures; (3) aspects of the coordination problem facing monetary and fiscal policy; (4) ways of financing paying interest on currency (reserves) at the market rate; (5) the "monetary theory of the exchange rate"; and (6) the problem of "exchange rate indeterminacy" in systems with extreme currency substitution.

The real structure of the model is identical to the Lucas tree model of Chapter 3, Section 7. In particular, equilibrium consumption allocations remain $c_t = \xi_t - g_t$, and the equilibrium asset-pricing kernel $q(x_{t+1}, x_t)$ continues to be given by Equation 3.53. From a mechanical point of view, there are two main additions to the model of Chapter 3, Section 7. First, there is appended a quantity theory equation of the form $M_{t+1} = p_t \xi_t$, where p_t is the price level at t and M_{t+1} is the per capita currency stock carried over from t to $(t + 1)$. Here ξ_t is the per capita dividend at time t, what we earlier (in Chapter 3) called x_t or d_t. Second, the government budget constraint is modified to include seignorage revenues in the following way:

$$g_t = \tau_t + \int q(x_{t+1}, x_t) b_{t+1}(x_{t+1}) \, dx_{t+1} - b_t(x_t) + \frac{M_{t+1} - M_t}{p_t}.$$

Seignorage $(M_{t+1} - M_t)/p_t$ will act as a lump-sum tax, leaving real asset prices and allocations unaltered. The model will be used to determine the implications for a host of nominal magnitudes of the quantity theory equation $M_{t+1} = p_t \xi_t$ and the implications for inflation and monetary and fiscal policies of the government budget constraint.

We begin with a description of the restrictions on exchange patterns that are used to support a positive demand for an unbacked currency in the face of the annihilating forces described at the beginning of Chapter 4. A special and fairly intricate combination of spatial, intertemporal, and legal restrictions provides this support. Once the model has been set forth, the various price level and irrelevance propositions will appear as relatively straightforward implications of the quantity theory equation and the government budget constraint.

5.1 A One-Country Model

The physical setup is identical with that described in Section 3.7. That is, the economy is a one-tree version of Lucas's model in which dividends ξ_t are governed by a positive stochastic process. There is also an exogenous stochastic process for government purchases g_t that satisfies $0 \leq g_t < \xi_t$. Let $x_t = (\xi_t, g_t)$. We assume that x_t is Markov with transition density $f(x', x)$ where prob$\{x_{t+1} \leq x' | x_t = x\} = \int_0^{x'} f(s', x) ds'$. A representative household maximizes $E_0 \Sigma_{t=0}^{\infty} \beta^t u(c_t)$. There is one tree per household, but a household does not consume the fruit from the tree located in its own yard. Each household consists of a worker-shopper pair. The worker stays home and sells the fruit from the tree in its own yard, eventually paying the proceeds in the form of dividends to the owners of the tree. The shopper leaves home and purchases goods (fruit) from trees located in other yards. Currency is introduced into the setup of Section 3.7 by imposing restrictions on the timing of exchange of securities, goods, and dividends. These restrictions are motivated partly by imagining that some exchanges must be decentralized in time and space. In addition, some exogenous restrictions must be imposed on the kinds of securities that private agents are permitted to issue.

The pattern of trading is summarized in Table 5.1. Each period ($t \geq 0$) is divided into three distinct and successive trading sessions. In the first session, only securities are traded. During this securities trading session, the consumption good cannot be traded, nor can firms pay out the period t dividends. The securities traded are shares in trees, government-issued currency, and one-period state-contingent claims to currency at the beginning of period ($t + 1$). During the second, or shopping, session, each household conducts goods shopping and selling in the following way. A shopper leaves home and purchases goods in exchange for currency accumulated during the securities trading session. A worker stays home and sells in exchange for currency the time t output from the tree that is located in the household's yard. A household is not permitted to consume the output from its own tree. During the third, or dividend-collecting, session, the household visits the "yard," or tree locations, in which it owns equity and receives its share of the currency that has been collected at that yard, or "firm." The tree yard, or firm, pays all of its cash receipts to its shareholders each period. After receiving these cash dividends, the household has no more opportunities to trade during period t. It is forced to carry the currency it has received in dividends into period ($t + 1$).

The division of the period into trading sessions is used to support a role for an unbacked government-supplied currency. As we shall see, forces present in this model tend to drive out government currency. These forces are assumed to be thwarted by the above-mentioned restrictions on the pattern of trading and by restrictions that prevent private agents from issuing currency.

All random variables dated t are assumed to be realized at the beginning of

Table 5.1 Events within a period in the cash-in-advance model

Session	Private agents	Government
Securities trading session		
Initial wealth	$s_{t-1} = 1$ tree, worth $s_{t-1}r_t(x_t) = r_t(x_t)$ M_t/p_t currency $l_t^p(x_t)/p_t$ state-contingent nominal government debt	$-l_t(x_t)/p_t$ state-contingent nominal debt $-M_t/p_t$ currency
Transaction	Purchases s_t "trees" worth $s_t r_t(x_t)$ and $l_{t+1}^p(x_{t+1})$ units of nominal state-contingent debt Pays τ_t in lump sum taxes Holds currency in amount $m_t^p \geq p_t c_t$	Imposes lump-sum tax of τ_t on each person Prints additional currency $M_{t+1} - M_t$ Borrows $l_{t+1}(x_{t+1})$ in state-contingent form Holds currency in amount $m_t^g = p_t g_t$
Equilibrium condition		
Currency	$m_t^p + m_t^g = M_{t+1}$	
Trees	$s_t = 1$	
State-contingent debt	$l_{t+1}^p(x_{t+1}) = l_{t+1}(x_{t+1})$ for all x_{t+1}.	
Shopping session		
Transaction	"Shopper": Purchases c_t in exchange for currency in amount $p_t c_t$ subject to $m_t^p \geq p_t c_t$ "Worker": Sells fruit to private agents or government at price p_t Total sales $= p_t \xi_t$	Government purchases g_t from "workers" in exchange for $m_t^g = p_t g_t$ units of currency
Dividend collection session		
Transaction	"Shopper" collects dividends in form of currency from workers who guard trees in which it owns shares: total dividends $= p_t \xi_t$ This currency is carried by household into next period	None Government carries no cash between periods

Note: Households consume none of the fruit produced in their own yard. Timing: at the beginning of t, ξ_t, τ_t, g_t, $M_{t+1} - M_t$, p_t are all realized.

period t, prior to the securities trading session, including $x_t = (\xi_t, g_t)$ as well as all endogenous variables depending on x_t. Private agents and the government are assumed to observe the same variables at the same time.

A government operates in the following way. There is a given stochastic process $\{g_t\}$ of government per capita purchases. The government imposes real lump-sum taxes $\{\tau_t\}$ on the representative agent. Both g_t and τ_t, denominated in units of time t consumption good, are realized at the beginning of period t, prior to the securities trading session. At the beginning of period t, each private agent arrives carrying over M_t units of currency from period $(t-1)$. At the beginning of period t, prior to securities trading, the government announces that it will print or destroy $(M_{t+1} - M_t)$ units of currency. At the beginning of period t, prior to securities trading, the government honors its preexisting obligation to pay $l_t(x_t)$ dollars to owners of one-period state-contingent nominal securities. Here $l_t(x_t)$ is the number of dollars that the government promised at $(t-1)$ to pay at time t when the state of the economy is x_t. At the beginning of period t, the government also determines the function $l_{t+1}(x_{t+1})$ giving state-contingent one-period nominal borrowing. Let p_t be the price level at t. Then the government budget constraint is

$$(5.1) \qquad g_t = \tau_t + \frac{1}{p_t} \int l_{t+1}(x_{t+1}) n(x_{t+1}, x_t)\, dx_{t+1}$$
$$- l_t(x_t) p_t^{-1} + (M_{t+1} - M_t) p_t^{-1},$$
$$t \geq 0.$$

We assume that $l_0(x_0)$ is given. Here $n(x_{t+1}, x_t)$ is the kernel for pricing one-step-ahead nominal claims. That is, at the beginning of time t, the price in time t dollars of one dollar at the beginning of time $(t+1)$, given that $x_{t+1} \in A$, is given by $\int_{x' \in A} n(x', x)\, dx'$. The government does not purchase shares in trees directly.

We assume that M_{t+1} and τ_t are each chosen to be stochastic processes that can be expressed as functions of x_t. Observing M_{t+1} and τ_t therefore adds no information to that contained in x_t.

During the securities trading session, the government acquires currency in the amount

$$m_t^g = p_t \tau_t + \int l_{t+1}(x_{t+1}) n(x_{t+1}, x_t)\, dx_{t+1} - l_t(x_t) + (M_{t+1} - M_t).$$

During the shopping session, the government is subject to the cash-in-advance constraint $m_t^g \geq p_t g_t$, where m_t^g is the quantity of currency held by the government at the end of the securities trading session. We assume that the government acts to satisfy this constraint with equality. If $m_t^g = p_t g_t$ in the preceding equation, we have Equation (5.1).

During the securities trading session, at the beginning of period t, the household chooses currency holdings m_t^p, holdings of shares in trees, s_t, and nominal state-contingent government debt $l_{t+1}^p(x_{t+1})$ subject to the wealth constraint

$$(5.2) \qquad \frac{m_t^p}{p_t} + \tau_t + r(x_t)s_t + \frac{1}{p_t} \int l_{t+1}^p(x_{t+1})n(x_{t+1}, x_t)\, dx_{t+1} \le \theta_t(x_t),$$

where θ_t is beginning of period wealth and $r(x_t)$ is the price of trees at t. Wealth evolves according to

$$(5.3) \qquad \theta_{t+1}(x_{t+1}) = \frac{p_t \xi_t}{p_{t+1}} s_t + \frac{m_t^p - p_t c_t}{p_{t+1}} + r(x_{t+1})s_t + \frac{l_{t+1}^p(x_{t+1})}{p_{t+1}}.$$

Here $p_t \xi_t s_t$ is the dollar value of dividends carried over from t to $(t + 1)$, whereas $(m_t^p - p_t c_t)$ is excess currency that was accumulated during securities trading in t but was not spent during the shopping session at t. During the shopping session at t, the household is subject to the restriction $m_t^p \ge p_t c_t$.

We can use (5.2) and (5.3) to derive pricing formulas via the approach of arbitrage pricing described in Chapter 3. Multiply (5.3) by $n(x_{t+1}, x_t)p_{t+1}/p_t$, integrate both sides with respect to x_{t+1}, solve for $[\int l_{t+1}^p(x_{t+1})n(x_{t+1}, x_t)\, dx_{t+1}]/p_t$, and substitute into (5.2) to obtain

$$(5.4) \qquad \left[1 - \int n(x_{t+1}, x_t)\, dx_{t+1}\right] m_t^p p_t^{-1} + \tau_t + c_t \int n(x_{t+1}, x_t)\, dx_{t+1}$$
$$+ s_t \left\{ r(x_t) - \int \left[r(x_{t+1}) \frac{p_{t+1}}{p_t} + \xi_t \right] n(x_{t+1}, x_t)\, dx_{t+1} \right\}$$
$$+ \int \theta_{t+1}(x_{t+1}) \frac{p_{t+1}}{p_t} n(x_{t+1}, x_t)\, dx_{t+1} \le \theta_t(x_t).$$

There is no restriction on the value of s_t that can be chosen by the household. If sure unbounded wealth-generating opportunities are not to be present, the term multiplying s_t in (5.4) must be zero, or

$$(5.5) \qquad r(x_t) = \int \left[r(x_{t+1}) + \xi_t \frac{p_t}{p_{t+1}} \right] \frac{p_{t+1}}{p_t} n(x_{t+1}, x_t)\, dx_{t+1}.$$

Defining $q(x_{t+1}, x_t) = n(x_{t+1}, x_t)p_{t+1}/p_t$ as the kernel for pricing one-step-ahead state-contingent inflation-indexed claims [time $(t + 1)$ goods per unit time t good], the above equation can be written

$$r(x_t) = \int \left[r(x_{t+1}) + \xi_t \frac{p_t}{p_{t+1}} \right] q(x_{t+1}, x_t) \, dx_{t+1}.$$

This is a functional equation in the pricing function $r(x_t)$, which we shall analyze more fully shortly.

Returning to (5.4), note that $\int n(x_{t+1}, x_t) \, dx_{t+1}$ is the reciprocal of the gross nominal one-period risk-free interest rate. Evidently, if the gross risk-free nominal interest rate exceeds unity [that is, if $1 > \int n(x_{t+1}, x_t) \, dx_{t+1}$], the household could earn arbitrage profits by setting m_t^p/p_t less than zero. That is, when $1 > \int n(x_{t+1}, x_t) \, dx_{t+1}$, the household has an incentive to issue a claim that duplicates the return stream offered by currency. This force is assumed to be blocked by means of a government legal restriction that prevents private agents from issuing currency. When $1 > \int n(x_{t+1}, x_t) \, dx_{t+1}$, (5.4) shows that the household has an incentive to minimize its holdings of currency m_t^p. The cash-in-advance restriction $m_t^p \ge p_t c_t$ will therefore be binding when $1 > \int n(x_{t+1}, x_t) \, dx_{t+1}$. In this case, using (5.5), (5.4) becomes

(5.6) $$\tau_t + c_t + \int \theta_{t+1}(x_{t+1}) q(x_{t+1}, x_t) \, dx_{t+1} \le \theta_t(x_t).$$

Except where otherwise noted, we shall work with equilibria in which $1 > \int n(x_{t+1}, x_t) \, dx_{t+1}$, so that the cash-in-advance restriction is binding. The condition that $1 > \int n(x_{t+1}, x_t) \, dx_{t+1}$ is an implicit restriction on β, u, and the $\{\xi_t, g_t\}_{t=0}^{\infty}$ and $\{M_{t+1}\}_{t=0}^{\infty}$ processes. Equation (5.14) below displays the restriction. Low values of β and low values of M_t/M_{t+1} (that is, high-inflation regimes), for example, lead to low values for $\int n(x', x) \, dx'$.

The household's optimization problem can now be represented as follows. The household chooses stochastic processes for $\{c_t, m_t^p, s_t, l_{t+1}^p\}_{t=0}^{\infty}$ to maximize

(5.7) $$E_0 \sum_{t=0}^{\infty} \beta^t u(c_t),$$

subject to

(5.2) $$\frac{m_t^p}{p_t} + \tau_t + r(x_t)s_t + \frac{1}{p_t} \int l_{t+1}^p(x_{t+1}) n(x_{t+1}, x_t) \, dx_{t+1} \le \theta_t(x_t),$$
$$t \ge 0,$$

(5.3) $$\theta_{t+1}(x_{t+1}) = \xi_t \frac{p_t}{p_{t+1}} s_t + r(x_{t+1})s_t + l_{t+1}^p(x_{t+1})/p_{t+1}$$
$$+ (m_t^p - p_t c_t)/p_{t+1}, \qquad t \ge 0$$

$$m_t^p \ge p_t c_t, \qquad t \ge 0.$$

Here $u(\cdot)$ is increasing, strictly concave, and differentiable. The maximization takes as given stochastic processes for $\{p_t, \xi_t, \tau_t\}_{t=0}^{\infty}$ and the pricing kernel $n(x_{t+1}, x_t)$. It is assumed that τ_t is a function of x_t. The household starts with given initial wealth $\theta_0(x_0) = r(x_0)s_{-1} + M_0/p_0 + l_0^g(x_0)/p_0$ and $s_{-1} = 1$.

Given a stochastic process for $\{g_t\}_{t=0}^{\infty}$, an initial stock of currency $M_0 > 0$, and nominal interest-bearing debt $l_0(x_0)$, the government selects tax and borrowing strategies $\{\tau_t, l_{t+1}(x_{t+1})\}_{t=0}^{\infty}$ that satisfy the government budget constraint

$$(5.1) \qquad g_t = \tau_t + \frac{1}{p_t} \int l_{t+1}(x_{t+1})n(x_{t+1}, x_t)\, dx_{t+1}$$
$$- l_t(x_t)p_t^{-1} + (M_{t+1} - M_t)p_t^{-1}.$$

We assume that τ_t and M_{t+1} are each chosen to be a function of x_t whenever $t \geq 0$. The government also chooses a stock of currency $m_t^g = p_t g_t$ that it carries from the securities trading session at t and spends during the shopping session at t.

Let us define an equilibrium.

DEFINITION. *An equilibrium is a set of initial conditions $M_0 > 0$, $l_0(x_0)$, and stochastic processes for $\{\xi_t,\ g_t,\ c_t,\ \tau_t,\ M_{t+1},\ m_t^g,\ m_t^p,\ s_t,\ p_t,\ l_{t+1}^p(x_{t+1}),\ l_{t+1}(x_{t+1})\}_{t=0}^{\infty}$, and pricing functions $n(x_{t+1}, x_t)$ and $r(x_t)$ such that*
   (i) The government budget constraint (5.1) is satisfied for all $t \geq 0$, and $m_t^g = p_t g_t$.
   (ii) Given the pricing functions $n(x_{t+1}, x_t)$ and $r(x_t)$, the stochastic processes for $\{\tau_t, p_t, \xi_t\}_{t=0}^{\infty}$ and the initial conditions M_0, $l_0(x_0)$, $s_{-1} = 1$, the stochastic processes $\{c_t, m_t^p, s_t, l_{t+1}^p\}_{t=0}^{\infty}$ solve the household's maximization problem.
   (iii) The markets for currency, one-period state-contingent loans, and trees each clear each period:

$$(5.8a) \qquad M_{t+1} = m_t^p + m_t^g$$

$$(5.8b) \qquad l_{t+1}^p(x_{t+1}) = l_{t+1}(x_{t+1})$$

$$(5.8c) \qquad s_t = 1, \qquad t \geq 0.$$

This completes the definition of equilibrium.[2]

Except in Section 5.5, we will focus on equilibria in which the currency-in-advance restriction $p_t c_t \leq m_t^p$ is met with equality because the risk-free net

---

2. Walras's law guarantees that goods market equilibrium $c_t + g_t = \xi_t$ is satisfied if conditions (i), (ii), and (iii) are satisfied.

nominal interest rate is positive $[1 - \int n(x_{t+1}, x_t) \, dx_{t+1} > 0]$ and because currency pays no interest. In this case, the equilibrium allocation and pricing functions are readily calculated. Equation (5.8a) becomes $M_{t+1} = p_t(c_t + g_t)$. Because the good is nonstorable, goods market equilibrium implies that $c_t + g_t = \xi_t$. This can be shown to be an implication of (5.1), (5.2), (5.3), assumptions on $u(\cdot)$, and the definition of equilibrium. In particular, we argue as follows. Write the household's budget constraint as

$$\frac{m_t^p}{p_t} + \tau_t + r(x_t)s_t + \frac{1}{p_t} \int l_{t+1}^p(x_{t+1})n(x_{t+1}, x_t) \, dx_{t+1}$$

$$= \xi_{t-1} \frac{p_{t-1}}{p_t} s_{t-1} + r(x_t)s_{t-1} + l_t^p(x_t)/p_t + (m_{t-1}^p - p_{t-1}c_{t-1})/p_t,$$

$$t \geq 1.$$

Substitute for τ_t from the government budget constraint (5.1), set $l_t^p(x_t) = l_t(x_t)$ and $s_t = 1$ for all t, evaluate at $m_t^p = p_t c_t$ for all t, and rearrange to obtain

$$c_t + g_t = \xi_{t-1} \frac{p_{t-1}}{p_t} + \frac{M_{t+1} - M_t}{p_t}.$$

Substitute the money market equilibrium condition $M_{t+1} = m_t^p + m_t^g$ or $M_{t+1} = p_t(c_t + g_t)$ to obtain

$$\frac{M_t}{p_{t-1}} = \xi_{t-1}.$$

In turn, we have $\xi_{t-1} = c_{t-1} + g_{t-1}$.

Thus we have $M_{t+1} = p_t \xi_t$, or the quantity theory pricing function

(5.9) $p_t = M_{t+1}/\xi_t.$

We also have the consumption allocation to the household

(5.10) $c_t = \xi_t - g_t.$

To obtain formulas for $r(x_t)$ and the pricing kernel $n(x_{t+1}, x_t)$, we use the procedure of Chapter 3. Associated with household's optimization problem is the functional equation

$$v(x, \theta) = \max\left\{ u(c) + \beta \int v(x', \theta')f(x', x) \, dx' \right\},$$

subject to $c + \tau + r(x)s + \frac{1}{p(x)} \int l^p(x')n(x', x) \, dx' \leq \theta$

$$\theta' = \xi' \frac{M}{M'} s + r(x')s + \frac{l^p(x')}{p(x')},$$

where $p(x) = M/\xi$. Here a prime denotes next period's values. In representing θ', we have used $p = M/\xi$ and $p' = M'/\xi'$ to eliminate p and p' from the expression for dividends. The first-order necessary conditions for the problem on the right side of the functional equation can be rearranged to give

$$u'(c)r(x) = \beta \int u'(c') \left[r(x') + \xi' \frac{M}{M'} \right] f(x', x) \, dx'$$

$$n(x', x) = \frac{p}{p'} \beta \frac{u'(c')}{u'(c)} f(x', x).$$

Upon substituting the equilibrium quantities $(c = \xi - g)$ and $(p = M/\xi)$, we obtain the pricing formulas

(5.11) $$r(x) = \frac{\beta}{u'(\xi - g)} \int u'(\xi' - g') \left[r(x') + \xi' \frac{M}{M'} \right] f(x', x) \, dx'$$

(5.12) $$n(x', x) = \beta \frac{M\xi'}{M'\xi} \frac{u'(\xi' - g')}{u'(\xi - g)} f(x', x).$$

Recalling that we have defined the real one-step-ahead contingent claims pricing kernel $q(x', x) = (p'/p)n(x', x)$, we have from (5.12) that

(5.13) $$q(x', x) = \beta \frac{u'(\xi' - g')}{u'(\xi - g)} f(x', x).$$

Note that (5.13) is exactly the same formula that we derived in Chapter 3 for the model without currency. In particular, note that $q(x', x)$ is independent of the government's financing strategy.

We have established that the equilibrium consumption allocation $c_t = \xi_t - g_t$, real balances $M_{t+1}/p_t = \xi_t$, and the kernel $q(x_{t+1}, x_t)$ for pricing real state-contingent claims do not depend on the government's financing strategy. We summarize these findings formally in the following proposition.

PROPOSITION 5.1. *Given $\bar{M}_0$, $\bar{l}_0(x_0)$, suppose that there exists an equilibrium $\{\bar{\xi}_t, \bar{g}_t, \bar{c}_t, \bar{s}_t, \bar{\tau}_t, \bar{M}_{t+1}, \bar{m}_t^g, \bar{m}_t^p, \bar{p}_t, \bar{l}_{t+1})\}_{t=0}^{\infty}$, $\bar{n}(x_{t+1}, x_t)$, $q(x_{t+1}, x_t)$ and $\bar{r}(x_t)$. Suppose that this macron-bearing equilibrium is one in which the net nominal interest rate is always positive $[1 - \int \bar{n}(x_{t+1}, x_t) \, dx_{t+1} > 0$ for all $x_t]$, so that the cash-in-advance restriction is always binding for the household. Consider any alternative financing strategies $\{\hat{\tau}_t, \hat{M}_{t+1} > 0, \hat{l}_{t+1}(x_{t+1})\}_{t=0}^{\infty}$ that satisfy*

$$\bar{g}_t = \hat{\tau}_t + \frac{\hat{M}_{t+1} - \hat{M}_t}{\hat{p}_t} + \frac{1}{\hat{p}_t} \int \hat{l}_{t+1}(x_{t+1}) \hat{n}(x_{t+1}, x_t) \, dx_{t+1} - \frac{\hat{l}_t(x_t)}{\hat{p}_t},$$

$$t \geq 0,$$

with given initial conditions $\overline{M}_0 > 0$, $\overline{l}_0(x_0)$, where $\hat{p}_t = \hat{M}_{t+1}/\overline{\xi}_t$. Then there exists an equilibrium given by $\{\overline{\xi}_t, \overline{g}_t, \overline{c}_t, \overline{s}_t, \hat{\tau}_t, \hat{M}_{t+1}, \hat{m}_t^p = \hat{p}_t\overline{c}_t, \hat{m}_t^g = \hat{p}_t\overline{g}_t, \hat{p}_t = \hat{M}_{t+1}/\overline{\xi}_t, \hat{l}_{t+1}(x_{t+1})\}_{t=0}^{\infty}$, with $\hat{n}(x_{t+1}, x_t) = \hat{p}_t\overline{q}(x_{t+1}, x_t)/\hat{p}_{t+1}$, $\overline{q}(x_{t+1}, x_t)$, and $\hat{r}(x_t)$ satisfying the appropriate version of (5.11).

This is a general version of a "neutrality" or "irrelevance" proposition. In effect the proposition delineates an equivalence class of government financial policies that support the same real allocation and real interest rates. By exploring various dimensions of the set of policies within this equivalence class, we shall be able to state various special neutrality propositions as corollaries to Proposition 5.1. Before studying such corollaries, let us examine the Fisher effect as represented in Equations (5.12) and (5.13).

5.2 Fisher Equations

The sure one-period nominal interest factor is given by $\int n(x', x)\, dx'$ or

$$(5.14) \qquad \phi(x) = \beta \int \frac{u'(\xi' - g')}{u'(\xi - g)} \frac{\xi'}{\xi} \frac{M}{M'} f(x', x)\, dx'.$$

The one-period sure real interest rate factor is given by $\int q(x', x)\, dx'$ or

$$(5.15) \qquad \psi(x) = \beta \int \frac{u'(\xi' - g')}{u'(\xi - g)} f(x', x)\, dx'.$$

Equation (5.9), (5.14), and (5.15) form a version of Irving Fisher's theory relating the nominal interest rate to the real rate of interest. To see this point, use the definition that, for two random variables z_1 and z_2, $E_t z_1 z_2 = \text{cov}_t(z_1, z_2) + E_t z_1 E_t z_2$, where $\text{cov}_t(z_1, z_2) = E_t(z_1 - E_t z_1)(z_2 - E_t z_2)$. Setting $z_1 = u'(\xi' - g')/u'(\xi - g)$ and $z_2 = \xi' M/\xi M' = p/p'$ and using (5.14) and (5.15), we obtain

$$\phi(x) = \psi(x)E_t(p/p') + \beta\, \text{cov}_t\left[\frac{u'(\xi' - g')}{u'(\xi - g)}, p/p'\right].$$

When

$$\text{cov}_t\left[\frac{u'(\xi' - g')}{u'(\xi - g)}, p/p'\right] = 0,$$

the nominal interest factor $\phi(x)$ is the product of the real interest factor $\psi(x)$ and the expected inverse of the gross inflation rate, p/p'. This is Irving Fisher's theory. We briefly mention two special cases in which $\text{cov}_t[u'(\xi' - g')/u'(\xi - g), p/p'] = 0$. The first occurs when there is no uncertainty about

p_t/p_{t+1} at time t. A second occurs when consumers are risk neutral, so that $u'(\xi - g)$ is a constant for all $(\xi - g)$.

Note that the prices $r(x)$ and $\phi(x)$ given by (5.11) and (5.14) depend on the government financing strategy by way of their dependence on the distribution of M/M'. The equity price $r(x)$ depends on the distribution of M/M' because ownership of equities at t entitles the owner to a claim to the dollar value of current dividends at t and later. Only *future* consumption is attainable from period t dividends because of the restrictions on trading that force the household to collect dividends in currency at the end of the period and to carry the currency into the next period. The time $(t + 1)$ consumption goods value of these dollar dividends depends on the time $(t + 1)$ price level, which in turn depends on the time $(t + 1)$ currency stock M'.

5.3 Inflation-Indexed Government Debt

To make the situation here more plainly comparable to that in Chapter 3, we may conveniently reinterpret the present model as one in which the government issues one-period state-contingent debt that is indexed against inflation. At time t, the government sells claims to $b_{t+1}(x_{t+1})$ worth of goods at $(t + 1)$ in state x_{t+1} or equivalently to $p_{t+1}b_{t+1}(x_{t+1})$ dollars at time $(t + 1)$ in state x_{t+1}. The value of such claims at time t in terms of time t dollars is

$$\int p_{t+1}b_{t+1}(x_{t+1})n(x_{t+1}, x_t)\, dx_{t+1}$$

$$= \int p_{t+1}b_{t+1}(x_{t+1})\frac{p_t}{p_{t+1}}\, q(x_{t+1}, x_t)\, dx_{t+1}$$

$$= p_t \int b_{t+1}(x_{t+1})q(x_{t+1}, x_t)\, dx_{t+1}.$$

Thus the value of such claims in terms of time t goods is $\int b_{t+1}(x_{t+1})q(x_{t+1}, x_t)\, dx_{t+1}$. These claims pay off in the securities trading session at time $(t + 1)$ and pay off in dollars, not in physical goods.

We can reformulate our previous results in terms of a model in which all debt is indexed by simply replacing $l_{t+1}(x_{t+1})$ by $p_{t+1}b_{t+1}(x_{t+1})$ and replacing $n(x_{t+1}, x_t)$ by $p_t q(x_{t+1}, x_t)/p_{t+1}$. In particular, the flow government budget constraint at t becomes

$$g_t = \tau_t + \int q(x_{t+1}, x_t)b_{t+1}(x_t)\, dx_{t+1} - b_t(x_t) + \frac{M_{t+1} - M_t}{p_t}.$$

In the succeeding sections, we shall work with the formulation in which all government debt is indexed.

The preceding remarks suggest that it is in one sense irrelevant whether the government issues indexed or nominal interest-bearing debt. To make this point more concrete, we briefly consider a setup in which the government can issue both indexed and nonindexed debt. Let the government budget constraint be

$$g_t = \tau_t + \int q(x_{t+1}, x_t) b_{t+1}(x_{t+1}) \, dx_{t+1}$$

$$+ \frac{1}{p_t} \int n(x_{t+1}, x_t) l_{t+1}(x_{t+1}) \, dx_{t+1} - b_t(x_t)$$

$$- \frac{l_t(x_t)}{p_t} + \frac{M_{t+1} - M_t}{p_t}, \quad t \geq 0$$

where $M_0 > 0$, $b_0(x_0)$, and $l_0(x_0)$ are given.

Here $b_{t+1}(x_{t+1})$ denotes indexed state-contingent claims sold at t, whereas $l_{t+1}(x_{t+1})$ denotes nominal claims sold at t. Let the household's budget constraint be modified similarly, by replacing $l_{t+1}^p(x_{t+1})$ by $l_{t+1}^p(x_{t+1}) + p_{t+1} b_{t+1}^p(x_{t+1})$. To the equilibrium conditions of the model we now add $b_{t+1}^p(x_{t+1}) = b_{t+1}(x_{t+1})$. We state a theorem that asserts the irrelevance of government open-market operations in indexed government debt. The theorem is a simple version of ones described by Peled (1985) in settings somewhat different from ours.

PROPOSITION 5.2. *Irrelevance of government-issued indexed bonds*
Given that $\overline{M}_0 > 0$, $\overline{l}_0(x_0) = 0$, $\overline{b}_0(x_0) = 0$, *suppose that there exists an equilibrium without indexed debt*

$$\{\overline{\xi}_t, \overline{g}_t, \overline{c}_t, \overline{\tau}_t, \overline{M}_{t+1}, \overline{m}_t^g, \overline{m}_t^p, \overline{p}_t, \overline{l}_{t+1}(x_{t+1}), \overline{b}_{t+1}(x_{t+1}) = 0\}_{t=0}^\infty,$$
$$\overline{n}(x_{t+1}, x_t), \overline{q}(x_{t+1}, x_t), \text{ and } \overline{r}(x_t).$$

Then for any $\{\hat{l}_{t+1}(x_{t+1}), \hat{b}_{t+1}(x_{t+1})\}_{t=0}^\infty$ *satisfying* $\hat{l}_{t+1}(x_{t+1}) + \overline{p}_{t+1} \hat{b}_{t+1}(x_{t+1}) = \overline{l}_{t+1}(x_{t+1})$, *there is an equilibrium given by*

$$\{\overline{\xi}_t, \overline{g}_t, \overline{c}_t, \overline{\tau}_t, \overline{M}_{t+1}, \overline{m}_t^g, \overline{m}_t^p, \overline{p}_t, \hat{l}_{t+1}(x_{t+1}), \hat{b}_{t+1}(x_{t+1})\}_{t=0}^\infty,$$
$$\overline{n}(x_{t+1}, x_t), \overline{q}(x_{t+1}, x_t), \text{ and } \overline{r}(x_t).$$

This proposition can be viewed as a corollary to Proposition 5.1. It can be proved directly by verifying that the asserted equilibrium satisfies all of the equilibrium conditions. Both private agents' budget sets and the government's budget sets are unaltered as between the macron- and caret-bearing equilibria.

Notice how fiscal policy, in particular both $\{\overline{g}_t, \overline{\tau}_t\}_{t=0}^\infty$, is being held constant in the experiment described in this proposition. The inflation tax is also being held constant.

Relying on the result of Proposition 5.2, we shall work in the remainder of this chapter with systems in which only indexed debt is issued by the government.

5.4 Interactions of Monetary and Fiscal Policies

We shall use the model to study the interactions of monetary and fiscal policies in determining the equilibrium price-level process. For this purpose it is convenient to recall the government's sequence budget constraint at t:

$$(5.16) \quad g_t = \tau_t + \int q(x_{t+1}, x_t)b_{t+1}(x_{t+1}) \, dx_{t+1} - b_t(x_t) + \frac{M_{t+1} - M_t}{p_t}.$$

The integrated form of this budget constraint at t is

$$\int q(x_{t+1}, x_t)b_{t+1}(x_{t+1}) \, dx_{t+1}$$

$$= \sum_{j=1}^{\infty} \int q^{(j)}(x_{t+j}, x_t)\left(\tau_{t+j} + \frac{M_{t+1+j} - M_{t+j}}{p_{t+j}} - g_{t+j}\right) dx_{t+j}.$$

Using the above equation to eliminate $\int q(x_{t+1}, x_t)b_{t+1}(x_{t+1}) \, dx_{t+1}$ from (5.16) gives the alternative form

$$(5.17) \quad g_t + \sum_{j=1}^{\infty} \int q^{(j)}(x_{t+j}, x_t)g_{t+j} \, dx_{t+j} + b_t(x_t)$$

$$= \tau_t + \frac{M_{t+1} - M_t}{p_t}$$

$$+ \sum_{j=1}^{\infty} \int q^{(j)}(x_{t+j}, x_t)\left(\tau_{t+j} + \frac{M_{t+1+j} - M_{t+j}}{p_{t+j}}\right) dx_{t+j}.$$

Equation (5.17) states that the present value of government purchases $\{g_{t+j}\}_{j=0}^{\infty}$, plus the value in goods at t of any government debt due at t, $b_t(x_t)$, equals the present value of revenues from the explicit tax $\{\tau_{t+j}\}_{j=0}^{\infty}$ and the inflation tax $\{(M_{t+j+1} - M_{t+j})/p_{t+j}\}_{j=0}^{\infty}$.

Equation (5.17) implies that monetary and fiscal policies must be coordinated in the sense that, given a process for g_t, processes for τ_t and M_{t+1} cannot be chosen independently if they are to satisfy (5.17). Thus even though in this model the strict quantity theory equation (5.9) holds, statements such as "inflation is entirely a monetary phenomenon" must be interpreted and qualified in the light of (5.17). A correct statement would be: "Because $p_t = M_{t+1}/\xi_t$, and because ξ_t is an exogenous process, insofar as government actions are concerned, the process for inflation can be regarded as solely a function of the process chosen by the government for M_{t+1}. Furthermore, given a choice of a process for M_{t+1}, there exist choices of processes for lump-sum tax collections τ_t that make the choice of M_{t+1} process consistent with (5.17)."

Two widely proposed simple alternative rules for coordinating monetary and fiscal policies are the fixed-M rule and the fixed-p rule. Under the fixed-M rule, the government provides that $M_t = M_0$ for all t. Under this rule, the present value of seignorage is zero, and (5.17) collapses to

$$g_t + \sum_{j=1}^{\infty} \int q^{(j)}(x_{t+j}, x_t) g_{t+j} \, dx_{t+j} + b_t(x_t)$$

$$= \tau_t + \sum_{j=1}^{\infty} \int q^{(j)}(x_{t+j}, x_t) \tau_{t+j} \, dx_{t+j}.$$

This equation states that the government budget deficit net of interest payments $(g_t - \tau_t)$ is zero in present value, thereby restricting the class of τ_t policies capable of supporting a fixed-M rule. Under the fixed-M rule, the gross inflation rate is given by $p_{t+1}/p_t = \xi_t/\xi_{t+1}$. In general, $E(\xi_t/\xi_{t+1}) | \xi_t \neq 1$, and $E(\xi_t/\xi_{t+1}) \neq 1$, so that the fixed-$M$ rule need not be consistent with the absence of expected inflation.

Under the fixed-p rule, the government chooses an M_{t+1} process to satisfy $p_t = M_{t+1}/\xi_t = \bar{p} = M_1/\xi_0$, and $M_{t+1} = \xi_t \bar{p}$ when $t \geq 0$. Using the asset-pricing formulas (5.13) and the recursion for $q^{(j)}(x_{t+j}, x_t)$, the present value of seignorage from time t onward under this policy can be calculated to be

$$K_t = (\xi_t - \xi_{t-1}) + E_t \left\{ \frac{1}{u'(\xi_t - g_t)} \right.$$

$$\left. \cdot \sum_{j=1}^{\infty} \beta^j [u'(\xi_{t+j} - g_{t+j})(\xi_{t+j} - \xi_{t+j-1})] \right\},$$

where $E_t\{\cdot\} = E\{\cdot\}|x_t$. In general, the present value of seignorage under a fixed-p rule is not zero in this model, as this expression shows. In an economy with stationary ξ_t process, K_t could be expected to be small or even negative. In an economy with expected growth in ξ_t, K_t could be larger. In any event, (5.17) implies that, in order to support a constant-p rule for monetary policy, the τ_t process must be chosen to satisfy

$$g_t + \sum_{j=1}^{\infty} \int q^{(j)}(x_{t+j}, x_t) g_{t+j} \, dx_{t+j} + b_t(x_t)$$

$$= \tau_t + \sum_{j=1}^{\infty} \int q^{(j)}(x_{t+j}, x_t) \tau_{t+j} \, dx_{t+j} + K_t.$$

Advocates of the fixed-M rule or the fixed-p rule can be interpreted not as ignoring the need to choose a conformable tax process but as considering a permanent commitment to one of these monetary rules a way to compel the fiscal authorities to choose a τ_t process that satisfies the appropriate version of (5.17). From this perspective, the claim that inflation is entirely a monetary phenomenon makes sense. Notice also that because (5.17) constrains present values, the current government deficit net of interest, $g_t - \tau_t$, has no necessary direct connection with the price level at t. When a claim is made that monetary policy "alone" is sufficient to manage the inflation rate process, however, it cannot be taken to apply "regardless of fiscal policy" where fiscal policy is regarded as a choice of strategies $g_t(x_t)$, $\tau_t(x_t)$, $t \geq 0$.

We now further explore several dimensions of the tradeoffs between monetary and fiscal policies that are imposed by (5.17). In fact, (5.17) imposes such intricate interconnections between "monetary" and "fiscal" policies that it is somewhat artificial in the current context even to speak of separate monetary and fiscal policies, especially inasmuch as our model has nothing to say about why authority for setting M_{t+1}, g_t, and τ_t might be decentralized across distinct government agencies. We shall state and prove propositions that are capable of representing alternative and superficially conflicting assertions that have been made about the choice of monetary and fiscal policies. Distinct definitions of open-market operations and government deficit are sometimes used in describing the results of these propositions, which explains why verbal descriptions of these propositions seem to oppose them to one another.

We first state what can be regarded as a standard "Ricardian" proposition for our model. The experiment involves comparing inflation processes for economies with alternative settings of τ_0. The proposition is simply a corollary of Proposition 5.1.

PROPOSITION 5.3. *Current government deficits financed by bond issues are not inflationary.*

Consider an economy with $\{g_t, \xi_t\}_{t=0}^{\infty}$ processes and M_0 and $b_0(x_0)$ given. Let an initial equilibrium be given by $\bar{q}(x_{t+1}, x_t)$, $\bar{q}^{(j)}(x_{t+j}, x_t)$, and $\int \bar{b}_{t+1}(x_{t+1})\bar{q}(x_{t+1}, x_t)\,dx_{t+1}$, $\bar{p}_t$, and $\bar{\tau}_t$ for $t \geq 0$. Consider alternative tax and borrowing strategies $\hat{\tau}_t$, $\hat{b}_{t+1}(x_{t+1})$ that satisfy

$$(5.18) \qquad \hat{\tau}_0 - \bar{\tau}_0 = \int [\bar{b}_1(x_1) - \hat{b}_1(x_1)]\bar{q}(x_1, x_0)\,dx_1$$

$$(5.19) \qquad \int [\hat{b}_{t+1}(x_{t+1}) - \bar{b}_{t+1}(x_{t+1})]\bar{q}(x_{t+1}, x_t)\,dx_{t+1}$$

$$= \sum_{j=1}^{\infty} \int (\hat{\tau}_{t+j} - \bar{\tau}_{t+j})\bar{q}^{(j)}(x_{t+j}, x_t)\,dx_{t+j}, \qquad t \geq 0.$$

Tax and borrowing strategies satisfying (5.18) and (5.19) are equilibrium strategies at a price level and at asset price functions of $\bar{p}_t$, $\bar{q}(x_{t+1}, x_t)$ and $\bar{q}^{(j)}(x_{t+j}, x_t)$.

The proof of this proposition follows directly when we note that, under conditions (5.18) and (5.19), the government budget constraints (5.16) and (5.17) remain satisfied with the initial pricing kernel and the same process for the stock of currency M_{t+1}, $t \geq 0$, as prevails in the initial equilibrium. The quantity theory equation (5.9) then implies that the price-level process remains equal to the initial equilibrium process.

Adding conditions (5.18) and (5.19) gives the condition that the present value of taxes is being held constant in the experiment described in Proposition 5.3. Thus Proposition 5.3 states that a contemporary deficit accompanied by prospective surpluses sufficient to leave unaltered the present value of $\{\tau_t\}_{t=0}^{\infty}$ will also leave the equilibrium price-level process unaffected.

We now state another corollary to Proposition 5.1. This corollary is directed toward defining open-market operations in a way that makes them neutral. A key part of any definition of an open-market operation is the sense in which fiscal policy is being held constant. In the following proposition, holding fiscal policy constant entails altering the stream of lump-sum taxes τ_{t+j}, $j \geq 0$, by just enough to offset for each j the change in government interest payments [if $\int b(x_{t+1})q(x_{t+1}, x_t)\, dx_{t+1} > 0$] or government interest earnings [if $\int b(x_{t+1})q(x_{t+1}, x_t)\, dx_{t+1} < 0$] that are consequent upon altering the value of $\int b(x_{t+1})q(x_{t+1}, x_t)\, dx_{t+1}$. Using this concept of a constant fiscal policy and the associated concept of an open-market operation, we have the following proposition.

PROPOSITION 5.4. *Variations in M_t accomplished through open-market operations are neutral.*

Consider an economy with $\{g_t, \xi_t\}_{t=0}^{\infty}$ processes and M_0 and $b_0(x_0)$ each given. Let an initial equilibrium be given by $\bar{q}(x_{t+1}, x_t)$, $\bar{q}^{(j)}(x_{t+j}, x_t)$, and $\int \bar{b}_{t+1}(x_{t+1})\bar{q}(x_{t+1}, x_t)\, dx_{t+1}$, $\bar{p}_t$, and $\bar{\tau}_t$ for $t \geq 0$. Consider alternative tax, currency-creation, and borrowing strategies that satisfy

(5.20) $\hat{\tau}_0 = \bar{\tau}_0$

(5.21) $\displaystyle \int [\hat{b}_1(x_1) - \bar{b}_1(x_1)]\bar{q}(x_1, x_0)\, dx_1 = -\frac{\hat{M}_1 - \hat{M}_0}{\hat{p}_0} + \frac{\overline{M}_1 - \overline{M}_0}{\bar{p}_0},$

$\overline{M}_0 = \hat{M}_0, \hat{M}_{t+1}/\hat{p}_{t+1} = \overline{M}_{t+1}/\bar{p}_t$ for $t \geq 0$

(5.22) $$\int [\hat{b}_{t+1}(x_{t+1}) - \bar{b}_{t+1}(x_{t+1})]\bar{q}(x_{t+1}, x_t) \, dx_{t+1}$$

$$= \sum_{j=1}^{\infty} \int (\hat{\tau}_{t+j} - \bar{\tau}_{t+j})\bar{q}^{(j)}(x_{t+j}, x_t) \, dx_{t+j}, \qquad t \ge 0.$$

Tax, borrowing, and currency processes satisfying (5.20), (5.21), and (5.22) are equilibrium strategies at a price level given by $\hat{p}_t = \hat{M}_{t+1}/\xi_t$ and have asset-pricing functions given by $\hat{q}(x_{t+1}, x_t) = \bar{q}(x_{t+1}, x_t)$, $\hat{q}^{(j)}(x_{t+j}, x_t) = \bar{q}^{(j)}(x_{t+j}, x_t)$. Furthermore, $\hat{p}_{t+1}/\hat{p}_t = \bar{p}_{t+1}/\bar{p}_t$ for $t \ge 0$.

To prove this proposition, add Equation (5.21) and Equation (5.22) for $t = 0$. The resulting equation verifies that the government budget constraint is satisfied under the proposed caret-bearing equilibrium values. Note that (5.22) implies that $(\hat{M}_{t+1} - \hat{M}_t)/\hat{p}_t = (\bar{M}_{t+1} - \bar{M}_t)/\bar{p}_t$ for $t \ge 1$. Note also that under the proposed caret-bearing equilibrium, the loss in seignorage at $t = 0$ vis-à-vis the macron-bearing equilibrium is exactly balanced by the gain in the present value of lump-sum taxes.

Proposition 5.4 delivers a concept of open-market operations that makes them neutral. That is, variations in the stock of currency brought about as in Proposition 5.4 lead only to proportional variations in the price level. A key assumption used to obtain Proposition 5.4 is the interdependence between the public's interest-bearing bond holdings and their prospective explicit tax liabilities, given in Equation (5.22). In Proposition 5.4, prospective taxes are always adjusted by just enough to offset the altered debt service charges that are incidental to the open-market exchanges brought about according to (5.21). To invoke the conditions of Proposition 5.4, it is in effect necessary to assume that the central bank or open-market authority possesses and exercises the authority to alter explicit tax rates according to (5.22) whenever it alters the public's holdings of interest-bearing debt. Under the concept of open-market operations associated with the exercise of this power to adjust taxes, Proposition 5.4 states that open-market policy can control the price level and can alter the present value of the seignorage tax collected by the government.

We now study a different definition of open-market operations that holds fiscal policy fixed in the sense of taking the processes $\{g_t, \tau_t\}_{t=0}^{\infty}$ as given. Let $\{\xi_t\}_{t=0}^{\infty}$ and $b_0(x_0)$ be given. Because (g_t, ξ_t) is given, $q(x_{t+1}, x_t)$ is determined, as stated in Equation (5.13). Because $\{\tau_t\}_{t=0}^{\infty}$ and $b_0(x_0)$ are given, Equation (5.17) implies that the path of currency $\{M_{t+1}\}$ must be such that the present value of seignorage, namely,

(5.23) $$\frac{M_1 - M_0}{p_0} + \sum_{j=1}^{\infty} \int q^{(j)}(x_j, x_0)\left(\frac{M_{j+1} - M_j}{p_j}\right) dx_j = \bar{K},$$

must be constant across all alternative equilibria. The term $\bar{K}$ is the present value of the government's net-of-interest deficit. Equation (5.23) states that the present value of seignorage equals the present value of the net-of-interest government deficit. If the present value of τ_t is less than or equal to the present value of g_t, Equation (5.17) implies that $\bar{K} \geq 0$. From Equation (5.9) we have that

$$\frac{M_1 - M_0}{p_0} = \xi_0 - \frac{M_0}{p_0}$$

$$\frac{M_{j+1} - M_j}{p_j} = \xi_j - \xi_{j-1} \frac{p_{j-1}}{p_j}, \qquad j \geq 1.$$

Substituting these into (5.23) gives

(5.24) $$\underbrace{\left(\xi_0 - \frac{M_0}{p_0} \right)}_{A} + \underbrace{\sum_{j=1}^{\infty} \int q^{(j)}(x_j, x_0) \left(\xi_j - \xi_{j-1} \frac{p_{j-1}}{p_j} \right) dx_j}_{B} = \bar{K}.$$

The lower the term A, the greater the extent to which bonds are being issued to finance g_0. Across equilibria satisfying (5.24), the term A can be lowered (p_0 can be lowered by decreasing M_1) only if the term B is increased, which requires that p_{j-1}/p_j be lowered for some $j \geq 1$, which in turn means that more inflation must be accepted in the future. In a positive real interest rate economy, $q^{(j)}(x_j, x_0)$ averages to less than unity and decreases with j, which implies that the longer into the future this inflation is postponed, the higher it must eventually be. Thus under the assumed circumstances, a reduction in M_1 achieves a lower initial price level p_0 only at the cost of higher inflation eventually. We use these considerations to formulate the following proposition.

PROPOSITION 5.5. *Unpleasant monetarist arithmetic: government deficits financed by bond issues are eventually more inflationary than those financed by creating currency.*

Consider an economy with processes for $\{g_t, \xi_t, \text{ and } \tau_t\}_{t=0}^{\infty}$ given exogenously from outside. In particular, assume that $g_t = g > 0$ and $\xi_t = \xi > 0$, with probability 1 for all $t \geq 0$. Let the present value of τ_t be less than the present value of g_t. Let $b_0(x_0)$ and M_0 be given. Consider time paths for M_t of the form

(5.25) $$M_t = M_1 < M_0 \quad \text{for } t \leq T$$
$$M_t = M_{T+1} \quad \text{for } t \geq T + 1.$$

Assume that it is feasible to finance the present value of the government deficit with at least some paths of the class (5.25), which requires that the deficit not be too large. Then the larger $\int b_1(x_1)q(x_1, x_0)\, dx_1$ and therefore the lower M_1 and p_0, the higher the price level must eventually become.

To prove the proposition, let $R^{-1} = \int q(x_{t+1}, x_t)\, dx_{t+1} = \beta u'(\xi - g)/u'(\xi - g) = \beta < 1$. Then Equation (5.24) becomes

$$(5.26) \qquad \left(\xi - \frac{M_0}{p_0}\right) + \xi \sum_{j=1}^{\infty} R^{-1}(1 - p_{j-1}/p_j) = \overline{K} > 0.$$

Substitute the assumed form for the currency stock path (5.25) and the quantity theory equation (5.9) into (5.26) to obtain

$$(5.27) \qquad \left(1 - \frac{M_1}{M_{T+1}}\right) = R^T \xi^{-1} \overline{K} - R^T\left(1 - \frac{M_0}{M_1}\right).$$

Note that $(1 - M_t/M_{t+1})\xi$ is the amount of seignorage that is raised at time t. Equation (5.27) states that reductions of seignorage by Δ at time 0 require increases in seignorage by $R^T\Delta$ at time T. Because $R > 1$, it follows that postponing resorting to the seignorage tax requires more revenues to be raised when it is finally levied. To restate the issue in more detail, using (5.27) and the quantity theory equation (5.9) to solve for p_T as a function of p_0, we have

$$p_T = \frac{p_0}{1 + R^T - R^T \xi^{-1}(\overline{K} + M_0/p_0)}.$$

Differentiating gives

$$(5.28) \qquad \frac{dp_T}{dp_0} = \frac{(1 + R^T) - (R^T \xi^{-1}\overline{K} + 2R^T M_0/M_1)}{[1 + R^T - R^T \xi^{-1}(\overline{K} + M_0/p_0)]^2}.$$

Because $\overline{K} \geq 0$ and $R > 1$, we have that, when $M_1 < M_0$,

$$(5.29) \qquad \frac{dp_T}{dp_0} < 0.$$

Thus given a class of policies of the form (5.25), a lower price level for $t = 0, \ldots, (T - 1)$ can be achieved only at the cost of a permanently higher price level from $t = T$ onward.[3] This completes the proof of Proposition 5.5.

3. It can also be shown that, within the class of policies indicated by (5.25), the later the date T, the higher the eventual price level p_T must be. We leave the demonstration as an exercise for the reader.

As our discussion of Equation (5.24) indicates, Proposition 5.5 is a special case of a more general class of situations in which, given a $\{g_t, \tau_t\}_{t=0}^{\infty}$ process that is in deficit in the present value sense, open-market exchanges of M_{t+1} for bonds can reduce the price level only temporarily.

Proposition 5.5 exhibits the "unpleasant arithmetic" described by Sargent and Wallace (1981) in a related context. The proposition requires first, that g_t and τ_t both be exogenous processes that do not vary with the value of interest-bearing bonds $\int b_{t+1}(x_{t+1})q(x_{t+1}, x_t)\,dx_{t+1}$ that are issued; second, that the present value of government purchases exceed the present value of explicit taxes $\{\tau_t\}_{t=0}^{\infty}$; and third, that R exceed unity.

Proposition 5.5 states conditions under which, with fiscal policy specified as given $\{g_t, \tau_t\}$ sequences, open-market operations are not capable of permanently lowering the price level. Here open-market operations at t are defined as changes in M_{t+1} and $\int b(x_{t+1})q(x_{t+1}, x_t)\,dx_{t+1}$ that satisfy the government budget constraint (5.16), with g_t and τ_t regarded as given processes for all t. The idea here is that the monetary authority can conduct asset exchanges subject to (5.16) but cannot influence the process for g_t or τ_t. This idea leads to a definition of an open-market operation as an asset exchange with the public that holds fiscal policy constant, where "fiscal policy" means a stochastic process for (g_t, τ_t).

The loose statements in the titles of Propositions 5.4 and 5.5 raise the question of how a "government deficit" is to be defined. One definition of the current government deficit is simply $(g_t - \tau_t)$. Equation (5.17) states that, if $M_{t+1} = M_t$ for all t, then the present value of the deficit defined as $(g_t - \tau_t)$ must equal $-b_t(x_t)$. In other words, if $b_0(x_0) \geq 0$, only temporary deficits $(g_t - \tau_t)$ are feasible when $M_{t+1} - M_t = 0$ for all $t \geq 0$.

McCallum (1984) has noted that it is common to use an alternative definition reached by including net interest payments in the definition of the government deficit. Following McCallum, the government budget constraint (5.5) when $M_{t+1} - M_t = 0$ can be written

$$\int b(x_{t+1})q(x_{t+1}, x_t)\,dx_{t+1}$$

$$= g_t - \tau_t + \left[b(x_t) - \int b(x_t)q(x_t, x_{t-1})\,dx_t \right]$$

$$+ \int b(x_t)q(x_t, x_{t-1})\,dx_t.$$

The term on the second line is the deficit gross of interest on the debt. McCallum noted that it *is* feasible to run a permanent deficit defined as

$d_m(t) = [b(x_t) - \int b(x_t)q(x_t, x_{t-1}) \, dx_t] + g_t - \tau_t$ while simultaneously keeping $(M_{t+1} - M_t)$ equal to zero for all $t \geq 1$. It is possible, for example, to set $d_m(t)$ equal to a positive constant $\bar{d}_m$ while keeping $M_{t+1} - M_t = 0$ for all t. When $d_m(t) = \bar{d} > 0$, the value of one-period debt per capita, $\int b(x_{t+1})q(x_{t+1}, x_t) \, dx_{t+1}$, is growing without bound, and so are interest payments $[b(x_t) - \int b(x_t)q(x_t, x_{t-1}) \, dx_t]$. Therefore, with $d_m(t)$ held constant, $(\tau_t - g_t)$ is also growing without bound. With a given process for g_t, the government must increase τ_t without bound over time just enough to cover the increased interest expenses associated with the growing stock of debt. It is feasible for the stock of one-period debt and taxes to grow without bound in this way while $M_{t+1} - M_t = 0$ for all $t \geq 0$ [that is, (5.17) and (5.4) remain satisfied].

Proposition 5.5 suggests a different and less powerful concept of open-market operations than is associated with Proposition 5.4. In Proposition 5.5, the open-market authority is bound to take the $\{\tau_t\}_{t=0}^{\infty}$ strategy as given and beyond its control. The open-market authority cannot alter the present value of seignorage that the government is to collect. If the government is running a permanent deficit, in the sense that the present value of $\{g_t - \tau_t\}_{t=0}^{\infty}$ is positive, then the present value of seignorage is bound to be positive. Under these circumstances, an open-market authority can only decide when to invoke the inflation tax. Roughly speaking, when real interest rates are positive, postponing the inflation tax tends to increase the inflation tax that must eventually be imposed at a rate equal to the gross real rate of interest.

On the other hand, under Proposition 5.4, variations in M_{t+1} are assumed to be accompanied by an alteration in the stream of taxes that is sufficient to offset the change in seignorage $(M_{t+1} - M_t)/p_t$. This change in taxes permits open-market operations permanently to influence the price level.

Propositions 5.4 and 5.5 provide a useful background for understanding Neil Wallace's characterization of monetary and fiscal policymakers in the United States as having engaged in a game of "chicken" since 1981. (Wallace offered this interpretation in remarks made orally in March 1981.) In the United States, authority for choosing processes for M_{t+1}, g_t, and τ_t is decentralized across three government agencies, the Federal Reserve, Congress, and the executive. As a technical matter of legal authority, the Federal Reserve cannot perform the powerful kind of open-market operations that were envisioned in Proposition 5.4, in which future tax changes are automatically triggered by open-market exchanges of currency for interest-bearing bonds. If Congress and the President "go first" and choose plans for $\{g_t\}$, $\{\tau_t\}$ that imply that the present value of the net-of-interest budget deficit is positive, then the situation is as described in Proposition 5.5, and it is simply not feasible for the Federal Reserve forever to stick to a constant-M rule. Furthermore, the longer the Fed delays in delivering to the Treasury seignorage revenues raised through inflation, the more inflation must eventually occur. On the other hand, if the Federal Reserve views itself as "going first" and as being able to sustain a constant-M rule, then despite its lack of formal authority to legislate tax or expenditure changes, the Fed can force the budget into balance in the present value sense. A game of chicken seemed to be occurring in the United States from 1981 to 1985 because the Fed announced a policy that is feasible only if the budget swings toward balance in a present value sense, whereas Congress and the President set in place plans for government expenditures and taxes that imply prospective net-of-interest deficits so large that they are feasible only if the Fed eventually creates more inflation. In such a situation, something has to give.

5.5 Interest on Reserves

There has been a recurrent proposal to pay interest on currency (or bank reserves) at the risk-free market rate of interest. Milton Friedman (1960) noted that a system of legal restrictions enforcing a government monopoly on the right to issue currency is subject to two difficulties when the government currency bears a lower rate of return than private debt. First, enforcement difficulties are associated with the incentive to avoid the restrictions. Second, "bad economic results" are associated with a situation in which two assets with similar risk characteristics offer different rates of return. Friedman proposed paying interest on reserves at the market interest rate as a way of overcoming both difficulties. He said that the interest payments could be financed either by levying taxes or by having the government hold a portfolio of private securities to back its currency, in which case the interest earnings on that portfolio could be passed to holders of currency.

The cash-in-advance model described in this chapter exhibits the first difficulty mentioned by Friedman but not the second. As we saw in Section 5.1, there is an arbitrage opportunity to private agents to issue currency that is assumed to go unexploited in equilibrium. The equilibrium consumption allocation in this model is optimal, however, despite the distortion in the structure of rates of return associated with the presence of the cash-in-advance restriction. This feature is special and is coincident with the fact that things have been carefully arranged to assure that the inflation tax is nondistorting. If the setup were altered to render the inflation tax distorting, then the model would also capture Friedman's second reason for paying interest on reserves. The inflation tax would be distorting if nontrivial labor supply or capital accumulation choices were added to the model. See Lucas and Stokey (1983) and Y. Eugene Yun (1985) for sample analyses of cash-in-advance models with distorting taxes.

The cash-in-advance model described above provides a convenient context within which to analyze the consequences of different methods of financing interest on reserves schemes. As one would expect in a general equilibrium context, much depends on the way in which interest payments are financed.

We consider a situation in which, beginning in period ($t = 0$), the government pays interest on currency held between t and ($t + 1$) at the gross nominal rate of $\alpha_t = R_t p_{t+1}/p_t$, where $R_t^{-1} = \int q(x_{t+1}, x_t) \, dx_{t+1}$. Currency thus has the same real gross rate of return R_t as risk-free interest-bearing securities. Because currency is not dominated in rate of return, $m_t^p \geq p_t c_t$ will not generally hold with equality. Instead the household's demand for real balances of currency is indeterminate: at t consumers are content to hold any level of real balances m_t^p/p_t exceeding c_t, since they can offset these holdings with sales of sure one-period securities and attain the same budget set.[4]

With the government paying interest on currency, the government's budget constraint (5.16) needs to be altered by adding to expenditures the real value of interest payments due at t. At this time t, the government must make real interest payments in the total amount $[R_{t-1} - (p_{t-1}/p_t)] (M_t/p_{t-1})$, in order to equate to R_{t-1} the real return on currency held from ($t - 1$) to t. We assume that these payments begin at $t = 1$, so that for $t \geq 1$, (5.16) must be altered to

$$g_t + \left(R_{t-1} - \frac{p_{t-1}}{p_t} \right) \frac{M_t}{p_{t-1}}$$

$$= \tau_t + \int q(x_{t+1}, x_t) b_{t+1}(x_{t+1}) \, dx_{t+1} - b_t(x_t) + \frac{M_{t+1} - M_t}{p_t}.$$

Rearranging this equation gives

$$(5.30) \qquad b_t(x_t) = (\tau_t - g_t) + \int b_{t+1}(x_{t+1}) q(x_{t+1}, x_t) \, dx_{t+1}$$

$$+ \left(\frac{M_{t+1}}{p_t} - \frac{M_t}{p_{t-1}} \right) + \frac{M_t}{p_{t-1}} (1 - R_{t-1}), \qquad t \geq 1.$$

4. The scheme analyzed in the text is one in which the government pays interest on currency at the risk-free real rate of interest. Alternative schemes can be imagined in which the government makes currency a risky asset but gives currency a return stream that makes it an asset not dominated in rate of return. The government could, for example, make currency pay off in nominal terms at the sure nominal rate of interest. Such modifications would still render the demand for real balances indeterminate. Versions of our Propositions 5.6 and 5.7 would continue to hold under such schemes.

For $t = 0$, we again have the budget constraint (5.16), since the interest payments are assumed to commence at $t = 1$. We represent (5.16) for $t = 0$ as

$$(5.31) \qquad b_0(x_0) = (\tau_0 - g_0) + \int b_1(x_1)q(x_1, x_0)\, dx_1 + \frac{M_1 - M_0}{p_0}.$$

Using (5.30) and (5.31) to derive the integrated form of the government budget constraint now leads to[5]

$$(5.32) \qquad \frac{M_0}{p_0} + b_0(x_0)$$

$$= (\tau_0 - g_0) + \sum_{j=0}^{\infty} \iint \cdots \int (\tau_{1+j} - g_{1+j})q(x_{1+j}, x_j)$$

$$\cdot q(x_j, x_{j-1}) \cdots q(x_1, x_0)\, dx_{1+j}\, dx_j \cdots dx_1.$$

This equation states that the value of initial government debt $M_0/p_0 + b_0(x_0)$ equals the present value of the government net-of-interest surplus. Under this interest-on-reserves scheme, currency is a perfect substitute for interest-bearing government and private debt and is valued accordingly.

In (5.32) it is understood that τ_t is a function of $x^t \equiv (x_t, x_{t-1}, \ldots, x_0)$, that is, the entire history of x_t. At time 0, the price of a claim on one unit of consumption at time t contingent on the history x^t assuming value $\bar{x}^t = (\bar{x}_t, \bar{x}_{t-1}, \ldots, \bar{x}_0)$ is given by $q(\bar{x}_t, \bar{x}_{t-1})q(\bar{x}_{t-1}, \bar{x}_{t-2}) \cdots q(\bar{x}_1, \bar{x}_0)$. This claim can be established by pursuing the sort of arbitrage pricing reasoning that we used repeatedly in Chapter 3. When a variable y_t depends only on x_t, by integrating with respect to $(x_{t-1}, \ldots, x_1)$ a term like

$$\int \cdots \int y(x_t)q(x_t, x_{t-1})q(x_{t-1}, x_{t-2}) \cdots q(x_1, x_0)dx_t \cdots dx_1$$

can be simplified to $\int y(x_t)q^{(t)}(x_t, x_0)\, dx_t$ by using the standard recursive formula for $q^{(j)}(x_{t+j}, x_t)$. When a variable y_t is indexed on the entire history up to time t, x^t, however, the formula cannot be simplified in this way. As a result, the present value of $\{\tau_t - g_t\}_{t=0}^{\infty}$ in (5.32) is represented differently from the way it is in (5.17). Note that it is useful to index τ_t by x^t because interest payments at t depend on R_{t-1}, which in turn depends on x_{t-1}.

Let $\bar{\phi}$ be the minimum value that any constant-for-all-time level of real balances can attain and still satisfy the cash-in-advance constraint for all $t \geq 0$. That is,

$$\bar{\phi} = \inf[\phi: \text{prob}\{\phi > \sup_t \xi_t\} = 1].$$

---

5. The identity described in Exercise 5.4 is used in deriving (5.32).

We now consider a scheme in which the government levies whatever lump-sum taxes are necessary to finance the interest payments on currency. Under this scheme, the price level, level of taxes, and real balances are all indeterminate. Consider potential equilibria in which real balances are constant over time. Given $b_0(x_0)$, a $\{g_t\}_{t=0}^{\infty}$ process, and also that $M_0 > 0$, we must find a p_0 where $\infty > p_0 > 0$ and a $\{\tau_t\}$ sequence that satisfy (5.32) and $M_0/p_0 \geq \overline{\phi}$. We can do so in infinitely many ways. Choose any p_0 satisfying $0 < p_0 \leq M_0/\overline{\phi}$. Then choose a tax sequence satisfying (5.32). Evidently this p_0 and tax sequence satisfy the government budget constraint with a given $q(x_{t+1}, x_t)$ kernel. It can also be verified that all such choices of p_0 and $\{\tau_t\}_{t=0}^{\infty}$ provide the private agent with the same budget set at a given $q(x_{t+1}, x_t)$ kernel. The reason is that the increased taxes and increased M_0/p_0 just offset each other as far as both the private agent's and the government's budget sets are concerned.

The reasoning establishes

PROPOSITION 5.6. *Indeterminacy of price level, real balances, and taxes under interest on reserves with tax financing.*

Let $\{g_t\}_{t=0}^{\infty}$, $M_0 > 0$, $b_0(x_0)$ be given. Let $\{\tau_t\}_{t=0}^{\infty}$ be chosen to satisfy (5.30)– (5.31), thereby financing interest payments on currency at the risk-free real rate of interest. Then for any initial price level satisfying $0 < p_0 \leq M_0/\overline{\phi}$, there exists an equilibrium with constant real balances over time. The present value of taxes varies directly with M_0/p_0 in the manner depicted by (5.32). This statement completes Proposition 5.6

The present value of taxes is indeterminate under this system because the level of real balances is indeterminate. As a result it is impossible to estimate the level of additional taxes needed to support this scheme by observing the levels of real balances and interest rates that prevail *before* the scheme is implemented. The reason is that implementing the scheme makes currency a good asset in terms of rate of return, thereby rendering the cash-in-advance restriction nonbinding and the demand for currency indeterminate and possibly much larger than it was before the scheme was introduced. The interest payments and the taxes needed to support them then become impossible to estimate.[6]

---

6. Robert Hall (1983) describes a system for linking payments on currency to a target price level in a systematic way. Hall's scheme names a target price level and systematically links interest payments on currency to the price level. Currency is dominated in rate of return when the price level is less than the target level, causing people to abandon currency and making the price level rise. Currency is a dominating asset when the price level exceeds the target price level, causing people to move into currency and making the price level fall. Under tax financing, Hall's scheme can be shown to render the price level and the present value of taxes determinate.

For each equilibrium described in Proposition 5.6, any $\{p_t, M_t\}$ sequence is an equilibrium, provided that it starts from the given p_0 and satisfies $M_{t+1}/p_t = M_1/p_0$. One example of such an equilibrium holds p_t constant at p_0 and M_{t+1} constant at M_1 for $t \geq 1$. In this equilibrium explicit interest is being paid on currency held between t and $(t + 1)$ at the gross interest rate R_t.

According to a second example of such an equilibrium, $p_{t+1}R_t/p_t = 1$ or $p_{t+1} = R_t^{-1}p_t$ and $M_{t+1} = R_{t-1}^{-1}M_t$ for $t \geq 1$. In this case no explicit interest is being paid because $[R_t - (p_t/p_{t+1})] = 0$. Real interest is paid on currency by producing a deflation through taxing and using the proceeds to retire currency. A further specialization of this example occurs when $R_t^{-1} = \beta$ for all t, which implies that $p_{t+1} = \beta p_t$ and $M_{t+1} = \beta M_t$.

We now briefly consider the suggestion that interest payments could be financed by having the government hold private securities to back the currency, passing along the interest on the securities to the holders of currency. The idea is to move to a system of paying interest on currency without raising taxes. To study this idea, it is useful to repeat and to compare the two forms of the intertemporal budget constraint at $t = 0$, the original one (5.17) pertinent where interest is not being paid on currency and the modified one (5.32), which holds under interest on reserves:

$$(5.17') \quad b_0(x_0) = (\tau_0 - g_0) + \sum_{j=0}^{\infty} \int \cdots \int (\tau_{1+j} - g_{1+j})$$
$$\cdot q(x_{1+j}, x_j)q(x_j, x_{j-1}) \cdots q(x_1, x_0)\, dx_{1+j}dx_j \cdots dx_1$$
$$+ \frac{M_1 - M_0}{p_0} + \sum_{j=0}^{\infty} \int \cdots \int \left(\frac{M_{2+j} - M_{1+j}}{p_{1+j}}\right) q(x_{1+j}, x_j)$$
$$\cdot q(x_j, x_{j-1}) \cdots q(x_1, x_0)\, dx_{1+j}dx_j \cdots dx_1$$

[(5.17) for $t = 0$: the government budget constraint without interest on currency] and

$$(5.32) \quad b_0(x_0) + \frac{M_0}{p_0} = (\tau_0 - g_0) + \sum_{j=0}^{\infty} \int (\tau_{1+j} - g_{1+j})q(x_{1+j}, x_j) \cdots$$
$$q(x_1, x_0)\, dx_{1+j} \cdots dx_1$$

(the government budget constraint with interest paid on currency).

Consider an equilibrium in which interest is not being paid on currency, and in which $M_t = M_0 > 0$ for all $t \geq 1$, so that no seignorage is being raised. Let the values of $M_0 > 0$, $b_0(x_0)$, $\{g_t\}_{t=0}^{\infty}$, and $\{\tau_t\}_{t=0}^{\infty}$ associated with this equilibrium be denoted by $\bar{M}_0$, $\bar{b}_0(x_0)$, $\{\bar{g}_t\}_{t=0}^{\infty}$, and $\{\bar{\tau}_t\}_{t=0}^{\infty}$. Now suppose that we fix M_0, $b_0(x_0)$, $\{g_t\}$, $\{\tau_t\}$ at their values in the macron-bearing equilibrium and seek an equilibrium with interest on currency at the risk-free market rate of interest. This procedure is equivalent to requiring that both (5.17′) and (5.32) hold at the values $\overline{M}_0$, $\overline{b}_0(x_0)$, $\{\overline{g}_t\}_{t=0}^{\infty}$, $\{\overline{\tau}_t\}_{t=0}^{\infty}$. The only way that both (5.17′) and (5.32) can hold at these values is if $\overline{M}_0/p_0 = 0$. No finite value of p_0 satisfies this equation. Therefore there exists no equilibrium with interest payments on currency. We may summarize these findings.

PROPOSITION 5.7. *Nonexistence of an equilibrium with interest payments on currency financed solely by interest earned on the government portfolio.*

Consider an initial equilibrium, denoted by macrons, with no interest being paid on currency. Let government expenditures and taxes be given by $\{\overline{g}_t, \overline{\tau}_t\}_{t=0}^{\infty}$. *Say that* $M_0 = \overline{M}_0 > 0$ *and* $b_0(x_0) = \overline{b}_0(x_0)$ *are given. Let* $M_{t+1} - M_t = 0$ *for all* $t \geq 0$ *so that no seignorage is being raised. Fix* $\{g_t, \tau_t\}_{t=0}^{\infty}$, M_0, *and* $b_0(x_0)$ *at their values for the macron-bearing economy. Then there exists no equilibrium with interest payments on reserves at the risk-free real rate being financed by earnings on the government's portfolio.*

This proposition can be generalized to dispense with the assumption that $\overline{M}_{t+1} - \overline{M}_t = 0$. We actually require that in the initial macron-bearing equilibrium, $R_{t-1} > \overline{p}_{t-1}/\overline{p}_t$ for all $t \geq 1$. Under this condition, there exists no equilibrium with $\{\overline{g}_t, \overline{\tau}_t\}_{t=0}^{\infty} = \{\hat{g}_t, \hat{\tau}_t\}_{t=0}^{\infty}$ and with interest payments being made on currency at the risk-free market rate.

Sargent and Wallace (1985) analyze Friedman's proposal to pay interest on reserves in the context of an overlapping-generations model. They obtain results related to but distinct from the present ones. With tax financing, Sargent and Wallace find indeterminacy even more pervasive than is indicated by Proposition 5.6: they find interest rates and consumption allocations indeterminate as well as real balances and the price level. With interest payments financed by government security holdings, they find that an equilibrium may or may not exist.

5.6 A Two-Country Model

We now describe a two-country version of the cash-in-advance model. The model is specified with the aim of representing a number of "classical" doctrines in international monetary theory. These doctrines include (1) "the monetary theory of the exchange rate," which is the notion that the exchange rate is proportional to the ratio of the currency stocks in the two countries; and (2) a two-country version of Irving Fisher's theory of interest, including the notion that the "real interest rate" is independent of the currency supply process, in particular, and the government's financing decision, in general, in each country. The nature of these results hinges delicately on the specification of the cash-in-advance constraints. Partly to highlight this delicacy, we shall see that a consequence of altering the form of those constraints in a simple way is to replace the uniquely determined exchange rate of the monetary theory of the exchange rate with the infinite number of equilibrium exchange rates encountered by Kareken and Wallace (1981).

There are two countries, each with its own currency. Each country has the same number of private agents. There is one representative private agent in each country. There is one good, which is exogenously produced by Lucas trees, one for each agent in each country. In country 1, ξ_t units of the consumption good are produced by each tree in period t, whereas in country 2, η_t units of the same consumption good are produced by the country 2 trees in period t. We shall assume that (ξ_t, η_t) are governed by a first-order Markov process. Residents in country i for $i = 1, 2$ have preferences summarized by

$$(5.33) \qquad E_0 \sum_{t=0}^{\infty} \beta^t u(c_{it}),$$

where c_{it} is time t consumption in country i. Notice that preferences are assumed to be identical across countries.

The government of country i purchases and uses consumption goods in amount g_t^i, imposes lump-sum taxes on residents of *both* countries in the amounts of $\tau_t^i/2$ each, and issues new currency in amount $(M_{t+1}^i - M_t^i)$ at the time t. Here g_t^i and τ_t^i are in units of the time t good, whereas M_t^i is in units of dollars for $i = 1$, and in units of pounds for $i = 2$. The assumption that each government taxes its own and foreign residents in equal amounts will be seen to play an important role in setting an analytically convenient equal initial distribution of wealth across the two countries. The state vector is now $x_t = (\xi_t, \eta_t, g_t^1, g_t^2)$. The government of country i is subject to the budget constraint

$$(5.34) \qquad g_t^i = \tau_t^i + \int q(x_{t+1}, x_t) b_{it+1}(x_{t+1}) \, dx_{t+1} - b_{it}(x_t) + \frac{M_{t+1}^i - M_t^i}{p_t^i},$$

where $b_{it+1}(x_{t+1})$ is the amount, measured in units of time $(t + 1)$ good, that the government of country i promises to pay at $(t + 1)$ contingent on the realization of state x_{t+1} at $(t + 1)$, and p_t^i is the price level in country i at t. An integrated form of the budget constraint for government i is

$$(5.35) \qquad g_t^i + \sum_{j=1}^{\infty} \int q^{(j)}(x_{t+j}, x_t) g_{t+j}^i \, dx_{t+j} + b_{it}(x_t)$$
$$= \tau_t^i + \frac{M_{t+1}^i - M_t^i}{p_t^i} + \sum_{j=1}^{\infty} \int q^{(j)}(x_{t+j}, x_t)$$
$$\cdot \left(\tau_{t+j}^i + \frac{M_{t+1+j}^i - M_{t+j}^i}{p_{t+j}^i} \right) dx_{t+j}.$$

We assume that each government always purchases consumption goods in the home market, using domestic currency to make the purchase.

Residents of country i are permitted to own shares in trees in either country as well as the currency and state-contingent debt issued by either country. Residents of country i owe taxes to the government of *both* countries. We assume that initially wealth of each kind is evenly divided between residents of the two countries. In particular, at time 0, residents of each country own one-half of each of the trees of country 1, the trees of country 2, the initial stocks of dollars and pounds, and the initial debt of countries 1 and 2.

The structure of trading is much as it is in the one-country model. At the beginning of t, the random variables $(\xi_t, \eta_t, g_t^i, \tau_t^i, M_{t+1}^i - M_t^i, i = 1, 2)$ are realized. Each period t is divided into three trading sessions. In the securities trading session, households of each country start out with the stocks of dollars and pounds that were paid to them as dividends by firms of countries 1 and 2, respectively, during the preceding period. Each household must pay $\tau_t^i/2$ in lump-sum taxes, denominated in units of the consumption good but payable in currency, to the government of country i during the securities trading session. During the securities trading session, currencies of both countries, shares in trees of both countries, and government debt are all traded. Residents of each country are free to hold securities and currency issued in the other country as well as in their own.

At the conclusion of securities trading, agents disperse, and the shopping session occurs. Each household consists of a shopper-dividend collector pair. The shopper takes the currencies of countries 1 and 2 purchased during the security trading period and uses them to purchase goods in the "yards" of the people in country 1 and country 2, respectively. The goods produced in country 1 can be purchased only with dollars, whereas the goods produced in country 2 can be purchased only with pounds. Households are thus subject to the following cash-in-advance constraints. Let c_{it}^j be the amount of the good produced in country j that is consumed by a resident of country i. We have $c_{it} = c_{it}^1 + c_{it}^2$, where c_{it} is time t consumption of a resident of country i. Let m_{it}^{pj} be the amount of currency of country j held by a (private) resident of country i at the conclusion of security trading at time t. Then we require

(5.36)
$$m_{1t}^{p1} \geq p_t^1 c_{1t}^1, \qquad m_{2t}^{p1} \geq p_t^1 c_{2t}^1$$
$$m_{1t}^{p2} \geq p_t^2 c_{1t}^2, \qquad m_{2t}^{p2} \geq p_t^2 c_{2t}^2.$$

The constraints on the left apply to residents of country 1, whereas those on the right apply to residents of country 2. The constraints in the top line of (5.36) pertain to currency of country 1, whereas those in the second line pertain to the currency of country 2. Letting m_t^{gj} be the stock of j-country currency held by the government of country j at the conclusion of security trading, we impose the following cash-in-advance constraints on the governments:

(5.37) $m_t^{g1} = p_t^1 g_t^1, \qquad m_t^{g2} = p_t^2 g_t^2.$

We are assuming that a government does not hold currency issued by the other country, thereby requiring the government to purchase all of its goods domestically. During the shopping session, the worker stays home and sells the output from her tree in exchange for domestic currency. At the end of the shopping session, the worker has accumulated currency in an amount equal to the value of current output. This cash must be paid out to owners of the tree.

After shopping concludes, the third, or dividend collection, session occurs. The shopper visits the domestic and foreign locations at which the household owns shares in trees to collect dividends. The dividends are payable in the currency of the country in which the tree is located. The household is forced to carry over all of the cash into the next period. The government owns no trees, so that households end up carrying all of the currency between periods.

We now analyze equilibrium price determination. Equilibrium conditions in the markets for currency are

(5.38) $m_{1t}^{p1} + m_{2t}^{p1} + m_t^{g1} = M_{t+1}^1$
$m_{1t}^{p2} + m_{2t}^{p2} + m_t^{g2} = M_{t+1}^2.$

Substituting (5.37) and (5.36) at equality into (5.38) gives

(5.39) $p_t^1(c_{1t}^1 + c_{2t}^1 + g_t^1) = M_{t+1}^1$
$p_t^2(c_{1t}^2 + c_{2t}^2 + g_t^2) = M_{t+1}^2.$

Equilibrium in the goods markets requires

(5.40) $c_{1t}^1 + c_{2t}^1 + g_t^1 = \xi_t$
$c_{1t}^2 + c_{2t}^2 + g_t^2 = \eta_t.$

Substituting (5.40) into (5.39) gives the quantity theory equations

(5.41) $p_t^1 = M_{t+1}^1/\xi_t$
$p_t^2 = M_{t+1}^2/\eta_t.$

Defining the exchange rate e_t as p_t^1/p_t^2 (measured in dollars per pound), we have

(5.42) $e_t = \dfrac{M_{t+1}^1}{M_{t+1}^2} \cdot \dfrac{\eta_t}{\xi_t}.$

This is a version of the monetary theory of the exchange rate.

We now study the decision problem of a household of country i. Let the household begin period t with wealth of θ_{it}, denominated in units of the consumption good. The household chooses securities subject to the constraint

(5.43) $\quad \dfrac{m_{it}^{p1}}{p_t^1} + \dfrac{m_{it}^{p2}}{p_t^2} + \dfrac{1}{2}(\tau_t^1 + \tau_t^2) + r_1(x_t)s_{it}^1 + r_2(x_t)s_{it}^2$

$\qquad + \displaystyle\int b_{it+1}^d(x_{t+1})q(x_{t+1}, x_t)\,dx_{t+1} \le \theta_{it}.$

Here $r_1(x_t)$ is the price in units of current consumption good of a title to current and all future dividends ξ_t, payable in dollars; $r_2(x_t)$ is the price in units of current consumption of the current and all future pound receipts from selling the η_t process; s_{it}^j is the number of shares of country j tree purchased at t by a resident of country i; and $b_{it+1}^d(x_{t+1})$ is state-contingent claims on time $(t + 1)$ goods purchased by a resident of country i.

The household chooses $\{c_{it}^1, c_{it}^2, m_{it}^{p1}, m_{it}^{p2}, s_{it}^1, s_{it}^2, b_{it+1}^d(x_{t+1})\}_{t=0}^{\infty}$ to maximize (5.33) subject to (5.43), the cash-in-advance constraints (5.36), and the law of motion for wealth. During the shopping period in t, the household collects $p_t^1\xi_t s_{it}^1$ of dividends in the form of dollars, and $p_t^2\eta_t s_{it}^2$ of dividends in the form of pounds. Next period's wealth, measured in units of time $(t + 1)$ consumption goods is then given by

$$\theta_{it+1} = p_t^1\xi_t s_{it}^1/p_{t+1}^1 + p_t^2\eta_t s_{it}^2/p_{t+1}^2$$
$$+ (m_{it}^{p1} - p_t^1 c_{it}^1)/p_{t+1}^1 + (m_{it}^{p2} - p_t^2 c_{it}^2)/p_{t+1}^2$$
$$+ r_1(x_{t+1})s_{it}^1 + r_2(x_{t+1})s_{it}^2 + b_{it+1}^d(x_{t+1}).$$

In the presence of assets bearing positive net nominal interest rates, households will choose to make (5.36) hold with equality. Substituting these equalities into the preceding equation then gives

(5.44) $\quad \theta_{it+1} = p_t^1\xi_t s_{it}^1/p_{t+1}^1 + p_t^2\eta_t s_{it}^2/p_{t+1}^2$
$\qquad + r_1(x_{t+1})s_{it}^1 + r_2(x_{t+1})s_{it}^2 + b_{it+1}^d(x_{t+1}).$

Households maximize (5.33) subject to (5.36), (5.43), and (5.44).

In order to describe an equilibrium of the model, we require an initial distribution of wealth. We have assumed that, initially, wealth of every kind is evenly divided between the residents of the two countries. In particular, at time 0, residents of each country own half of each and every asset, namely, the trees of country 1, the trees of country 2, the stocks of dollars and pounds, and the debt $b_{10}(x_0)$ and $b_{20}(x_0)$ of countries 1 and 2, respectively. Given this equality of initial wealth, and the assumption that preferences are identical in the two countries, the distribution of wealth will remain unaltered as time passes. The assumption that individuals in both countries are taxed equally by the governments of each country is made to equalize the distribution of wealth in the two countries.

Given this equal initial distribution of wealth, the equilibrium consumption allocation will be

(5.45) $\quad c_{1t} = c_{2t} = [(\xi_t + \eta_t) - (g_t^1 + g_t^2)]/2.$

With equilibrium consumption given by (5.45), the balance of payments of country 1, measured in dollars, is given by

$$p_t^1(c_{1t}^1 + c_{2t}^1 + g_t^1) - (p_t^1 \xi_t + e_t p_t^2 \eta_t)/2,$$

where $p_t^1(c_{1t}^1 + c_{2t}^1 + g_t^1) = p_t^1 \xi_t$ is total dollar value of purchases of goods in country 1, whereas $(p_t^1 \xi_t + e_t p_t^2 \eta_t)/2$ is the dollar value of dividends received by residents of country 1. When we use (5.45), the above expression becomes equal to

(5.46) $\quad \dfrac{1}{2} p_t^1(\xi_t - \eta_t).$

Symmetrically, the balance of payments of country 2, measured in pounds, is given by

$$\frac{1}{2} p_t^2(\eta_t - \xi_t).$$

With equilibrium allocations given by (5.45), equilibrium asset-pricing formulas become

(5.47) $\quad q(x', x) = \beta \dfrac{u'([(\xi' + \eta') - (g^{1'} + g^{2'})]/2)}{u'([(\xi + \eta) - (g^1 + g^2)]/2)} f(x', x).$

$$r_1(x) = u'[(\xi + \eta)/2 - (g^1 + g^2)/2]^{-1}$$

$$\cdot \beta \int u'([(\xi' + \eta') - (g^{1'} + g^{2'})]/2)$$

$$\cdot \left[r_1(x') + \xi' \frac{M^1}{M^{1'}} \right] f(x', x) \, dx'$$

$$r_2(x) = u'[(\xi + \eta)/2 - (g^1 + g^2)/2]^{-1}$$

$$\cdot \beta \int u'([(\xi' + \eta') - (g^{1'} + g^{2'})]/2)$$

$$\cdot \left[r_2(x') + \eta' \frac{M^2}{M^{2'}} \right] f(x', x) \, dx'.$$

Letting $\phi_1(x)$ be the current price in dollars of a dollar tomorrow, and $\phi_2(x)$ be the current price in pounds of a pound tomorrow, we obtain

$$(5.48) \qquad \phi_1(x) = \beta \int \frac{u'([(\xi' + \eta') - (g^{1'} + g^{2'})]/2)}{u'([(\xi + \eta) - (g^1 + g^2)]/2)} \frac{\xi'}{\xi} \frac{M^1}{M^{1'}} f(x', x) \, dx'$$

$$\phi_2(x) = \beta \int \frac{u'([(\xi' + \eta') - (g^{1'} + g^{2'})]/2)}{u'([(\xi + \eta) - (g^1 + g^2)]/2)} \frac{\eta'}{\eta} \frac{M^2}{M^{2'}} f(x', x) \, dx',$$

which are versions of Irving Fisher's decomposition of the gross nominal interest rate into the product of a gross real rate and a gross inflation rate.

The results in this model hinge on imposing a great deal of symmetry on agents in the two countries. In particular, the initial distribution and composition of wealth are equal, with the two countries' currencies initially being equally distributed among residents of both countries and with taxes being assumed to be levied in a way consistent with this assumption. Furthermore, agents in one country are free to trade assets and goods originating in the other country. The exchange rate and individual country price levels, however, are rendered determinate by prescribing that consumption goods in each country can be purchased only with domestic country currency accumulated in advance. In the next section, we alter the rules to permit domestic consumption goods to be purchased with the currency of the foreign country.

5.7 Exchange Rate Indeterminacy

We retain all features of the preceding model except that we alter the nature of the cash-in-advance constraint. In particular, we make currency of either country acceptable for goods in both countries at the market exchange rate during the shopping period. We also make dividends in each country payable at the market exchange rate in the currency of both countries. Thus in place of the cash-in-advance constraints (5.36), we now posit

$$(5.49) \qquad m_{1t}^{p1} + e_t m_{1t}^{p2} \geq p_t^1 c_{1t}^1 + e_t p_t^2 c_{1t}^2$$
$$m_{2t}^{p1} + e_t m_{2t}^{p2} \geq p_t^1 c_{2t}^1 + e_t p_t^2 c_{2t}^2.$$

The first inequality restricts agents in country 1, the other restricts agents in country 2. We retain the constraint (5.37) on the governments, for convenience. The equilibrium condition in the money market now becomes

$$(m_{1t}^{p1} + m_{2t}^{p1} + m_t^{g1}) + e_t(m_{1t}^{p2} + m_{2t}^{p2} + m_t^{g2}) = M_{t+1}^1 + e_t M_{t+1}^2.$$

Substituting (5.37), (5.40), and (5.49) at equality into the above equation gives

(5.50) $$p_t^1 = \frac{(M_{t+1}^1 + e_t M_{t+1}^2)}{(\eta_t + \xi_t)},$$

which relates the price level in country 1 to the world money supply $(M_{t+1}^1 + e_t M_{t+1}^2)$.

Given the form of the cash-in-advance restraints (5.49), equilibrium will require that neither currency dominates the other one in rate of return. Otherwise, no private agent would hold the dominated currency. The rate of return on currency i is p_t^i/p_{t+1}^i. A sufficient condition for lack of dominance is equality of these stochastic rates of return,

$$\frac{p_t^1}{p_{t+1}^1} = \frac{p_t^2}{p_{t+1}^2}, \qquad t \geq 0.$$

Rearranging this condition gives

$$e_t = \frac{p_t^1}{p_t^2} = \frac{p_{t+1}^1}{p_{t+1}^2} = e_{t+1}, \qquad t \geq 0,$$

which states that the exchange rate is constant over time. We shall study the structure of the class of constant exchange rate equilibria for the model. (In general, there may be additional equilibria outside of this class.)

We begin by repeating (5.35) and also writing a weighted sum of (5.35) for $i = 1, 2$:

(5.35) $$g_t^i + \sum_{j=1}^{\infty} \int q^{(j)}(x_{t+j}, x_t) g_{t+j}^i \, dx_{t+j} + b_{it}(x_t)$$

$$= \tau_t^i + \frac{M_{t+1}^i - M_t^i}{p_t^i} + \sum_{j=1}^{\infty} q^{(j)}(x_{t+j}, x_t)$$

$$\cdot \left(\tau_{t+j}^i + \frac{M_{t+1+j}^i - M_{t+j}^i}{p_{t+j}^i} \right) dx_{t+j},$$

$$t \geq 0 \qquad i = 1, 2$$

(5.51) $$\sum_{i=1}^{2} \left[\left(g_t^i - \tau_t^i + \sum_{j=1}^{\infty} \int q^{(j)}(x_{t+j}, x_t)(g_{t+j}^i - \tau_{t+j}^i) \, dx_{t+j} + b_{it}(x_t) \right) \right]$$

$$= \frac{(M_{t+1}^1 + e_t M_{t+1}^2) - (M_t^1 + e_t M_t^2)}{p_t^1} + \sum_{j=1}^{\infty} \int q^{(j)}(x_{t+j}, x_t)$$

$$\cdot \left[\frac{(M_{t+j+1}^1 + e_{t+j} M_{t+1+j}^2) - (M_{t+j}^1 + e_{t+j} M_{t+j}^2)}{p_{t+j}^1} \right] dx_{t+j}$$

Let us define the (worldwide) per capita quantities

$$g_t = (g_t^1 + g_t^2)2^{-1}$$
$$\tau_t = (\tau_t^1 + \tau_t^2)2^{-1}$$
$$b_t(x_t) = [b_{1t}(x_t) + b_{2t}(x_t)]2^{-1}$$
$$M_t^*(e) = (M_t^1 + eM_t^2)2^{-1}.$$

These are the per capita amounts of worldwide government purchases, taxes, state-contingent borrowings, and the world money supply, respectively. Furthermore, define the worldwide per capita dividend process ξ_t^* as $\xi_t^* = (\xi_t + \eta_t)2^{-1}$. Notice that with $M_t^*(e)$ and ξ_t^* replacing M_t and ξ_t, respectively, and with g_t, τ_t, and $b_t(x_t)$ defined as above, the two-country model of this section becomes identical with the one-country model of Sections 5.1 and 5.2. Evidently, this is true for any value of the constant exchange rate $e_t = e \in (0, \infty)$. It follows that, whenever the processes (g_t, τ_t, ξ_t^*) are such that an equilibrium exists for the one-country model, there will also exist an equilibrium for the two-country model described in this section; indeed, there will exist an equilibrium for any $e \in (0, \infty)$. We formalize and expand upon this reasoning in the following theorem, which is a variant of one established by Kareken and Wallace (1981) in the context of an overlapping-generations model.

PROPOSITION 5.8 Kareken-Wallace Exchange Rate Indeterminacy

Consider an economy with $\{g_t^i, \tau_t^i\}_{t=0}^{\infty}$, $i = 1, 2$ and $\{\xi_t, \eta_t\}_{t=0}^{\infty}$ processes given. Let $b_{i0}(x_0)$, M_0^i be given for $i = 1, 2$. Let $b_{it+1}(x_{t+1})$ be given for $i = 1, 2$, $t \geq 0$. Let the cash-in-advance constraints be (5.49) and (5.37). Let there exist an initial equilibrium, denoted the macron-bearing equilibrium, with a constant exchange rate $e(t) = \bar{e} > 0$ for $t \geq 0$. Suppose that in the macron-bearing equilibrium (5.50) holds with equality. Then for any $\hat{e} \in (0, \infty)$, there exists another equilibrium, denoted the caret-bearing equilibrium, in which $e(t) = \hat{e}$ for all $t \geq 0$, starting from the same initial values for currency $\hat{M}_0^1 = \overline{M}_0^1$, $\hat{M}_0^2 = \overline{M}_0^2$. In general, $\hat{M}_{t+1}^i/\hat{p}_t^i \neq \overline{M}_{t+1}^i/\overline{p}_t^i$. The world real money supply sequences, however, are equal: $(\hat{M}_{t+1}^1 + \hat{e}\hat{M}_{t+1}^2)/\hat{p}_t^1 = (\overline{M}_{t+1}^1 + \bar{e}\overline{M}_{t+1}^2)/\overline{p}_t^1$ for all $t \geq 0$. Also, the sequences of rates of return on currency are equal in the two equilibria.

To prove the proposition, we shall show that, for a given $\hat{e} \in (0, \infty)$, we can construct (p_t^i, M_t^i) sequences that satisfy the equilibrium conditions. Use (5.34) for $i = 1$ and 2 and $t = 0$, to obtain

$$\frac{\overline{M}_0^1 + \hat{e}\overline{M}_0^2}{\hat{p}_0^1} = \sum_{i=1}^{2} [g_0^i - \tau_0^i - \int b_{i1}(x_1)q(x_1, x_0) \, dx_1 + b_{i0}(x_0)]$$

$$- \frac{\hat{M}_1^1 + \hat{e}\hat{M}_1^2}{\hat{p}_0^1}.$$

From (5.50), however, in equilibrium $(\hat{M}_1^1 + \hat{e}\hat{M}_1^2)/\hat{p}_0^1 = \xi_0 + \eta_0$. Substituting this formula into the above equation and solving for $\hat{p}_0^1$ gives

$$(\hat{p}_0^1)^{-1} = (\overline{M}_0^1 + \hat{e}\overline{M}_0^1)^{-1} \left\{ -(\xi_0 + \eta_0) \right.$$
$$\left. + \sum_{i=1}^{2} [g_0^i - \tau_0^i - \int q(x_1, x_0)b_{i1}(x_1, x_0) \, dx_1 + b_{i0}(x_0)] \right\}.$$

Choose $\hat{p}_0^1 = \hat{e}\hat{p}_0^2$, and set $\hat{p}_t^i/\hat{p}_0^i = \overline{p}_t^i/\overline{p}_0^i$ for all $t \geq 1$ and $i = 1, 2$. Use (5.34) to solve for stocks of currency for $t \geq 0$:

(5.52) $\qquad \hat{M}_{t+1}^i = \hat{M}_t^i + \hat{p}_t^i[g_t^i - \tau_t^i - \int q(x_{t+1}, x_t)b_{it+1}(x_{t+1}) \, dx_{t+1} + b_{it}(x_t)]$

for $i = 1, 2$. This equation is to be solved for stocks of currency $\hat{M}_{t+1}^i$ for $t \geq 0$ for $i = 1, 2$, subject to the initial conditions $\hat{M}_0^i = \overline{M}_0^i$, $i = 1, 2$. It remains to be verified that equilibrium condition (5.50) obtains for $t \geq 1$ with the proposed settings of $\hat{M}_{t+1}^i$, $\hat{p}_t^i$ for $t \geq 0$, $i = 1, 2$. Use (5.34) for $i = 1$ and 2 to obtain

(5.53) $\qquad \hat{M}_{t+1}^1 + \hat{e}\hat{M}_{t+1}^2 = \hat{M}_t^1 + \hat{e}\hat{M}_t^2 + \hat{p}_t^1 A_t^1 + \hat{p}_t^1 A_t^2, \qquad t \geq 0,$

where, for $i = 1, 2$,

$$A_t^i \equiv g_t^i - \tau_t^i - \int q(x_{t+1}, x_t)b_{it+1}(x_{t+1}) \, dx_{t+1} + b_{it}(x_i).$$

Note that the A_t^i process is assumed constant between the caret- and macron-bearing equilibria. Note also that (5.53) holds because all terms $\hat{M}_{t+1}^i$ have been chosen to satisfy (5.34). Rewrite (5.53) as

(5.54) $\qquad \dfrac{\hat{M}_{t+1}^1 + \hat{e}\hat{M}_{t+1}^2}{\hat{p}_t^1} = \dfrac{\hat{M}_t^1 + \hat{e}\hat{M}_t^2}{\hat{p}_{t-1}^1} \cdot \dfrac{\hat{p}_{t-1}^1}{\hat{p}_t^1} + A_t^1 + A_t^2, \qquad t \geq 1.$

Because $\hat{p}_{t-1}^1/\hat{p}_t^1 = \overline{p}_{t-1}^1/\overline{p}_t^1$ for $t \geq 1$, and because $(\hat{M}_1^1 + \hat{e}\hat{M}_1^2)/\hat{p}_0^1 = (\xi_0 + \eta_0) = (\overline{M}_1^1 + \overline{e}\overline{M}_1^2)/\overline{p}_0^1$, it follows from (5.54) that $(\hat{M}_2^1 + \hat{e}\hat{M}_2^2)\hat{p}_1^1 = (\xi_1 + \eta_1)$. By recursions on (5.54), it follows that $(\hat{M}_{t+1}^1 + \hat{e}\hat{M}_{t+1}^2)/\hat{p}_t^1 = (\xi_t + \eta_t)$ for all $t \geq 0$. We have thus constructed sequences $(\hat{M}_{t+1}^i, \hat{p}_t^i, i = 1, 2; t \geq 0)$ that with $e(t) = \hat{e}$ for all $t \geq 0$ satisfy (5.34) and the equilibrium condition (5.50). We have constructed an equilibrium with the asserted properties, thereby completing the proof of Proposition 5.8.

The results of Proposition 5.8 are usefully compared with the "monetary theory of the exchange rate" embodied in Equation (5.42). Proposition 5.8 asserts that there is a continuum of equilibrium exchange rates, e, each of them constant over time and therefore uncorrelated with the path of M^1_{t+1}/M^2_{t+1} over time. In the setup leading to Equation (5.42), exchange rates can be expected to correlate with M^1_{t+1}/M^2_{t+1} in a manner determined by the dependence between M^1_{t+1}/M^2_{t+1} and (η_t/ξ_t). These strikingly different implications for exchange rate behavior stem directly from assumptions made about the cash-in-advance restriction.

5.8 Conclusions

The cash in the models of this chapter is issued only by the government. Evidences of private indebtedness — such as private bank notes or checks — are assumed not to qualify as the cash needed to finance consumption purchases. If the cash-in-advance restriction were altered to permit evidences of private indebtedness to qualify freely as cash, government currency would not be valued. The model would collapse to a version of the model of Section 4.1. Theories of the price level thus hinge sensitively on the way in which cash is defined and precisely on the way in which the cash-in-advance constraint is set up in these models.

The cash-in-advance model is a convenient one for representing aspects of classical monetary theory in the context of an intertemporal model. In this model, government financial policy is irrelevant, as Proposition 5.1 states. Government policy impinges on real interest rates and consumption allocations only insofar as concerns a choice of a government expenditure process $\{g_t\}^\infty_{t=0}$. In this model, what the government purchases, the public must pay for, but the form taken by the payment is irrelevant.

Exercises

Exercise 5.1. **Private Wealth**

Prove that in equilibrium the wealth $\theta_t(x_t)$ that appears in Equation (5.6) satisfies

$$\theta_t(x_t) = (\tau_t + \xi_t - g_t) + \sum_{j=1}^{\infty} \int q^{(j)}(x_{t+j}, x_t)(\tau_{t+j} + \xi_{t+j} - g_{t+j})\, dx_{t+j}.$$

Exercise 5.2. **Unpleasant Monetarist Arithmetic**

Describe what is happening to the quantity of one-period government bonds in the example in Proposition 5.5.

Exercise 5.3. **A Permanent (McCallum) Government Deficit**

Consider McCallum's definition of the government deficit, $d_m(t) = [b_t(x_t) - \int b_t(x_t)q(x_t, x_{t-1})\, dx_t] + g_t - \tau_t$. Let $\{g_t, \xi_t\}_{t=0}^\infty$ be a given stochastic process. Given g_t, let the government run a constant "deficit" $d_m(t) = \bar{d}_m$ for all $t \geq 0$.

a. Show that the equilibrium values of c_t, p_t, and $q(x_{t+1}, x_t)$ are independent of the deficit $\bar{d}_m$.

b. Calculate the present value of the constant sequence $\{\bar{d}_m\}$.

c. Show that, taking the stochastic process $\{M_t\}$ as given, the present value of taxes at time zero is independent of d_m. Argue that this is no longer true for $t > 0$.

Exercise 5.4. **A Useful Identity under Interest on Reserves**

Prove that for the model of Section 5.5

$$\sum_{j=1}^\infty \int (R_{j-1} - 1)q(x_j, x_{j-1})q(x_{j-1}, x_{j-2}) \cdots$$

$$q(x_1, x_0)\, dx_j\, dx_{j-1} \cdots dx_1 = 1.$$

Exercise 5.5. **Defining the State Vector (Optional)**

Assume that the state vector contains (M_{t+1}, τ_t) in addition to (ξ_t, g_t). Denote $(\xi_t, g_t) = X_t$; $(M_{t+1}, \tau_t) = V_t$ and $Z_t = (V_t, X_t)$. Assume that Z_t is Markov, with transition density $h(z'; z)$. Furthermore assume that the x-component of z is itself an independent Markov process with the same transition function as in the text, $f(x', x)$. We assume that $P[X_{t+1} \leq x' | V_t = v, X_t = x] = P[X_{t+1} \leq x' | V_t = v', X_t = x]$ for every (v, v').[7] Then we can decompose the transition density $h(\cdot)$ as follows:

$$h(z'; z) = h(v', x'; v, x) = f(x', x)g(v'; x', v, x),$$

where $g(v'; x', v, x)$ is interpreted as the density of V_{t+1}, given $(X_{t+1} = x', V_t = v, X_t = x)$, and therefore has the property that[8]

$$\int g(v'; x', v, x)\, dv' = 1.$$

---

7. As the purpose of this exercise is to show that the neutrality Proposition 5.1 still holds, we must assume that the "real" aspects of the economy, as represented by X_t, are independent of the financial decisions represented by V_t. If that were not the case, then we would be *assuming* the nonneutrality of the government financial decision, as we would be asserting that the distribution of today's X_t depends on yesterday's financial mix, V_{t-1}.

8. Here and below we assume that every finite dimensional distribution of the stochastic process $\{Z_t\}$ possesses a density.

For this new setup, show that the following version of Proposition 5.1 holds. Given a stochastic process for $X_t = (\xi_t, g_t)$, the equilibrium values of $(c_t, M_{t+1}/p_t, t \geq 0)$ are independent of the government's financing method. That is, all choices of $[\tau_t, M_{t+1}, b_{t+1}(z_{t+1}), t \geq 0]$ that satisfy the government budget constraint — the relevant version of (5.16) in the text — give rise to the same equilibrium processes for $(c_t, M_{t+1}/p_t, t \geq 0)$. Moreover, the pricing kernel $\eta(z', z)$ can be decomposed as $q(x', x)$ times $g(v'; x', v, x)$. Among other things the implication is that

(1) $$\int \eta(v', x'; v, x)\, dv' = q(x', x).$$

The intertemporal prices given by the right side of (1) are independent of the government's method of financing expenditures.

Exercise 5.6 Computing an Equilibrium

Consider a one-nonstorable-good nonstochastic Lucas cash-in-advance economy. A single representative household maximizes $\sum_{t=0}^{\infty} \beta^t u(c_t)$, $0 < \beta < 1$, where $u'(c) > 0$, $u''(c) < 0$, $u'(0) = +\infty$. The good is produced by a tree that lasts forever and produces a constant stream of ($\xi > 0$) units of the consumption good each period. If a household owns s_t shares of the tree, it receives $p_t \xi s_t$ units of currency from the firm during the "shopping stage" of period t. Here p_t is the price level at t. This cash cannot be spent at t but must be carried over into $(t + 1)$. There is a securities trading period at the beginning of t during which taxes are paid and cash and other securities are traded. The household's budget constraints are

$$r_t s_t + \frac{m_t^p}{p_t} + \tau_t + \frac{b_{t+1}^p}{R_t} \leq \theta_t$$

$$\theta_{t+1} = \frac{p_t \xi s_t}{p_{t+1}} + r_{t+1} s_t + b_{t+1}^p + \frac{m_t^p - c_t p_t}{p_{t+1}}$$

$$c_t \leq \frac{m_t^p}{p_t},$$

where c_t is consumption at t, r_t is the price of a claim on the current and all future dollar dividends from a tree (paid during the securities trading period), m_t^p is the household's cash at the close of security trading at t, b_{t+1}^p is the real value at $(t + 1)$ of "tax anticipation" certificates purchased at t, R_t is the rate of return on tax anticipation certificates, τ_t is a lump-sum tax or transfer, and θ_t is real wealth at the beginning of period t.

A government purchases a constant per capita stream of $g_t = g < \xi$ for each $t \geq 0$. These purchases give no utility to private agents. The economy begins with an outstanding stock of unbacked currency of $M_0 = \overline{M}_0$ at the beginning of period zero. The government's budget constraint is

$$g = \tau_t + \frac{b_{t+1}}{R_t} + \frac{M_{t+1} - M_t}{p_t} - b_t, \qquad t \geq 1,$$

and for $t = 0$

$$g = \tau_0 + \frac{b_1}{R_0} + \frac{M_1 - M_0}{p_0}.$$

The government faces the cash-in-advance constraint

$$m_t^g = p_t g_t.$$

The equilibrium condition in the cash market is

$$M_{t+1} = m_t^g + m_t^p.$$

When the economy begins, each household owns one tree and the currency stock M_0. In all questions below assume that

$$M_{t+1} = \mu M_t, \qquad t \geq 1,$$

where $\mu > 1$.

   a. Define an equilibrium for this economy.
   b. Prove that the following prices are equilibrium ones:

$$r_t = \frac{\beta \xi \mu^{-1}}{1 - \beta}$$

$$R_t = \beta^{-1}$$

$$p_t = \frac{M_1}{\xi} \mu^t.$$

   c. Prove the following proposition. Consider an economy with (g, ξ) given and with M_0 given. Let an initial equilibrium be given by $\overline{R}_t, \overline{b}_{t+1}, \overline{M}_{t+1}, \overline{p}_t$, $\overline{\tau}_t, \overline{c}_t, \overline{r}_t$ for $t \geq 0$. Consider any alternative tax, currency-creation, and borrowing strategies that satisfy

(1) $\qquad \hat{\tau}_0 = \overline{\tau}_0$

(2) $\qquad \dfrac{\hat{b}_1 - \overline{b}_1}{\overline{R}_1} = \dfrac{-(\hat{M}_1 - \overline{M}_0)}{\hat{p}_0} + \dfrac{\overline{M}_1 - \overline{M}_0}{\overline{p}_0}$

(3) $\qquad \dfrac{\hat{b}_{j+1} - \overline{b}_{j+1}}{\overline{R}_1} = \displaystyle\sum_{t=1}^{\infty} \dfrac{(\hat{\tau}_{j+t} - \overline{\tau}_{j+t})}{\overline{R}_1^t}, \qquad \text{for all } j \geq 0,$

(4) $$\frac{\hat{M}_{t+1}}{\hat{M}_t} = \mu, \qquad t \geq 1.$$

Any strategies satisfying (1), (2), and (3) are also equilibria, with

$$\hat{p}_t = \frac{\hat{M}_1 \mu^t}{\xi}, \qquad \hat{R}_t = \bar{R}_t = \bar{R}_1 \quad \text{for all } t, \qquad \hat{c}_t = \bar{c}_t, \qquad \hat{r}_t = \bar{r}_t.$$

Interpret this proposition as characterizing the neutrality of open-market operations.

Exercise 5.7 Interest on Reserves and Stock Prices

Under the interest-on-reserves scheme described in Proposition 5.6, find a formula for the price $r(x_t)$ of a share in trees at time t.

Exercise 5.8. Incentives for "Private Currencies"

The cash that appears in the model of this chapter is all issued by the government, with the printing of government notes assumed to be costless. Suppose that private agents have access to the same costless technology for printing "notes." Show that, at equilibrium prices for the one-country model of Section 5.1, it is feasible for a safe private bank to issue a private bank note, that is, a piece of paper that can be converted to a specified amount of government currency during any subsequent security trading period. Show that, at the equilibrium prices for the model of Section 5.1, a private bank would have an incentive to issue such notes. Given the full array of markets in state-contingent securities that is assumed to operate in this model, to what forces can we refer in order to interpret the absence of private bank notes in this model?

Exercise 5.9. Other Interest-on-Reserve Schemes

Consider three different schemes for paying interest on reserves as in Section 5.5. The first guarantees a real return similar to the return on a risk-free claim to one unit of consumption. This scheme is the one analyzed in Section 5.5 and pays interest on currency at the rate

$$\alpha^1(x_t, x_{t+1}) = R(x_t) \frac{p_{t+1}(x_{t+1})}{p_t(x_t)},$$

where $R(x_t) = [\int q(s, x_t) \, ds]^{-1}$. The second scheme guarantees a real rate of return similar to the rate of growth of the economy. Specifically, $\alpha^2(x_t, x_{t+1})$ is given by

$$\alpha^2(x_t, x_{t+1}) = \frac{\xi_{t+1}}{\xi_t} \frac{p_{t+1}(x_{t+1})}{p_t(x_t)}.$$

Finally, in the third scheme, currency earns a known nominal rate of interest. In particular this nominal rate of interest is set equal to the nominal risk-free rate in an equilibrium where currency does not earn interest. In other words

$$\alpha^3(x_t) = \left[\int g(x_{t+1}, x_t) \frac{p_t(x_t)}{p_{t+1}(x_{t+1})} dx_{t+1} \right]^{-1}.$$

Find formulas for the price $r^i(x_t)$ of a share in trees under scheme i. Compare it to the prices under the scheme of Section 5.1 (no interest paid on reserves) and to the price in the economy with no currency of Chapter 3.

Exercise 5.10. **Stock Prices and Inflation**

Consider a one-country version of Lucas's cash-in-advance model. The household's preferences are

(1)
$$E \sum_{t=0}^{\infty} \beta^t \ln c_t, \qquad 0 < \beta < 1.$$

Government purchases $g_t = 0$ for all t. The endowment of the one good ξ_t is Markov.

The stock of currency evolves according to the Markov law

(2)
$$\frac{M_{t+1}}{M_{t+2}} = \rho \frac{M_t}{M_{t+1}} + \epsilon_{t+1}, \qquad 0 < \rho < 1,$$

where ϵ_{t+1} is a serially independent random process distributed independently of M_t/M_{t+1} and ϵ_{t+1} has bounded support on the interval $[\epsilon, \bar{\epsilon}]$. The currency changes through lump-sum transfers and taxes. Define

$$\bar{x} = \frac{\bar{\epsilon}}{1-\rho} \quad \text{and} \quad x = \frac{\epsilon}{1-\rho}.$$

Notice that, if M_t/M_{t+1} is in $[x, \bar{x}]$, then M_{t+j}/M_{t+j+1} are in $[x, \bar{x}]$ for all j.

The timing of transactions remains exactly as in Lucas's model. In particular, a share in a tree purchased during the securities trading session at t represents a claim to the dividends payable in currency from t on.

a. Assume that M_0/M_1 belongs to $[x, \bar{x}]$ and that $\bar{x} < 1/\beta\rho$. Show that the strong form of the quantity theory holds, that is,

$$p_t = \frac{M_{t+1}}{\xi_t}.$$

b. Let r_t be the price of trees at time t, denominated in units of the consumption good at t. Assume that M_0/M_1 belongs to $[x, \bar{x}]$ and that

$\bar{x} < 1/\beta\rho$. Show that

$$r_t = \xi_t \cdot \frac{\beta\rho}{1 - \rho\beta} \cdot \frac{M_t}{M_{t+1}}.$$

c. Describe a sense in which an increase in the rate of growth of currency increases the rate of inflation and decreases the price of trees.

d. Interpret the dependence of trees (stock prices) on the rate of currency creation. How does an increase in the rate of growth of currency, and the attendant effects on the price of trees and the rate of inflation, affect the welfare of the representative consumer?

References and Suggested Readings

Clower, Robert W. 1967. A reconsideration of the microfoundations of monetary theory. *Western Economic Journal* 6:1–9.

Friedman, Milton. 1960. *A Program for Monetary Stability.* Bronx: Fordham University Press.

Hall, Robert E. 1983. Optimal fiduciary monetary systems. *Journal of Monetary Economics* 12(1):33–50.

Kareken, John H., and Neil Wallace. 1981. On the indeterminacy of equilibrium exchange rates. *Quarterly Journal of Economics* 96(2):207–222.

Liviatan, Nissan. 1984. Tight money and inflation. *Journal of Monetary Economics* 13(1):5–15.

Lucas, Robert E., Jr. 1978. Asset prices in an exchange economy. *Econometrica* 42(2):1429–45.

——— 1980. Equilibrium in a pure currency economy. *Economic Inquiry* 18(2):203–220. (Reprinted in *Models of Monetary Economies,* ed. J. H. Kareken and N. Wallace, pp. 131–146. Minneapolis: Federal Reserve Bank of Minneapolis, 1980.)

——— 1982. Interest rates and currency prices in a two-country world. *Journal of Monetary Economics* 10(3):335–359.

Lucas, Robert E., Jr., and Nancy L. Stokey. 1983. Optimal fiscal and monetary policy in an economy without capital. *Journal of Monetary Economics* 12(1):55–93.

——— 1985. Money and interest in a cash-in-advance economy. Working Paper 1618. National Bureau of Economic Research, Chicago.

McCallum, Bennett T. 1984. Are bond-financed deficits inflationary? A Ricardian analysis. *Journal of Political Economy* 92(1):123–135.

Peled, Dan. 1985. Stochastic inflation and government provision of indexed bonds. *Journal of Monetary Economics* 15(3):291–308.

Sargent, Thomas J., and Neil Wallace. 1981. Some unpleasant monetarist arithmetic. Federal Reserve Bank of Minneapolis *Quarterly Review* 5(3):1–17.

——— 1984. Interest on reserves. *Journal of Monetary Economics* 15(3):279–290.

Yun, Y. Eugene. 1985. Business cycles in a cash-in-advance model. University of Minnesota, Minneapolis.

6 | Credit and Currency with Long-Lived Agents

The cash-in-advance model envisions a situation in which neither centralized goods trading nor autarky occurs.[1] The idea is that agents are heterogeneous with regard to their preferences or endowment pattern, which gives a motive for exchange, but that agents are locationally separated, at least during the "shopping session," which prevents centralized exchange of goods. Although heterogeneity of agents with respect to preferences, endowments, and location provides the motivation for using currency, the precise nature of this heterogeneity remains partly implicit.[2] In particular, explicit locational itineraries or traveling and search technologies are not described. The idea in the cash-in-advance model is that the heterogeneity of preferences, endowments, and locations can be imagined to occur in a way that leads to an outcome for which the real side of the economy behaves like a one-good Lucas tree model.

This chapter pursues the idea that heterogeneity of preferences, endowments, and locations can be used to create a model of currency. The approach of the present chapter is more primitive in the sense that much less is left implicit than in the cash-in-advance model. The present chapter begins

1. In the Lucas tree model of Chapter 3, an equilibrium allocation occurs when each household consumes the output of the tree in its own yard each period. In the cash-in-advance model, preferences are assumed to be such that a household does not want to consume any of the output from the tree in its own yard.

2. Lucas (1980) describes an interpretation of preferences over different "colors" of the same good that rationalizes a heterogeneity of preferences consistent with maintaining preferences for a representative household.

by precisely describing the nature of the heterogeneity across agents. The basic idea is that when endowment patterns over time differ sufficiently across agents, borrowing and lending occur in response to agents' desire to smooth consumption over time. If something prevents loan markets from operating, it is possible that an unbacked currency can play a role in helping agents smooth their consumption over time. The present chapter will eventually appeal to locational heterogeneity as the force that causes loan markets to fail in this way.

The model of this chapter is a simplified version of one that was proposed by Truman Bewley (1980) and Robert Townsend (1980). We shall use the model to study a number of interrelated issues and theories. We use the model to describe: (1) the "permanent income" theory of consumption, (2) the "Ricardian doctrine" that government borrowing and taxes have equivalent economic effects, (3) the restrictions on the operation of private loan markets needed in order that unbacked currency be valued, and (4) a theory of the optimal inflation rate and the optimal behavior of the currency stock over time.

6.1 The Physical Setup

Assume that there is a discrete-time, pure exchange, one-good economy consisting of N individuals, each of whom lives for the $(T+1)$ periods $\{t = 0, 1, \ldots, T\}$. There is no uncertainty.

All agents have identical preferences of the additively time separable form $\sum_{t=0}^{T} \beta^t u(c_t^h)$, where c_t^h is consumption of the one good in period t by agent h, $0 < \beta < 1$ is a common discount factor, and u is a utility function that obeys $u' > 0, u'' < 0, u'(\infty) = 0, u'(0) = +\infty$. Notice that all agents have the same β and u and that all agents are assumed to live lives that are identical in length. Furthermore all agents are assumed to be born and to die in the same periods. We will examine some versions of the model in which T is finite and others in which T is infinite.

Although the agents are identical in their preferences, life spans, and times of living, they are assumed heterogeneous with respect to the time streams of their endowments of the one good in the model. The good is assumed to be perishable and so cannot be stored. For simplicity, we assume that there are two groups of agents. Let y_t^h be the endowment of the good at time t of an agent of type h. The first group consists of a number N^A agents each of whom is endowed as

(6.1a) $\qquad y_t^A = \begin{cases} 1, & t \text{ even,} \\ 0, & t \text{ odd,} \end{cases} \qquad 0 \le t \le T.$

The second group consists of N^B agents, each of whom is endowed according to

(6.1b) $$y_t^B = \begin{cases} 0, & t \text{ even,} \\ 1, & t \text{ odd,} \end{cases} \qquad 0 \le t \le T.$$

6.2 Optimal Allocations

We shall characterize only a subset of all optimal allocations, restricting ourselves to those allocations that treat each of the type A agents identically with one another and each of the type B agents identically with one another. We define optimal allocations by imagining that there is a social planner and solving his optimum problem. The fictitious social planner seeks to maximize the "welfare function"

$$\omega_A \sum_{t=0}^{T} \beta^t u(c_t^A) + \omega_B \sum_{t=0}^{T} \beta^t u(c_t^B),$$

subject to the feasibility constraints

$$\begin{aligned} N^A c_t^A + N^B c_t^B &\le N^A, & t \text{ even,} \quad & 0 \le t \le T \\ N^A c_t^A + N^B c_t^B &\le N^B, & t \text{ odd,} \quad & 0 \le t \le T. \end{aligned}$$

Here $1 > \omega_A > 0$, $\omega_B = 1 - \omega_A$ are positive weights, giving the social planner's preferences for utility for agents of classes A and B, respectively. Dividing the feasibility constraints by N^A gives

$$\begin{aligned} c_t^A + \rho c_t^B &\le 1, & t \text{ even} \\ c_t^A + \rho c_t^B &\le \rho, & t \text{ odd}, \quad \text{where } \rho = N^B/N^A. \end{aligned}$$

The reader is invited to solve this constrained-maximization problem. The solution is to say that $u'(c_{t+1}^A)/u'(c_t^A) = u'(c_{t+1}^B)/u'(c_t^B)$ for $t = 0, 1, \ldots,$ $T - 1$ and to satisfy the feasibility constraints at equality for all t. Using the feasibility constraints in the above marginal condition, the optimality condition can be completely expressed

$$\frac{u'(c_{t+1}^A)}{u'(c_t^A)} = \frac{u'[(\rho - c_{t+1}^A)/\rho]}{u'[(1 - c_t^A)/\rho]}, \qquad t \ge 0, \quad t \text{ even.}$$

We note that for $\rho = 1$ ($N^A = N^B$), these conditions are satisfied for any constant level $c_t^A = c^A$ for all t where $0 \le c^A \le 1$. Then $c_t^B = c^B = 1 - c^A$ for all t. For $\rho = 1$, it is thus optimal for the planner completely to smooth the consumption paths of the agents of both types A and B. The value of c^A chosen depends on the social planner's weight ω^A. If $\rho \ne 1$, then in general the optimal time path of consumption depends on the value of p, the form of the utility function u, and the weight ω_A but *not* on the value of the discount factor β.

6.3 Competitive Equilibrium

We now analyze the competitive equilibrium of this model, assuming that all mutually beneficial trades between members of the two groups occur. Given the nature of preferences, and the uneven nature of endowment streams, there is room for a loan market to emerge. We let l_t^h be the amount of one-period consumption loans purchased by agent h at time t, measured in units of the t-period consumption good. Here $l_t^h > 0$ means that agent h is lending in period t, and $l_t^h < 0$ means that he is borrowing. The one-period net interest rate in period t is $r(t)$, measured in units of time $(t + 1)$ good per unit of time t goods. If an agent lends l_t^h at time t, he is repaid $[1 + r(t)]l_t^h$ at time $(t + 1)$. Agent h's problem is thus to maximize

(6.2)
$$\sum_{t=0}^{T} \beta^t u(c_t^h),$$

subject to the sequence of budget constraints

(6.3)
$$c_t^h + l_t^h \le y_t^h + l_{t-1}^h [1 + r(t - 1)], \qquad T \ge t \ge 1$$
$$c_0^h + l_0^h \le y_0^h,$$

where the last constraint amounts to adding the requirement that $l_{-1}^h = 0$, which says that individuals come into the world neither owing nor owning any debt. The agent faces the interest rates $r(t), t = 0, \ldots, T - 1$ as a price taker.

We now define a competitive equilibrium as sequences $\{c_t^h, l_t^h, h = A, B, t = 0, \ldots, T\}$ and $\{r(t), t = 0, \ldots, T - 1\}$ such that (1) Agents of each type are solving their constrained maximum problem and (2) The loan market clears each period, which requires

$$N^A l_t^A + N^B l_t^B = 0, \qquad t = 0, 1, \ldots, T.$$

We find conditions for solving the agent's choice problem by forming the Lagrangian

(6.4)
$$J = \sum_{t=0}^{T} \beta^t (u(c_t^h) + \lambda_t^h (y_t^h + l_{t-1}^h [1 + r(t - 1)] - c_t^h - l_t^h)),$$

subject to $c_t^h \ge 0$, with no inequality constraint on l_t^h, where $\lambda_t^h, t = 0, \ldots, T$ is a sequence of nonnegative Lagrange multipliers, and $l_{-1}^h = 0$ is understood as an initial condition. The first-order necessary conditions for this problem are

(6.5) $\qquad \dfrac{\partial J}{\partial c_t^h} = \beta^t [u'(c_t^h) - \lambda_t^h] \leq 0, \qquad = 0 \quad \text{if } c_t^h > 0, \qquad 0 \leq t \leq T$

(6.6) $\qquad \dfrac{\partial J}{\partial l_t^h} = -\beta^t \lambda_t^h + \beta^{t+1} \lambda_{t+1}^h [1 + r(t)] = 0, \qquad t = 0, 1, \ldots, T-1$

(6.7) $\qquad \dfrac{\partial J}{\partial l_T^h} = -\beta^T \lambda_T^h = 0.$

Equation (6.7) instructs the agent to set $\lambda_T = 0$, which by virtue of (6.6) implies that $\lambda_t = 0$ for all $t = 0, \ldots, T$, which in turn by (6.5) implies that $u'(c_t^h) = 0$ and $c_t^h = +\infty$. Because the agent is regarded as facing the interest rates $r(t)$ as a price taker, the agent has an incentive to borrow unlimited amounts and to end life with $l_T^h = -\infty$. Obviously, agents of both types A and B have the incentive to try to behave in this way. Equally obviously, in market equilibrium they cannot all behave in this way, because this is a closed system, with the A's and B's borrowing and lending only to one another. *No* agent wants to lend in period T, regardless of the interest rate $r(T)$. Therefore, when we put the agents of types A and B together, the only quantities that satisfy the loan market equilibrium condition and constrained maximization can be

(6.8) $\qquad l_T^A = l_T^B = 0.$

An agent's consumption-lending plan can be determined by solving Equations (6.5), (6.6), and (6.8). We note that upon imposing the boundary conditions (6.8), the budget constraints portrayed in difference equation (6.3) at equality have the representation

(6.9) $\qquad c_0^h + \displaystyle\sum_{t=1}^{T} \dfrac{c_t^h}{\displaystyle\prod_{s=1}^{t} [1 + r(s-1)]}$

$\qquad\qquad = y_0^h + \displaystyle\sum_{t=1}^{T} \dfrac{y_t^h}{\displaystyle\prod_{s=1}^{t} [1 + r(s-1)]}, \qquad h = A, B.$

Equation (6.9) states that the present value of consumption equals the present value of income. It is the "stock form" of the consumer's budget constraint and emerges upon imposing the market equilibrium condition $l_T^A = l_T^B = 0$ on the agents' budget constraints in "flow form" (6.3).

We now specialize the model in order to be able to compute an equilibrium explicitly. We assume that T is an odd number greater than or equal to unity. Because the economy runs for $(T + 1)$ periods, in other words, each of the A's and B's has $(T + 1)/2$ periods in which he is endowed with zero and $(T + 1)/2$ periods in which he is endowed with one unit of the good. We also assume that $N^A = N^B$, so that in each period there are equal numbers of borrowers and lenders.

We now proceed to calculate an equilibrium for this version of the model. An equilibrium of the model must satisfy (6.5), (6.6), and (6.9) for $h = A, B$ and also the loan market equilibrium condition $N^A l_t^A + N^B l_t^B = 0$ for $t = 0, \ldots, T$. The loan market equilibrium condition and (6.3) are readily rearranged to yield the equivalent goods market equilibrium condition $c_t^A + c_t^B = 1$ for all $0 \le t \le T$. Thus we seek a solution to (6.5), (6.6), (6.9), and $c_t^A + c_t^B = 1$.

From (6.5) and (6.6) we have that

(6.10) $$\frac{u'(c_{t+1}^h)}{u'(c_t^h)} = \frac{1}{\beta[1 + r(t)]} \quad \text{for } t = 0, 1, \ldots, T - 1,$$

and for $h = A, B$. From the loan market equilibrium conditions $N^A l_t^A + N^B l_t^B = 0$, (6.8), and $N^A = N^B$, we have that $l_t^A = -l_t^B$ and $c_t^A + c_t^B = 1$. Substituting this last equation into (6.10) for $h = A, B$ gives

(6.11) $$\frac{u'(c_{t+1}^A)}{u'(c_t^A)} = \frac{u'(1 - c_{t+1}^A)}{u'(1 - c_t^A)} = \frac{1}{\beta[1 + r(t)]}, \qquad t = 0, 1, \ldots, T - 1.$$

Equations (6.11) are solved by

(6.12) $$c_t^A = c^A, \qquad t = 0, \ldots, T$$

and $$1 + r(t) = \frac{1}{\beta}, \qquad t = 0, \ldots, T - 1.$$

The constant level of c^A must satisfy the present value constraint (6.9). When we set $[1 + r(s)]$ equal to its equilibrium value of $1/\beta$ for $s = 0, 1, \ldots, T - 1$, (6.9) becomes

(6.13) $$c_0^h + \sum_{t=1}^{T} c_t^h \beta^t = y_0^h + \sum_{t=1}^{T} y_t^h \beta^t.$$

For $h = A$, the right side is $1 + \beta^2 + \beta^4 + \ldots + \beta^{T-1} = (1 - \beta^{T+1})/(1 - \beta^2)$. Thus we determine the constant level of $c_t^A = c^A$ by solving

(6.14) $$c^A \cdot \frac{1 - \beta^{T+1}}{1 - \beta} = \frac{1 - \beta^{T+1}}{1 - \beta^2}$$

or $\qquad c^A = \dfrac{1-\beta}{1-\beta^2} = \dfrac{1}{1+\beta}.$

We solve for the constant level of $c_t^B = c^B$ from (6.13) with $h = B$ or from

(6.15) $\qquad c^B = 1 - c^A = \dfrac{\beta}{1+\beta}.$

Note that the equilibrium consumption allocation is optimal.

This special version of the model has specified the endowment patterns and preferences of the agents in such a manner as to yield precisely a version of the permanent income model of consumption. In spite of their having very uneven income streams, agents of both types A and B are able to smooth their consumption over time completely. The reason is that the endowment patterns and relative numbers of the two types of agents are such that one plus the interest rate ends up being a constant, equal to the reciprocal of the common discount factor of time preference.

We now describe a somewhat modified version of the model. We keep T odd but now have $N_A \neq N_B$. The loan market equilibrium conditions now imply that

$$N^A c_t^A + N^B c_t^B = N^A, \qquad t \text{ even}, \qquad T \geq t \geq 0$$
$$N^A c_t^A + N^B c_t^B = N^B, \qquad t \text{ odd}, \qquad T \geq t \geq 0.$$

Dividing by N^A and letting $\rho = N^B/N^A$, these statements can be written

(6.16) $\qquad \begin{aligned} c_t^A + \rho c_t^B &= 1, & t \text{ even}, & \qquad T \geq t \geq 0 \\ c_t^A + \rho c_t^B &= \rho, & t \text{ odd}, & \qquad T \geq t \geq 0. \end{aligned}$

We shall seek a stationary equilibrium in which $c_t^A = c_e^A$ for t even, $c_t^A = c_0^A$ for t odd, $c_t^B = c_e^B$ for t even, $c_t^B = c_0^B$ for t odd, $1 + r(t) = 1 + r_e$ for t even, and $1 + r(t) = 1 + r_0$ for t odd. Conditions (6.5), (6.6), (6.8), and (6.16) imply that

(6.17) $\qquad \dfrac{u'(\rho - \rho c_0^B)}{u'(1 - \rho c_e^B)} = \dfrac{u'(c_0^B)}{u'(c_e^B)} = \dfrac{1}{\beta(1+r_e)} = \beta(1+r_0).$

Notice that (6.17) implies that $(1+r_e)(1+r_0) = 1/\beta^2$, so that the two-period rate of interest is pinned down by the rate of time preference.

Equations (6.17) and (6.9) for $h = B$ provide a system that can be solved for c_0^B, c_e^B, $1 + r_e$, and $1 + r_0$. To specialize the model more, suppose that $u(c) = \ln c$. Then (6.17) becomes

$$\dfrac{1 - \rho c_e^B}{\rho - \rho c_0^B} = \dfrac{c_e^B}{c_0^B} = \dfrac{1}{\beta(1+r_e)} = \beta(1+r_0).$$

The first equality implies that $\rho c_e^B = c_0^B$. Then the remaining two equalities imply

$$\frac{1}{\rho} = \frac{1}{\beta(1 + r_e)} = \beta(1 + r_0).$$

Therefore we have that

(6.18) $\quad 1 + r_e = \dfrac{\rho}{\beta}$

$$1 + r_0 = \frac{1}{\beta\rho}$$

$$\rho c_e^B = c_0^B$$
$$\rho c_e^A = c_0^A,$$

where the last equality follows from the marginal conditions for agent A. The levels of c_0^B, c_e^B, c_0^A, and c_e^A can be computed using (6.9) and the equilibrium interest rates in (6.18). For agent A, this is easy, because the two-period gross interest rate is $1/\beta^2$, and therefore the present value of income is $(1 - \beta^{T+1})/(1 - \beta^2)$. At the equilibrium interest rates, we have that the present value of consumption is

$$c_e^A + c_0^A \frac{\beta}{\rho} + c_e^A \beta^2 + c_0^A \frac{\beta^3}{\rho} + \ldots + c_0^A \frac{\beta^T}{\rho}.$$

Using $c_0^A = \rho c_e^A$ from (6.18), we have that the present value of consumption is $c_e^A(1 - \beta^{T+1})/(1 - \beta)$. Therefore, c_e^A is determined from

$$c_e^A \frac{1 - \beta^{T+1}}{1 - \beta} = \frac{1 - \beta^{T+1}}{1 - \beta^2}$$

or $\quad c_e^A = \dfrac{1}{1 + \beta}$,

which implies that

$$c_0^A = \rho \left(\frac{1}{1 + \beta} \right).$$

The solution for c_0^B is found from $c_0^B = (1 - 1/\rho)c_0^A$, which gives

$$c_0^B = \frac{\beta}{1 + \beta}$$

$$c_e^B = \frac{1}{\rho} \cdot \frac{\beta}{1 + \beta}.$$

The reader can verify that these values for c_0^B, c_e^B satisfy the agent's present-value budget constraint, (6.9).

Recall that $\rho = N_B/N_A$. Assume that $\rho > 1$. Then the solution of Equation (6.18) says the interest rate is high in even periods and low in odd periods. In even periods the aggregate endowment is $N_A = N_B/\rho < N_B$. Even periods are thus periods of scarcity when the demand for loans is high. The interest rate rises to allocate the available goods. Notice that, according to (6.18), each individual agent consumes less in even periods than in odd periods when $\rho > 1$.

This example illustrates the restrictions on the distribution and patterns of endowments that are needed in order for individuals to be able to achieve the kind of smoothing of consumption upon which the permanent income theory focuses. In this model, agents would like to smooth their consumption completely if the interest rate were $1 + r(t) = 1/\beta$ for all t. Because the aggregate endowment fluctuates according to the sequence $\{N_A, N_B, N_A, N_B, \ldots\}$, the interest rate must adjust to reconcile individual agents' consumption path with this fluctuating endowment stream.

6.4 A Digression on the Balances of Trade and Payments

It is possible to reinterpret our model as one describing international trade in a pure exchange environment. Let us regard the A's all as living in one country and the B's as living in another country. The agents are free to trade, as before. On this interpretation, all borrowing and lending is international. The budget constraint (6.3) can be represented as

$$(y_t^h - c_t^h) + r(t-1)l_{t-1}^h - (l_t^h - l_{t-1}^h) = 0, \qquad h = A, B.$$

The first term is the trade balance of country h. The second term is the service balance, the sum of the first two terms being the current account. The third term is the capital account surplus, or capital movement.

6.5 The Ricardian Doctrine about Taxes and Government Debt

We shall now use our model as a vehicle for explaining the Ricardian doctrine that, under particular circumstances, the government's decision about whether to finance a current expenditure by taxes or borrowing is irrelevant as far as equilibrium interest rates and individual consumption streams are concerned.

There is assumed to be a government that taxes and borrows and uses the proceeds to purchase the good in the economy. The government is assumed to exist from $t = 0$ to $t = T$ and so lives exactly as long as the private agents do in the model and during the same periods. At time t, the government purchases goods at the rate of g_t units of good per capita. The government throws these goods away or uses them in a way that generates no utility for consumers. This last assumption is made only for simplicity. It could be relaxed and is not a critical one in delivering the Ricardian results.[3] At time t, each agent of type A pays a lump-sum tax of τ_t^A, measured in time t goods, whereas each agent of type B pays a lump-sum tax of τ_t^B. The government also borrows an amount of $-l_t^g$ per capita at time t, where $-l_t^g$ denotes the amount of one-period bonds per capita, measured in time t goods, that are issued by the government at time t. The government operates in the loan market on an equal footing with private agents. The government's budget constraint is

(6.19) $(N^A + N^B)(g_t + l_t^g) = N^A \tau_t^A + N^B \tau_t^B + (N^A + N^B) l_{t-1}^g$
$\cdot [1 + r(t-1)], \qquad 0 \le t \le T, \qquad l_{-1}^g = 0.$

We will specialize the model still further by assuming that $\tau_t^A = \tau_t^B = \tau_t$ for all t, so that the agents of types A and B are taxed equally. Substituting this specialization into (6.19) and dividing by $(N^A + N^B)$ gives

(6.20) $g_t + l_t^g = \tau_t + l_{t-1}^g [1 + r(t-1)],$
$0 \le t \le T, \qquad l_{-1}^g = 0.$

Because the government competes in the loan market on the same basis as private agents, by the same logic that we used above to argue that in equilibrium we must have $l_T^A = l_T^B = 0$, we must have that $l_T^g = 0$. Neither the A's nor the B's will supply loans at any interest rate at time T, and the government will therefore be unable to borrow at T. Solving the difference equation (6.20) "forward" subject to the boundary conditions $l_T^g = 0$ and $l_{-1}^g = 0$ gives the present-value constraint

(6.21) $g_0 + \sum_{t=1}^{T} g_t \left(\prod_{s=1}^{t} [1 + r(s-1)] \right)^{-1}$
$= \tau_0 + \sum_{t=1}^{T} \tau_t \left(\prod_{s=1}^{t} [1 + r(s-1)] \right)^{-1}.$

The individual consumer of type h now faces the budget constraints

(6.22) $c_t^h + l_t^h \le y_t^h - \tau_t + l_{t-1}^h [1 + r(t-1)], \qquad l_{-1}^h = 0.$

3. Agents' preferences, for example, could be modified to take the form $\sum_{t=0}^{T} \beta^t u(c_t, g_t)$. The experiment in the Ricardian proposition holds the sequence $\{g_t\}_{t=0}^{T}$ fixed and proceeds by verifying that no agent's budget set is altered by present-value-preserving changes in the time stream of taxes. Consequently, private agents' choices are not altered by such changes in the timing of taxes. This logic would continue to hold if preferences were altered as has been indicated.

(Eventually we will assume, as we did earlier, that $\{y_t^A\}$ is given by the sequence $\{1, 0, 1, 0, \ldots\}$ and $\{y_t^B\}$ by the sequence $\{0, 1, 0, 1, \ldots\}$.) A representation of (6.22) that satisfies the boundary condition $l_T^h = 0$ is

$$
(6.23) \quad c_0^h + \sum_{t=1}^{T} c_t^h \left(\prod_{s=1}^{t} [1 + r(s-1)] \right)^{-1}
$$

$$
= y_0^h + \sum_{t=1}^{T} y_t^h \left(\prod_{s=1}^{t} [1 + r(s-1)] \right)^{-1}
$$

$$
- \tau_0 - \sum_{t=1}^{T} \tau_t \left(\prod_{s=1}^{t} [1 + r(s-1)] \right)^{-1},
$$

which is the consumer's present-value constraint in terms of after-tax income. Substituting (6.21) into (6.23) gives

$$
(6.24) \quad c_0^h + \sum_{t=1}^{T} c_t^h \left(\prod_{s=1}^{t} [1 + r(s-1)] \right)^{-1}
$$

$$
= y_0^h + \sum_{t=1}^{T} y_t^h \left(\prod_{s=1}^{t} [1 + r(s-1)] \right)^{-1}
$$

$$
- g_0 - \sum_{t=1}^{T} g_t \left(\prod_{s=1}^{t} [1 + r(s-1)] \right)^{-1}.
$$

The consumer's maximum problem can be formulated in the "isoperimetric" form: to maximize $\sum_{t=0}^{T} \beta^t u(c_t^h)$ subject to (6.24). To solve this problem, we form the Lagrangian

$$
(6.25) \quad J = \sum_{t=0}^{T} \beta^t u(c_t^h) + \mu^h \left(\left\{ \tilde{y}_0^h + \frac{\tilde{y}_1^h}{1 + r(0)} + \ldots \right. \right.
$$

$$
+ \frac{\tilde{y}_T^h}{[1 + r(0)] \ldots [1 + r(T-1)]} \right\}
$$

$$
\left. - \left\{ c_0^h + \frac{c_1^h}{1 + r(0)} + \ldots + \frac{c_T^h}{[1 + r(0)] \ldots [1 + r(T-1)]} \right\} \right),
$$

subject to $c_t^h \geq 0$, where $\tilde{y}_t^h = y_t^h - g_t$ and where μ^h is a nonnegative Lagrange multiplier. The first-order necessary conditions for (6.25) are

$$
(6.26) \quad \frac{\partial J}{\partial c_0^h} = u'(c_0^h) - \mu^h \leq 0, \qquad = 0 \quad \text{if } c_0^h > 0
$$

$$
\frac{\partial J}{\partial c_t^h} = \beta^t u'(c_t^h) - \frac{\mu^h}{[1 + r(0)] \ldots [1 + r(t-1)]} \leq 0,
$$

$$
= 0 \quad \text{if } c_t^h > 0, \qquad t = 1, 2, \ldots, T.
$$

The equilibrium condition in the goods market at t is

(6.27) $N^A c_t^A + N^B c_t^B + (N^A + N^B) g_t = (N^A y_t^A + N^B y_t^B)$.

An equivalent equilibrium condition in terms of the loan market is $N^A l_t^A + N^B l_t^B + (N^A + N^B) l_t^g = 0$ for $t = 0, \ldots, T$. For an equilibrium to exist, it is necessary to assume that $(N^A + N^B) g_t < (N^A y_t^A + N^B y_t^B)$ so that the government is not trying to purchase more goods than are available at time t.

Let us now describe an equilibrium of the model formally. We shall take as the exogenous variables of the model $\{y_t^A, y_t^B, t = 0, \ldots, T\}$, and $\{g_t, t = 0, \ldots, T\}$. The endogenous variables are $\{1 + r(t), t = 0, \ldots, T - 1\}$, $\{c_t^A, c_t^B, t = 0, \ldots, T\}$, and a sequence of per capita tax rates $\{\tau_t, t = 0, \ldots, T\}$. We make the following definition.

DEFINITION. *A competitive equilibrium of the model is a set of sequences for $c_t^A, c_t^B, y_t^A, y_t^B, g_t,$ and τ_t for $t = 0, \ldots, T,$ and $r(t)$ for $t = 0, \ldots, T - 1$ such that*

(i) *Given the $[1 + r(t)]$ sequence, c_t^h solves the agents' maximization problem (6.25), for $h = A, B$.*
(ii) *Given the $[1 + r(t)]$ sequence, the τ_t sequence satisfies the government's present-value constraint (6.21).*
(iii) *The goods market clears every period, that is, Equation (6.27) holds.*

Condition (i) is satisfied when Equations (6.26) are satisfied with equality and (6.24) holds. Rearranging these equations and repeating (6.21) and (6.27), we have the following set of equilibrium conditions:[4]

(6.28) $\dfrac{u'(c_{t+1}^h)}{u'(c_t^h)} = \dfrac{1}{\beta[1 + r(t)]}$ $t = 0, \ldots, T - 1, h = A, B$.

(6.24) $c_0^h + \displaystyle\sum_{t=1}^{T} c_t^h \left(\prod_{s=1}^{t} [1 + r(s - 1)] \right)^{-1}$

$= y_0^h + \displaystyle\sum_{t=1}^{T} y_t^h \left(\prod_{s=1}^{t} [1 + r(s - 1)] \right)^{-1}$

$- g_0 - \displaystyle\sum_{t=1}^{T} g_t \left(\prod_{s=1}^{t} [1 + r(s - 1)] \right)^{-1}$.

(6.27) $N^A c_t^A + N^B c_t^B + (N^A + N^B) g_t = (N^A y_t^A + N^B y_t^B)$,
$\quad\quad t = 0, \ldots, T$.

---

4. The above assumptions about the shape of u may be used to deduce that (6.26) will hold at equality.

$$(6.21) \qquad g_0 + \sum_{t=1}^{T} g_t \left(\prod_{s=1}^{t} [1 + r(s-1)] \right)^{-1}$$

$$= \tau_0 + \sum_{t=1}^{T} \tau_t \left(\prod_{s=1}^{t} [1 + r(s-1)] \right)^{-1}.$$

These equations have a recursive structure. In particular, the $\{\tau_t\}$ sequence appears only in the last equation. Furthermore, the first three equations are precisely those that we studied in Section 6.3 above, with the modification that y_t^h in Section 6.3 is to be reinterpreted as $(y_t^h - g_t)$. As long as $(N^A + N^B)g_t < (N^A y_t^A + N^B y_t^B)$, the first three equations in general produce a solution for sequences $\{c_t^A, c_t^B, t = 0, \ldots T; 1 + r(t), t = 0, \ldots, T-1\}$. The role of the last equation (6.21) is then simply to define a menu of tax sequences, and implicitly a sequence of government borrowing sequences, that are sufficient to finance the government budget. This reasoning establishes the following proposition.

RICARDIAN PROPOSITION. *Given the sequence of per capita government expenditures $\{g_t, t = 0, \ldots, T\}$, neither the equilibrium interest rates $\{1 + r(t), t = 0, \ldots, T-1\}$ nor the equilibrium consumption allocations depend on the particular sequence of per capita taxes $\{\tau_t, t = 0, \ldots, T\}$ that is chosen by the government subject to (6.21). The equilibrium interest rates and consumption allocations depend on the path of per capita government expenditures g_t but not on how they are financed, whether by current taxes or borrowing.*

Consider the following experiment. Start with an initial equilibrium and a particular path of per capita taxes $\{\tilde{\tau}_t, t = 0, \ldots, T\}$ that satisfies (6.21). Let the associated equilibrium path of per capita government borrowing be given by $\{-\tilde{l}_t^g, t = 0, \ldots, T\}$. Now consider an alternative path in which τ_0 is lowered, say, to $\hat{\tau}_0 < \tilde{\tau}_0$, which means that $-\tilde{l}_0^g$ must be raised, so that the government is doing additional borrowing at $t = 0$ to finance its expenditures. According to our model, this operation leaves equilibrium interest rates and consumption allocations unaltered and via Equation (6.21) causes $\sum_{t=1}^{T} \tau_t (\prod_{s=1}^{t} [1 + r(s-1)])^{-1}$ to *rise* by exactly $(\tilde{\tau}_0 - \hat{\tau}_0)$. The present value of each agent's tax liabilities is not altered by the change in taxes at time 0, and so each agent's budget set is unaltered at the old equilibrium interest rates. There is thus no reason to disturb the old equilibrium consumption plans. Because the present value of per capita taxes is entirely pinned down by (6.21) and the choice of the $\{g_t\}$ sequence, the choice of τ_t at a particular t is irrelevant for the determination of any of the real variables of the model.

Let us compute the equilibrium of our model for a particular example. We take T odd, $y_t^A = \{1, 0, 1, 0, \ldots, 0\}$, $y_t^B = \{0, 1, 0, 1, \ldots, 1\}$, $N_A = N_B$, and a constant $g_t = g$ for all t. The reader is invited to verify that the equilibrium of the model is $[1 + r(t)] = \beta^{-1}$ for all $t = 0, \ldots, T - 1$, $c_t^A + g = 1/(1 + \beta)$, $c_t^B + g = \beta/(1 + \beta)$ for all $t = 0, \ldots, T$. This example illustrates the way in which the level of government expenditures g affects consumption allocations, but the way in which they are financed does not.

Two assumptions are important for delivering the Ricardian proposition: first, the assumption that lump-sum taxes are used rather than distorting taxes; and second, the assumption that, when the timing of tax payments is changed by the government, the distribution of taxes across agents is not changed in the present value sense. In the above proposition, we assumed that all individuals were taxed at the common rate τ_t, but this condition is not necessary for the proposition to hold. If the A's and the B's can be taxed at different rates, then the way in which those different rates are chosen will influence equilibrium consumption allocations and interest rates. Even with different tax rates across agents of different types, however, it will still be possible to obtain a version of the Ricardian proposition, provided that the choice between debt-financed government expenditures and tax-financed government expenditures is not permitted to influence the present value of the taxes paid by an agent of type A or type B.

6.6 The Model with Valued Currency and No Private Debt

We now consider a version of the model in which ex cathedra all private loan markets are shut down. This device is admittedly artificial, inasmuch as our description of the preferences and situations of agents leaves nothing in the environment of the model to prevent loan markets from coming into being. Later we shall consider precisely the same mathematics as describing a different but related economy in which private loan markets simply could not operate. For now let us simply shut down all loan markets. In so doing we will be able to provide a potential role for unbacked or fiat money to perform and a force that can make it valued. In the above version of the model with private loan markets, markets operate "well" in the sense of delivering a Pareto-optimal equilibrium. If an unbacked currency is introduced into that model, it will be worthless in any competitive equilibrium, even if $T = +\infty$. (The skeptical reader should do Exercise 6.1.) Later we shall see in several contexts that the existence of a Pareto-optimal equilibrium without fiat money precludes the existence of an equilibrium in which unbacked currency is valued.

We consider a pure exchange economy in which $N^A = N^B = N$, $y_t^A = \{1,$

$0, 1, 0, \ldots, \}, y_t^B = \{0, 1, 0, 1, \ldots \}$. The agents of type B are each initially endowed with m units of unbacked, intrinsically useless, inconvertible pieces of paper called dollars at the beginning of period 0. We let m_t^h be the currency that agent h chooses to hold from period t to period $(t + 1)$. We require that $m_t^h \geq 0$, with initial endowments $m_{-1}^A = 0$, $m_{-1}^B = m$. The total currency supply is $M_t = mN$. For now, we assume that the currency supply is constant for all time. The price level at time t is denoted p_t, measured in dollars per unit of time t good. We begin by analyzing an economy in which T is finite.

The problem of an agent of type h is to maximize $\Sigma_{t=0}^T \beta^t u(c_t^h)$ subject to

(6.29) $p_t c_t^h + m_t^h \leq p_t y_t^h + m_{t-1}^h, \qquad m_{-1}^h$ given; $m_t^h \geq 0$.

The agent faces the sequence of nonnegative prices p_t as a price taker. Notice that (6.29) permits the agent to smooth her consumption stream only via the holding of currency. To solve this choice problem, we form the Lagrangian

(6.30) $$J = \sum_{t=0}^T \beta^t [u(c_t^h) + \lambda_t^h(p_t y_t^h + m_{t-1}^h - p_t c_t^h - m_t^h)],$$

subject to $c_t^h \geq 0$, $m_t^h \geq 0$, where λ_t^h is a sequence of nonnegative Lagrange multipliers. The first-order necessary conditions for this problem are:

(6.31a) $\dfrac{\partial J}{\partial c_t^h} = \beta^t[u'(c_t^h) - \lambda_t^h p_t] \leq 0, \qquad = 0 \quad \text{if } c_t^h > 0,$

   $t = 0, \ldots, T$

(6.31b) $\dfrac{\partial J}{\partial m_t^h} = -\beta^t \lambda_t^h + \beta^{t+1} \lambda_{t+1}^h \leq 0, \qquad = 0 \quad \text{if } m_t^h > 0,$

   $t = 0, \ldots, T-1$

(6.31c) $\dfrac{\partial J}{\partial m_T^h} = -\beta^T \lambda_T^h \leq 0, \qquad = 0 \quad \text{if } m_T^h > 0 \text{ (or } -\beta^T \lambda_T^h m_T^h = 0).$

We use the following definition of an equilibrium with valued currency.

DEFINITION. *An equilibrium with valued currency is a collection of sequences* $\{c_t^A \geq 0, c_t^B \geq 0, \infty > p_t > 0, m_t^A \geq 0, m_t^B \geq 0\}_{t=0}^T$ *such that*

   (a) given $\{p_t\}_{t=0}^T$, $\{c_t^h, m_t^h\}_{t=0}^T$ *solves agent h's constrained-maximization problem*
   (b) $\{m_t^A, m_t^B\}_{t=0}^T$ *satisfies the market-clearing condition*

(6.32) $N^A m_t^A + N^B m_t^B = M_t, \qquad t = 0, \ldots, T,$

   where $M_t = Nm$ is the supply of currency.

We now show that there exists no equilibrium with valued currency when T is finite. The last condition of (6.31) states that $\lambda_T^h \geq 0$, and $\lambda_T^h = 0$ if $m_T^h > 0$. From the money market equilibrium condition (6.32), $m_T^A > 0$ or $m_T^B > 0$ or both if there is to be an equilibrium where $p_T < +\infty$. Suppose there is an equilibrium and $p_T < +\infty$. Take an agent h for which $m_T^h > 0$. For such an agent, (6.31) implies that $\lambda_T^h = 0$ and $u'(c_T^h)/p_T \leq \lambda_T^h = 0$. Because $u' > 0$ for $c_t^h < +\infty$, in equilibrium this inequality cannot be satisfied when $p_T < +\infty$. Therefore, the assumption that $p_T < +\infty$ has led us to a contradiction. For this model, $p_T = +\infty$ and $p_t = +\infty$ whenever $t < T$ is the only equilibrium. Currency is worthless in equilibrium. With the loan markets shut down, and no other store of value available, the equilibrium of the model is an autarkic one, with each agent consuming her own endowment.

This outcome is readily understandable. Despite the impetus to create a store of value because private loan markets are absent, no one wants to hold money in period T. The budget constraint (6.29) tells the agent that, for any finite p_t path she faces, she can easily improve upon a plan that involves a positive setting of m_T^h simply by disposing of currency and consuming more in the last period. For this reason no one wants to hold currency in period T, at any price, and so its value $1/p_T$ is bid down to zero. As a result, however, currency is useless as a store of value in period $T - 1$, and so there will be no demand for it then, either, implying that $1/p_{T-1} = 0$, and so on.

To construct an economy in which unbacked currency is valued, we shall set $T = +\infty$. Because there is no "last period," the preceding argument no longer prevents the existence of an equilibrium in which currency is valued. We shall confront the individual agent with the problem of maximizing the limit of the right side of (6.30) as T approaches $+\infty$. Our first-order necessary conditions are now

(6.33a) $\beta^t[u'(c_t^h) - \lambda_t^h p_t] \leq 0, \qquad = 0$ if $c_t^h > 0, \qquad t = 0, 1, \ldots$

(6.33b) $-\beta^t \lambda_t^h + \beta^{t+1} \lambda_{t+1}^h \leq 0, \qquad = 0$ if $m_t^h > 0, \qquad t = 0, 1, \ldots$

(6.33c) $\lim_{T \to \infty} - \beta^T \lambda_T^h \leq 0, \qquad \lim_{T \to \infty} \beta^T \lambda_T^h m_T^h = 0,$

where $\{\lambda_t^h\}$ is now an infinite sequence of nonnegative multipliers. The first two equations can be rearranged to read

(6.34) $u'(c_t^h) \leq \lambda_t^h p_t, \qquad =$ if $c_t^h > 0$

$\dfrac{\lambda_{t+1}^h}{\lambda_t^h} \leq \dfrac{1}{\beta}, \qquad =$ if $m_t^h > 0.$

Assuming an interior solution for consumption in all periods, these equations imply that

(6.35) $\qquad \dfrac{u'(c_{t+1}^h)}{u'(c_t^h)} = \dfrac{\lambda_{t+1}^h p_{t+1}}{\lambda_t^h p_t}$ for all $t \geq 0$.

We begin by seeking an equilibrium with valued currency in which the consumption allocation is optimal. We continue to assume that $N^A = N^B$. From Section 6.1, we recall that a necessary condition for an optimal consumption allocation is $u'(c_{t+1}^h)/u'(c_t^h) = 1$ for $h = A, B$ and for $t \geq 0$. By virtue of (6.35), this equality implies that

(6.36) $\qquad \dfrac{\lambda_{t+1}^h}{\lambda_t^h} \dfrac{p_{t+1}}{p_t} = 1, \qquad h = A, B.$

Equation (6.34), (6.36), and the equilibrium condition (6.32) imply that, in an optimal currency equilibrium,

(6.37) $\qquad \dfrac{p_{t+1}}{p_t} = \beta$

and $\qquad \dfrac{\lambda_{t+1}^h}{\lambda_t^h} = \dfrac{1}{\beta} \qquad$ for $h = A, B, \qquad t \geq 0,$

with $\lambda_0^h > 0$. [This result follows because, in equilibrium, $m_t^h > 0$ for either A or B or for both for each t. For one h for which $m_t^h > 0$, (6.34) and (6.36) imply $p_{t+1}/p_t = \beta$, but for the other h, (6.36) can then hold only if $\lambda_{t+1}^h/\lambda_t^h = 1/\beta$.] In such an equilibrium, however, the boundary condition (6.33c) for an optimum would be violated, implying that individuals are not maximizing their utility. Heuristically, in such an equilibrium, per capita real balances are growing without limit over time [see Equation (6.32)]. The implication is that either the A's or the B's or both are accumulating real balances over time. This situation cannot be optimal, because the consumption path associated with such a plan for real balances is easily dominated by a plan that temporarily arrests the accumulation of real balances and consumes the proceeds. Therefore there exists no optimal equilibrium with valued currency and a constant stock of currency.

Although an optimal valued currency equilibrium does not exist, a nonoptimal monetary equilibrium does exist. To find it we begin by depicting the indifference curve between c_t^h and c_{t+1}^h, holding levels of c_s^h for $s \neq t$, $t + 1$ constant. From the utility function $\Sigma_{t=0}^T \beta^t u(c_t^h)$ we have that the indifference curve has slope $dc_{t+1}^h/dc_t^h = -u'(c_t^h)/\beta u'(c_{t+1}^h)$. The indifference curve is convex and has slope equal to $-1/\beta$ along a 45° line through the origin (see Figure 6.1). Note that, because the indifference curve is convex,

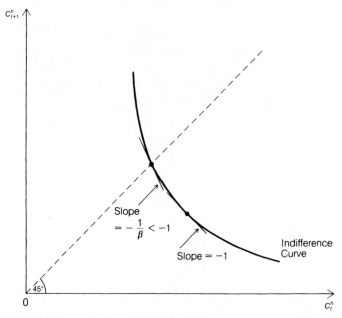

Figure 6.1. The tradeoff between time t and time $(t + 1)$ consumption faced by agent h.

the slope of the indifference curve attains the value -1 in the region in which $c_t^h > c_{t+1}^h$ and that, in the region in which $c_{t+1}^h > c_t^h$, the slope is less than $-1/\beta$.

Because $N^A = N^B$, and because the preferences of agents and their endowments have been rigged to deliver a great deal of symmetry between classes of agents and stationarity over time, it is natural to seek an equilibrium of the "quantity theory" form in which $p_t = kM_t$, where k is a constant to be determined and where M_t is the aggregate stock of currency at t. We have specified that M_t is a constant M, so that we are now able to seek an equilibrium with a constant price level $p_t = p$. For an equilibrium in which $p_t = p$, the first-order necessary conditions imply

$$\frac{u'(c_{t+1}^h)}{u'(c_t^h)} = \frac{\lambda_{t+1}^h}{\lambda_t^h} \le \frac{1}{\beta}, \quad = \text{ if } m_t^h > 0.$$

Now consider the situation of agents of class A. When $p_t = p$ whenever $t \ge 0$, the budget constraints of the A's are equivalent to the system of constraints

$$c_0^A + c_1^A + \cdots + c_s^A \le (s + 2)/2 - m_s^A/p; \quad s \text{ even}, \quad s \ge 0$$
$$c_0^A + c_1^A + \cdots + c_s^A \le (s + 1)/2 - m_s^A/p; \quad s \text{ odd}, \quad s \ge 1.$$

The structure of these constraints reveals that it cannot be optimal to have $m_t^A > 0$ for all t, for the consumption plan associated with a currency plan with $m_t^A > 0$ for all t can readily be dominated by a feasible plan with the same consumption in all periods but one and a greater consumption in that one period. Therefore, for at least one time subscript $\tilde{t}$, we must have $m_{\tilde{t}}^A = 0$. Heuristically, this finding corresponds to the commonsense observation that if, in this nonstochastic economy, an agent is always holding positive amounts of currency, then he must sometimes be holding too much currency.

Next, by virtue of the above reasoning and the periodic structure to the agent's endowments, it is natural to seek an optimal policy for demanding currency and for consuming of the periodic form

$$m_t^A = m^A > 0, \qquad c_t^A = c^*, \qquad t \text{ even}$$
$$m_t^A = 0, \qquad c_t^A = c^{**}, \qquad t \text{ odd.}$$

The agent must hold zero currency balances sometimes if he is to be behaving optimally. The assumption of a periodic policy then means that he will hold zero balances every other period. If we restrict him to a periodic policy, it is sensible to guess that he will hold zero balances in odd periods, when he is expecting to receive a unit of the good next period, and will hold positive amounts of currency in even periods, when he expects to receive zero units of endowment the following period. If we make these guesses, adding agent A's budget constraints for two successive periods gives .

$$c_t^A + c_{t+1}^A \leq 1, \qquad t \geq 0.$$

Because our guess requires that $m_t^A = m^A > 0$ for t even, we have, from the first-order necessary condition,

(6.38) $$\frac{u'(c_{t+1}^A)}{u'(c_t^A)} = \frac{u'(c^{**})}{u'(c^*)} = \frac{1}{\beta}, \qquad t \text{ even.}$$

Thus (c^*, c^{**}) are chosen to satisfy (6.38) and $c^* + c^{**} = 1$, as depicted in Figure 6.2. We have $m_t^A = pc^{**}$, for t even. For t odd, we immediately have

(6.39) $$\frac{u'(c_{t+1}^A)}{u'(c_t^A)} = \frac{u'(c^*)}{u'(c^{**})} = \beta < \frac{1}{\beta},$$

which is consistent with $m_t^A = 0$ for t odd, as required.

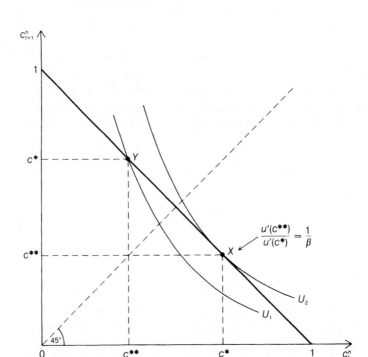

Figure 6.2. The tradeoff between time t and time $(t + 1)$ consumption faced by agent A (B) in equilibrium for t even (odd). For t even, $c_t^A = c^*$, $c_{t+1}^A = c^{**}$, $m_t^A = pc^{**}$, and $m_{t+1}^A = 0$. The slope of the indifference curve at X is $-u'(c_t^h)/\beta u'(c_{t+1}^h) = -u'(c^*)/\beta u'(c^{**}) = -1$, and the slope of the indifference curve at Y is $-u'(c^{**})/\beta u'(c^*) = -1/\beta^2$.

We also have that

$$(6.40) \qquad \frac{\lambda_{t+1}^A}{\lambda_t^A} = \frac{1}{\beta}, \qquad t \text{ even}$$

$$\frac{\lambda_{t+1}^A}{\lambda_t^A} = \beta, \qquad t \text{ odd}.$$

Therefore we have that the shadow price λ_t^A oscillates periodically but is constant on average because $\lambda_{t+2}^A = \lambda_t^A$ for all t. This shadow price is the marginal utility of currency and is constant on average. As a consequence of (6.40), we also have that the first-order necessary condition (6.33c) is satisfied when A's planned consumption and currency holdings are:

$$(6.41) \qquad c_t^A = \begin{cases} c^*, & t \text{ even} \\ c^{**}, & t \text{ odd} \end{cases}$$

$$m_t^A = \begin{cases} c^{**}p, & t \text{ even} \\ 0, & t \text{ odd.} \end{cases}$$

The analysis readily suggests how the B's must behave if there is to be the kind of constant price-level equilibrium that we seek. Because $N^A = N^B$, it follows that $c_t^A + c_t^B = 1$ for all t. It then follows that

$$(6.42) \qquad c_t^B = \begin{cases} c^{**}, & t \text{ even} \\ c^*, & t \text{ odd.} \end{cases}$$

Because the B agents each begin with an endowment of $m_{-1}^B = m$ units of currency, whereas the A's start with none, an equilibrium seems possible in which (6.42) holds and also

$$(6.43) \qquad m_t^B = \begin{cases} 0, & t \text{ even} \\ c^{**}p, & t \text{ odd.} \end{cases}$$

Thus, Figure 6.2 applies to the B agents with the reinterpretation that in even periods the B's find themselves in the situation of the A's in odd periods and vice versa.

The equilibrium condition for the money market, $N^A m_t^A + N^B m_t^B = M = mN$ becomes, with (6.41) and (6.43), $N^A c^{**}p = M$, or

$$(6.44) \qquad p = \frac{M}{c^{**}N^A}.$$

Equation (6.43) is a version of the quantity theory of money guess with which we began the search for an equilibrium. We have now verified that such an equilibrium exists and have characterized it.

In summary, we have constructed an equilibrium in which unbacked currency is valued and the A's and the B's pass currency back and forth in order to try to smooth their consumption paths. This model captures the heuristic story that, because incomes are not perfectly synchronized with consumption streams, there is a motive to hold "money" to bridge the gap. In this model, the impetus to smooth consumption is converted into a force for valuing an unbacked currency by ruling out markets in private consumption loans (or "inside money").

We note that this equilibrium is not an optimal one, for we have

$$\frac{u'(c_{t+1}^A)}{u'(c_t^A)} = \frac{1}{\beta} > \frac{u'(c_{t+1}^B)}{u'(c_t^B)} = \beta, \qquad t \text{ even}$$

$$\frac{u'(c_{t+1}^A)}{u'(c_t^A)} = \beta < \frac{u'(c_{t+1}^B)}{u'(c_t^B)} = \frac{1}{\beta}, \qquad t \text{ odd}.$$

The marginal rates of substitution are not equal for different agents, and Pareto-improving redistributions are therefore possible. Notice, however, that, as β approaches unity, the extent of suboptimality of the stationary monetary equilibrium diminishes.

6.7 An Interventionist Optimal Monetary Equilibrium

The problem with the monetary equilibrium described above is that the gross rate of return on money, which is $p(t)/p(t+1) = 1$, is too low. A necessary condition for optimality in this economy is that the gross rate of return on money be $p(t)/p(t+1) = \beta^{-1}$. As we saw earlier, with a fixed supply of money over time, there does not exist such an equilibrium with the value of currency appreciating over time. In this section, we describe a scheme by which the government levies lump-sum taxes and transfers in a special way on the A's and B's each period and uses the proceeds to vary the currency stock. The scheme is adopted with the aim of delivering deflation at the optimal rate of $p(t+1)/p(t) - 1 = \beta - 1$. We shall examine a scheme with enough free parameters for any optimal equilibrium to be supported under it.

Lump-sum taxes paid by agent h in period t in units of time t goods are denoted z_t^h. The following pattern of taxes is used:

(6.45) $z_t^A = \begin{cases} 1 - \lambda, & t \text{ even} \\ 0, & t \text{ odd} \end{cases}$

$z_t^B = \begin{cases} 0, & t \text{ even} \\ 1 - \mu, & t \text{ odd}, \end{cases}$

where λ and μ are chosen to satisfy $0 < \lambda < 1 + \beta$ and also

(6.46) $\dfrac{\lambda}{1+\beta} + \dfrac{\mu}{1+\beta} = 1.$

The meaning of (6.46) is as follows. The parameter λ is the after-tax even-period endowment of the A's, while μ is the after-tax odd-period endowment of the B's. It will turn out in equilibrium that

(6.47) $\qquad c_t^A = c^A = \dfrac{\lambda}{1+\beta}, \qquad t = 0, \ldots, T$

$\qquad\qquad c_t^B = c^B = \dfrac{\mu}{1+\beta}, \qquad t = 0, \ldots, T.$

Equation (6.46) is the condition that total consumption exhausts the endowment each period.

The individual agent's budget constraint is now

(6.48) $\qquad p_t c_t^h + m_t^h \le p_t y_t^h + m_{t-1}^h - z_t^h p_t$

$\qquad\qquad m_{-1}^A = 0$

$\qquad\qquad m_{-1}^B = m_{-1}^s.$

The per capita supply of money m_t^s obeys

(6.49) $\qquad m_t^s = m_{t-1}^s - (z_t^A p_t + z_t^B p_t),$

which expresses the idea that the government is using the proceeds of the lump-sum taxes to retire money.

We claim that an equilibrium of the model is a consumption allocation given by (6.47) and a price-level sequence obeying

(6.50) $\qquad p_{t+1} = \beta p_t, \qquad t \ge 0.$

We begin verifying this guess by first guessing that the demands for money are given by

(6.51) $\qquad m_t^A = \begin{cases} p_t(\lambda - c^A) = p_t \lambda \dfrac{\beta}{1+\beta}, & t \text{ even} \\[2mm] 0, & t \text{ odd} \end{cases}$

$\qquad\qquad m_t^B = \begin{cases} 0, & t \text{ even} \\[2mm] p_t(\mu - c^B) = p_t \dfrac{\mu\beta}{1+\beta}, & t \text{ odd}. \end{cases}$

The money market equilibrium condition is

$$N^B m_t^s = N^A m_t^A + N^B m_t^B,$$

or, by virtue of $N^A = N^B$ and Equation (6.51),

(6.52) $\qquad \begin{aligned} m_t^s &= m_t^A, & t \text{ even} \\ m_t^s &= m_t^B, & t \text{ odd} \end{aligned}$

Using the equilibrium condition (6.52), the law of motion (6.49) for m_t^s, and the tax scheme (6.45), we can express the equilibrium condition in the money market as

(6.53) $\quad m_t^A = m_{t-1}^B - (1 - \lambda)p_t, \qquad t$ even
$\qquad\quad m_t^B = m_{t-1}^A - (1 - \mu)p_t, \qquad t$ odd.

The first equation of (6.53) states that in equilibrium the demand for money of the A's in even periods equals the amount that the B's carried over last period minus the amount that is taxed away. A symmetrical interpretation applies to the second equation of (6.53). Substituting the second equations of (6.51) into (6.53) and rearranging gives

$$p_t\left[\frac{\lambda\beta}{1+\beta} + (1-\lambda) - \frac{p_{t-1}}{p_t}\frac{\mu\beta}{1+\beta}\right] = 0, \qquad t \text{ even}$$

$$p_t\left[\frac{\mu\beta}{1+\beta} + (1-\mu) - \frac{p_{t-1}}{p_t}\frac{\lambda\beta}{1+\beta}\right] = 0, \qquad t \text{ odd}.$$

Using (6.46), or $\lambda = 1 + \beta - \mu$, in the above equations, we find that $p_{t-1}/p_t = \beta^{-1}$, or $p_t = \beta p_{t-1}$ for *all* t. The consumption plans given by (6.46) thus imply that $p_t = \beta p_{t-1}$.

We have now to verify that the consumption plans (6.47) are optimal. From (6.51) and (6.52), prices obey

(6.54) $\quad p_t = m_t^s\dfrac{(1+\beta)}{\lambda\beta}, \qquad t$ even

$\qquad\quad p_t = m_t^s\dfrac{(1+\beta)}{\mu\beta}, \qquad t$ odd.

Substituting (6.54) into (6.53) and rearranging verifies that the money supply obeys

(6.55) $\quad m_t^s = \dfrac{\lambda\beta}{\mu} m_{t-1}^s, \qquad t$ even, $\quad t \geq 0$

$\qquad\quad m_t^s = \dfrac{\mu\beta}{\lambda} m_{t-1}^s, \qquad t$ odd, $\quad t \geq 1,$

with initial condition $m_{-1}^s = m$. In particular, $m_0^s = \lambda\beta m/\mu$. Now the present value of an A's endowment is $(\lambda + \beta^2\lambda + \ldots) = \lambda/(1 - \beta^2)$. We saw in Section 6.3 that, when confronted with a rate of return of β^{-1}, it was optimal for an agent with this present value of endowments to consume a constant level of $c_t^A = c^A = \lambda/(1 + \beta)$.

The present value of a B's endowment is $(\mu\beta + \mu\beta^3 + \ldots) + m/p_0$, because each B is initially endowed with m units of currency. Using (6.54) for

$t = 0$, and $m_0^s = (\lambda\beta/\mu)m$, we find that $m/p_0 = \mu/(1 + \beta)$. Thus the present value of a B's endowment is $\mu\beta/(1 - \beta^2) + \mu/(1 + \beta) = \mu/(1 - \beta^2)$. It follows again, as in Section 6.3, that the optimal plan for an agent B confronted with a constant rate of return on money of β^{-1} is to consume at a constant rate of $c_t^B = c^B = \mu/(1 + \beta)$. Thus we have verified the optimality of (6.47) for both A and B. We summarize these results in the following proposition.

PROPOSITION. *Given the model with $N^A = N^B$, and the loan markets arbitrarily shut down, let the money supply process be given by*

$$(6.55) \qquad m_t^s = \frac{\lambda\beta}{\mu} m_{t-1}^s, \qquad t \text{ even}, \qquad t \geq 0$$

$$m_t^s = \frac{\mu\beta}{\lambda} m_{t-1}^s, \qquad t \text{ odd}, \qquad t \geq 1,$$

with $m_{-1}^s = m$, and where $\mu + \lambda = 1 + \beta$, with $0 < \lambda < 1 + \beta$. This money supply process is achieved via a pattern of real lump-sum taxes (or transfers if $\lambda > 1$) of $(1 - \lambda)$ on the A's in even periods, and $(1 - \mu)$ on the B's in the odd periods, as indicated in (6.45), with the proceeds being used to shrink or expand the money supply as in (6.49). A competitive equilibrium of this model is given by

$$(6.47) \qquad c_t^A = c^A = \frac{\lambda}{1 + \beta}, \qquad t \geq 0$$

$$c_t^B = c^B = \frac{\mu}{1 + \beta}, \qquad t \geq 0$$

$$(6.54) \qquad p_t = \begin{cases} \dfrac{1 + \beta}{\lambda\beta} m_t^s, & t \text{ even} \\[2ex] \dfrac{1 + \beta}{\mu\beta} m_t^s, & t \text{ odd}. \end{cases}$$

The equilibrium is an optimal one. Furthermore, by varying λ suitably in the interval $(0, 1 + \beta)$, any optimal equilibrium can be supported by this scheme.

According to (6.54), a quantity theory equation of the form $p_t = km_t^s$ for constant k holds only in the special case that $\mu = \lambda$. When $\mu \neq \lambda$, p_t is seen to be a time-varying function of m_t^s in equilibrium. In this model, the nature of the relation between the price level and the money supply depends on the precise method that is used to alter the stock of currency over time. This dependence occurs in (6.54), via the appearance of λ and μ, which represent the distribution of taxes and transfers across agents of types A and B.

A feature of this equilibrium that Robert Townsend has emphasized is that it requires detailed intervention by the authorities to support it. In particular, the stream of lump-sum taxes must be chosen to depend on the agents' endowment patterns in just the correct ways. Townsend has shown that it will not work simply to tax all agents each period at a single common rate $z = z_t^A = z_t^B$. Indeed, to achieve our optimal monetary equilibrium requires precisely the same detailed knowledge about the agents and the same order of discriminatory lump-sum taxation that would be involved in using lump-sum taxes and subsidies to achieve an optimal allocation. In this sense, the optimal monetary equilibrium is not achieved by a set of macroeconomic measures that is blind to the situation of individual agents.

6.8 Townsend's "Turnpike" Interpretation

The preceding analysis of currency is artificial in the sense that it depends entirely on our having arbitrarily ruled out the existence of markets for private loans. The physical setup of the model itself provided no reason for those loan markets not to exist and indeed every incentive for them to exist. In addition, for many questions that we want to analyze, we want a model in which private loans and currency coexist, with currency being valued.[5]

Robert Townsend has proposed a model whose mathematical structure is identical with the above model, but in which a global market in private loans cannot emerge because agents are spatially separated. Townsend's setup can accommodate local markets for private loans, so that it meets the objections to the model expressed above.

In Townsend's version of the model, the economy starts at time $t = 0$, with N east-heading migrants and N west-heading migrants physically located at each of the integers along a "turnpike" of infinite length extending in both directions. Each of the integers $n = 0, \pm 1, \pm 2, \ldots$ is a trading post number. Agents can trade the one good only with agents at the trading post at which they find themselves at a given date. An east-heading agent at an even-numbered trading post is endowed with one unit of the consumption good and an odd-numbered trading post has an endowment of zero units (see Table 6.1). A west-heading agent is endowed with zero units at an even-numbered trading post and with one unit of the consumption good at an odd-numbered trading post. Finally, at the end of each period, each east-

5. In the United States today, for example, M_1 consists of the sum of demand deposits (a part of which is backed by commercial loans and another, smaller part of which is backed by reserves or currency) and currency held by the public. Thus M_1 is not interpretable as the m in our model.

Table 6.1 Endowments of agents in the Townsend turnpike model

Trading post	Endowment	
	Of east-heading agent	Of west-heading agent
. . .	. . .	. . .
−3	0	1
−2	1	0
−1	0	1
0	1	0
1	0	1
2	1	0
3	0	1
. . .	. . .	. . .

heading agent moves one trading post to the east, whereas each west-heading agent moves one trading post to the west. The turnpike along which the trading posts are located is of infinite length in each direction, implying that the east-heading and west-heading agents who are paired at time t will never meet again. This feature means that there can be no private debt between agents moving in opposite directions. An IOU between agents moving in opposite directions can never be collected because a potential lender never meets the potential borrower again; nor does the lender meet anyone who ever meets the potential borrower, and so on, ad infinitum.

Let an agent who is endowed with one unit of the good at $t = 0$ be called an agent of type A and an agent who is endowed with zero units of the good at $t = 0$ be called an agent of type B. Agents of type h have preferences summarized by $\sum_{t=0}^{\infty} \beta^t u(c_t^h)$. Finally, start the economy at time 0 by having each agent of type B endowed with $m_1^B = m$ units of unbacked currency and each agent of type A endowed with $m_1^A = 0$ units of unbacked currency.

With the symbols thus reinterpreted, this model involves precisely the same mathematics as that which was analyzed above. Agents' spatial separation and their movements along the turnpike have been set up to produce a physical reason that a global market in private loans cannot exist. The various propositions about the equilibria of the model and their optimality that were proved above apply equally to the present turnpike version.

A version of the model could be constructed in which local private markets for loans coexist with valued unbacked currency. To build such a model, one would assume some heterogeneity in the time patterns of the endowment of agents who are located at the same trading post and are headed in the same direction. If half of the east-headed agents located at trading post i at time t have present and future endowment pattern $y_t^h = (\alpha, \gamma, \alpha, \gamma \ldots)$, for example, whereas the other half of the east-headed agents have $(\gamma, \alpha, \gamma, \alpha, \ldots)$ with $\gamma \neq \alpha$, then there is room for local private loans among this cohort of east-headed agents. Whether or not there exists an equilibrium with valued currency depends on how nearly Pareto optimal the equilibrium with local loan markets is. Exercise 6.5 involves the analysis of such a model. In the following chapter, we shall return to the same subject in the context of a simpler model in which "local" private loans again compete with unbacked currency, and annihilate the value of currency if loan markets operate too well in the sense of delivering Pareto-optimal outcomes.

In summary, Townsend's version of the model is one in which competitive equilibria without currency fail to be Pareto optimal. The spatial separation of agents and their endowment patterns give a setting in which private loan markets are restricted by the requirement for agents who trade IOU's to be linked together, if only indirectly, repeatedly over time and space. Spatial separation is the "friction" that provides a potential social role for a valued unbacked currency.

6.9 Conclusions

Townsend's interpretation of the model in this chapter provides an explicit description of an economic environment in which markets in private loans alone will not support an optimal allocation. This limitation on the achievements of markets in private loans leaves room for a consumption-smoothing role to be performed by a valued fiat currency.

In the next chapter, we study a model with a friction analytically related to Townsend's. The idea will be to induce decentralized exchange and a role for an unbacked currency by having agents separated in time rather than in space. In order to simplify the analysis of saving behavior, households will be assumed to live only two periods. Currency will form a vehicle for achieving intergenerational exchanges not possible through private loan markets. In return for the sacrifice of generality in terms of the saving decision facing agents, we may hope to be compensated by a gain in the ease with which heterogeneity across agents in the same generation or cohort (see Section 6.8 and Exercise 6.5) can be analyzed.

Exercises

Exercise 6.1. Value of Unbacked Currency

Prove that, in the $T = +\infty$ version of the model of Section 6.3 in which private loan markets are permitted to operate and $N^A = N^B$, there exists no equilibrium in which unbacked currency is valued.

Exercise 6.2. **Computing Equilibrium Interest Rates**

Suppose that there are N^A agents with endowment stream $\{y_t^A\}$, $t = 0$, . . . , T, and N^B agents with endowment stream $\{y_t^B\}$, $t = 0$, . . . , T. We require that $y_t^h \geq 0$ but otherwise leave the streams of endowments unrestricted. Assume that the preferences of all agents are described by $\sum_{t=0}^T \beta^t u(c_t^h)$, where

$$u(c_t) = u_0 + u_1 c_t - (u_2/2)c_t^2, \qquad u_1, u_2 > 0.$$

Compute the sequence of equilibrium one-period interest rates for the consumption loans model of Section 6.2, and show that it is given by

$$1 + r(t-1) = \frac{(N^A + N^B)u_1 - u_2(N^A y_{t-1}^A + N^B y_{t-1}^B)}{\beta[(N^A + N^B)u_1 - u_2(N^A y_t^A + N^B y_t^B)]}$$

for $t = 1, 2, \ldots, T$.

Hints.

a. Formulate each agent's problem as a discrete-time calculus-of-variations problem using the methods of Sargent (1979, chap. 9) and using l_t^h as agent h's state variable, or as a dynamic programming problem. Obtain the Euler equations. (See Section 1.4 on the way to derive the Euler equations in a dynamic programming setup.)

b. Multiply agent A's Euler equation for l_t^A by N^A and add it to N^B times agent B's Euler equation for l_t^B.

c. Impose the equilibrium condition that $N^A l_t^A + N^B l_t^B = 0$ for $t = 0, \ldots, T$, and solve for $1 + r(t-1)$.

Exercise 6.3. **"Self-Insurance" and the Permanent Income Theory**

Consider the following modification of the model of Section 6.3. Assume that $N^A = N^B$, that $T = +\infty$, and that y_t^A for $t = 0, 1, \ldots$ is now a sequence of independently and identically distributed random variables, each of which is distributed uniformly on the interval $[0, 1]$. Assume that $y_t^B = 1 - y_t^A$, so that y_t^B is also uniformly distributed on $[0, 1]$. Notice that there is no aggregate risk, although there is risk for each individual. An agent of type h seeks to maximize

$$E_0 \sum_{t=0}^\infty \beta^t u(c_t^h),$$

where E_t is the mathematical expectation operator conditional on $(y_t^h, y_{t-1}^h, \ldots, y_0^h)$, $u(c_t) = u_0 + u_1 c_t - \frac{u_2}{2} c_t^2$, and $0 < \beta < 1$. Let there be a market in perfectly safe one-period consumption loans, with a one-period gross interest rate of $[1 + r(t)]$ between periods t and $(t + 1)$. The agent's budget constraint in period t is $c_t^h + l_t^h \leq y_t^h + [1 + r(t-1)]l_{t-1}^h$, with boundary conditions

$$\lim_{T \to \infty} E_t \phi(T, t) l_t^h = 0, \qquad l_{-1}^h = 0, \quad \text{where}$$

$$\phi(T, t) = \left(\prod_{s=1}^{T} [1 + r(t+s-1)] \right)^{-1}.$$

The flow budget constraint with these terminal conditions can be solved to give

(a)
$$c_z^h + E_z \sum_{t=1}^{\infty} c_{t+z}^h \left(\prod_{s=1}^{t} [1 + r(z+s-1)] \right)^{-1}$$

$$= y_z^h + E_z \sum_{t=1}^{\infty} y_{t+z}^h \left(\prod_{s=1}^{t} [1 + r(z+s-1)] \right)^{-1}$$

$$+ l_{z-1}^h [1 + r(z-1)],$$

$$z = 0, 1, 2, \ldots$$

The equilibrium condition for the model can be expressed as either

$$N^A l_t^A + N^A l_t^B = 0$$

or $c_t^A + c_t^B = 1$ for $t = 0, 1, \ldots$

Prove that an equilibrium is given by

(b)
$$\frac{1}{1 + r(t)} = \beta, \qquad t = 0, 1, \ldots$$

(c)
$$c_t^h = \frac{1}{2} + \frac{1-\beta}{\beta} l_{t-1}^h + (1 - \beta)\left(y_t^h - \frac{1}{2} \right), \qquad t = 0, 1, \ldots,$$

$$h = A, B.$$

Hint. Obtain the stochastic Euler equations, using the methods of Section 1.3 or Sargent (1979, chap. 14). Notice that given (b), (c) satisfies (a) and the stochastic Euler equations and also implies market clearing.

Notice that the interest rate is certain, despite the appearance of randomness in the model. Notice also that (c) is a version of the "permanent income" theory. The agent's permanent income is

$$\frac{1}{2} + \frac{1-\beta}{\beta} l_{t-1}^h = \frac{1}{2} + r(t-1)l_{t-1}^h,$$

which equals the sum of Ey_t^h for all t plus the expected interested income from his initial assets of l_{t-1}^h. The agent's transitory income in period t is $(y_t^h - 1/2)$. The marginal propensity to consume out of permanent income is unity, whereas the marginal propensity to consume out of transitory income is $(1 - \beta)$.

Exercise 6.4. The Distribution of Currency

Consider the model of Section 6.6 with $T = +\infty$ and with $N^A = N^B$. Keep all aspects of the model as in Section 6.6 except for the initial stocks of currency. Let each type A agent begin with $m_{-1}^A = m/2$ units of currency and each type B agent begin with $m_{-1}^B = m/2$ units of currency.

a. Find equilibrium consumption allocations and a price path in which currency is valued. How is currency redistributed over time in this equilibrium?

b. How do this equilibrium consumption allocation and price path compare with those computed in Section 6.6?

Exercise 6.5. Rate-of-Return Dominance

Consider a version of the turnpike model of Section 6.8 modified as follows: two agents travel in the same direction and can therefore engage in intertemporal trades. These agents share the same preferences but have different endowments. East-heading agents: agents 1 and 2 have endowment streams given by

$$y_t^1 = 1, \qquad t = 0, 1, \ldots$$

$$y_t^2 = \begin{cases} 0, & t \text{ even} \\ w, & t \text{ odd.} \end{cases}$$

West-heading agents: agents 3 and 4 have endowments given by

$$y_t^3 = 1, \qquad t = 0, 1, \ldots$$

$$y_t^4 = \begin{cases} w, & t \text{ even} \\ 0, & t \text{ odd.} \end{cases}$$

Preferences are given by $\Sigma \beta^t u(c_t^h)$, where $u(c) = (c^{1-\rho} - 1)/(1 - \rho)$.

a. Assume that there is no outside debt. Compute the competitive equilibrium of this model

b. Now endow agent 2 with m units of currency. Specify under what conditions there exists an equilibrium in which currency is valued and the price level is constant.

c. Compare the rates of return on different assets — currency and loans — faced by east- and west-heading agents. What accounts for the difference?

d. Argue that neither the part (a) equilibrium nor the part (b) equilibrium is optimal when we restrict ourselves to allocations that treat all agents of a given type identically.

References and Suggested Readings

Bewley, Truman. 1980. The optimum quantity of money. In *Models of Monetary Economies,* ed. J. H. Kareken and N. Wallace, pp. 169–210. Minneapolis: Federal Reserve Bank of Minneapolis.

Friedman, Milton. 1969. The optimum quantity of money. In *The Optimum Quantity of Money and Other Essays,* pp. 1–50. Chicago: Aldine.

Lucas, Robert E., Jr. 1980. Equilibrium in a pure currency economy. In *Models of Monetary Economies,* ed. J. H. Kareken and N. Wallace, pp. 131–146. Minneapolis: Federal Reserve Bank of Minneapolis.

Sargent, Thomas J. 1979. *Macroeconomic Theory.* New York: Academic Press.

Townsend, Robert. 1980. Models of money with spatially separated agents. In *Models of Monetary Economies,* ed. J. H. Kareken and N. Wallace, pp. 265–304. Minneapolis: Federal Reserve Bank of Minneapolis.

7 | Credit and Currency with Overlapping Generations

This chapter uses the two-period-lived overlapping-generations model introduced by Paul Samuelson to study a variety of issues in monetary theory. This chapter uses a version of the overlapping-generations model that has been described by Neil Wallace (1980). Like Townsend's turnpike model, the overlapping-generations model uses a structure with missing links among agents to inhibit the operation of loan and insurance markets and to open up a potential role for an unbacked government-issued currency. Like Townsend's model, the missing trading links create the possibility that endowment and preferences make the economy short of borrowers. When it is, there is a potential role for an unbacked government-issued currency. By assuming the role of permanent borrower, the government adds a means of reallocating goods that ameliorates the missing trading links. The advantages of the two-period-lived overlapping-generations model are that the missing links are structured in an analytically manageable way and that the saving and portfolio choices faced by agents are simplified by the assumed two-period life span. These simplifications render it possible to analyze situations in which there is heterogeneity among agents' preferences and endowments, which can be much more difficult to analyze in contexts such as that of Townsend's turnpike model (see Exercise 6.5). Heterogeneity among agents' preferences and endowments is something that we want to study partly in order to attain a theory to help us to understand variations over time in the volume of "inside" indebtedness and their implications for price-level fluctuations and welfare.

In overlapping-generations models, equilibria exist in which unbacked currency is valued and coexists with private loans. In equilibrium, private loans neither dominate nor are dominated by currency in rate of return. Such equilibria with no dominance in rate of return satisfy conditions needed to deliver Modigliani-Miller theorems for government open-market operations. The structure of these Modigliani-Miller theorems, which rely on logic similar to that underlying the Ricardian equivalence theorem, will be explored in this chapter and in Chapter 8. The exchange rate indeterminacy proposition of Kareken and Wallace (1981), which we study further in both chapters, is another version of an irrelevance proposition, one that stems directly from equilibrium conditions requiring no dominance in rate of return.

7.1 The Overlapping-Generations Model

The economy consists of overlapping generations of two-period-lived agents. The economy operates in discrete time, starts at time $t = 1$, and ends at time $t = T + 1$. There is no uncertainty. We shall usually consider the case in which $T = +\infty$, which will be necessary if we want unbacked government debt or currency to be valued. At each date t with $1 \le t \le T$, there are born $N(t)$ young people, said to be of generation t, who are young in period t, old in period $(t + 1)$, and dead in period $(t + 2)$ and beyond. Agent h of generation t is endowed with $w_t^h(t)$ of a single consumption good at time t, and $w_t^h(t + 1)$ of the good at $(t + 1)$. There is only one consumption good at each date t. A government imposes a lump-sum tax of $\tau_t^h(t)$ on agent h of generation t when he is young and $\tau_t^h(t + 1)$ when he is old. The taxes $\tau_t^h(t)$ and $\tau_t^h(t + 1)$ can be negative, in which case they are transfers. We shall denote the after-tax endowments as $\tilde{w}_t^h(t) = w_t^h(t) - \tau_t^h(t)$ and $\tilde{w}_t^h(t + 1) = w_t^h(t + 1) - \tau_t^h(t + 1)$. Agent h of generation t consumes $c_t^h(t)$ when young and $c_t^h(t + 1)$ when old.

The preferences of agent h of generation t are described by a utility function $u_t^h[c_t^h(t), c_t^h(t + 1)]$. We assume that u_t^h is characterized by (1) indifference curves that are convex to the origin, (2) absence of satiation, (3) $u_{t1}^h / u_{t2}^h \to \infty$ as $c_t^h(t)/c_t^h(t + 1) \to 0$, and $u_{t1}^h / u_{t2}^h \to 0$ as $c_t^h(t)/c_t^h(t + 1) \to \infty$, and (4) positive income effects on both goods, so that both $c_t^h(t)$ and $c_t^h(t + 1)$ are "normal goods." Property (4) implies, in Figure 7.1, that the indifference curves become steeper as we move northward along a line parallel to the $c_t^h(t)$ axis and become less steep as we move eastward along a line parallel to the $c_t^h(t + 1)$ axis. Thus in Figure 7.1, the indifference curve is steeper at B than at A and steeper at A than at C. These four properties are in general not sufficient to imply that first-period saving, $w_t^h(t) - \tau_t^h(t) - c_t^h(t)$, will rise with an increase in the rate of interest. Whether saving rises with the interest

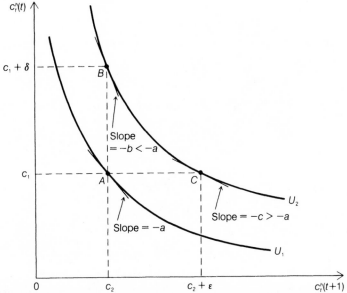

Figure 7.1. Indifference curves of agent h. The slope of the tangent to the indifference curve for the utility level U_1 at the point $A = (c_2, c_1)$ is $-a$. Let B be a point $(c_2, c_1 + \delta)$, where $\delta > 0$. B is on the indifference curve for some utility level $U_2 > U_1$. The slope of the tangent to the indifference curve at B is $-b$, and $-b < -a$. Similarly, let C be a point $(c_2 + \epsilon, c_1)$, where $\epsilon > 0$. Then C is on the indifference curve for some utility level $U_2 > U_1$. The slope of the tangent to the indifference curve at C is $-c$, with $-c > -a$.

rate depends on whether the substitution effect of the higher interest rate is sufficient to counterbalance the income effect, which, if the agent is relatively well endowed in the first period of life, can cause him to increase first-period consumption in response to a higher interest rate. We shall sometimes want to add the following additional assumption about preferences that is illustrated in Figure 7.2: (5) preferences are such that first-period saving, $w_t^h(t) - \tau_t^h(t) - c_t^h(t)$, always increases with an increase in the rate of interest. This statement is equivalent to the assumption that $c_t^h(t)$ and $c_t^h(t + 1)$ are gross substitutes (see Varian 1978). The role of this optional assumption will be to help to reduce the number of equilibria.

In addition to the generations born at times $t \geq 1$, at time $t = 1$ there exist $N(0)$ old people, of whom the hth agent is endowed with $w_0^h(1)$ units of the time 1 consumption good. An old agent h at time 1 simply maximizes $c_0^h(1)$.

There is a constant-returns-to-scale technology for storing goods between times t and $(t + 1)$. If agent h stores $k_t^h(t)$ good at time t, then at time $(t + 1)$,

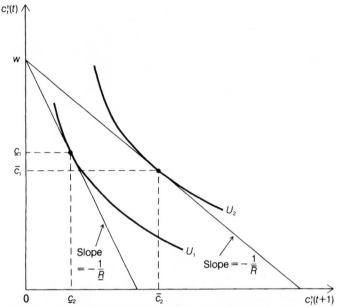

Figure 7.2. Savings of agent h. Agent h's after-tax endowment is $[\tilde{w}_t^h(t+1), \tilde{w}_t^h(t)] = (0, w)$. At a low interest rate $\underline{R}$, h chooses $[c_t^h(t+1),$ $c_t^h(t)] = (\underline{c}_2, \underline{c}_1)$, and at a higher interest rate $\overline{R}$, h chooses $(\overline{c}_2, \overline{c}_1)$. Savings, $\tilde{w}_t^h(t) - c_t^h(t)$, is greater at the higher interest rate.

$k_t^h(t)$ $[1 + p(t)]$ goods become available, where $p(t) \geq -1$ for $t \geq 1$. The sequence $p(t)$ is exogenous and nonstochastic. All agents are imagined to have access to this technology.

The temporal arrangement of private agents and their endowments is depicted in Figure 7.3. A salient feature of this economy is that agents have been placed so that private intertemporal trading can occur only between members of the same generation. If there is heterogeneity in the endowment patterns and/or the preferences of the agents of generation t, private borrowing and lending between members of the same generation can occur. Borrowing or lending cannot occur, however, between members of different generations. On the one hand, at time t, the old will not want to lend to the young, at any interest rate, because it is the old person's last period on earth. On the other hand, the young will not be willing to lend to the old, because the old have nothing of value to offer in exchange because they will be gone from the scene in period $(t+1)$. To reallocate goods across generations, it is therefore necessary to resort to some governmental or social mechanism rather than to markets in private loans. As we shall see, there can be socially desirable reallocations of endowments that cannot be achieved by private

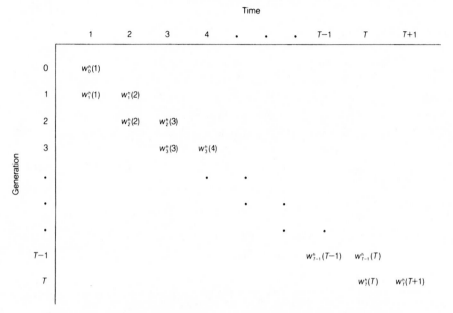

Figure 7.3. Temporal arrangement of private agents and their endowments.

borrowing and lending arrangements. This limit on what private loan markets can accomplish permits a role for the "social contrivance" of unbacked currency. The intertemporal location pattern of agents serves a purpose similar to that of Townsend's device of sending differently endowed agents traveling along a turnpike forever in different directions.

We assume that a government transcends generations and operates as long as the economy, namely throughout periods $t = 1, \ldots, T + 1$. Note that the government lives longer than any individual if $T > 1$. We shall assume that the government purchases $G(t) \geq 0$ units of goods at time t. These purchases do not yield utility to private agents. The government consumes all of $G(t)$ and stores none of it. (In the next chapter, we will study the effects of government storage.) At time t, the government imposes lump-sum taxes of $\tau_t^h(t)$ on agent h of generation t and of $\tau_{t-1}^h(t)$ on agent h of generation $(t - 1)$. The government lends $L^g(t)$ [or borrows if $L^g(t)$ is negative] via one-period loans at time t, being repaid $[1 + r(t)]L^g(t)$ at time $(t + 1)$, where $1 + r(t)$ is the gross rate of interest on loans at time t. The government's budget constraint is

$$(7.1) \qquad G(t) + L^g(t) = \sum_h \tau_{t-1}^h(t) + \sum_h \tau_t^h(t) + [1 + r(t-1)]L^g(t-1),$$

$$t \geq 1 \quad \text{with } L^g(0) = 0.$$

The national income identity or feasibility condition is

(7.2) $$G(t) + \sum_h c_t^h(t) + \sum_h c_{t-1}^h(t) + \sum_h k_t^h(t)$$
$$\leq \sum_h w_t^h(t) + \sum_h w_{t-1}^h(t) + [1 + \rho(t-1)] \sum_h k_{t-1}^h(t-1),$$

subject to $\sum_h k_0^h(0) = 0$, so that we are assuming that the old at time 1 had stored zero units when they were young at time 0 [there is no loss of generality in making this assumption, because $w_0^h(1)$ and $[1 + \rho(0)]k_0^h(0)$ play the same role in the model].

Agent h of generation t maximizes $u_t^h[c_t^h(t), c_t^h(t+1)]$, subject to the constraints

(7.3) $$c_t^h(t) + l_t^h(t) + k_t^h(t) \leq w_t^h(t) - \tau_t^h(t)$$

(7.4) $$c_t^h(t+1) \leq w_t^h(t+1) - \tau_t^h(t+1) + [1 + r(t)]l_t^h(t)$$
$$+ [1 + \rho(t)]k_t^h(t),$$

with $k_t^h(t) \geq 0$, $c_t^h(t) \geq 0$, $c_t^h(t+1) \geq 0$, and $l_t^h(t)$ unconstrained. Here $l_t^h(t)$ is the amount of one-period loans made by agent h in period t, whereas $[1 + r(t)]$ is the gross real rate of return on one-period loans, measured in units of time $(t + 1)$ good per unit of time t good. The agent is a perfect competitor and views the sequence of market rates of return $[1 + r(t)]$ and physical rates of return $1 + \rho(t)$ as beyond his influence. The agent maximizes u_t^h over $c_t^h(t)$, $c_t^h(t+1)$, $k_t^h(t)$, and $l_t^h(t)$ subject to (7.3) and (7.4), and $k_t^h(t) \geq 0$. Solving (7.4) for $l_t^h(t)$ and substituting the result into (7.3) gives the present value form of the budget constraint:

$$c_t^h(t) + \frac{c_t^h(t+1)}{1 + r(t)}$$
$$\leq [w_t^h(t) - \tau_t^h(t)] + \frac{w_t^h(t+1) - \tau_t^h(t+1)}{1 + r(t)} + \left[\frac{1 + \rho(t)}{1 + r(t)} - 1\right]k_t^h(t).$$

The preceding inequality implies that, if $\rho(t) > r(t)$, then there exist arbitrage opportunities: an individual could attain unbounded consumption by storing an indefinitely large amount, financing the acquisition by borrowing. Equilibrium requires the absence of any such arbitrage opportunities. Therefore, in an equilibrium we must have $\rho(t) \leq r(t)$. Furthermore, if $\rho(t) < r(t)$, it is clear from the above budget constraint that an individual will want to store a zero amount. In solving the agent's optimum problem, we shall require that $\rho(t) \leq r(t)$.

To solve the agent's problem, we form the Lagrangian

(7.5)
$$J = u_t^h[c_t^h(t), c_t^h(t+1)] + \mu_t^h(t)[w_t^h(t) - \tau_t^h(t) - c_t^h(t) \\
- l_t^h(t) - k_t^h(t)] + \mu_t^h(t+1)[w_t^h(t+1) - \tau_t^h(t+1) \\
+ [1 + r(t)]l_t^h(t) + [1 + p(t)]k_t^h(t) - c_t^h(t+1)],$$

which is to be maximized subject to $c_t^h(t) \geq 0$, $c_t^h(t+1) \geq 0$, $k_t^h(t) \geq 0$, and where $\mu_t^h(t)$, $\mu_t^h(t+1)$ are nonnegative multipliers. (For convenience, we now drop the t subscript from u_t^h.) The first-order necessary conditions associated with maximizing (7.5) are

(7.6a) $\quad c_t^h(t)$: $u_1^h[c_t^h(t), c_t^h(t+1)] - \mu_t^h(t) \leq 0,\quad = 0\quad$ if $c_t^h(t) > 0$

(7.6b) $\quad c_t^h(t+1)$: $u_2^h[c_t^h(t), c_t^h(t+1)] - \mu_t^h(t+1) \leq 0,$
$\qquad\qquad = 0\quad$ if $c_t^h(t+1) > 0$

(7.6c) $\quad l_t^h(t)$: $-\mu_t^h(t) + [1 + r(t)]\mu_t^h(t+1) = 0$

(7.6d) $\quad k_t^h(t)$: $-\mu_t^h(t) + [1 + p(t)]\mu_t^h(t+1) \leq 0,\quad = 0\quad$ if $k_t^h(t) > 0$.

The assumptions that we made about preferences imply that $c_t^h(t) > 0$, $c_t^h(t+1) > 0$. Conditions (7.6a)–(7.6c) can be stated as

$$\frac{u_2[c_t^h(t), c_t^h(t+1)]}{u_1[c_t^h(t), c_t^h(t+1)]} = \frac{1}{1 + r(t)},$$

which expresses tangency between the slope of the indifference curve $-u_2/u_1$ in the $[c_t^h(t+1), c_t^h(t)]$ plane and the slope of the budget line $-1/[1 + r(t)]$. The situation is as depicted in Figure 7.4 where we have assumed that $r(t) > p(t)$.

We note that, if $1 + r(t) < 1 + p(t)$, then every agent h has an incentive to store an indefinitely large amount and to finance it by borrowing an indefinitely large amount. This observation permits us to complete our description of the supply of loans. Write the constraint (7.3) at equality as

(7.7) $\quad l_t^h(t) = w_t^h(t) - \tau_t^h(t) - c_t^h(t) - k_t^h(t).$

For $r(t) > p(t)$, we have from (7.6c) and (7.6d) that $k_t^h(t) = 0$. Therefore, for $r(t) > p(t)$, $l_t^h(t)$ is a continuous function of the arguments $[1 + r(t)$, $w_t^h(t) - \tau_t^h(t), w_t^h(t+1) - \tau_t^h(t+1)]$ (because excess demand functions are continuous functions; see Varian 1978). By the normal goods assumption, this function is increasing in $w_t^h(t) - \tau_t^h(t)$ and decreasing in $w_t^h(t+1) - \tau_t^h(t+1)$. Under assumption (5), the function is also increasing in $[1 + r(t)]$. For $r(t) < p(t)$, the supply of loans becomes an indefinitely large negative number. For $r(t) = p(t)$, the supply of loans is indeterminate. Let $v^h(t)$ be the

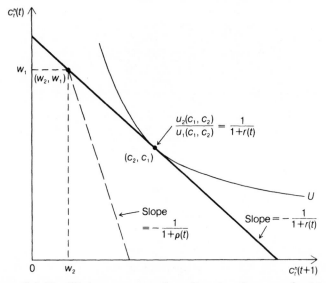

Figure 7.4. Equilibrium consumption allocation for agent h with no storage. The after-tax endowment of agent h, $[w_t^h(t+1) - \tau_t^h(t+1),$ $w_t^h(t) - \tau_t^h(t)] = (w_2, w_1)$. The dashed line with slope $-1/[1 + \rho(t)]$ is the consumption possibility frontier when agent h can store goods at the rate of return $[1 + \rho(t)]$. The solid line with slope $-1/[1 + r(t)] > -1/$ $[1 + \rho(t)]$ is the consumption possibility frontier when h can lend or borrow at the rate $1 + r(t) > 1 + \rho(t)$.

amount of saving that would be done if $\rho(t) = r(t)$, as depicted in Figure 7.6. Then the supply of loans can be any number less than or equal to $v^h(t)$, equaling $v^h(t)$ if $k_t^h(t) = 0$ and equaling $v^h(t) - k_t^h(t)$ if $k_t^h(t) > 0$ units are stored. Thus the individual's supply function for loans is as depicted in Figure 7.5 and Figure 7.7. Figure 7.5 depicts the excess supply curve of loans for someone who is relatively well endowed in the first period of life (a "lender"), while Figure 7.7 depicts the excess supply curve of loans for someone who is relatively well endowed in the second period of life (a "borrower"). We describe the excess supply curve [really a "correspondence," because it is multiple valued at $\rho(t) = r(t)$] by

(7.8) $l_t^h(t) = f_t^h[r(t), w_t^h(t) - \tau_t^h(t), w_t^h(t+1) - \tau_t^h(t+1)],$

where f is continuous for $r(t) > \rho(t)$ by the property of continuity of demand functions (for example, Varian 1978) and increasing in $r(t)$, under property (5). Under the normal goods assumption (4), f_t^h is increasing in $w_t^h(t) - \tau_t^h(t)$ and decreasing in $w_t^h(t+1) - \tau_t^h(t+1)$, so that increases in the

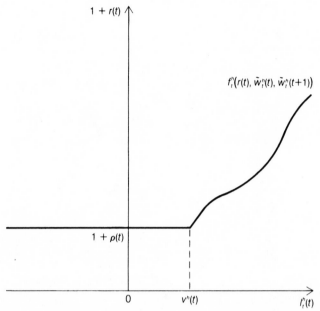

Figure 7.5. Supply of loans for an agent relatively well endowed in the first period of life. Here $v^h(t) = \tilde{w}_t^h(t) - c_t^h(t) > 0$, where $c_t^h(t)$ is the optimal first-period consumption when $r(t) = \rho(t)$. For $r(t) < \rho(t)$, $f_t^h(\cdot) = -\infty$.

first-period endowment increase the supply of loans, ceteris paribus, whereas increases in the second-period endowment decrease the supply of loans.

The government budget constraint (7.1), the national income identity (7.2), and the budget constraints (7.3) and (7.4) can be rearranged to yield

$$L^g(t) + \sum_h l_t^h(t) = [1 + r(t-1)][L^g(t-1) + \sum_h l_{t-1}^h(t-1)],$$

$$t \geq 1.$$

In addition, we have the initial condition $L^g(0) = \sum_h l_0^h(0) = 0$. The conditions $L^g(0) = 0$ and $\sum_h l_0^h(0) = 0$ amount to starting out the system at time 1 with zero maturing government debt and zero maturing private debt. The solution of the above difference equation with this initial condition is the loan market equilibrium condition

(7.9) $$L^g(t) + \sum_h l_t^h(t) = 0, \qquad t = 0, \ldots, T+1.$$

The variables of the model include the population size, endowment pat-

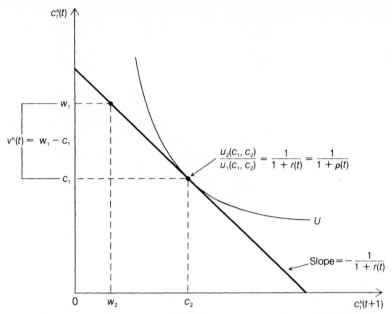

Figure 7.6. Equilibrium consumption when $r(t) = \rho(t)$. The after-tax endowment of agent h, $[\tilde{w}_t^h(t+1), \tilde{w}_t^h(t)] = (w_2, w_1)$. When $r(t) = \rho(t)$, agent h chooses $[c_t^h(t+1), c_t^h(t)] = (c_2, c_1)$. First-period savings is $v^h(t) = w_1 - c_1$.

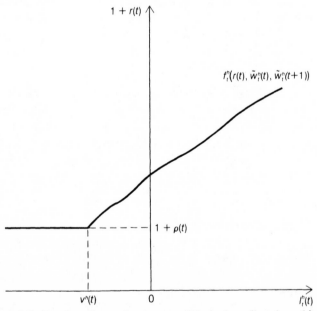

Figure 7.7. Supply of loans for an agent relatively well endowed in the second period of life. Here $v^h(t) = \tilde{w}_t^h(t) - c_t^h(t) < 0$. For $r(t) < \rho(t)$, $f_t^h(\cdot) = -\infty$.

terns, lump-sum tax rates, consumption allocations, private lending amounts, rates of storage, net physical rates of return, interest rates, rates of government purchases, and government borrowing sequences

$$\{N(t), w_0^h(1), w_t^h(t), w_t^h(t+1), \tau_0^h(1), \tau_t^h(t), \tau_t^h(t+1), c_0^h(1),$$
$$c_t^h(t), c_t^h(t+1), l_t^h(t), k_t^h(t), p(t), r(t), G(t), L^g(t)\},$$

where h runs from 1 to $N(t)$ and where t runs from 1 to T or to $(T + 1)$, as indicated above. We shall adopt different partitions of these variables into sets of endogenous and exogenous variables, depending on the example under study. In particular, the sequences of government expenditures, lump-sum tax rates, and government borrowing will usually contain some exogenous and some endogenous variables, depending on the example. Population $N(t)$ and endowment patterns $w_t^h(s)$, however, will always be treated as exogenous in this book. We now define an equilibrium.

DEFINITION. *An equilibrium is a horizon T satisfying $0 < T \le \infty$ and a collection of sequences*

$$\{N(t), w_0^h(1), w_t^h(t), w_t^h(t+1), \tau_0^h(1), \tau_t^h(t), \tau_t^h(t+1),$$
$$c_0^h(1), c_t^h(t), c_t^h(t+1), l_t^h(t), k_t^h(t), p(t), r(t), G(t), L^g(t)\}$$

such that

(i) *Given $\{r(t)\}_{t=1}^T$ and $\{p(t)\}_{t=1}^T$, the consumption allocation $\{c_t^h(t),$ $c_t^h(t+1)\}_{t=1}^T$, lending amounts $\{l_t^h(t)\}_{t=1}^T$, and storage rates $\{k_t^h(t)\}_{t=1}^T$ solve agent h's problem of maximizing $u_t^h[c_t^h(t), c_t^h(t+1)]$ subject to (7.3) and (7.4).*

(ii) *The government budget constraint (7.1) is satisfied for $t = 1, \ldots,$ $T + 1$, with $L^g(0) = 0$.*

(iii) *The loan market clears, that is, (7.9) holds for $t = 1, \ldots, T + 1$.*

This definition is equivalent to the following more compact one.

ALTERNATIVE DEFINITION. *An equilibrium is a horizon T satisfying $0 < T \le \infty$ and a set of sequences that satisfy*

(7.10) $$G(t) + L^g(t) = \sum_h \tau_t^h(t) + \sum_h \tau_{t-1}^h(t) + L^g(t-1)[1 + r(t-1)],$$
$$t = 1, \ldots, T + 1.$$

(7.11) $$l_t^h(t) = f_t^h[1 + r(t), w_t^h(t) - \tau_t^h(t), w_t^h(t+1) - \tau_t^h(t+1)],$$
$$t = 1, \ldots, T, \qquad h = 1, \ldots, N(t)$$

(7.12) $$\sum_h l_t^h(t) + L^g(t) = 0, \qquad t = 1, \ldots, T + 1$$

(7.13) $L^g(T+1) = 0$.

Condition (7.10) assures that the government's budget constraint is satisfied for all t. Condition (7.11) assures that private agents are choosing amounts of lending to maximize their utility subject to their constraints. Condition (7.12) assures that the loan market clears each period. To find an equilibrium, it is sufficient to solve Equations (7.10), (7.11), and (7.12) for sequences for $r(t)$, $L^g(t)$, $l^h_t(t)$, $\tau^h_0(1)$, $\tau^h_t(t)$, $\tau^h_t(t+1)$, starting from the initial condition $L^g(0) = 0$.

As an example, consider an economy in which $T = +\infty$, $\rho(t) = -1$ for all $t \geq 1$. Because $\rho(t) = -1$, we must have $k^h_t(t) = 0$ in equilibrium. We assume that preferences are given by $u^h_t[c^h_t(t), c^h_t(t+1)] = \ln c^h_t(t) + \ln c^h_t(t+1)$. We suppose that $N(t) = N_1 + N_2$ for all $t \geq 1$. For each $t \geq 1$, there are N_1 agents ("lenders"), each with endowment pattern $[w^h_t(t), w^h_t(t+1)] = (\alpha, 0)$, where $\alpha > 0$. There are N_2 agents ("borrowers"), each with endowment pattern $[w^h_t(t), w^h_t(t+1)] = (0, \beta)$, $\beta > 0$. We set $G(t) = 0$ for all $t \geq 1$. For taxes, we guess that one solution will be $[\tau^h_t(t), \tau^h_t(t+1)] = (0, 0)$ for all h and all $t \geq 1$. We restrict $\tau^h_0(1)$ to be nonpositive. The government budget constraint (7.1) with these specifications for taxes and expenditures becomes

(7.14) $L^g(1) = \sum_h \tau^h_0(1) \leq 0$

(7.15) $L^g(t) = [1 + r(t-1)]L^g(t-1), \quad t \geq 2$.

With the preceding specification of endowments, taxes, and preferences, the loan supply functions of our two types of agents become $\alpha/2$ for the N_1 lenders, and $-\beta/\{2[1 + r(t)]\}$ for the N_2 borrowers. The loan market equilibrium condition (7.12) then becomes

(7.16) $N_1 \dfrac{\alpha}{2} - N_2 \dfrac{\beta}{2[1 + r(t)]} + L^g(t) = 0, \quad r(t) > -1$

or $1 + r(t) = \dfrac{N_2 \beta}{N_1 \alpha + 2L^g(t)}, \quad t \geq 1$.

An equilibrium is a nonpositive setting for $\tau^h_0(1)$ and sequences for $L^g(t)$, $1 + r(t)$ that satisfy (7.14), (7.15), and (7.16).

One solution of (7.14), (7.15), and (7.16) is given by $\tau^h_0(1) = 0$ for all h, $L^g(t) = 0$ for all t, and

$$1 + r(t) = \frac{N_2 \beta}{N_1 \alpha}.$$

If $N_2 \beta / N_1 \alpha \geq 1$, this is the unique solution, as we shall soon show. This equilibrium is just a sequence of two-period consumption loan economies of the kind analyzed by Irving Fisher ([1907]1930). There are no interactions or reallocations across different generations, only trades between borrowers and lenders of the same generation.

When $N_2\beta/N_1\alpha < 1$, there are other solutions of (7.14), (7.15), and (7.16). For one additional solution, set $r(t) = 0$ for all $t \geq 1$ in (7.16), implying that

$$L^g(t) = \frac{N_2\beta}{2} - \frac{N_1\alpha}{2} < 0, \qquad t \geq 1,$$

where the inequality occurs because $N_2\beta/N_1\alpha < 1$. Determine a set of transfers $\tau_0^h(1)$ to the members of the old generation that satisfies (7.14) with $L^g(1) = (N_2\beta - N_1\alpha)/2 < 0$. This is a stationary equilibrium with $L^g(t)$ and $1 + r(t)$ unchanging for $t \geq 1$. In this equilibrium, goods are being reallocated across generations, as the young of generation $(t + 1)$ accept government debt $L^g(t)$ that is passed to them by the old of generation t. This equilibrium is not simply a sequence of Irving Fisher's two-period equilibria.

Evidently, when $N_2\beta/N_1\alpha < 1$, there are additional nonstationary equilibria that are associated with any initial interest rate $[1 + r(t)] \in (N_2\beta/N_1\alpha, 1)$. These equilibria are constructed as follows. Select $[1 + r(1)] \in (N_2\beta/N_1\alpha, 1)$. Solve (7.16) for $L^g(1) < 0$, and (7.14) for a set of transfers to the initial old that support this amount of public borrowing. Then solve (7.15) for $L^g(2)$, where $1 + r(1) < 1$ implies that $0 > L^g(2) > L^g(1)$. Then solve (7.16) for $1 + r(2)$, where $L^g(2) > L^g(1)$ implies that $1 + r(2) < 1 + r(1)$. If we continue in this way, one generates sequences $1 + r(t)$, $L^g(t)$, each of which is declining monotonically in absolute value.

It was asserted above that, when $N_2\beta/N_1\alpha \geq 1$, there is a unique equilibrium with $\tau_0^h(1) \leq 0$, the one associated with $L^g(t) = 0$, $1 + r(t) = N_2\beta/N_1\alpha$. To show this point, note that, when $N_2\beta/N_1\alpha \geq 1$, saying that $L^g(1) < 0$ implies a sequence $1 + r(t) > 1 + r(t - 1) > \ldots > 1 + r(1) > 1$, and $L^g(t) < L^g(t - 1) < \ldots < L^g(1) < 0$. It follows that eventually $L^g(t)$ will exceed $N_1\alpha$ in absolute value. At that point, (7.16) cannot be satisfied by any positive $1 + r(t)$.[1] Therefore, when $N_2\beta/N_1\alpha \geq 1$, there can be no equilibrium with $L^g(1) < 0$.

---

1. The government is caught in a vicious circle in which, at time t, because $1 + r(t) > 1$, it must promise to pay more next period $\{L^g(t)[1 + r(t)]\}$ than it owes this period $[L^g(t)]$. This additional government borrowing causes interest rates to rise over time, however, which in turn requires more borrowing. The process cannot continue indefinitely, because if it did, government borrowing would be growing without bound. Such growth is not feasible, because there is an upper bound of $N_1\alpha/2$ on the willingness of young people at t to lend to the government. Sargent and Wallace (1981) analyze some of the dynamic implications of this vicious circle.

Eventually, we shall characterize the circumstance under which there exist multiple equilibria. We postpone doing so until we have acquired a better understanding of the economic issues involved in interpreting a multiplicity of equilibria.

7.2 The Ricardian Doctrine about Taxes and Government Debt Again

We consider three example economies that will give us practice in computing equilibria. The examples will also provide a vehicle for studying aspects of the Ricardian doctrine.

EXAMPLE 7.1. Set $N(t) = N$ for all t; $[w_t^h(t), w_t^h(t + 1)] = (y - \epsilon, \epsilon)$ for all h and all $t = 1, \ldots, T$, where $0 < \epsilon < y/2$; $w_0^h(1) = w_0$ for all h; $\rho(t) = -1$ for $t = 1, \ldots, T$; $T < +\infty$; $G(t) = 0$ for $t = 1, \ldots, T + 1$; $\tau_t^h(s) = 0$ for all t, s, h. Finally, we set $u_t^h[c_t^h(t), c_t^h(t + 1)] = \ln c_t^h(t) + \ln c_t^h(t + 1)$ for all h and $t = 1, \ldots, T$.

For this specification of preferences, the saving function can be computed to be

$$w_t^h(t) - \tau_t^h(t) - c_t^h(t)$$
$$= \frac{w_t^h(t) - \tau_t^h(t)}{2} - \frac{w_t^h(t + 1) - \tau_t^h(t + 1)}{2[1 + r(t)]}, \qquad \text{for } r(t) > -1.$$

Therefore, for our example, we have

$$(7.17) \qquad l_t^h(t) = \frac{y - \epsilon}{2} - \frac{\epsilon}{2[1 + r(t)]}, \qquad \text{for } r(t) > -1.$$

Because we have $G(t) = 0$ for $t = 1, \ldots, T + 1$, and $\tau_t^h(s) = 0$ for all h, t, s, we can set $L^g(t) = 0$ for all t. The loan market equilibrium condition (7.12), together with (7.17), then implies that $r(t) + 1 = \epsilon/(y - \epsilon)$ for $t = 1, 2, \ldots, T$. The equilibrium consumption allocation is thus the autarkic one

$$c_t^h(t) = y - \epsilon, \qquad c_t^h(t + 1) = \epsilon, \qquad c_0^h(1) = w_0.$$

It is instructive to compare the present example to the example in Section 7.1. The present example contains only "lenders," each of whom has identical endowments and preferences. There are no "borrowers" as there were in the example of Section 7.1. The economy has a low interest rate for this reason.

EXAMPLE 7.2. As our second example, we take an economy identical to the preceding one, except that we set $G(1) = N[(y/2) - \epsilon]$, $G(t) = 0$, $t = 2, \ldots, T + 1$. We also guess that a tax scheme that will work is $\tau_T^h(T) = [(y/2) - \epsilon]$ for all h, with all other taxes being zero. The government thus purchases goods at time 1, borrows continuously during periods 1, 2, ..., T, and eventually repays its loans at time T with taxes imposed on members of the last generation when they are young. From the preceding calculations and the assumed structure of taxes, we see that the supply functions of loans are

$$l_t^h(t) = \frac{y - \epsilon}{2} - \frac{\epsilon}{2[1 + r(t)]}, \qquad r(t) > -1$$
$$t = 1, \ldots, T - 1.$$

$$l_T^h(T) = y/4 - \frac{\epsilon}{2[1 + r(T)]}, \qquad r(T) > -1.$$

With these supply functions, equilibrium is characterized by

$$N[(y/2) - \epsilon] + L^g(1) = 0 \quad \text{Equation (7.1) for } t = 1]$$
$$L^g(t) = [1 + r(t - 1)]L^g(t - 1), \quad [\text{Equation (7.1) for } t = 2,$$
$$3, \ldots, T - 1]$$

(7.18)
$$L^g(T) = [1 + r(T - 1)]L^g(T - 1) + N[(y/2) - \epsilon] \quad [\text{Equation (7.1)}$$
$$\text{for } t = T]$$

$$L^g(t) + \sum_h l_t^h(t) = 0, \qquad t = 1, \ldots, T + 1.$$

A solution of these equations is given by $r(t) = 0$, $t = 1, \ldots, T - 1$; $1 + r(T) = 2\epsilon/y$; $L^g(t) = -N[(y/2) - \epsilon]$ for $t = 1, \ldots, T - 1$; $L^g(T) = 0$; $l_T^h(T) = 0$.

Examples 7.1 and 7.2 are depicted in Figures 7.8 and 7.9. Figure 7.8 shows the time and generation structure of the endowments and the consumption allocations of the autarkic equilibrium of Example 7.1. Figure 7.9 shows the consumption allocation of the Example 7.2 equilibrium. This allocation is achieved, via the intermediation of government borrowing and repayment, by having each member of generation one hand over $[(y/2) - \epsilon]$ units of time 1 good to the government and then each member h of generation t for $1 \leq t \leq T$ hand over $[(y/2) - \epsilon]$ units of time t good to the member of generation $(t - 1)$ with the same h index. The government acts as an intermediary in this process by rolling over its debt. Notice that, relative to the Example 7.1 equilibrium, each member of each generation t for $t = 1, \ldots, T - 1$ is better off in the Example 7.2 equilibrium, because

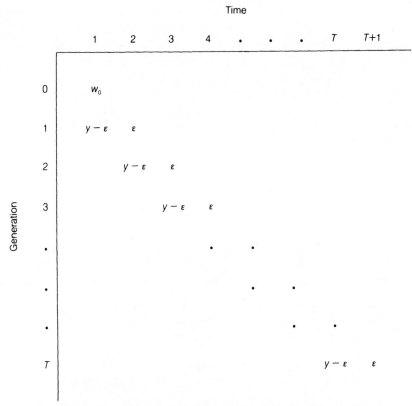

Figure 7.8. Equilibrium consumption allocation for Example 7.1. In this autarkic economy, $c_0^h(1) = w_0^h(1) = w_0$ and $[c_t^h(t), c_t^h(t+1)] = [w_t^h(t), w_t^h(t+1)] = (y - \epsilon, \epsilon)$ for all h and all $t = 1, 2, \ldots, T$.

$[c_t^h(t), c_t^h(t+1)] = (y/2, y/2)$ is preferred to the allocation $(y - \epsilon, \epsilon)$. Only the members of generation T are worse off in Example 7.2, because they consume $(y/2, \epsilon)$ instead of $(y - \epsilon, \epsilon)$. The government extracts some resources from the Example 7.2 economy but not from the Example 7.1 economy.

EXAMPLE 7.3. The third example is identical to the second except that we now set $\tau_T^h(T) = 0$ for all h and instead set $\tau_{T-j}^h(T-j) = y/2 - \epsilon$ for some j satisfying $1 < j < T - 1$, retaining all other tax rates at zero. Thus we tax only members of generation $(T - j)$ and pay off the government debt at that time. The equilibrium of this economy is directly calculated from the counterparts of (7.17) to be $r(t) = 0$, $t = 0, \ldots, T - j - 1$; $1 + r(T - j) = 2\epsilon/y$; $r(t) + 1 = \epsilon/(y - \epsilon)$, $t = T - j + 1, \ldots, T$; $L^g(t) = -N(y/2 - \epsilon)$, $t = 1, \ldots, T - j - 1$; $L^g(t) = 0$, $t = T - j, \ldots, T + 1$. The equilibrium

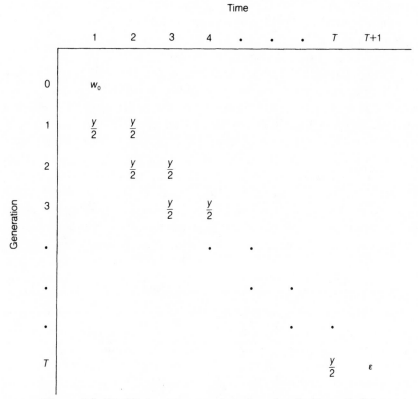

Figure 7.9. Equilibrium consumption allocation for Example 7.2.

consumption allocations are $c_0^h(1) = w_0^h(1)$, $[c_t^h(t), c_t^h(t + 1)] = (y/2, y/2)$ for $t = 1, \ldots, T - j - 1$; $[c_{T-j}^h(T - j), c_{T-j}^h(T - j + 1)] = (y/2, \epsilon)$, $[c_t^h(t), c_t^h(t + 1)] = (y - \epsilon, \epsilon)$, $t = T - j + 1, \ldots, T$. We invite the reader to put the Example 7.3 consumption allocations on a graph like that shown in Figure 7.9.

A comparison of Examples 7.2 and 7.3 reveals a couple of important things. First, the only difference is the choice of the taxing and government borrowing strategy that is used to finance identical paths of government purchases $G(t)$. The equilibrium consumption allocations and the interest rates, however, are different across the two examples. Thus for this economy, the Ricardian doctrine about the equivalence of government borrowing and taxing as ways of financing expenditures fails to hold. The fundamental reason is that the government lives longer than the individual agents and that the choice of the timing of taxes affects the incidence of their burden and so alters the distribution of wealth across generations. Such changes in distribution, then, in general affect the time pattern of interest rates.

Second, although the members of generation T are better off under the Example 7.3 equilibrium, those of generations $T - j, \ldots, T - 1$ are better off under the Example 7.2 equilibrium. Under a social welfare function that weights all generations equally, the Example 7.2 equilibrium is the better one. The generation that pays the taxes is equally well off in each economy, whereas the generations that are present before the government debt is repaid are better off because government debt, being available, provides them with a vehicle for smoothing their consumption streams over time. Notice that, without some government intervention, private loan markets are not able to provide such a facility in this economy (recall the Example 7.1 equilibrium). The Example 7.2 and 7.3 economies suggest a case for issuing government debt and postponing its repayment until the last possible date. Notice that there is no need for the government to make any purchases of goods at $t = 1$. Instead, it could issue the debt at $t = 1$ and simply hand over the proceeds to the old people in the form of transfers to be achieved by setting $\tau_0^h(1) = -y/2 + \epsilon$.

Now consider an economy in which $T = +\infty$, and imagine counterparts to our economies of Examples 7.1, 7.2, and 7.3. Suppose again that $G(1) = N[(y/2) - \epsilon]$ and $G(t) = 0$ for $t > 1$. The preceding argument suggests that there is a welfare reason to attempt to refinance the government debt indefinitely, that is, to attempt never to pay it off. Evidently when $T = +\infty$, an equilibrium exists in which the debt is never repaid, taxes never being levied to repay it. Retaining the specification of preferences in our example, the loan market equilibrium condition becomes

$$(7.19) \qquad N[(y/2) - \epsilon] = -L^g(t), \qquad t = 1, 2, \ldots,$$

whereas the government budget constraint becomes

$$(7.20) \qquad L^g(t) = [1 + r(t - 1)]L^g(t - 1), \qquad t = 2, 3, \ldots,$$

with initial condition $L^g(1) = -N[(y/2) - \epsilon]$. A solution of (7.19) and (7.20) is given by the interest rate sequence $r(t) = 0$ and by government borrowing of $-L^g(t) = N(y/2 - \epsilon)$ for all $t \geq 1$. This is the counterpart to the Example 7.2 equilibrium for the case in which $T = +\infty$. The consumption allocations are given by $c_0^h(1) = w_0^h(1)$ and $[c_t^h(t), c_t^h(t + 1)] = (y/2, y/2)$ for all $t \geq 1$. When $T = +\infty$, the allocation associated with the Example 7.2 equilibrium evidently Pareto dominates the allocation that is associated with the autarkic equilibrium of Example 7.1.

It is useful at this point to formulate a present-value version of the government budget constraint. Define total lump-sum taxes collected at time t as

(7.21) $\quad \tau(t) = \sum_h \tau^h_{t-1}(t) + \sum_h \tau^h_t(t).$

Recursions on the government budget constraint (7.1) imply that

(7.22) $\quad G(1) + [1 + r(1)]^{-1}G(2) + \ldots + \prod_{t=1}^{T}[1 + r(t)]^{-1}G(T+1)$

$$= \tau(1) + [1 + r(1)]^{-1}\tau(2) + \ldots + \prod_{t=1}^{T}[1 + r(t)]^{-1}\tau(T+1)$$

$$+ \prod_{t=1}^{T}[1 + r(t)]^{-1}[-L^g(T+1)].$$

In the economy with finite T, the loan market equilibrium condition for $t = T + 1$ implies that $L^g(T+1) = 0$. The reason is that $\Sigma_h l^h_{T+1}(T+1) = 0$, because there are no young people alive in period $(T + 1)$, only old ones, who do not save. Therefore, for the finite T economy, $L^g(T+1) = 0$ and (7.22) imply that the present value of government expenditures equals the present value of total tax collections.

For $1 \le s \le T$, $L^g(T+1) = 0$ in (7.22) and (7.1) imply that

(7.23) $\quad -L^g(s) = [1 + r(s)]^{-1}[\tau(s+1) - G(s+1)]$

$$+ \ldots + \prod_{j=0}^{T-s}[1 + r(s+j)]^{-1}[\tau(T+1) - G(T+1)],$$

which states that the value of government bonds outstanding at time s equals the present value of prospective net-of-interest government surpluses.

In the case that $T = +\infty$, Equation (7.22) becomes

(7.24) $\quad G(1) + \sum_{t=2}^{\infty} \prod_{s=1}^{t-1}[1 + r(s)]^{-1}G(t)$

$$= \tau(1) + \sum_{t=2}^{\infty} \prod_{s=1}^{t-1}[1 + r(s)]^{-1}\tau(t)$$

$$+ \lim_{T \to \infty} \prod_{s=1}^{T}[1 + r(s)]^{-1}[-L^g(T+1)].$$

When $T = +\infty$, as we have seen, there may exist equilibria in which

$$\lim_{T \to \infty} \prod_{s=1}^{T}[1 + r(s)]^{-1}[-L^g(T+1)] > 0.$$

In this case, for $s \ge 1$, the value of government debt obeys

(7.25) $$-L^g(s) = \sum_{j=1}^{\infty} \prod_{t=s}^{s+j-1} [1 + r(t)]^{-1}[\tau(s+j) - G(s+j)]$$

$$+ \lim_{T \to \infty} \prod_{v=s}^{T} [1 + r(v)]^{-1}[-L^g(T+1)].$$

Expression (7.24) indicates that, in an equilibrium for which

$$\lim_{T \to \infty} \prod_{s=1}^{T} [1 + r(s)]^{-1}[-L^g(T+1)] > 0,$$

the present value of government expenditures exceeds the present value of tax collections. In this case, the value of government debt at time s, given by (7.25), exceeds the present value of future government surpluses. In this case, government debt is said partly to consist of "net wealth," that is, wealth created over and above that which represents a claim on the future net revenues of the government. In an economy in which (7.25) holds, with

$$\lim_{T \to \infty} \prod_{s=1}^{T} [1 + r(s)]^{-1}[-L^g(T+1)] > 0,$$

government bonds need not be fully "backed" by prospective taxes in order to be valued by the market.

We have already encountered two examples of economies for which equilibria exist in which $\lim_{T \to \infty} \Pi_{s=1}^{T} [1 + r(s)]^{-1}[-L^g(T+1)] > 0$. These examples share the properties that $r(s) = 0$ for all s in this equilibrium and that there exist other equilibria in which $r(s) < 0$ for all s and in which $L^g(t)$ is either always zero or approaches zero as t grows large. Possibly government debt can be valued without full backing in "low-interest-rate economies." We shall see later that this characterization of the situation is essentially correct.

7.3 A Ricardian Proposition

The preceding section indicates that in one sense a Ricardian proposition fails to characterize the overlapping-generations model. Even though we held the sequence of government purchases $G(t)$ fixed, alterations in the paths of $\{\tau_t^h(t), \tau_{t-1}^h(t), L^g(t)\}$ altered the budget sets of some private agents. The paths of $\{\tau_t^h(t), \tau_t^h(t+1), L^g(t)\}$ were altered in a way that shifted the tax burden across generations and across people. By affecting some private agents' budget sets, these changed the equilibrium interest rate sequence and consumption allocation.

In the representative-agent model of Chapters 3, 4, and 5, variations in the stream of taxes over time were not permitted to alter the distribution of taxes across agents. The reasons were that the representative agents have a life span in common with one another and with the government and that all agents were sent an identical lump-sum tax bill each period, so that redistributions of taxes across agents were not permitted.

These observations suggest that a version of a Ricardian proposition can be stated for the overlapping-generations model. Such a proposition can be discovered by searching for an equivalence class of government tax and borrowing strategies that leave each agent's budget set unaltered at an initial equilibrium interest rate sequence. In order to state such a proposition, it is convenient to summarize the equilibrium conditions of the model by the following four equations.

(7.26)
$$\sum_h c_t^h(t) + \sum_h c_{t-1}^h(t) + G(t) + K(t)$$
$$= [1 + p(t-1)]K(t-1) + \sum_h w_{t-1}^h(t) + \sum_h w_t^h(t),$$
$$t \geq 1, \qquad K(0) \text{ given}$$

(7.27)
$$G(t) + L^g(t)$$
$$= \sum_h \tau_{t-1}^h(t) + \sum_h \tau_t^h(t) + [1 + r(t-1)]L^g(t-1),$$
$$L^g(0) = 0, \qquad t \geq 1$$

(7.28)
$$c_t^h(t) = g_t^h\{[w_t^h(t) - \tau_t^h(t)] + \frac{w_t^h(t+1) - \tau_t^h(t+1)}{1 + r(t)}, 1 + r(t)\}$$
$$\text{all } h, \text{ all } t \geq 1$$

(7.29)
$$[w_t^h(t) - \tau_t^h(t)] + \frac{w_t^h(t+1) - \tau_t^h(t+1)}{1 + r(t)}$$
$$= c_t^h(t) + \frac{c_t^h(t+1)}{1 + r(t)}, \qquad \text{all } h, \text{ all } t \geq 1.$$

In (7.26), $K(t) \equiv \sum_h k_t^h(t)$. Equation (7.26) is the "national income identity" or "goods market" equilibrium condition. Condition (7.27) is the government's budget constraint. Conditions (7.28) and (7.29) describe the optimal consumption decisions of private agents: condition (7.29) is private agents' budget constraint, whereas Equation (7.28) expresses first-period consumption as a function of the present value of after-tax endowments and the real rate of interest. The function g_t^h is agent h's demand function for first-period consumption.

An equilibrium can be defined as a set of sequences for

$$\{c_t^h(t), c_{t-1}^h(t), G(t), K(t), r(t), \rho(t), L^g(t), \tau_{t-1}^h(t), \tau_t^h(t)\}_{t=1}^{\infty}$$

that satisfy (7.26), (7.27), (7.28), and (7.29).

The following version of a Ricardian proposition holds for this model.

PROPOSITION 7.1. *Let there exist an initial equilibrium, called the macron-bearing equilibrium, given by*

$$\{\bar{c}_t^h(t), \bar{c}_{t-1}^h(t), \overline{G}(t), \overline{K}(t), \bar{r}(t), \bar{\rho}(t), \overline{L}^g(t), \bar{\tau}_{t-1}^h(t), \bar{\tau}_t^h(t)\}_{t=1}^{\infty}.$$

Then there exists another equilibrium, called the caret-bearing equilibrium, given by

$$\{\bar{c}_t^h(t), \bar{c}_{t-1}^h(t), \overline{G}(t), \overline{K}(t), \bar{r}(t), \bar{\rho}(t), \hat{L}^g(t), \hat{\tau}_{t-1}^h(t), \hat{\tau}_t^h(t)\}_{t=1}^{\infty},$$
$$\hat{\tau}_0^h(1) = \hat{\tau}_0^h(1),$$

for any sequences $\hat{L}^g(t)$, $\hat{\tau}_{t-1}^h(t)$, $\hat{\tau}_t^h(t)$ that satisfy the following conditions:

(7.30) $$\hat{\tau}_t^h(t) + \frac{\hat{\tau}_t^h(t+1)}{1 + \bar{r}(t)} = \bar{\tau}_t^h(t) + \frac{\bar{\tau}_t^h(t+1)}{1 + \bar{r}(t)}, \quad \text{all } h, \quad \text{all } t \ge 1$$

(7.31) $$\sum_h \hat{\tau}_{t-1}^h(t) + \sum_h \hat{\tau}_t^h(t) - \left(\sum_h \bar{\tau}_{t-1}^h(t) + \sum_h \bar{\tau}_t^h(t) \right)$$
$$= \{\hat{L}^g(t) - [1 + \bar{r}(t-1)]\hat{L}^g(t-1)\}$$
$$- \{\overline{L}^g(t) - [1 + \bar{r}(t-1)]\overline{L}^g(t)\}, \quad \text{all } t \ge 1, \quad \text{and}$$

$$\hat{L}^g(0) = \overline{L}^g(0) = 0.$$

To prove this proposition, we proceed as follows. Note that condition (7.30) implies that, at the original interest rate $\bar{r}(t)$, the present value of each private agent's after-tax endowment in the caret-bearing equilibrium is unaltered vis-à-vis the macron-bearing equilibrium. Therefore, (7.28) and (7.29) are satisfied with $\hat{c}_t^h(t) = \bar{c}_t^h(t)$, $\hat{c}_t^h(t+1) = \bar{c}_t^h(t+1)$ for all h and all $t \ge 1$. Evidently (7.26) is satisfied with these values for $\hat{c}_t^h(t), \hat{c}_t^h(t+1)$ for $t \ge 1$ and all h and with $\hat{c}_0^h(1) = \bar{c}_0^h(1)$ for all h. Finally, condition (7.31) implies that the government's budget constraint (7.27) is satisfied for all $t \ge 1$. This statement completes the proof.

Heuristically, condition (7.30) ensures that each private agent's budget set is the same in the two equilibria, whereas condition (7.31) ensures that the government's budget set is the same. Because no agent's budget set is affected, equilibrium interest rates and consumption allocations are unaffected.

It is useful to compare the structure of this theorem with that of the Ricardian proposition described for the Lucas tree model of Chapter 3. Each of these theorems can be viewed as follows. An initial equilibrium is considered. The allocation (that is, the consumption stream of the government and each private agent) associated with this equilibrium is taken as given. Then a class of several government tax and borrowing strategies that also supports this allocation as an equilibrium is discovered. Choices of tax and borrowing strategies within this equivalence class are said to be irrelevant.

In the next chapter, this logical structure will be used to study a variety of "neutrality" or "irrelevance" theorems.

7.4 Currency, Bonds, and Open-Market Operations

We now add unbacked government currency to the model in the following way. We set $T = +\infty$. At the beginning of time 1, there are in the hands of the government $H(1) > 0$ units of pieces of paper measured in dollars. (Later, with minor adjustments to our arguments, we will start the system off with all of the currency initially in the hands of the old people at $t = 1$.) Let the price level at time t be denoted $p(t)$, measured in dollars per time t good. The government issues new currency or retires old currency according to the modified version of the government budget constraint

$$(7.32) \qquad G(t) = \sum_h \tau_{t-1}^h(t) + \sum_h \tau_t^h(t) + [1 + r(t-1)]L^g(t-1) - L^g(t)$$
$$+ [H(t) - H(t-1)]/p(t), \qquad \text{for all } t \geq 1,$$

where $H(0) = 0$, $H(t) \geq 0$, and all terms are as defined previously. We permit the possibility that $p(t) = +\infty$ for all $t \geq 1$, in which case currency is not valued and (7.32) collapses to (7.1).

There are now four potential stores of value in this model: private loans, storage, government loans, and, if $p(t) < +\infty$ for all t, currency. Because there is no uncertainty in this model, if it is to be held, currency must yield the same real gross rate of return as do private and government one-period loans, namely $[1 + r(t)]$. Because the gross real rate of return on currency is $p(t)/p(t + 1)$, denominated in time $(t + 1)$ goods per unit of time t good, we have the arbitrage condition

$$(7.33) \qquad 1 + r(t) = p(t)/p(t + 1) \qquad \text{if } 0 < p(t) < +\infty, \qquad t \geq 1.$$

Substituting (7.33) into (7.32) and rearranging, we have

$$(7.34) \qquad G(t) = \sum_h \tau_{t-1}^h(t) + \sum_h \tau_t^h(t) + $$
$$[1 + r(t-1)] \cdot \left[L^g(t-1) - \frac{H(t-1)}{p(t-1)} \right] - \left[L^g(t) - \frac{H(t)}{p(t)} \right],$$
$$t \geq 1, \qquad H(0) = 0, \qquad L^g(0) = 0.$$

The equilibrium condition (7.9) or (7.12) must now be modified to take into account that there is an additional abode for savings, namely currency. Thus (7.12) needs to be modified to become

(7.35)
$$\sum_h f_t^h[1 + r(t), w_t^h(t) - \tau_t^h(t), w_t^h(t + 1) - \tau^h(t + 1)]$$

$$= - L^g(t) + \frac{H(t)}{p(t)},$$

which states that the excess supply of private loans equals total real government indebtedness at time t. We define an equilibrium with valued currency, or "currency equilibrium," in the following way.

DEFINITION. *A currency equilibrium is a set of sequences for government expenditures $\{G(t) \geq 0, \ t \geq 1\}$, tax rates $\{\tau_{t-1}^h(t), \ \tau_t^h(t), \ h = 1, \ldots, N(t), \ t \geq 1\}$, government loans $\{L^g(t), \ t \geq 1\}$, positive stocks of currency $\{H(t) > 0, \ t \geq 1\}$, finite positive price levels $\{0 < p(t) < +\infty, \ t \geq 1\}$, and interest rate sequences $\{r(t) > -1, \ t \geq 1\}$ that satisfy (7.33), (7.34), and (7.35).*

Notice that the definition builds in market clearing, private agents' optimization, and respect for the budget constraints of both the government and private agents.

We state the following proposition, which is a version of one that has been utilized by Bryant and Wallace (1979) and Wallace (1981a).

PROPOSITION 7.2. *Suppose that the model possesses an equilibrium in which currency has no value [$p(t) = +\infty$ for all t] and in which $- L^g(t) = - \overline{L}^g(t) > 0$ for all $t \geq 1$. Then the model also possesses a currency equilibrium.*

Proof. [Note that the equilibrium with $p(t) = +\infty$ is just the equilibrium of the model studied in Sections 7.1–7.2.] Let $\overline{r}(t)$ be the equilibrium interest rate sequence. A currency equilibrium is readily found by setting

$$\frac{H(t)}{p(t)} = - \overline{L}^g(t)$$

$$L^g(t) = 0.$$

[Notice that we have $H(t)/p(t) > 0$.] It is readily verified that (7.32) [or (7.34)], (7.33), and (7.35) are satisfied with $p(t)/p(t + 1) = \overline{r}(t) + 1$. The initial price level is determined from (7.35) with $r(1) = \overline{r}(1)$:

$$\sum_h f_1^h[1 + \overline{r}(1), w_1^h(1) - \tau_1^h(1), w_1^h(2) - \tau_1^h(2)] = \frac{H(1)}{p(1)},$$

given the initial stock of currency, $H(1)$, which is an arbitrary positive number. This statement completes the proof.

Notice that the last equation and Equation (7.33) imply a special and qualified version of the quantity theory, amounting to the statement that the initial price level $p(1)$ and all subsequent price levels $p(t)$, $t > 1$, are proportional to the initial stock of currency. We state another proposition that again stems from the work of Bryant and Wallace (1979) and Wallace (1981a).

PROPOSITION 7.3. *Under the assumptions of Proposition 7.2, there exist many currency equilibria. Let $\bar{p}(t)$ be the equilibrium price level for the Proposition 7.2 equilibrium. For a fixed value of $H(1) > 0$ and fixed settings for the fiscal policy variables $\{G(t), \tau_{t-1}^h(t), \tau_t^h(t), t \ge 1\}$, there exists a continuum of equilibria, all with a price-level sequence identical to the price-level sequence $\bar{p}(t)$ of the Proposition 7.2 equilibrium but with different values for $H(t)$, $t \ge 2$, and $L^g(t)$, $t \ge 2$. For $t \ge 2$, the values of $L^g(t)$ and $H(t)$ can be arbitrary as long as they obey $H(t) > 0$ and the constraint on government open-market operations, namely,*

$$(7.36) \qquad -L^g(t) + \frac{H(t)}{p(t)} = -\bar{L}^g(t).$$

Proof. The reader is asked to verify this proposition as an exercise.

This proposition is a version of Wallace's proposition that government open-market operations in currency and government bonds are irrelevant for the determination of rates of return, consumption allocations, or the price level. The proposition holds fiscal policy fixed. We shall encounter a generalized version of this proposition in the next chapter, where we study a stochastic model.

Consider a particular equilibrium among those described in Proposition 7.3, namely the one in which $L^g(t) = 0$. In this equilibrium, we have that real balances are given by

$$\frac{\bar{H}(t)}{\bar{p}(t)} = -\bar{L}^g(t) > 0,$$

where $\bar{L}^g(t)$ is the sequence of net government borrowing described in Proposition 7.2. Let $\hat{H}(t)$, $\hat{L}^g(t)$ be the stocks of nominal balances and real government loans, respectively, in another of the Proposition 7.3 equilibria with $\hat{L}^g(t) > 0$. Proposition (7.3) implies that in the caret-bearing equilibrium

$$(7.37) \qquad \frac{\hat{H}(t)}{\bar{p}(t)} = \frac{\bar{H}(t)}{\bar{p}(t)} + \hat{L}^g(t).$$

Because $\hat{L}^g(t) > 0$, it must be true that $\hat{H}(t) > \overline{H}(t)$. Equation (7.37) states that increases in the stock of currency accomplished through government open-market purchases of private loans have no effect on the equilibrium price level. This is a version of the "real bills" doctrine, which states that, if the government central bank increases the stock of currency by buying safe private loans (real bills), the price level will not rise.[2] The proposition depends on the equal rates of return on private loans and currency in the initial equilibrium. (For a discussion of how the proposition needs to be modified when the initial equilibrium is one with unequal rates of return on currency and private loans, see Sargent and Wallace 1982. Sargent and Wallace 1983 assert that the relevance of government open-market operations can be tested by checking whether there are arbitrage profits available to a central bank at initial equilibrium prices.)

In the equilibria described in Proposition 7.2 and 7.3 the net worth of the government is negative. This point is highlighted by Equation (7.37), in which the value of total liabilities of a central bank, $\hat{H}(t)/\overline{p}(t)$, exceeds the value of its assets, $\hat{L}^g(t)$, by an amount $\overline{H}(t)/\overline{p}(t)$. (See the balance sheet depicted below.)

Assets	*Liabilities*
Private loans held by bank, $\hat{L}^g(t)$	Real value of outstanding stock of currency, $\hat{H}(t)/\overline{p}(t)$
	Net worth, $-\overline{H}(t)/\overline{p}(t)$

The variations in the stock of currency envisioned in Proposition 7.3 are

---

2. The real bills doctrine originated with Adam Smith (1776, bk. 2, chap. 2) and was extensively discussed by John Stuart Mill (1848). Sargent and Wallace (1982) use an overlapping-generations model to study the real bills doctrine and to compare it with the quantity theory of money. Sargent and Wallace's model is one in which fluctuations in the demand and supply for private credit cause price-level fluctuations due to variations in the stock of private indebtedness that compete with currency. In their model, the sum of currency and inside indebtedness correlates perfectly with the price level. Sargent and Wallace describe a legal restriction representing a prohibition against private bank notes (that is, low-denomination intermediated private securities that compete with currency). The restriction separates the private credit market from the currency market and permits the government to stabilize the price level by simply stabilizing the stock of currency. Under this legal restriction, currency is dominated in rate of return by private securities, and government open-market operations in private securities affect equilibrium rates of return and the price-level sequence (that is, the "real bills" conclusions of Proposition 7.3 do not obtain). Open-market operations have these effects because they partly undo or partly strengthen the legal restriction. Sargent and Wallace describe the welfare effects of the legal restriction, which are ambiguous on the Pareto criterion because they shift utilities across agents. The legal restriction studied by Sargent and Wallace (1982) is a stylized version of aspects of Peel's Bank Act of 1844, which is discussed by Mill (1844).

fully "backed" by variations in the stock of privately issued claims held by the government. This backing prevents variation of the currency stock from having any price-level effects. Private agents in effect "see through" the central bank's balance sheet and realize that the increased stock of currency leaves unaltered the government's stream of net indebtedness at the initial equilibrium price-level sequence.

Variations in the stock of currency that are not fully backed in general have price-level consequences. To take a simple example, return to Proposition 7.2 and its proof. Note that there is a distinct initial price level $p(1)$ and a distinct price-level path $p(t)$ for every distinct value of the initial currency stock $H(1) > 0$. The initial price level is determined from $p(1) = H(1)/\Sigma_h$ $f_1^h[1 + \bar{r}(1), w_1^h(1) - \tau_1^h(1), w_1^h(2) - \tau_1^h(2)]$, whereas subsequent price levels are determined from $p(t)/p(t + 1) = 1 + \bar{r}(t)$. Evidently variations in $H(1)$ lead to proportional variations in $p(t)$ for all $t \geq 1$ and in $H(t)$, $t \geq 2$. Such variations in the initial currency stock are thus consistent with the price-level consequences associated with the quantity theory of money.

One message of these experiments is that, in the present model, the price-level consequences associated with changes in the stock of currency depend on how the alterations in the stock of currency are engineered. In determining price-level consequences, it is particularly important to study the changes in government-held assets (including prospective net tax receipts) that are associated with alternative paths of the currency stock. Section 7.8 will return to and expand upon this theme.[3]

7.5 Computing Equilibria

Let us now specialize the model in order to construct some examples for which equilibria can be computed and for which the senses in which multiple equilibria occur can be illustrated concretely. We assume that population evolves according to

(7.38) $N(t) = (1 + n)N(t - 1)$ for $t \geq 1$,

where n is a constant obeying $n > -1$ and $N(0) > 0$ is given. We further assume that taxes and endowments are stationary in the weak sense that the

---

3. In 1844, John Stuart Mill asserted: "The issues of a *Government* paper, even when not permanent, will raise prices; because Governments usually issue their paper in purchases for consumption. If issued to pay off a portion of the national debt, we believe they would have no effect." (Mill 1844, p. 589, as quoted in Friedman and Schwartz 1982, p. 30; Friedman and Schwartz take issue with the opinion expressed by Mill.) The assertion in Mill's second sentence can be interpreted in terms of Proposition 7.3. The assertion in the first sentence is also consistent with the predictions of the model of this chapter (see Section 7.10 on seignorage).

per capita aggregate savings function,

$$\frac{\sum_h f_t^h[1 + r(t), w_t^h(t) - \tau_t^h(t), w_t^h(t + 1) - \tau_t^h(t + 1)]}{N(t)},$$

is a time-invariant function of $[1 + r(t)]$. Denote the per capita aggregate saving function as $f[1 + r(t)]$. Let us invoke our optional assumption (5) on preferences, which is sufficient to imply that $f[(1 + r(t)]$ is monotonically increasing in $[1 + r(t)]$. Let us denote this condition as $f' > 0$.

Denote the per capita real government indebtedness at t as $h(t)$, and define it as

$$(7.39) \qquad h(t) = \frac{-L^g(t) + \dfrac{H(t)}{p(t)}}{N(t)}.$$

Denote the per capita government deficit at t, net of interest on the government debt, as $d(t)$, and define it as

$$(7.40) \qquad d(t) = \frac{G(t) - \sum_h \tau_{t-1}^h(t) - \sum_h \tau_t^h(t)}{N(t)}.$$

With definitions (7.39) and (7.40), the government budget constraint (7.34) can be expressed as

$$(7.41) \qquad h(t) = \frac{1 + r(t - 1)}{1 + n} h(t - 1) + d(t), \qquad t \geq 1,$$

subject to $h(0) = 0$. The loan market equilibrium condition becomes

$$(7.42) \qquad h(t) = f[1 + r(t)], \qquad t \geq 1.$$

Equations (7.41) and (7.42) form a system of difference equations that potentially determine the time path of $\{h(t), 1 + r(t); t \geq 1\}$, given an exogenously determined sequence for the government deficit $\{d(t); t \geq 1\}$. Initially think of setting $H(t)/p(t) = 0$ for all t, and consider per capita government debt $h(t)$ as consisting entirely of loans. Section 7.6 will reinterpret some of our results in terms of economies with currency.

We first study system (7.41)–(7.42) under the zero deficit path, $d(t) = 0$ for all $t \geq 2$. Because $h(0) = 0$, (7.41) implies that $h(1) = d(1)$. We begin by studying stationary solutions, seeking solutions of (7.41)–(7.42) that satisfy $h(t) = h(t - 1) = h$, $r(t) = r$ for all $t \geq 1$. Evidently one such solution is given by $r = n$ and $h = f(1 + n)$. Another stationary solution is given by

$h = 0$, $1 + r = f^{-1}(0)$. When $f(1 + n) < 0$, there does not exist a stationary equilibrium with positive government indebtedness, because we have assumed that $f'(1 + r) > 0$.

Whether $f(1 + n)$ is greater than or less than zero influences the possible behavior of nonstationary solutions. We have assumed that $f[1 + r(t)]$ is monotonically increasing in $[1 + r(t)]$. Without loss of generality, we may say that $f[1 + r(t)]$ is bounded from above as $[1 + r(t)]$ approaches $+\infty$. The after-tax per capita endowment $\Sigma_h[w_t^h(t) - \tau_t^h(t)]/N(t)$ is such a bound, one that would be attained only when the entire first-period endowment was saved by each agent. Continue to assume that $d(t) = 0$ for all $t \geq 2$. If $f(1 + n) < 0$, there exists no equilibrium with $h(1) > 0$, for if $h(1) > 0$, from the monotonicity of f, we have $1 + r(1) > 1 + n$, which by (7.41) implies that $h(2) > h(1)$. This statement in turn implies that $1 + r(2) > 1 + r(1)$, which via (7.41) implies that $h(3) > h(2)$. It follows that government borrowing $h(t)$ is growing without bound and would exceed per capita savings in finite time. Such a path is not feasible and therefore cannot be an equilibrium.

We can characterize the dynamics of the system in a single equation by first inverting (7.42) to obtain $1 + r(t) = f^{-1}[h(t)]$ and then substituting the result into (7.41) to obtain the difference equation

$$h(t) = \frac{f^{-1}[h(t-1)]}{1+n} h(t-1) + d(t), \qquad t \geq 2, \qquad h(1) = d(1).$$

To analyze this equation, we write it as

(7.43) $\qquad h(t) = \phi[h(t-1)] + d(t),$

where $\phi[h(t-1)] = f^{-1}[h(t-1)]h(t-1)/(1+n)$. We note that

(7.44) $\qquad \phi'[h(t-1)] = \dfrac{f^{-1}[h(t-1)]}{1+n} + \dfrac{h(t-1)}{1+n} f^{-1\prime}[h(t-1)] > 0$

$\qquad \phi''[h(t-1)] = \dfrac{2f^{-1\prime}[h(t-1)]}{1+n} + \dfrac{h(t-1)}{1+n} f^{-1\prime\prime}[h(t-1)].$

We shall temporarily assume that $\phi''[h(t-1)] > 0$. The condition that $f^{-1\prime\prime}[h(t-1)] > 0$ is sufficient to guarantee that $\phi''[h(t-1)] > 0$. We note that

(7.45) $\qquad \phi'(0) = \dfrac{f^{-1}(0)}{1+n}.$

In addition, $\phi[h(t-1)]$ will have an asymptote at the upper bound on per capita savings.

We have graphed $\phi[h(t-1)]$ for the case $f^{-1}(0)/(1+n) < 1$ in Figure 7.10. The graph is upward sloping and concave by (7.44) and by assumption. If we choose initial conditions for the system by setting $h(1) = d(1)$, the evolution of $h(t)$ for the deficit policy $\{d(t) = 0, t \geq 2\}$ can be found from the graph. There are two stationary points, where $\phi[h(t-1)]$ crosses the $45°$ line. One is at $h(t-1) = 0$, the other at $h(t-1) = h_\infty = f(1+n) > 0$. The graph indicates that the higher stationary point is unstable, whereas the lower one is stable.

For the case in which $f^{-1}(0)/(1+n) > 1$, $\phi[h(t+1)]$ is graphed in Figure 7.11. Once again there are two stationary points, one at zero and the other at $h_\infty = f(1+n)$. The lower stationary point is again the stable one, which is a reflection of the convexity of $\phi[h(t-1)]$.

That there are only two stationary points results from our having assumed that $\phi''[h(t-1)] > 0$ everywhere. If this assumption is abandoned, then

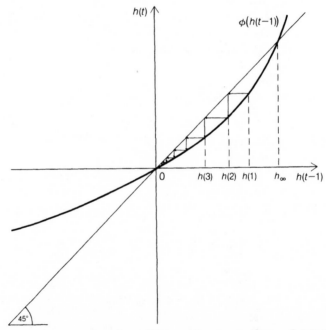

Figure 7.10. The function $\phi[h(t-1)]$ when $\phi'(0) = f^{-1}(0)/(1+n) < 1$. The function ϕ has two stationary points, $\phi(0)$ and $\phi(h_\infty)$. $\phi(0)$ is stable, and $\phi(h_\infty)$ is unstable. Thus when $h(1) \in [0, h_\infty)$, $h(t) \to 0$ as $t \to \infty$. If $h(1) \in (h_\infty, \infty)$, $h(t) \to \infty$ as $t \to \infty$, which is not feasible. The path of $h(t)$ converging to 0 is shown for $h(1) \in (0, h_\infty)$.

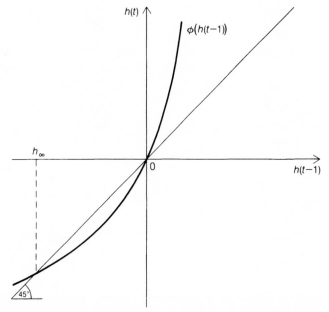

Figure 7.11. The function $\phi[h(t-1)]$ when $\phi'(0) = f^{-1}(0)/(1 + n) > 1$. The function ϕ has two stationary points, $\phi(0)$ and $\phi(h_\infty)$. Here $\phi(0)$ is unstable and $\phi(h_\infty)$ is stable. For any $h(1) > 0$, $h(t) \to \infty$ as $t \to \infty$; therefore, $h(1) > 0$ is not feasible.

multiple stationary points can emerge, as a $\phi[h(t-1)]$ can then be drawn with $\phi' > 0$ but with many crossings of the 45° line.

We now analyze the system when the government runs positive deficits each period. Consider an example in which the government sets $d(t) = d > 0$ for all $t \geq 2$. If $f^{-1}(0)/(1 + n) < 1$ and if d is set at a sufficiently low level, then the situation is as in Figure 7.12, which graphs $\phi[h(t-1)] + d$. There exist two stationary points that satisfy (7.41) and (7.42) with $h_\infty = h(t)$ for all t and $r_\infty = r(t)$ for all t, or

$$h_\infty \left(\frac{n - r_\infty}{1 + n} \right) = d$$

$$h = f(1 + r_\infty).$$

The lower stationary point for h is the stable one. As is evident from these equations and the graph, the stationary values of h and r depend on the value of d. This is another way to see that the Ricardian proposition does not hold for this model. Note that across economies, as d increases, the lower stationary values of h_∞ and r_∞ increase but the upper stationary values decrease. In

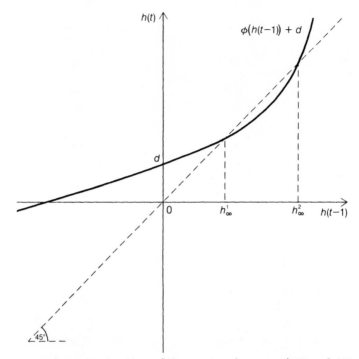

Figure 7.12. The function $\phi[h(t-1)] + d$ when $\phi'(0) = f^{-1}(0)/$ $(1 + n) < 1$. With $d > 0$ sufficiently low, there are two stationary points, $\phi(h_\infty^1)$ and $\phi(h_\infty^2)$. Whereas $\phi(h_\infty^1)$ is stable, $\phi(h_\infty^2)$ is unstable.

Section 7.9 below, we relate these findings to a Laffer curve that is associated with government seignorage.

Next note that if $f^{-1}(0)/(1 + n) > 1$, then it is not feasible to run a positive deficit forever. Also, even if $f^{-1}(0)/(1 + n) < 1$, it is not feasible to run too large a positive deficit forever. We ask the reader to verify these claims by studying appropriate versions of graphs of $\phi[h(t-1)] + d(t)$.

If the assumption that $\phi'' > 0$ is abandoned, it is possible for the slope of $\phi[h(t-1)]$ to change sign in a way that creates cyclical equilibria. Applying the results of Sonnenschein (1973), we are free to specify *any* continuous function $f[1 + r(t)]$ as the aggregate savings function and are assured that there is an admissible specification of the endowments and preferences $u_t^h[c_t^h(t), c_t^h(t + 1)]$ that generates this savings function. With such freedom to specify the savings function, one can produce $\phi[h(t-1)]$ functions that lead to complicated cyclical dynamics, which depend delicately on initial conditions. An example is given by the $\phi[h(t-1)]$ function depicted in Figure 7.13. With such a ϕ function, it is possible to have many equilibrium se-

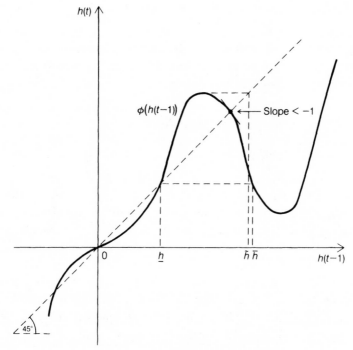

Figure 7.13. A $\phi[h(t-1)]$ function that gives rise to "chaotic dynamics." Here we have relaxed the assumption that $f' > 0$, which permits ϕ' to be negative. If the system starts at the initial condition $0 < h(0) < \underline{h}$, then $h(t)$ converges monotonically to 0. If $h(0) \in (\underline{h}, \bar{h})$, however, then the system oscillates forever, never converging but always remaining within the interval $(\underline{h}, \bar{h})$. Furthermore, associated with each initial condition $h(0) \in (\underline{h}, \bar{h})$ there is a distinct equilibrium path for $\{h(t)\}$. Each of these paths is a high-interest-rate equilibrium that is Pareto optimal.

quences for $h(t)$, $r(t)$, many of which are cyclical and involve $h(t)$ bounded away from zero for all $t \geq 1$. Furthermore, many of these cyclical equilibria can be "high interest rate" equilibria that satisfy the Balasko-Shell criterion for Pareto optimality. See Section 7.7 below.

Researchers such as Benhabib and Day (1982) and Grandmont (1985) have studied such cycles in the context of overlapping-generations models.[4]

---

4. In oral remarks at the 1984 summer meeting of the Econometric Society, Christopher Sims pointed out that the mechanism generating these cycles requires that the cycle have a duration that is long relative to the life span of the agents. He questioned the value of this mechanism as a tool for understanding observed business cycles, which are short relative to agents' life spans.

7.6 Interpretations as Currency Equilibria

We reinterpret the results of the preceding section in terms of an economy in which $L^g(t) = 0$ for all $t \geq 0$, so that $h(t)$ must be nonnegative for all t, and all government debt must be in the form of currency. We have that (7.41) and (7.42) of the preceding section hold with

$$h(t) = \frac{H(t)}{p(t)N(t)}, \qquad t \geq 1$$

and $1 + r(t) = p(t)/p(t+1), \qquad t \geq 1, \quad$ provided that $0 < p(t) < +\infty$.

We first reconsider a version of the scheme that we analyzed in Figure 7.10. We assume that $f(1 + n) > 0$, that $d(1) \geq 0$ and that $d(t) = 0$ for $t \geq 2$. The deficit at time 1 is endogenous and is determined as follows. At time 1, the government offers to exchange the initial stock of $H(1)$ units of currency for goods at the exchange rate given by the price level $p(1)$. After period 1, the government abstains from printing any more currency, so that we have $H(t) = H(1)$ for $t \geq 2$ and $d(t) = 0$ for $t \geq 2$. The value of $d(1)$ is determined by the price level $p(1)$, which is endogenous. With these specifications, the preceding analysis survives intact. In particular, one stationary equilibrium is given by $p(t) = +\infty$ for all t. Another stationary equilibrium is given by the solution to

$$h(1) \equiv \frac{H(1)}{p(1)N(1)} = f(1 + n)$$

or

(7.46) $$p(1) = \frac{H(1)}{N(1)f(1 + n)} \equiv p^*(1)$$

and

(7.47) $$p(t)/p(t+1) = 1 + n, \qquad t \geq 1.$$

Any initial price level $p(1)$ greater than $p^*(1)$ given by (7.46) is also an equilibrium price level, one that results in $h(1) < f(1 + n)$ and $\lim_{t \to \infty} h(t) = 0$.

There is thus a continuum of currency equilibria indexed by initial price levels $p(1)$ in the interval $[p^*(1), \infty]$. We ask the reader to verify that $p(1) < p^*(1)$ cannot be an equilibrium. Notice that all of the equilibria with an initial price level greater than $p^*(1)$ converge to situations in which currency is valueless.

Notice that the $p^*(1)$ stationary equilibrium given by (7.46) and (7.47) is one in which a version of the quantity theory of money holds. Doubling the value of $H(1)$ doubles the value of $p(1)$ and all subsequent price levels $p(t)$, $t \geq 2$. Equivalently, changing the units in which $H(1)$ is measured (for example, from dollars to pesos) leaves real balances unaltered for every $t \geq 1$.

It is evident from the preceding analysis that, in the situation in which $d(1) > 0$, $d(t) = 0$ for $t \geq 2$, and $f(1 + n) < 0$, there will exist no equilibria with valued currency. The reader is asked to verify this point.

To take an example, let us assume that

$$f[1 + r(t)] = \frac{w_1}{2} - \frac{w_2}{2[1 + r(t)]},$$

with $w_1 > w_2$. Such a per capita saving function emerges from a setup in which $u_t^h[c_t^h(t), c_t^h(t + 1)] = \ln c_t^h(t) + \ln c_t^h(t + 1)$, for all t and h, with time-invariant per capita endowments $w_1 = \Sigma_h w_t^h(t)/N(t)$, $w_2 = \Sigma_h w_t^h(t + 1)/N(t)$. Under this specification, the equilibrium condition $f[1 + r(t)] = H(t)/p(t)N(t)$ becomes

$$\frac{H(1)}{p(t)N(t)} = \frac{w_1}{2} - \frac{w_2}{2}\frac{p(t + 1)}{p(t)}.$$

Multiplying both sides by $p(t)$ and rearranging, we have the linear difference equation

$$p(t) = \frac{2}{w_1}\frac{H(1)}{N(t)} + \frac{w_2}{w_1}p(t + 1).$$

From Sargent (1979, chap. 9), we have that the general solution of this difference equation is

$$p(t) = \frac{2}{w_1}\sum_{s=0}^{\infty}\left(\frac{w_2}{w_1}\right)^s\frac{H(1)}{N(t + s)} + c\left(\frac{w_1}{w_2}\right)^t$$

for any constant c. Using $N(t) = (1 + n)N(t - 1)$ or $N(t) = \theta N(t - 1)$, where $\theta \equiv 1 + n$, we have

$$p(t) = \frac{2}{w_1}\left[\sum_{s=0}^{\infty}\left(\frac{w_2}{w_1\theta}\right)^s\right]\frac{H(1)}{N(t)} + c\left(\frac{w_1}{w_2}\right)^t, \qquad t \geq 1.$$

The infinite sum converges, provided that $w_2/(w_1\theta) < 1$, in which case solutions exist and are given by

$$p(t) = \frac{2}{w_1}\left(\frac{1}{1 - \dfrac{w_2}{w_1\theta}}\right)\frac{H(1)}{N(t)} + c\left(\frac{w_1}{w_2}\right)^t.$$

These solutions for the price level satisfy $0 < p(t) < +\infty$ for $1 \leq t < \infty$ for *any* constant $c \geq 0$. The parameter c is arbitrary and thus serves to index a continuum of equilibria. The stationary equilibrium emerges if $c = 0$. Notice that all of the equilibria with $c > 0$ have $\lim_{t \to \infty}[p(t)/p(t+1)] = (w_2/w_1)$, which is the equilibrium gross interest rate for the economy without valued currency.

We now move on to consider a currency equilibrium interpretation of a version of the situation depicted in Figure 7.12 in which $d(t) = d > 0$ for all $t \geq 2$. The first-period real government deficit can be regarded as endogenous and determined by $d(1) = h(1) = H(1)/[p(1)N(1)]$. If $p(1) = +\infty$, the deficit d simply cannot be financed because currency is not valued. For any $p(1) < +\infty$, the deficit can be financed by creation of new currency according to Equation (7.41). Real balances per capita will approach the lower stationary point if the initial price level is above the value that sets initial per capita real balances equal to its value at the upper stationary point. Along an equilibrium path, the inflation rate is determined by

$$\frac{p(t)}{p(t+1)} = 1 + r(t) = f^{-1}[h(t)]$$

or

$$\frac{p(t+1)}{p(t)} = \{f^{-1}[h(t)]\}^{-1}.$$

The inflation rate thus varies inversely with real balances per capita. The stationary inflation rate associated with the larger stationary point value for $h(t)$ is therefore lower than the inflation rate sequence associated with any other $h(t)$ sequence that finances the government deficit. If we interpret the inflation rate as a tax, the multiplicity of inflation rate sequences that serve to finance the same deficit of $d > 0$ from time $t \geq 2$ amounts to a dynamic version of the phenomenon described by the Laffer curve. We shall explore this phenomenon more in Section 7.9.

7.7 Optimality

We shall briefly discuss criteria for the optimality of competitive equilibria in overlapping-generations models. There is a close connection between the conditions under which there fails to exist an optimal equilibrium without valued fiat currency and under which there exists an equilibrium with valued currency.

We begin by studying an economy consisting of agents who have identical preferences and endowment patterns when young and for which $N(t) = (1 + n)N(t - 1)$ for $t \geq 1$. Under this circumstance, the per capita savings correspondence $f[1 + r(t)]$ is also the savings correspondence of the representative agent. We begin by assuming that the net rate of return on storage $\rho(t) = \rho$ for all $t \geq 1$. We assume that $G(t) = 0$ for all $t \geq 1$. The equilibrium interest rate for the economy without valued currency is determined by

$$f[1 + r(t)] = 0.$$

Because f and ρ do not depend on time, the solution of this equation is a time-invariant interest rate

$$1 + r(t) = 1 + r, \qquad t \geq 1.$$

We now establish the proposition that, if $1 + r < (1 + n)$, then the equilibrium fails to be Pareto optimal. This point is established by assuming that $1 + r < 1 + n \equiv \theta$ and by constructing a feasible consumption allocation that Pareto dominates the equilibrium allocation. This superior allocation is constructed by redistributing at least some goods from young to old for each generation.[5] Thus, in Figure 7.14, let the equilibrium consumption allocation be $[c_t^h(t), c_t^h(t + 1)] = (\bar{c}_1, \bar{c}_2)$ for all h and all $t \geq 1$ and $c_0^h(1) = \bar{c}_0$ for all h. This allocation is feasible, which means that it satisfies the following special case of (7.2):

$$N(t)\bar{c}_1 + N(t - 1)\bar{c}_2 + K(t) = Y(t) + (1 + \rho)K(t - 1),$$

with $K(t) \geq 0$, and where $Y(t) = \Sigma_h w_t^h(t) + \Sigma_h w_{t-1}^h(t) = N(t)w_1 + N(t - 1)w_2$ and $K(t) = \Sigma_h k_t^h(t)$. Now hold the $K(t)$ sequence fixed at its original value and consider the alternative allocation $c_0^h(1) = \bar{c}_0 + \theta\delta$, $[c_t^h(t), c_t^h(t + 1)] = (\bar{c}_1 - \delta, \bar{c}_2 + \theta\delta)$. For $\delta > 0$, any such alternative allocation is preferred by generation 0. It is also possible to select a $\delta > 0$ so that such an allocation is preferred by all generations born in $t \geq 1$, because this amounts to a southwesterly move along a straight line of slope $-1/(1 + n) = -\theta^{-1}$ through the initial consumption allocation $(\bar{c}_1, \bar{c}_2)$ (see Figure 7.14). Select $(\bar{c}_1 - \delta, \bar{c}_2 + \theta\delta)$ as the utility-maximizing pair along this line. Furthermore, such an allocation is feasible and also holds the $K(t)$ sequence fixed at its initial value, for we have that the proposed new allocation satisfies

$$N(t)(\bar{c}_1 - \delta) + N(t - 1)[\bar{c}_2 + (1 + n)\delta] + K(t)$$
$$= Y(t) + (1 + \rho)K(t - 1),$$

which is equivalent with the feasibility condition for the original equilib-

---

5. A version of this graphical argument appears in Wallace (1980b, p. 58–59). For discussions of optimality in overlapping-generations models, see Shell (1971), Starret (1972), and Wilson (1981).

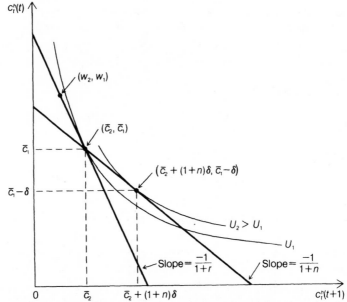

Figure 7.14. Inefficiency when the equilibrium interest rate without currency is less than the growth rate of the economy. With initial endowment (w_2, w_1) and the equilibrium interest rate without currency given by $1 + r < 1 + n$, the equilibrium consumption allocation is $(\bar{c}_2, \bar{c}_1)$. The equilibrium allocation $(\bar{c}_2, \bar{c}_1)$ is not Pareto optimal, because there exists some $\delta > 0$ such that a feasible allocation $[\bar{c}_2 + (1 + n)\delta, \bar{c}_1 - \delta]$ Pareto dominates it.

rium. Thus for an equilibrium with $1 + r < (1 + n)$, we have constructed a feasible allocation that Pareto dominates the equilibrium allocation.

When $f' > 0$ everywhere, the condition that the solution r of $f(1 + r) = 0$ satisfies $1 + r < (1 + n)$ is evidently equivalent to the condition that $f(1 + n) > 0$. Subsequently, when $f' > 0$, $f(1 + n) > 0$ will sometimes be used as a characterization of the situation in which the equilibrium without valued currency is not Pareto optimal. In the present example it is also possible to show that, if $1 + r \geq (1 + n)$, then the equilibrium without valued currency is Pareto optimal. This point will not be established here.

For the case in which $N(t) = N(0)$ and $\rho(t) = -1$ for all $t \geq 1$, Balasko and Shell (1980) have established a convenient general criterion for testing whether allocations are optimal. Balasko and Shell permit diversity among agents in terms of endowments $[w_t^h(t), w_t^h(t + 1)]$ and utility functions $u_t^h[c_t^h(t), c_t^h(t + 1)]$. They impose several kinds of technical conditions that serve to rule out possible pathologies. The two main categories are these.

First, they assume that indifference curves have neither flat parts nor kinks, and they also rule out indifference curves with flat parts or kinks as limits of sequences of indifference curves for given h as $t \to \infty$. Second, they assume that the aggregate endowments $\Sigma_h w_{t-1}^h(t) + \Sigma_h w_t^h(t)$ are uniformly bounded from above and that there exists an $\epsilon > 0$ such that $w_t^h(s) > \epsilon$ for all t, h, s. They consider consumption allocations uniformly bounded away from the axes. With these conditions, Balasko and Shell consider the class of allocations in which all young agents at t share a common marginal rate of substitution $1 + r(t) = u_{t1}^h/u_{t2}^h$ and in which all of the endowments are consumed. Then Balasko and Shell show that an allocation is Pareto optimal if and only if

$$(7.48) \qquad \sum_{t=1}^{\infty} \prod_{s=1}^{t} [1 + r(s)] = +\infty,$$

that is, if and only if the infinite sum of t-period gross interest rates, $\prod_{s=1}^{t}[1 + r(s)]$, diverges.

The Balasko-Shell criterion for optimality succinctly summarizes the sense in which low-interest-rate economies are not optimal. We have already encountered repeated examples of the situation that, before an equilibrium with valued currency can exist, the equilibrium without valued currency must be a low-interest-rate economy in just the sense identified by Balasko-Shell's criterion, (7.48). Furthermore, by applying the Balasko-Shell criterion, (7.48), or by applying generalizations of it to allow for a positive net growth rate of population n, it can be shown that, among equilibria with valued currency, only equilibria with high rates of return on currency are optimal. Let $n = 0$, for example, in the model described in Figure 7.10. Then the Balasko-Shell criterion establishes that, among all equilibria with $h(t) > 0$, only the stationary equilibrium with $h(t) = f(1 + n)$ is optimal. All of the nonstationary equilibria with $h(t) \to 0$ have rate-of-return sequences on currency that are too low.

Neil Wallace (1980b) discusses the connection between nonoptimality of the equilibrium without valued currency and existence of equilibria with valued currency. Further developments of this connection are described by Koda (1985), Manuelli (1984), and Millan (1981).

7.8 Four Examples on Inflation and Its Causes

We study a sequence of simple examples designed partly to illustrate the close connection between the conditions for nonoptimality of equilibria without valued currency and the conditions for the existence of equilibria with valued currency. The examples illustrate the kinds of special assumptions that are required to yield "neutrality" of real variable with respect to variations in the rate of expansion of currency. The examples illustrate the "Lucas critique" in that they show that no single function expresses velocity as a function of expected inflation and is independent of the way that that new currency is injected into the system. Finally, the examples illustrate that whether or not inflation is "bad" (not Pareto optimal) depends on how new currency is injected into the system. Thus the Example 7.5 inflation leaves the equilibrium optimal, whereas the Example 7.6 equilibrium is evidently suboptimal.

EXAMPLE 7.4. *Fixed Supply of Currency*

Consider an economy in which $H(t) = H$ for all $t \geq 1$, $G(t) = 0$ for all $t \geq 1$, $\tau_t^h(s) = 0$ for all t, h, s. Assume that $N(t) = (1 + n)N(t - 1)$ and that there is a time-invariant per capita saving correspondence $f[1 + r(t)]$. Assume that the entire currency stock H is initially in the hands of the old at $t = 1$. We seek a stationary equilibrium with valued currency, that is, one with a constant real rate of return and constant per capita real balances. The equilibrium condition is

$$(7.49) \qquad f\left[\frac{p(t)}{p(t + 1)}\right] = \frac{H}{p(t)N(t)}.$$

We solve this equation for a stationary equilibrium by guessing a solution for the price level of the quantity theory form $p(t) = kH/N(t)$, where $k > 0$ is a constant to be determined. With this guess, we have that

$$\frac{p(t)}{p(t + 1)} = \frac{\dfrac{kH}{N(t)}}{\dfrac{kH}{N(t + 1)}} = 1 + n.$$

Substituting this equation into (7.49) gives $f(1 + n) = H/[p(t)N(t)]$, which can be solved to yield

$$p(t) = [f(1 + n)]^{-1}\frac{H}{N(t)},$$

which is of the form of the quantity theory guess with $k = f(1 + n)^{-1}$. Because we require that $k > 0$, it follows that a necessary condition for the existence of a stationary valued-currency equilibrium is $f(1 + n) > 0$. When $f' > 0$, this is equivalent to the condition that the equilibrium without valued currency fails to be Pareto optimal.

EXAMPLE 7.5. *Nominal Transfers Proportional to Initial Holdings of Currency*

Consider an economy in which $G(t) = 0, t \geq 1$, and $\tau_t^h(s) = 0$ for all t, s, h. Assume that $N(t) = (1 + n)N(t - 1)$ for $t \geq 1$ and that there is a time-invariant per capita saving correspondence $f[1 + r(t)]$. Assume that the currency stock at $t = 1$ is $H(1) > 0$ and is initially in the hands of the old at $t = 1$. Assume that $H(t) = zH(t - 1), t \geq 2$, where $z > 1$. The increase in the currency stock is neither spent by the government nor handed out via lump-sum transfers, because $G(t) = 0$, and $\tau_t^h(s) = 0$ for all t, h, s. Instead, the new currency is handed out each period to the old in direct proportion to the balances of currency that they chose when young. This principle is known in advance and is taken into account by the young when they choose their currency balances. Thus an agent h who chooses to hold $m_t^h > 0$ units when young is given an additional $(z - 1)m_t^h$ and ends up with zm_t^h units when old. It is as if currency paid interest at the nominal gross rate of return z. The real gross rate of return on currency is therefore $zp(t)/p(t + 1)$.

We seek a stationary equilibrium of the model with valued currency. The equilibrium condition is

$$f[zp(t)/p(t + 1)] = \frac{H(t)}{p(t)N(t)}.$$

We again guess a solution of the quantity theory form $p(t) = kH(t)/N(t)$, $k > 0$. This guess implies that $zp(t)/p(t + 1) = (1 + n)$, which in turn implies that

$$p(t) = [f(1 + n)]^{-1} \frac{H(t)}{N(t)},$$

which verifies the guess with $k = f(1 + n)^{-1}$, provided that $f(1 + n) > 0$. Notice that this is exactly the same formula for k that we encountered in the previous example. The gross rate of inflation $p(t + 1)/p(t) = z/(1 + n)$, which equals the gross rate of currency creation divided by the gross rate of real growth. The currency is being handed out, however, in such a way that "currency is neutral" in the sense that the equilibrium interest rate on consumption loans, $1 + r(t) = (1 + n)$, is independent of z, as is velocity, which equals $f(1 + n)^{-1}$.

EXAMPLE 7.6. *Seignorage*

Next we consider an economy in which the government attempts to finance a flow of expenditures by creating currency. In particular, we assume that $N(t) = (1 + n)N(t - 1)$ for $t \geq 1$, and $\tau_t^h(s) = 0$ for all t, h, s. Let the initial stock of currency $H(1) > 0$ be in the hands of the government at the beginning of period 1. We assume that

$$H(t) = zH(t - 1), \qquad z > 1, \qquad t \geq 2.$$

The rate of government purchases of goods $G(t)$ is endogenous and is determined by the special case of (7.32):

$$G(t) = \frac{H(t) - H(t - 1)}{p(t)} = \frac{(z - 1)H(t - 1)}{p(t)}.$$

We once again assume that there is a time-invariant per capita savings function $f[1 + r(t)]$. The equilibrium condition in the loan market is

$$f\left[\frac{p(t)}{p(t + 1)}\right] = \frac{H(t)}{p(t)N(t)}.$$

We again seek a stationary solution and guess at the quantity theory form $p(t) = kH(t)/N(t)$, $k > 0$. This guess implies that $p(t)/p(t + 1) = (1 + n)/z$. Substituting this into the loan market equilibrium condition and rearranging gives

$$p(t) = f\left[\frac{(1 + n)}{z}\right]^{-1} \frac{H(t)}{N(t)},$$

which is of the quantity theory form provided that $f[(1 + n)/z] > 0$. Because $z > 1$, a necessary condition for such an equilibrium to exist is $f(1 + n) > 0$, which is the case in which the equilibrium without valued currency fails to be Pareto optimal. For specifications of f such that $f(R) < 0$ for $R \leq \overline{R}$, there exists a z sufficiently high that no stationary equilibrium with valued currency exists, namely z for which $z \geq (1 + n)/\overline{R}$.

Notice that, for this example, the equilibrium gross interest rate on consumption loans equals $[(1 + n)/z]$ and so depends on the rate of expansion of currency, z. Velocity $f[(1 + n)/z]^{-1}$ is also a function of z. The stationary value of $G(t)/N(t)$ is readily computed to be $(z - 1)f[(1 + n)/z]/z$. For a given specification of f, the value of z that maximizes seignorage could be computed.

An argument like those in Section 7.7 can be used to show that the equilibrium of this example is not Pareto optimal because the gross rate of return falls short of the growth rate $(1 + n)$ when $z > 1$. Here Pareto optimality refers to a comparison among alternative allocations, each of which assigns the same consumption stream to the government.

EXAMPLE 7.7. *Lump-Sum Currency Transfers to the Old*

For our next example, we take up the case in which $G(t) = 0$ for all $t \geq 1$, $N(t) = (1 + n)N(t - 1)$ for $t \geq 1$. We now assume that all agents have identical preferences and endowments, $w_t^h(t) = w_1$, $w_t^h(t + 1) = w_2$, so that the per capita saving schedule $f(1 + r)$ is the saving schedule of the representative young agent.

We assume that $H(t) = zH(t - 1)$ when $t > 1$ and that the increase in currency is distributed lump sum in the equal amounts $\tau_{t-1}(t)$ to each old agent in each period:

$$\frac{H(t) - H(t - 1)}{p(t)} = -\sum_h \tau_{t-1}^h(t) = -N(t - 1)\tau_{t-1}(t).$$

In particular the amount of the transfer received by an agent is independent of the agent's choice of currency holdings when the agent is young. We assume that the currency stock is initially all in the hands of the old at $t = 1$.

Letting $h(t)$ be per capita real balances, we derive the following special version of (7.34):

$$(7.50) \qquad h(t) = \frac{1 + r(t - 1)}{1 + n} h(t - 1) - \frac{1}{1 + n} \tau_{t-1}(t).$$

The law of motion $H(t) = zH(t - 1)$ implies $h(t) = \{z[1 + r(t - 1)]/(1 + n)\}h(t - 1)$. Substituting this into (7.50) then gives

$$-\tau_{t-1}(t) = (z - 1)[1 + r(t - 1)]h(t - 1).$$

The loan market equilibrium condition then becomes

$$f\left[\frac{p(t)}{p(t + 1)}, w_1, w_2 + (z - 1)\frac{p(t)}{p(t + 1)}\frac{H(t)}{p(t)N(t)}\right] = \frac{H(t)}{N(t)p(t)},$$

where, inconsistently, we have included the endowments explicitly as arguments of f. A stationary equilibrium with valued currency, if it exists, satisfies

$$f\left[\frac{1 + n}{z}, w_1, w_2 + (z - 1)\frac{1 + n}{z} h\right] = h > 0,$$

where $h = H(t)/[p(t)N(t)]$. In such an equilibrium, velocity f^{-1} is a complicated function of z. For instance, with our logarithmic preference example,

$$f[1 + r(t), w_1, w_2 - \tau_t^h(t + 1)] = \frac{w_1}{2} - \frac{w_2 - \tau_t^h(t + 1)}{2[1 + r(t)]}.$$

Then the stationary value of h is given by

$$\frac{H(t)}{N(t)p(t)} = \left[w_1 - w_2 \frac{z}{1+n} \right] \cdot \frac{1}{1+z}.$$

The condition that an equilibrium exists is $w_1 > w_2 z/(1+n)$, which in this special case is the condition that $f[(1+n)/z] > 0$. Notice that in the present case of lump-sum transfers to the old, we have that velocity is given by

$$\left\{ \left[w_1 - w_2 \frac{z}{(1+n)} \right] \frac{1}{1+z} \right\}^{-1},$$

whereas with the same specification of preferences and the same motion of currency $H(t) = zH(t-1)$ being used to finance government purchases that we saw in Example 7.6, we would have that velocity is given by

$$2\left[w_1 - w_2 \frac{z}{1+n} \right]^{-1}.$$

These two examples again illustrate the general principle that velocity depends not only on the gross rate of creation of currency z but also on the precise way in which the new currency enters the system.

EXAMPLE 7.8. *Lump-Sum Transfers to the Young*

In the government budget constraint, we now set $G(t) = 0$, $\tau_t^h(t+1) = 0$, and

$$\tau_t^h(t)N(t) = -\frac{H(t) - H(t-1)}{p(t)}.$$

Here lump-sum transfers financed by money creation are being given to the young. We also assume that

$$H(t) = zH(t-1).$$

In conjunction with the previous equation, this equation implies that

$$\tau_t^h(t) = -\frac{(z-1)H(t-1)}{N(t)p(t)}.$$

Consider the special case of identical logarithmic preferences and identical endowments $[w_t^h(t), w_t^h(t+1)] = (w_1, w_2)$. Then the aggregate saving function with $\tau_t^h(t)$ given as above is

$$N(t)\left[\frac{w_1}{2} + \frac{(z-1)H(t-1)}{2N(t)p(t)} - \frac{w_2}{2} \frac{p(t+1)}{p(t)} \right].$$

Table 7.1. Values of $H(t)/[p(t)N(t)]$ for different sources of money creation when $H(t) = zH(t-1)$

Source	Value
Example 7.5. Second-period transfers proportional to initial holdings	$\dfrac{w_1}{2} - \dfrac{w_2}{2}\dfrac{1}{1+n}$
Example 7.6. Seignorage	$\dfrac{w_1}{2} - \dfrac{w_2}{2}\dfrac{z}{1+n}$
Example 7.7. Lump-sum transfers to the old	$w_1\left(\dfrac{1}{z+1}\right)\left[1 - \dfrac{w_2}{w_1}\dfrac{z}{1+n}\right]$
Example 7.8. Lump-sum transfers to the young	$w_1\left(\dfrac{z}{z+1}\right)\left[1 - \dfrac{w_2}{w_1}\dfrac{z}{1+n}\right]$

Note: Preferences for all agents are assumed to be given by $\ln c_t^h(t) + \ln c_t^h(t+1)$, and before-tax endowments are assumed to be given by $(w_1, w_2) = [w_t^h(t), w_t^h(t+1)]$.

Equating aggregate saving to $H(t)/p(t)$ and solving for $H(t)/p(t)N(t)$ gives

$$\frac{H(t)}{p(t)N(t)} = w_1\left(\frac{z}{z+1}\right)\left(1 - \frac{w_2}{w_1}\frac{z}{1+n}\right).$$

We summarize the results of Examples 7.4–7.8 in Table 7.1, which shows the stationary values of $H(t)/[p(t)N(t)]$ that are associated with money creation achieved through differing means when preferences are identical and logarithmic and when endowment patterns are identical and given by (w_1, w_2). The table indicates that it is impossible to find a function that can express $H(t)/[p(t)N(t)]$ (velocity) as a function of the expected rate of inflation $z/(1+n)$ alone and that does not depend on precisely how new currency is injected into the system. Instead, the relationship between velocity and $z/(1+n)$ depends precisely on the manner in which currency is injected into the system.

7.9 Seignorage and the Laffer Curve

We now consider an economy in which $N(t) = N > 0$ and $p(t) = -1$ for all $t \geq 1$.[6] We suppose that each agent born in $t \geq 1$ is endowed with $w_t^h(t) = w_1$ when young and $w_t^h(t+1) = w_2$ when old, where $0 < w_2 < w_1$. Each young agent born in $t \geq 1$ has identical preferences $u[c_t^h(t), c_t^h(t+1)]$. For $t \geq 1$, a young agent's saving function is given by $w_1 - c_t^h(t) = f[R(t)]$, where $R(t)$ is the one-period gross rate of return on saving between t and $(t+1)$ and where

6. This section is based on the paper by Bryant and Wallace (1984).

$f' > 0$. The saving function f solves the equation

(7.51) $$\frac{u_1[w_1 - f(R),\, w_2 + f(R)R]}{u_2[w_1 - f(R),\, w_2 + f(R)R]} = R,$$

which is the representative household's first-order necessary condition evaluated at the boundary of its budget set.

The government is imagined to finance a constant level of purchases, $G(t) = G > 0$, $t \geq 1$, by printing new base money. The government's budget constraint is

$$G = \frac{H(t) - H(t-1)}{p(t)},$$

subject to $H(0)$ given. The budget constraint can be rearranged to assume the form

$$G = \frac{H(t)}{p(t)} - \frac{H(t-1)}{p(t-1)}\frac{p(t-1)}{p(t)}$$

or

(7.52) $$G = \frac{H(t)}{p(t)} - \frac{H(t-1)}{p(t-1)} R(t-1), \qquad t \geq 2,$$

where $R(t-1) \equiv p(t-1)/p(t)$ is the gross rate of return on holding currency between $(t-1)$ and t.

Substituting the equilibrium condition $H(t)/p(t) = f[R(t)]/N$ into (7.52) gives

(7.53) $$\frac{G}{N} = f[R(t)] - f[R(t-1)]R(t-1), \quad \text{for } t \geq 2.$$

We shall seek a stationary inflation rate $R(t) = R$ for all $t \geq 1$ that finances the deficit G. Substituting $R(t) = R$ for $t \geq 1$ into (7.53) for $t \geq 2$ gives

(7.54) $$\frac{G}{N} = f(R)(1 - R).$$

For $t = 1$, government budget constraint can be expressed as

(7.55) $$\frac{G}{N} = f[R(1)] - \frac{H(0)}{p(1)N}.$$

We seek a solution of (7.54) and (7.55) for $R > 0$ and $p(1) > 0$. Given the resulting R and $p(1)$, the price level for $t > 1$ can be found from $p(t+1) = R^{-1}p(t)$.

To characterize a solution of (7.54) and (7.55), it is helpful to study Figures 7.15–7.17. Figure 7.15 depicts a young household's offer curve through the initial endowment point (w_2, w_1). The vertical distance between the point A or (w_2, w_1) and the point C on the offer curve equals saving, $f(R)$. The gross interest rate associated with a point on the offer curve equals the negative of the reciprocal of the slope of the straight line connecting (w_2, w_1) and the point on the offer curve. If the government manages to confront the household with a rate of return $R \leq 1$ on its savings $f(R)$, all held in the form of currency, the government collects revenues of $f(R)(1 - R)$. Geometrically, $f(R)(1 - R)$ is found as the base AB of the triangle ABC in Figure 7.15. The point B is found by projecting a line of slope -1 through point C to the line that is parallel to the $c_i^h(t)$ axis and that goes through point A. The intersection of the line of slope -1 through point C with the $c_i^h(t)$ axis is evidently at $[0, w_1 + w_2 - f(R)(1 - R)]$.

From Figure 7.16 it follows that a gross interest rate that raises a given amount of revenue G/N per capita can be found as follows. Draw the line of slope -1 connecting the points $(0, w_1 + w_2 - G/N)$ on the $c_i^h(t)$ axis with the

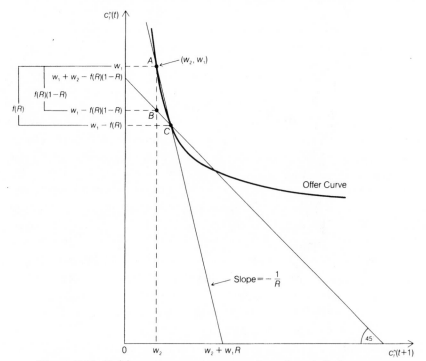

Figure 7.15. Raising government revenue through an inflationary tax.

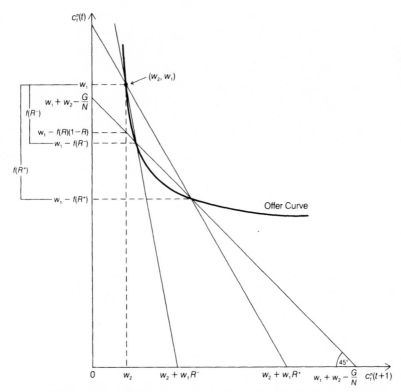

Figure 7.16. Two inflationary tax rates that raise the same government revenue.

point $(w_1 + w_2 - G/N, 0)$ on the $c_t^h(t + 1)$ axis. The intersections of this line with the offer curve through (w_2, w_1) are associated with $[R, f(R)]$ combinations that satisfy (7.54). This situation is depicted in Figure 7.16. As Figure 7.16 suggests, in general if there is one rate of return R that satisfies $G/N = f(R)(1 - R)$, then there are at least two. Each crossing of the offer curve through (w_2, w_1) with the $-45°$ line through the points $(0, w_1 + w_2 - G/N)$ and $(w_1 + w_2 - G/N, 0)$ determines an R that satisfies $G/N = f(R)(1 - R)$. If the offer curve through (w_2, w_1) cuts this $-45°$ line once from above, it must necessarily cut it at least once more from below (why?). Following Bryant and Wallace (1984), we let R^- be the lowest R that satisfies (7.54) and R^+ the highest R that satisfies (7.54). Figure 7.17 plots $f(R)(1 - R)$ against R and depicts two values of R, namely R^+ and R^-, that satisfy (7.54). Evidently, $f(R)(1 - R)$ is zero at $R = 0$ and at $R = 1$.

From Figures 7.15, 7.16, and 7.17 it is evident that many values of G/N are simply too high to be financed on a sustained basis through currency cre-

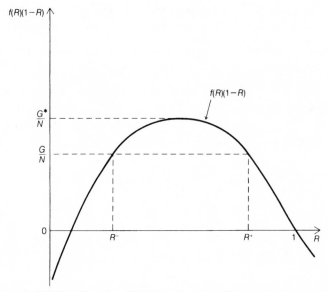

Figure 7.17. The function $f(R)(1 - R)$ when f is continuous and increasing in R, with $f(0) = -\infty$. For $0 < G/N < G^*/N$, two values of $R \in (0, 1)$ satisfy $G/N = f(R)(1 - R)$. G^*/N is the highest sustained level of G/N that can be financed by currency creation and satisfies $G^*/N = f(R^*)(1 - R^*) = \max f(R)(1 - R)$ with respect to R.

ation. The highest sustained level of G/N that can be financed by currency creation is the one associated with the point on the offer curve that intersects the line connecting $(w_1 + w_2 - G/N, 0)$ and $(0, w_1 + w_2 - G/N)$ that is closest to the origin.

Given an R that satisfies (7.54), (7.55) can be used to solve for $p(1)$:

$$p(1) = \frac{H(0)}{Rf(R)N}$$

or

(7.56) $$p(1) = \frac{H(0)}{[f(R) - GN^{-1}]N}.$$

From (7.56) it follows that the solution of (7.54) and (7.55) with the largest value of R is associated with the uniformly lowest price level $p(t)$ for $t \geq 1$. It follows that the solution of (7.54) and (7.55) with the largest value of R Pareto dominates solutions with a smaller value of R. Because $R < 1$ for any solution to (7.54) and (7.55) with $G/N > 0$, however, any such equilibrium fails to be Pareto optimal. The symptom of failure of Pareto optimality is that the equilibrium gross rate of return R falls short of the gross growth rate, unity.

EXAMPLE. Consider the special case in which preferences are given by $\ln c_t^h(t) + \ln c_t^h(t+1)$. We then have the saving function $f(R) = w_1/2 - w_2/2R$. Equation (7.54) becomes

$$g = (1 - R)\left(\frac{w_1}{2} - \frac{w_2}{2R}\right),$$

where $g \equiv G/N$. This equation can be rearranged to be

$$\frac{w_2}{w_1}\frac{1}{R} - \left(1 + \frac{w_2}{w_1} - \frac{2g}{w_1}\right) + R = 0$$

or $$\frac{b}{R} + \left[\frac{2g}{w_1} - (1 + b)\right] + R = 0,$$

where we have defined $b \equiv w_2/w_1$. (Here b will play a role similar to the discount factor in the problems described by Sargent 1979, chap. 9.) To find the stationary values of R that finance the per capita government deficit g, we have to find the zeros of the above equation. It can be verified directly that if R_0 is a zero of this equation, then so is b/R_0. Thus the stationary rates of return on currency that finance the deficit occur in "b-reciprocal pairs." Let λ denote a zero of the above equation. Then evidently the above equation is equivalent to

$$0 = -\lambda^{-1}\left[(\lambda - R)\left(\lambda - \frac{b}{R}\right)\right] = \frac{b}{R} - \left(\lambda + \frac{b}{\lambda}\right) + R.$$

By matching coefficients with the preceding equation, we find that λ is determined from

$$\lambda + \frac{b}{\lambda} = \frac{-2g}{w_1} + (1 + b).$$

For convenience, define $\lambda^{-1} = \pi$, where π now has an interpretation as a gross inflation rate, because $p(t+1) = \lambda^{-1}p(t) = \pi p(t)$. Then the above equation can be expressed as

$$(\pi^{-1} + b\pi) = \frac{-2g}{w_1} + (1 + b).$$

The solutions of this equation are depicted in Figure 7.18, which is identical to Figure 4 of Sargent (1979, chap. 9). The function $\pi^{-1} + b\pi$ attains a minimum at a value of π of $\sqrt{1/b}$, assuming a value of $2\sqrt{b}$ there. For $g = 0$, there are two solutions, one at $\pi = 1$, the other at $\pi = 1/b = w_1/w_2 > 1$. The two solutions between them capture the multiplicity of equilibria in the model without government deficits that we described earlier. For values of g that satisfy $(1 + b) - 2g/w_1 > 2\sqrt{b}$ or

$$g < \frac{w_1}{2}[(1 + b) - 2\sqrt{b}],$$

the government deficit is small enough to be financed through inflation. Government deficits that violate the preceding inequality are simply too large to be financed by the inflation tax alone.

7.10 Dynamics of Seignorage

To investigate nonstationary equilibria, we now seek solutions of (7.53) and (7.54) for $p(1)$ and a sequence $R(t)$. Express (7.53) and (7.55) as

(7.57) $f[R(t)] = \dfrac{G}{N} + f[R(t - 1)]R(t - 1), \qquad t \geq 2$

(7.58) $f[R(1)] = \dfrac{G}{N} + \dfrac{H(0)}{p(1)N}.$

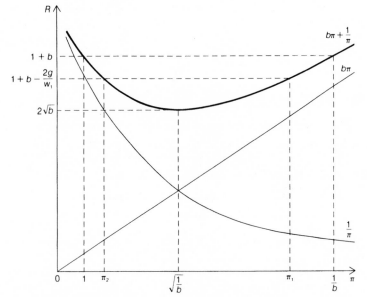

Figure 7.18. The function $b\pi + \pi^{-1}$ (not to scale).

Given an initial $p(1)$, (7.57) and (7.58) describe a difference equation in $f[R(t)]$. We study the evolution of this system with the aid of Figure 7.19. We have drawn the system as having two stationary points. In general, if there is one stationary point, then there are at least two, as we saw from our analysis of Figures 7.15–7.17. Note from Figure 7.17 that if $R^- < R(t-1) < R^+$, then $f[R(t-1)]$ $[1 - R(t-1)] > G/N$ or $G/N + R(t-1)f[R(t-1)] < f[R(t-1)]$. Figure 7.19 is drawn to reflect this last inequality. Evidently the stationary point with the lower value of $f(R)$, and therefore also the lower value of R, is stable. The higher stationary value for $f(R)$ is not stable. The starting point for $f[R(1)]$ is determined via (7.58) by selection of a $p(1)$.

The dynamics reflected in Figure 7.19 capture what Stanley Fischer (1984) has called the "slippery side" of the Laffer curve. There are two stationary tax rates on real balances $[1 - R(t)]$ that finance the deficit. The range of feasible values of $p(1)$ are given by the solutions of (7.58) that satisfy $R(1) \le R^+$. Among these values for $p(1)$, if the system begins at a $p(1)$ less than the singular value of $p(1)$ that solves (7.58) with $R(1)$ at R^+, the system eventually converges to the higher and less efficient inflation tax rate $(1 - R^-)$. Sargent

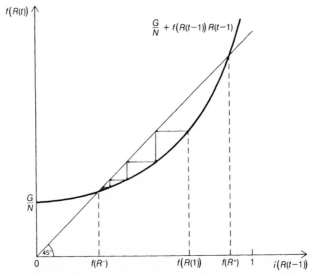

Figure 7.19. The function $G/N + f[R(t-1)]R(t-1) = f[R(t)]$. For G/N sufficiently small, the function $G/N + f[R(t-1)]R(t-1)$ has two stationary points, $f(R^-)$ and $f(R^+)$. Because f is increasing in $R(t)$, for any $R(1) \in [0, R^+)$, $f[R(t)] \to f(R^-)$ as $t \to \infty$. Thus $f(R^-)$ is locally stable, whereas $f(R^+)$ is unstable.

and Wallace (1984) use a stochastic version of this model, which has a continuum of equilibria, to study the dynamics of hyperinflation.

7.11 Forced Saving

Bryant and Wallace (1984) showed that the government can correct the suboptimality associated with the inflation tax by issuing government bonds with a higher yield and also by imposing a set of legal restrictions that cause "forced saving." The heart of Bryant and Wallace's argument appears in Figure 7.20. The government issues bonds in minimal denominations of amount F and offers a gross rate of return of $R_2 > R^+$ on these bonds. The government confronts the household with the all-or-none option of remaining at (w_2, w_1) or moving along the segment $\{w_2 + [w_1 - c_t^h(t)]R_2, w_1 - c_t^h(t)\}$ as long as $w_1 - c_t^h(t) \geq F$. A legal restriction is passed prohibiting private agents from borrowing or lending among themselves. The force of

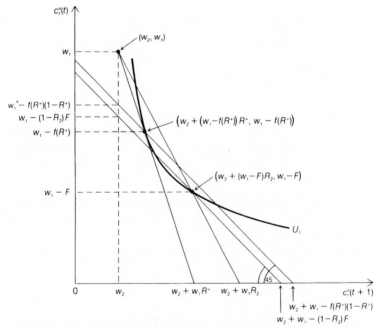

Figure 7.20. Forced savings. Endowed with (w_2, w_1) and faced with an interest rate R^+, the agent chooses consumption allocation $[w_2 + f(R^+)R^+, w_1 - f(R^+)]$. With the F-legal restriction and the interest rate $R_2 > R^+$, the agent chooses the corner solution $[w_2 + FR_2, w_1 - F]$. The government raises per capita revenue $f(R^+)(1 - R^+)$ without a legal restriction and $(1 - R_2)F > f(R^+)(1 - R^+)$ with the F-legal restriction.

this restriction is to prevent several households from sharing a large-denomination bond, thereby undoing the legal restriction. Notice that F and R_2 can be chosen as in Figure 7.20, so that the household remains on the same indifference curve as in the stationary monetary equilibrium with $R(t) = R^+$ but with the government raising more revenue. As Figure 7.20 is drawn, the household is maximizing at the corner $[c_t^h(t), c_t^h(t+1)] = (w_1 - F, w_2 + FR_2)$. The government raises more revenue because evidently $F(1 - R_2) > f(R^+)(1 - R^+)$. Here F is the base of the tax, and $(1 - R_2)$ is the tax rate on savings.

Figure 7.20 indicates that the government can choose F and R_2 to satisfy $G/N = F(1 - R_2)$ and leave all households born in $t \geq 1$ better off than in the inflation tax equilibrium with $R(t) = R^+$ for $t \geq 1$. For $t \geq 2$, the government's budget constraint is $G/N = F - FR_2(t - 1)$, where $R_2(t - 1) = R_2$ is the gross rate of return on bonds. For $t = 1$, the government's budget constraint can be construed to be

$$(7.59) \qquad \frac{G}{N} = F - \frac{H(0)}{Np(1)},$$

where it is understood that at $t = 1$, the government redeems the initial outstanding stock of currency $H(0)$ and issues bonds in its place. Because $F > f(R^+)$, it follows from a comparison of (7.56) and (7.59) that the initial price level $p(1)$ is lower when only bonds are issued. The initial old are thus better off under this scheme, as is each generation born in $t \geq 1$.

Evidently under this scheme, given a G/N that is feasible to finance under a currency-only inflation tax, it is possible to set F and R_2 so that G/N is financed and so that the resulting consumption allocation is Pareto optimal among all those having $N(w_1 + w_2 - G/N)$ to allocate among consumers at each $t \geq 1$. To establish this point, it is sufficient to invoke Balasko-Shell's criterion, (7.48), and to show that F and R_2 can be selected so that the utility-maximizing corner in Figure 7.20 occurs at a $u_1(w_1 - F, w_2 + FR_2)/u_2(w_1 - F, w_2 + FR_2) \geq 1$. Readers should convince themselves that this can be done.

Bryant and Wallace's analysis might be used directly to provide a defense for the kind of forced saving program that John Maynard Keynes (1940) advocated to finance the war. Bryant and Wallace (1984) used their analysis to suggest why a government might want to offer different rates of return on its debt to different lenders. They wanted to explain the widely observed dominance in rate of return of large-denomination government debt (interest-bearing government securities) over low-denomination government debt (currency). They proposed that these observations be interpreted as reflecting a set of legal restrictions designed to enforce a price discrimination scheme that permits the government to offer different rates of return to different lenders. In a setup with two classes of lenders, poor and rich, Bryant and Wallace show that a scheme in which rich lenders alone are offered higher-yielding government securities while the poor can only hold lower-yielding currency can Pareto dominate a scheme without such price discrimination. The equilibria with both currency and higher-yielding bonds that Bryant and Wallace analyze are ones with imperfect price discrimination and could in principle be Pareto dominated by a finer set of all-or-none choices that supports an equilibrium in which all young agents at each t share a common marginal rate of substitution of current consumption for future consumption. Implicitly, Bryant and Wallace have in mind a setting in which there is much heterogeneity and uncertainty and in which the information required to support such a perfect price discrimination scheme is not available to the government.

7.12 International Exchange Rates

In a two-country version of an overlapping-generations model with free trade in goods, loans, and currencies, how is the exchange rate determined? Equivalently, in this setting, how many currencies are there room for? Kareken and Wallace (1981) studied these questions and found that the exchange rate is indeterminate, or put differently, that there is room for at most one unbacked currency in the overlapping-generations model with heterogeneous agents. A two-country overlapping-generations model has a structure virtually identical to that of a one-country model with heterogeneous agents. We have seen that in many circumstances the effects of the trading "friction" in the overlapping-generations model are cured when a single outside asset is supplied by the government and that it is irrelevant whether this asset is currency or bonds.[7] The Kareken-Wallace exchange rate indeterminacy results can be interpreted as another reflection of the situation that there is room for only one outside asset in this model.[8]

Consider a two-country, one-nonstorable-good version of the model described in the preceding section. In each country $i = 1, 2$, there are overlap-

---

7. The sense in which the friction is cured is that the equilibrium with government indebtedness can be an optimal one when the equilibrium without government indebtedness is not optimal.

8. The logic of the exchange rate indeterminacy result was set forth in a note by Russell Boyer (1971) entitled "Nickels and Dimes." Boyer pointed out that the exchange rate between nickels and dimes is indeterminate if left to market forces. He noted that nickels and dimes are analogous to dollars and pounds.

ping generations of two-period-lived agents. Let the aggregate net saving function of the young at time t in country i be $F_t^i[R^i(t)]$ where $R^i(t)$ is the gross rate of return in country i on assets held between times t and $(t + 1)$. At time $t \geq 1$, the government of country i purchases $G_i(t) \geq 0$ units of the consumption good, financing its purchases by issuing currency. The budget constraint of government i is

$$(7.60) \qquad G_i(t) = \frac{H_i(t) - H_i(t - 1)}{p_i(t)}, \qquad t \geq 1, \qquad H_i(0) > 0 \text{ given,}$$

where $H_i(t)$ is the stock of currency of government i at time t, and $p_i(t)$ is the price level in country i at time t.

Consider a free-trade regime in which residents of each country are free to hold the assets, including currency, emanating from the other country. Because there is no uncertainty in the model, as an equilibrium condition we require equal rates of return on all assets, $R^1(t) = R^2(t) = R(t)$. In particular, we require equal rates of return on currency:

$$(7.61) \qquad \frac{p_1(t)}{p_1(t + 1)} = \frac{p_2(t)}{p_2(t + 1)}, \qquad t \geq 1,$$

a condition that is necessary if $p_1(t)$ and $p_2(t)$ are both to be finite for all t (that is, if both currencies are to be voluntarily held). Rearranging this equality gives

$$(7.62) \qquad \frac{p_1(t + 1)}{p_2(t + 1)} = \frac{p_1(t)}{p_2(t)}, \qquad t \geq 1.$$

When we define the exchange rate $e(t) = p_1(t)/p_2(t)$, Equation (7.62) implies that the equilibrium exchange rate is constant over time.

$$(7.63) \qquad e(t) = e, \qquad t \geq 1.$$

Let $R(t) = p_1(t)/p_1(t + 1) = p_2(t)/p_2(t + 1)$. The equilibrium condition in the loan (or currency) market is

$$(7.64) \qquad F_t^1[R(t)] + F_t^2[R(t)] = \frac{H_1(t)}{p_1(t)} + \frac{H_2(t)}{p_2(t)}.$$

[Notice that this is a version of Equation (7.12): $\Sigma_h l_t^h(t) + L^g(t) = 0$.] Define the worldwide saving function at time t, $F_t[R(t)] = F_t^1[R(t)] + F_t^2[R(t)]$. Then (7.64) becomes

$$(7.65) \qquad F_t[R(t)] = \frac{H_1(t)}{p_1(t)} + \frac{H_2(t)}{p_2(t)}.$$

Express the government budget constraint as

(7.66) $\quad G_i(t) = \dfrac{H_i(t)}{p_i(t)} - \dfrac{H_i(t-1)}{p_i(t-1)} R(t-1), \qquad t \geq 2$

(7.67) $\quad G_i(1) = \dfrac{H_i(1)}{p_i(1)} - \dfrac{H_i(0)}{p_i(1)}, \qquad i = 1, 2.$

Adding (7.66) for $i = 1, 2$ and using (7.65) gives

(7.68) $\quad G_1(t) + G_2(t) = F_t[R(t)] - F_{t-1}[R(t-1)]R(t-1).$

Adding (7.67) for $i = 1, 2$ and using (7.63) and the definition of the exchange rate $e(t) = p_1(t)/p_2(t)$ gives

(7.69) $\quad G_1(1) + G_2(1) = F_1[R(1)] - \dfrac{H_1(0) + eH_2(0)}{p_1(1)}.$

Collecting equations, we may formulate the following definition.

DEFINITION. *An equilibrium is a collection of real positive and bounded sequences for* $\{R(t), p_1(t), p_2(t), H_1(t), H_2(t), G_1(t), G_2(t)\}_{t=1}^{\infty}$, *a real number* $e \in (0, \infty)$ *and given positive real numbers* $H_1(0), H_2(0)$, *and a saving function* $F_t[R(t)]$ *that satisfy*

(7.70) $\quad G_1(t) + G_2(t) = F_t[R(t)] - F_{t-1}[R(t-1)]R(t-1), \qquad t \geq 2$

(7.71) $\quad G_1(1) + G_2(1) = F_1[R(1)] - \dfrac{H_1(0) + eH_2(0)}{p_1(1)}$

(7.72) $\quad p_2(t) = e^{-1}p_1(t), \qquad t \geq 1$

(7.73) $\quad R(t) = \dfrac{p_i(t)}{p_i(t+1)}, \qquad i = 1, 2, \qquad t \geq 1$

(7.74) $\quad G_i(t) = \dfrac{H_i(t) - H_i(t-1)}{p_i(t)}, \qquad i = 1, 2, \qquad t \geq 1.$

The following proposition, due to Kareken and Wallace (1981), establishes that the equilibrium exchange rate is indeterminate.

PROPOSITION 7.4. *Let* $\{\overline{R}(t), \overline{p}_1(t), \overline{p}_2(t), \overline{H}_1(t), \overline{H}_2(t), \overline{G}_1(t), \overline{G}_2(t)\}_{t=1}^{\infty}$ *and* $\overline{e}$, $\overline{H}_1(0), \overline{H}_2(0)$ *be an equilibrium. Then for any* $\hat{e} \in (0, \infty)$ *there exists an equilibrium with* $\hat{G}_i(t) = \overline{G}_i(t), \hat{R}(t) = \overline{R}(t)$, *but with* $\hat{p}_i(t) \neq \overline{p}_i(t), \hat{H}_i(t) \neq \overline{H}_i(t).$

Proof. Note that (7.71) is solved with $\hat{G}_i(t) = \overline{G}_i(t)$, $i = 1, 2$, and $\hat{R}(t) =$

$\overline{R}(t)$. Use a version of (7.71) to solve for $\hat{p}_1(1)$:

$$\frac{\overline{H}_1(0) + \hat{e}\overline{H}_2(0)}{\hat{p}_1(1)} = F_1[\overline{R}(1)] - [\overline{G}_1(1) + \overline{G}_2(1)].$$

Because $\bar{p}_1(1) > 0$, the right side of this equation is known to be positive. Therefore, for any $\hat{e} \in (0, \infty)$, this equation has a solution for a positive, finite price level $\hat{p}_1(1)$. Solve for $\hat{p}_2(1)$ using (7.72): $\hat{p}_2(1) = \hat{e}^{-1}\hat{p}_1(1)$. Then use (7.73) to solve for $\hat{p}_i(t)$, $i = 1, 2, t \geq 1$. Finally, use (7.74) with $\hat{G}_i(t) = \overline{G}_i(t)$ and $p_i(t) = \hat{p}_i(t)$ to solve for $\hat{H}_i(t)$, $i = 1, 2; t \geq 1$. This statement concludes the proof.

This proposition states that the exchange rate e_t is indeterminate. If there is an equilibrium in which each country is succeeding in financing its expenditures via equations (7.66)–(7.67), and in which both currencies are valued, then the equilibrium exchange rate must be constant over time [Equation (7.64)]. *Any* constant exchange rate $e \in (0, \infty)$, however, is an equilibrium that supports the same streams of government purchases $G_i(t)$ and the same equilibrium gross rates of return $R(t)$ for $t \geq 1$.

In the equilibria described in Proposition 7.4, one country may be raising seignorage revenues from the residents of the other country. Condition (7.62) or (7.63) states that there is a single worldwide inflation rate, which is influenced by the $G_i(t)$ streams chosen by both countries. This situation means that there is scope for coordination of national economic policies. Indeed, one way or another the macroeconomic policies of the two countries must be coordinated. Sebastian (1985) and Miller and Wallace (1985) describe various games that the authorities of the two countries may play.

One way to coordinate policies, which would be in the interest of people who reside in a country with a small $G_i(t)$ sequence and who are also lenders, would be for there to be portfolio autarky. That is, residents of each country would be prohibited from holding private or governmental evidences of indebtedness emanating from the other country. These restrictions would convert the model of this section simply to a pair of noninteracting economies of the kind described in Section 7.10, each with its own price level and rate-of-return process. The equilibrium exchange rate between currencies would be determined from $e(t) = p_1(t)/p_2(t)$ and would vary over time. In this model, the rates of return in one country could exceed those in the other country. This model of portfolio autarky generates a version of the "monetary theory of the exchange rate" similar to that which we encountered in our study of cash-in-advance models in Chapter 5.

Kareken and Wallace (1981) and Nickelsburg (1980) describe the ways in which legal restrictions on portfolios of various kinds would render the exchange rate determinate.

7.13 Conclusions

The cash-in-advance models of Chapter 5 are created by grafting unbacked government currency onto the Lucas tree model in a way that leaves intact all of the real properties of the model. In particular, consumption allocations and all real state-contingent future prices are left unaltered by the addition of a monetary sector. This cash-in-advance construction is inspired by the wish to have a theory of the price level that requires minimal alterations in the real equilibrium associated with some version of an Arrow-Debreu economy.

Models with the Bewley-Townsend or overlapping-generations structure embody a perspective on the dependence between "real" and "monetary" phenomena that differs from that of the cash-in-advance model. In the Bewley-Townsend and overlapping-generations models, when there exists an equilibrium with valued unbacked currency, there typically also exists an equilibrium in which currency is not valued. The allocations and real rates of return typically differ between these equilibria with and without valued government currency. In these models, things do not dichotomize into a "real" and "monetary" side. Furthermore, the existence of an equilibrium with valued unbacked government currency hinges on how well the economy operates without valued currency. In particular, if the equilibrium without valued currency is Pareto optimal, then no equilibrium with valued currency will exist. The existence of an equilibrium with valued currency thus shows that something is "wrong" with the allocation in which there is no valued currency.

The cash-in-advance model of Chapter 5 exhibits rate-of-return dominance of other assets over one government's currency. Such dominance does not occur in overlapping-generations models without legal restrictions.[9]

The rate-of-return dominance in cash-in-advance models, however, can also be regarded as reflecting a legal restriction. As we saw in Chapter 5, an arbitrage opportunity in the cash-in-advance model can be interpreted in terms of an incentive to set up private banks that issue bank notes. Some force must be present to prevent this arbitrage opportunity from being exploited. A costlessly enforced legal prohibition against issuing private bank notes is one possibility and perhaps the most natural one in light of the

9. See Exercise 6.5 for an endowment pattern that delivers rate-of-return dominance in a Townsend turnpike model.

physical description of the model.[10] There seem to be no physical or techno-
logical impediments to issuing and using such private bank notes in the
description of the economic environment of the cash-in-advance model.[11]

In a variety of contexts using overlapping-generations models, Neil Wallace has recently posited legal restrictions that render a government-issued
currency a dominated asset. Versions of his analyses were inspired by a desire
to rationalize Fisher effects, determinate exchange rates, and other manifes-
tations of rate-of-return dominance in the context of overlapping-generations models. Other parts of his work were aimed at providing a normative
reason that a government might want to impose legal restrictions on portfolios in order to finance its expenditures most efficiently in a world in which
lump-sum taxation is not possible. Wallace finds that the structure of legal
restrictions influences the distribution of wealth and welfare across different
classes of agents, for example, "borrowers" and "lenders." In examples that
Wallace has studied with heterogeneous agents, it is impossible to evaluate
legal restrictions on the financial system according to macroeconomic criteria such as price-level stability alone.[12]

Exercises

Exercise 7.1 Credit Controls

Consider the following overlapping-generations model. At each date $t \geq 1$
there appear N two-period-lived young people, said to be of generation t, who
live and consume during periods t and $(t + 1)$. At time $t = 1$ there exist N old

10. The assertion that free banking produces bad outcomes and that legal restrictions prohibiting free banking are a good idea has a long tradition. See Friedman (1960). At a theoretical
level, Sargent and Wallace's model (1982) can be used to represent parts of the case against free
banking (that it might cause larger price-level fluctuations and might reduce the utility attained
by some parties). That model can also be used to represent some advantages of free banking
(that it permits a Pareto-optimal equilibrium, whereas its prohibition does not). At an empirical
level, Rolnick and Weber (1983) have reexamined the actual performance of free banking in the
United States in the days before the Civil War and have found evidence that the system was
orderly.

11. Sargent and Wallace (1983) construct an overlapping-generations models of commodity
money economies. They describe several propositions designed to shed light on the aspects of a
commodity (depreciation rate and supply conditions) that determine whether a particular
commodity is used as "money." (They have difficulty discovering a version of Gresham's law
without appealing to a structure of legal restrictions; for empirical evidence about Gresham's
law, see Rolnick and Weber 1985.) The reader is invited to consider how a commodity money
system would be modeled in a cash-in-advance structure.

12. See Wallace (1980a) and Sargent and Wallace (1982). A general finding that has emerged
from Wallace's work is that the equilibrium price level, rates of return, and consumption
allocations depend intricately on the details of the legal restrictions on the financial system.

people who are endowed with $H(0)$ units of paper "dollars," which they offer to supply inelastically to the young of generation 1 in exchange for goods. Let $p(t)$ be the price of the one good in the model, measured in dollars per time t good. For each $t \geq 1$, $N/2$ members of generation t are endowed with $y > 0$ units of the good at t and 0 units at $(t + 1)$, whereas the remaining $N/2$ members of generation t are endowed with 0 units of the good at t and $y > 0$ units when they are old. All members of all generations have the same utility function:

$$u[c_t^h(t), c_t^h(t + 1)] = \ln c_t^h(t) + \ln c_t^h(t + 1),$$

where $c_t^h(s)$ is the consumption of agent h of generation t in period s. The old at $t = 1$ simply maximize $c_0^h(1)$. The consumption good is nonstorable. The currency supply is constant through time, so $H(t) = H(0)$, $t \geq 1$.

a. Define a competitive equilibrium without valued currency for this model. Who trades what with whom?

b. Compute the nonvalued-currency competitive equilibrium values of the gross return on consumption loans, the consumption allocation of the old at $t = 1$, and that of the "borrowers" and "lenders" for $t \geq 1$.

c. Define a competitive equilibrium with valued currency. Who trades what with whom?

d. Prove that for this economy there does not exist a competitive equilibrium with valued currency.

e. Now suppose that the government imposes the restriction that $l_t^h(t)[1 + r(t)] \geq -y/4$, where $l_t^h(t)[1 + r(t)]$ represents claims on $(t + 1)$-period consumption purchased (if positive) or sold (if negative) by household h of generation t. This is a restriction on the amount of borrowing. For an equilibrium without valued currency, compute the consumption allocation and the gross rate of return on consumption loans.

f. In the setup of (e), show that there exists an equilibrium with valued currency in which the price level obeys the quantity theory equation $p(t) = qH(0)/N$. Find a formula for the undetermined coefficient q. Compute the consumption allocation and the equilibrium rate of return on consumption loans.

g. Are lenders better off in economy (b) or economy (f)? What about borrowers? What about the old of period 1 (generation 0)?

Exercise 7.2 Inside Money and Real Bills

Consider the following overlapping-generations model of two-period-lived people. At each date $t \geq 1$ there are born N_1 individuals of type 1 who are endowed with $y > 0$ units of the consumption good when they are young and zero units when they are old; there are also born N_2 individuals of type 2 who are endowed with zero units of the consumption good when they are young and $Y > 0$ units when they are old. The consumption good is nonstorable. At time $t = 1$, there are N old people, all of the same type, each endowed with zero units of the consumption good and H_0/N units of unbacked paper called "fiat currency." The populations of type 1 and 2 individuals, N_1 and N_2, remain constant for all $t \geq 1$. The young of each generation are identical in preferences and maximize the utility function $\ln c_t^h(t) + \ln c_t^h(t + 1)$ where $c_t^h(s)$ is consumption in the sth period of a member h of generation t.

a. Consider the equilibrium without valued currency (that is, the equilibrium in which there is no trade between generations). Let $[1 + r(t)]$ be the gross rate of return on consumption loans. Find a formula for $[1 + r(t)]$ as a function of N_1, N_2, y, and Y.

b. Suppose that N_1, N_2, y, and Y are such that $[1 + r(t)] > 1$ in the equilibrium without valued currency. Then prove that there can exist no quantity-theory-style equilibrium where fiat currency is valued and where the price level $p(t)$ obeys the quantity theory equation $p(t) = q \cdot H_0$, where q is a positive constant and $p(t)$ is measured in units of currency per unit good.

c. Suppose that N_1, N_2, y, and Y are such that in the nonvalued-currency equilibrium, $1 + r(t) < 1$. Prove that there exists an equilibrium in which fiat currency is valued and that there obtains the quantity theory equation $p(t) = q \cdot H_0$, where q is a constant. Construct an argument to show that the equilibrium with valued currency is not Pareto superior to the nonvalued-currency equilibrium.

d. Suppose that N_1, N_2, y, and Y are such that, in the above nonvalued-currency economy, $[1 + r(t)] < 1$, so that there exists an equilibrium in which fiat currency is valued. Let $\bar{p}$ be the stationary equilibrium price level in that economy. Now consider an alternative economy, identical with the preceding one in all respects except for the following feature: a government each period purchases a constant amount L_g of consumption loans and pays for them by issuing debt on itself, called "inside money" M_I, in the amount $M_I(t) = L_g \cdot p(t)$. The government never retires the inside money, using the proceeds of the loans to finance new purchases of consumption loans in subsequent periods. The quantity of outside money, or currency, remains H_0, whereas the "total high-power money" is now $H_0 + M_I(t)$.

   (i) Show that in this economy there exists a valued-currency equilibrium in which the price level is constant over time at $p(t) = \bar{p}$, or equivalently, as in the economy in (c), $p(t) = qH_0$.
   (ii) Explain why government purchases of private debt are not inflationary in this economy.

(iii) In standard macroeconomic models, once-and-for-all government open-market operations in private debt normally affect real variables and/or the price level. What accounts for the difference between those models and the one in this problem?

Exercise 7.3 Social Security and the Price Level

Consider an economy ("economy I") that consists of overlapping generations of two-period-lived people. At each date $t \geq 1$ there are born a constant number N of young people, who desire to consume both when they are young, at t, and when they are old, at $(t + 1)$. Each young person has the utility function $\ln c_t(t) + \ln c_t(t + 1)$, where $c_s(t)$ is time t consumption of an agent born at s. For all dates $t \geq 1$, young people are endowed with $y > 0$ units of a single nonstorable consumption good when they are young and zero units when they are old. In addition, at time $t = 1$ there are N old people endowed in the aggregate with H units of unbacked fiat currency. Let $p(t)$ be the nominal price level at t, denominated in dollars per time t good.

a. Define and compute an equilibrium with valued fiat currency for this economy. Argue that it exists and is unique. Now consider a second economy ("economy II") that is identical to the above economy except that economy II possesses a social security system. In particular, at each date $t \geq 1$, the government taxes $\tau > 0$ units of the time t consumption good away from each young person and at the same time gives τ units of the time t consumption good to each old person then alive.

b. Does economy II possess an equilibrium with valued fiat currency? Describe the restrictions on the parameter τ, if any, that are needed to ensure the existence of such an equilibrium.

c. If an equilibrium with valued fiat currency exists, is it unique?

d. Consider the *stationary* equilibrium with valued fiat currency. Is it unique? Describe how the value of currency or price level would vary across economies with differences in the size of the social security system, as measured by τ.

Exercise 7.4 Seignorage

Consider an economy consisting of overlapping generations of two-period-lived agents. At each date $t \geq 1$, there are born N_1 "lenders" who are endowed with $\alpha > 0$ units of the single consumption good when they are young and zero units when they are old. At each date $t \geq 1$, there are also born N_2 "borrowers" who are endowed with zero units of the consumption good when they are young and $\beta > 0$ units when they are old. The good is nonstorable, and N_1 and N_2 are constant through time. The economy starts at time 1, at which time there are N old people who are in the aggregate endowed with $H(0)$ units of unbacked, intrinsically worthless pieces of paper called dollars. Assume that α, β, N_1, and N_2 are such that

$$\frac{N_2\beta}{N_1\alpha} < 1.$$

Assume that everyone has preferences

$$u[c_t^h(t), c_t^h(t+1)] = \ln c_t^h(t) + \ln c_t^h(t+1),$$

where $c_t^h(s)$ is consumption of time s good of agent h born at time t.

a. Compute the equilibrium interest rate on consumption loans in the equilibrium without valued currency.

b. Construct a *brief* argument to establish whether or not the equilibrium without valued currency is Pareto optimal.

The economy also contains a government that purchases and destroys G_t units of the good in period t, $t \geq 1$. The government finances its purchases entirely by currency creation. That is, at time t,

$$G_t = \frac{H(t) - H(t-1)}{p(t)},$$

where $[H(t) - H(t-1)]$ is the additional dollars printed by the government at t and $p(t)$ is the price level at t. The government is assumed to increase $H(t)$ according to

$$H(t) = zH(t-1), \qquad z \geq 1,$$

where z is a constant for all time $t \geq 1$.

At time t, old people who carried over $H(t-1)$ dollars between $(t-1)$ and t offer these $H(t-1)$ dollars in exchange for time t goods. Also at t the government offers $H(t) - H(t-1)$ dollars for goods, so that $H(t)$ is the total supply of dollars at time t, to be carried over by the young into time $(t+1)$.

c. Assume that $1/z > N_2\beta/N_1\alpha$. Show that under this assumption there exists a continuum of equilibria with valued currency.

d. Display the unique stationary equilibrium with valued currency in the form of a "quantity theory" equation. Compute the equilibrium rate of return on currency and consumption loans.

e. Argue that if $1/z < N_2\beta/N_1\alpha$, then there exists no valued-currency equilibrium. Interpret this result. (Hint: Look at the rate of return on consumption loans in the equilibrium without valued currency.)

f. Find the value of z that *maximizes* the government's G_t in a stationary equilibrium. Compare this with the largest value of z that is compatible with the existence of a valued-currency equilibrium.

Exercise 7.5. **Oscillating Physical Returns**

Consider an overlapping-generations model with $N(t) = N(0) > 0$ for $t \geq 1$. Let the net rate of return on storage $p(t)$ be given by the periodic sequence

$$p(t) = \begin{cases} p(1) > 0, & \text{for } t \text{ odd} \\ p(2) < 0, & \text{for } t \text{ even}, \end{cases}$$

with $[1 + p(1)] \cdot [1 + p(2)] < 1$. Let the per capita saving function be $f[1 + r(t)]$ for $r(t) > p(t)$. Let the saving function satisfy $f'[1 + r(t)] > 0$ for $r(t) > p(t)$ and

$$\lim_{\substack{r(t) \to p(2) \\ r(t) > p(2)}} f[1 + r(t)] > 0.$$

Let there be a fixed stock of government-supplied unbacked currency in the amount H that is initially in the hands of the old people at $t = 1$. Assume that $G(t) = 0$ for all $t \geq 1$ and $H(t) = H$ for all $t \geq 1$.

a. Describe the equilibrium in which currency is valueless. Compute the equilibrium rate of return on loans and the equilibrium amounts of storage.

b. Let $p(t)$ be the price level and $K(t)$ the storage amount at t. Prove that there exists a stationary or periodic equilibrium of the form

$$p(t) = \begin{cases} p(1), & t \text{ odd} \\ p(2), & t \text{ even}, \end{cases}$$

with $0 < p(2) < p(1) < \infty$, and with $K(t) = K(1) > 0$ for t odd and $K(t) = 0$ for t even.

c. Assume that all agents are identical, so that $f[1 + r(t)]$ is the saving function of the representative agent. Prove that the equilibrium in (b) Pareto dominates the equilibrium in (a).

d. (Optional.) Indicate in what sense the assumption that

$$\lim_{\substack{r(t) \to p(2) \\ r(t) > p(2)}} f[1 + r(t)] > 0$$

is necessary for the existence proof to go through. Notice that this statement is *not* equivalent to saying that without that assumption an equilibrium does not exist. It just says that without the assumption we cannot establish existence.

e. (Optional.) Prove that no equilibrium exists with valued currency and with zero storage at every t, that is, $K(t) = 0$ for all t.

f. (Optional.) Prove that there exists a continuum of equilibria with valued currency and such that $K(t) > 0$ for all t. These equilibria are such that they all "converge" to the equilibrium computed in part (a). This argument establishes nonuniqueness of the result in (b).

g. (Optional.) Prove that there exist no equilibria such that $K(t) = 0$ and $r(t - 1) = p(2)$ if t odd.

Exercise 7.6. Indeterminacy of Exchange Rates

Consider a two-country, one-nonstorable-good, overlapping-generations model of two-period-lived agents. In country i there is a constant number N_i of young people born at each $t \geq 1$. Agents in both countries have the common preferences $u[c_t^h(t), c_t^h(t + 1)] = \ln c_t^h(t) + \ln c_t^h(t + 1)$. The per capita endowments in country i are time invariant and are given by $[\Sigma w_t^h(t)/N_1, \Sigma w_t^h(t + 1)/N_1] = (\alpha_1, \alpha_2)$ for country 1, and by $[\Sigma w_t^h(t)/N_2, \Sigma w_t^h(t + 1)/N_2] = (\beta_1, \beta_2)$ for country 2. At time 0, the old of country i are endowed with $H_i(0)$ units of inconvertible currency. The currency of country 1 is called "pounds," whereas the currency of country 2 is called "dollars." The government of country i makes the currency supply grow according to $H_i(t) = z_i H_i(t - 1)$ for $t \geq 1$, where $z_i \geq 1$. The currency is used to finance government purchases of the good. No explicit taxes are imposed, and the government budget constraints are $G_i(t) = [H_i(t) - H_i(t - 1)]/p_i(t)$, where $p_i(t)$ is the price level in country i's currency. Define the exchange rate as $e(t) = p_1(t)/p_2(t)$.

Consider a free-trade, flexible-exchange-rate regime in which agents in the two countries are permitted freely to borrow and to lend to each other and to hold each other's currency.

a. Write down the condition for equilibrium in the world currency-consumption loans market.

b. Prove that $[(\beta_2 N_2 + \alpha_2 N_1)/(\beta_1 N_2 + \alpha_1 N_1)] < 1$ is a necessary condition for the existence of an equilibrium with valued currency if $z_1 \geq 1$ and $z_2 \geq 1$.

c. Find conditions on $(z_1, z_2, \alpha_1, \alpha_2, N_1, N_2, \beta_1, \beta_2)$ such that there exists an equilibrium in which

(i) both countries' currencies are valued
(ii) country 1's currency is valued but there exists no equilibrium in which country 2's currency is valued.

d. Under conditions in which an equilibrium exists, with both currencies being valued, prove that any constant exchange rate $e(t) = e$, $t \geq 1$ in the interval $(0, \infty)$ is an equilibrium exchange rate.

e. Give a formula for:

(i) the balance of trade
(ii) the balance of payments.

Exercise 7.7. **Asset Prices and Volatility**

Consider an economy with overlapping generations of two-period-lived agents. At time $t \geq 1$, there are born $N(t)$ young, each of whom is endowed with w units of the one consumption good in the model in the first period of life and zero units in the second period of life. The consumption good can be productively invested under the following conditions: if $k(t)$ units of the good are stored at t, then $(1 + p)k(t)$ units become available at time $(t + 1)$, where $p \geq -1$. Each agent of each generation has the utility function $\ln c_t(t) + \ln c_t(t + 1)$ where $c_t(s)$ is consumption of the s-period good of an agent born in t.

In addition, there is a small and constant number T of "trees," all of which are initially in the hands of the initial old at time $t = 1$. These trees live forever. At time $t \geq 1$, each tree drops (pays dividends) d_t units of the consumption good to its owner as of the beginning of the period. Notice that d_t is measured in units of time t consumption good per tree. Assume that $\{d_t\}_{t=1}^{\infty}$ is a positive and bounded sequence. Let the price of trees at t be v_t, measured in units of the consumption good at t per tree. Assume that the number of trees is relatively small, in the sense that for any $\epsilon > 0$,

$$T \cdot \sum_{j=1}^{\infty} \left(\frac{1}{1 + \epsilon} \right)^j d_{t+j} < \frac{N(t)w}{2} \qquad \text{for all } t \geq 1.$$

a. Assume $N(t) = N$ and that $p > 0$ is constant for all time. Describe the equilibrium of this economy. Show formally that the following formula describes the evolution of the price of trees:

(1)
$$v_t = \sum_{j=1}^{\infty} \left(\frac{1}{1 + r} \right)^j d_{t+j},$$

where r is the real rate of interest. Prove that r is constant over time, and give a formula for it.

b. Assume now that $p = -1$, so that the consumption good is nonstorable. Derive a formula for v_t in this economy, and compare it with (1). How is the real rate of interest behaving in this economy? Describe an example in which dividends are constant ($d_t = d > 0$ for all $t \geq 1$) but in which v_t varies through time.

c. Prove that in model (b) the share price still obeys the following generalization of (a):

$$v_t = \sum_{j=1}^{\infty} \prod_{s=1}^{j} \left(\frac{1}{1 + r(t + s - 1)} \right) d_{t+j},$$

where now the real rate $r(s)$ varies over time. Describe the way in which $r(s)$ varies over time.

Exercise 7.8. Unpleasant Monetarist Arithmetic

Consider an economy in which the aggregate demand for government currency for $t \geq 1$ is given by $[M(t)p(t)]^d = g[R_1(t)]$, where $R_1(t)$ is the gross rate of return on currency between t and $(t + 1)$, $M(t)$ is the stock of currency at t, and $p(t)$ is the value of currency in terms of goods at t (the reciprocal of the price level). The function $g(R)$ satisfies

(1) $g(R)(1 - R) = h(R) > 0$ for $R \in (\underline{R}, 1)$,
          $h(R) \leq 0$ for $R < \underline{R}$, $R \geq 1$, $\underline{R} > 0$.
          $h'(R) < 0$ for $R > R_m$
          $h'(R) > 0$ for $R < R_m$
          $h(R_m) > D$,   where D is a positive number to be defined shortly.

The government faces an infinitely elastic demand for its interest-bearing bonds at a constant over time gross rate of return $R_2 > 1$. The government finances a budget deficit D, defined as government purchases minus explicit taxes, that is constant over time. The government's budget constraint is

(2) $D = p(t)[M(t) - M(t - 1)] + B(t) - B(t - 1)R_2$, $t \geq 1$,

subject to $B(0) = 0$, $M(0) > 0$. In equilibrium,

(3) $M(t)p(t) = g[R_1(t)]$.

The government is free to choose paths of $M(t)$, $B(t)$, subject to (2) and (3).
   a. Prove that, for $B(t) = 0$, for all $t > 0$, there exist two stationary equilibria for this model.
   b. Show that there exist values of $B > 0$, such that there exist stationary equilibrium with $B(t) = B$, $M(t)p(t) = Mp$.
   c. Prove a version of the following proposition: among stationary equilibria, the lower the value of B, the lower the stationary rate of inflation consistent with equilibrium. (You will have to make an assumption about Laffer curve effects to obtain such a proposition.)

This problem displays some of the ideas used by Sargent and Wallace (1981). Sargent and Wallace argue that, under assumptions like those leading to the proposition stated under (c), the "looser" money is today [that is, the higher $M(1)$ and the lower $B(1)$], the lower the stationary inflation rate.

Exercise 7.9. Grandmont

Consider a nonstochastic, one-good overlapping-generations model consisting of two-period-lived young people born in each $t \geq 1$ and an initial group of old people at $t = 1$ who are endowed with $H(0) > 0$ units of unbacked currency at the beginning of period 1. The one good in the model is not storable. Let the aggregate first-period saving function of the young be time invariant and be denoted $f[1 + r(t)]$ where $[1 + r(t)]$ is the gross rate of return on consumption loans between t and $(t + 1)$. The saving function is assumed to satisfy $f(0) = -\infty$, $f'(1 + r) > 0$, $f(1) > 0$.

Let the government pay interest on currency, starting in period 2 (to holders of currency between periods 1 and 2). The government pays interest on currency at a nominal rate of $[1 + r(t)] p(t + 1)/\bar{p}$, where $[1 + r(t)]$ is the real gross rate of return on consumption loans, $p(t)$ is the price level at t, and $\bar{p}$ is a target price level chosen to satisfy

$$\bar{p} = H(0)/f(1).$$

The government finances its interest payments by printing new money, so that the government's budget constraint is:

$$H(t + 1) - H(t) = \left\{[1 + r(t)]\frac{p(t + 1)}{\bar{p}} - 1\right\}H(t), \qquad t \geq 1,$$

given $H(1) = H(0) > 0$. The gross rate of return on consumption loans in this economy is $1 + r(t)$. In equilibrium, we have that $[1 + r(t)]$ must be at least as great as the real rate of return on currency

$$[1 + r(t)]p(t)/\bar{p} = [1 + r(t)]\frac{p(t + 1)}{\bar{p}}\frac{p(t)}{p(t + 1)}$$

with equality if currency is valued,

$$1 + r(t) \geq [1 + r(t)]p(t)/\bar{p}, \qquad 0 < p(t) < \infty.$$

The loan market-clearing condition in this economy is

$$f[1 + r(t)] = H(t)/p(t).$$

a. Define an equilibrium.

b. Prove that there exists a unique monetary equilibrium in this economy and compute it.

Exercise 7.10. **Bryant-Keynes-Wallace**

Consider an economy consisting of overlapping generations of two-period-lived agents. There is a constant population of N young agents born at each date $t \geq 1$. There is a single consumption good that is not storable. Each agent born in $t \geq 1$ is endowed with w_1 units of the consumption good when young and with w_2 units when old, where $0 < w_2 < w_1$. Each agent born at $t \geq 1$ has identical preferences $\ln c_t^h(t) + \ln c_t^h(t + 1)$, where $c_t^h(s)$ is time s consumption of agent h born at time t. In addition, at time 1, there are alive N

old people who are endowed with $H(0)$ units of unbacked paper currency and who want to maximize their consumption of the time 1 good.

A government attempts to finance a constant level of government purchases $G(t) = G > 0$ for $t \geq 1$ by printing new base money. The government's budget constraint is

$$G = [H(t) - H(t-1)]/p(t),$$

where $p(t)$ is the price level at t, and $H(t)$ is the stock of currency carried over from t to $(t+1)$ by agents born in t. Let $g = G/N$ be government purchases per young person. Assume that purchases $G(t)$ yield no utility to private agents.

a. Define a stationary equilibrium with valued fiat currency.

b. Prove that, for g sufficiently small, there exists a stationary equilibrium with valued fiat currency.

c. Prove that, in general, if there exists one stationary equilibrium with valued fiat currency, with rate of return on currency $1 + r(t) = 1 + r_1$, then there exists at least one other stationary equilibrium with valued currency with $1 + r(t) = 1 + r_2 \neq 1 + r_1$.

d. Tell whether the equilibria described in (b) and (c) are Pareto optimal, among those allocations that allocate among private agents what is left after the government takes $G(t) = G$ each period. (A proof is not required here: an informal argument will suffice.)

Now let the government institute a forced saving program of the following form. At time 1, the government redeems the outstanding stock of currency $H(0)$, exchanging it for government bonds. For $t \geq 1$, the government offers each young consumer the option of saving at least F worth of time t goods in the form of bonds bearing a constant rate of return $(1 + r_2)$. A legal prohibition against private intermediation is instituted that prevents two or more private agents from sharing one of these bonds. The government's budget constraint for $t \geq 2$ is

$$G/N = B(t) - B(t-1)(1 + r_2),$$

where $B(t) \geq F$. Here $B(t)$ is the saving of a young agent at t. At time $t = 1$, the government's budget constraint is

$$G/N = B(1) - \frac{H(0)}{Np(1)},$$

where $p(1)$ is the price level at which the initial currency stock is redeemed at $t = 1$. The government sets F and r_2.

Consider stationary equilibria with $B(t) = B$ for $t \geq 1$ and r_2 and F constant.

e. Prove that if g is small enough for an equilibrium of type (a) to exist, then a stationary equilibrium with forced saving exists. (Either a graphic argument or an algebraic argument is sufficient.)

f. Given g, find the values of F and r_2 that maximize the utility of a representative young agent for $t \geq 1$.

g. Is the equilibrium allocation associated with the values of F and $(1 + r_2)$ found in (f) optimal among those allocations that give $G(t) = G$ to the government for all $t \geq 1$? (Here an informal argument will suffice.)

References and Suggested Readings

Aiyagari, S. Rao. 1985. Deficits, interest rates, and the tax distribution. *Federal Reserve Bank of Minneapolis Quarterly Review* 9(1):5–14.

Balasko, Y., and K. Shell. 1980. The overlapping-generations model I: the case of pure exchange without money. *Journal of Economic Theory* 23(3):281–306.

Barro, Robert J. 1974. Are government bonds net wealth? *Journal of Political Economy* 82(6):1095–1117.

Benhabib, Jess, and Richard H. Day. 1982. A characterization of erratic dynamics in the overlapping generations model. *Journal of Economic Dynamics and Control* 4(1):37–55.

Boyer, Russell. 1971. Nickels and dimes. University of Western Ontario, London, Ontario.

Bryant, J., and N. Wallace. 1979. The inefficiency of interest-bearing national debt. *Journal of Political Economy* 87(2):365–381.

———— 1984. A price discrimination analysis of monetary policy. *Review of Economic Studies* 51(2):279–288.

Fischer, Stanley. 1984. The economy of Israel. In *Monetary and Fiscal Policies and Their Applications,* Carnegie-Rochester Conference Series 20, ed. K. Brunner and A. H. Meltzer, pp. 7–52. Amsterdam: North-Holland.

Fisher, Irving. [1907] 1930. *The Theory of Interest.* London: Macmillan.

Friedman, Milton. 1960. *A Program for Monetary Stability.* New York: Fordham University Press.

Friedman, Milton, and Anna J. Schwartz. 1982. *Monetary Trends in the United States and the United Kingdom: Their Relation to Income, Prices, and Interest Rates, 1867–1975.* Chicago: University of Chicago Press.

Grandmont, Jean-Michel. 1985. On endogenous competitive business cycles. *Econometrica* 53(5):995–1046.

Kareken, J. H., and N. Wallace. 1981. On the indeterminacy of equilibrium exchange rates. *Quarterly Journal of Economics* 96(2):207–222.

Keynes, John Maynard. 1940. *How to Pay for the War: A Radical Plan for the Chancellor of the Exchequer.* London: Macmillan.

Koda, Keiichi. 1984. A note on the existence of monetary equilibria in overlapping generations models with storage. *Journal of Economic Theory* 34(2):388–395.

Lucas, Robert E., Jr. 1972. Expectations and the neutrality of money. *Journal of Economic Theory* 4(2):103–124.

—— 1976. Econometric policy evaluation: a critique. In *The Phillips Curve and Labor Markets,* Carnegie-Rochester Conference Series 1, ed. K. Brunner and A. H. Meltzer, pp. 19–46. Amsterdam: North-Holland.

Manuelli, Rodolfo. 1984. A note on the relationship between existence of monetary equilibrium and optimality of the nonmonetary equilibrium in stochastic overlapping generations models. Northwestern University, Evanston, Ill.

Mill, John Stuart. 1844. Review of books by Thomas Tooke and R. Toriens. *Westminster Review* 41(June):593.

—— [1848] 1965. *Principles of Political Economy.* New York: A. Kelley.

Millan, Teodoro. 1981. On the existence of optimal competitive equilibria in the overlapping-generations model. Ph.D. diss., University of Minnesota.

—— 1982. The role of currency reserve requirements in precluding the occurrence of inefficient equilibria. Working Paper 37. Universidad Autonoma de Barcelona. (Forthcoming in *Journal of Economic Theory.*)

Miller, P., and N. Wallace. 1985. The international coordination of macroeconomic policies: a welfare analysis. Federal Reserve Bank of Minneapolis *Quarterly Review* 9(2):14–32.

Nickelsburg, Gerald. 1980. Flexible exchange rates and uncertain government policies: a theoretical and empirical analysis. Ph.D. diss., University of Minnesota.

Peled, Dan. 1982. Information diversity over time and the optimality of monetary equilibria. *Journal of Economic Theory* 28(2):255–274.

Rolnick, A. J., and W. E. Weber. 1983. New evidence on the free banking era. *American Economic Review* 73(5):1080–1091.

—— 1984. The causes of free bank failures: a detailed examination. *Journal of Monetary Economics* 14(3):267–291.

—— 1985. Explaining the demand for free bank notes. Staff Report 97. Federal Reserve Bank of Minneapolis.

—— Forthcoming. Gresham's law. *Journal of Political Economy.*

Samuelson, Paul A. 1958. An exact consumption-loan model of interest with or without the social contrivance of money. *Journal of Political Economy* 66(6):467–482.

Sargent, Thomas J. 1979. *Macroeconomic Theory.* New York: Academic Press.

Sargent, Thomas J. and N. Wallace. 1981. Some unpleasant monetarist arithmetic. Federal Reserve Bank of Minneapolis *Quarterly Review* 5(3):1–17.

—— 1982. The real bills doctrine vs. the quantity theory: a reconsideration. *Journal of Political Economy* 90(6):1212–1236.

—— 1983. A model of commodity money. *Journal of Monetary Economics* 12(1):163–187.

—— 1984. Identification and estimation of a model of hyperinflation with a continuum of "sunspot" equilibria. Working Paper. Federal Reserve Bank of Minneapolis.

—— 1985. Interest on reserves. *Journal of Monetary Economics* 15(3):279–290.

Sebastian, Miguel. 1985. Fixed exchange rates and non-cooperative monetary policies. University of Minnesota, Minneapolis.

Shell, Karl. 1971. Notes on the economics of infinity. *Journal of Political Economy* 79(5):1002–1011.

Smith, Adam. [1776] 1937. *An Inquiry into the Wealth of Nations.* New York: Modern Library.

Sonnenschein, Hugo. 1973. Do Walras' identity and continuity characterize the class of community excess demand functions? *Journal of Economic Theory* 6(4):345–354.

Starrett, David A. 1972. On golden rules, the "biological theory of interest," and competitive inefficiency. *Journal of Political Economy* 80(2):276–291.

Varian, Hal. 1978. *Microeconomic Analysis.* New York: Norton.

Wallace, Neil. 1978. Models of overlapping generations: an exposition. University of Minnesota, Minneapolis.

———— 1980a. Integrating micro and macroeconomics: an application to credit controls. Federal Reserve Bank of Minneapolis *Quarterly Review* 4(4):16–29.

———— 1980b. The overlapping-generations model of fiat money. In *Models of Monetary Economies,* ed. J. H. Kareken and N. Wallace, pp. 49–82. Minneapolis: Federal Reserve Bank of Minneapolis.

———— 1981a. A Modigliani-Miller theorem for open market operations. *American Economic Review* 71(3):267–274.

———— 1981b. A hybrid fiat-commodity monetary system. *Journal of Economic Theory* 25(3):421–430.

———— 1983. A legal restrictions theory of the demand for "money" and the role of monetary policy. Federal Reserve Bank of Minneapolis *Quarterly Review* 7(1):1–7.

Wilson, Charles A. 1981. Equilibrium in dynamic models with an infinity of agents. *Journal of Economic Theory* 24(1):95–111.

8 | Government Finance in Stochastic Overlapping-Generations Models

This chapter describes a stochastic version of the overlapping-generations model that Neil Wallace (1981) has used. The model is a generalization of the one studied in the previous chapter. In the model of the present chapter, uncertainty is introduced by making the rate of return on storage a random process. The model can be viewed as embodying a general equilibrium version of Tobin's "Liquidity Preference as Behavior towards Risk" (1958) as a model of the demand for unbacked currency. We shall use the model to discuss a variety of issues about government debt management. The model will be used to present Wallace's Modigliani-Miller theorem for government open-market operations as well as a related theorem of Chamley and Polemarchakis (1984) that depicts a different class of "neutral" open-market operations. We shall also use the model to study the idea of Peled (1985) and Liviatan (1983) that introduction of government-supplied indexed bonds by itself makes no difference. Finally, we obtain a version of the Ricardian theorem.

These "irrelevance" theorems of Wallace, Chamley and Polemarchakis, Peled and Liviatan, and Ricardo all have a common structure, which it is the purpose of this chapter to study. The theorems assume an economy in which government and private securities exist and are valued in an initial equilibrium, with a given specification of government policy strategies. Holding the consumption allocations associated with this initial equilibrium fixed, one solves the equilibrium conditions for the class of government policies that supports this same consumption allocation in equilibrium. If this class of government policies is singular, the implication is that government policy is relevant (at least in the vicinity of the initial equilibrium). If several distinct government policies are associated with the same equilibrium consumption allocations, however, the implication is that choices of government policy from among this collection of policies are irrelevant. For the economy to be analyzed there turns out to be a wide class of government policies associated with an initial equilibrium that satisfies some regularity conditions. The different irrelevance theorems mentioned above correspond to movements in alternative directions within the equivalence class of government policies that is associated with an initial equilibrium.

For convenience, we will follow Wallace (1981) and will view the analysis in the context of a particular class of stochastic overlapping-generations economies. As Chamley and Polemarchakis (1984) have emphasized, however, similar results would hold in a wide variety of economies with an initial equilibrium that satisfies conditions like the ones that we assume. In particular, it is sufficient for the initial equilibrium to be one in which government and private securities of various types are voluntarily chosen by private agents and in which enough private agents are at interior maxima. The overlapping-generations economy is one that potentially satisfies these requirements and has equilibrium conditions that are simple to work with.

8.1 The Economy

The economy consists of overlapping generations of two-period-lived agents. At each date $t \geq 1$, there are born $N(t) > 0$ agents. An agent h born at time t is endowed (after taxes and transfers) with $w_t^h(t)$ of a single date t consumption good when young and receives (after taxes and transfers) an endowment of $w_{ti}^h(t + 1)$ units of the single date $(t + 1)$ consumption good when a random variable $x(t + 1) = x_i$.[1] Thus for $t \geq 1$, each young agent's second-period endowment is a random variable that is a function of the realization of the random variable $x(t + 1)$. The random variable $x(t + 1)$ governs the rate of return on storage of the single consumption good between dates t and $(t + 1)$. If an agent stores $k^h(t) \geq 0$ units of the consumption good at t, then "nature" returns $x(t + 1)k^h(t)$ units of the time $(t + 1)$ good. We assume that for $t \geq 1$, $x(t + 1)$ is nonnegative, is independently and identically distributed through time, and is described by the discrete probability distribution

$$\text{prob}\{x(t + 1) = x_i\} = f_i, \qquad i = 1, \ldots, I$$

$$\sum_{i=1}^{I} f_i = 1.$$

---

1. Notice that in notation this chapter differs from the previous chapter, where $w_t^h(t)$ denoted the *pretax* endowment.

It is assumed that $x(t + 1)$ is observed at the beginning of time $(t + 1)$, before time $(t + 1)$ decisions are taken.

Agent h of generation t consumes $c_t^h(t)$ when young and an x-contingent amount $c_{ti}^h(t + 1)$ when old if $x(t + 1) = x_i$. Agent h at $t \geq 1$ is assumed to maximize

$$Eu^h[c_t^h(t), c_{ti}^h(t + 1)] = \sum_{i=1}^{I} f_{ti} u^h[c_t^h(t), c_{ti}^h(t + 1)],$$

where $u^h[c_t^h(t), c_{ti}^h(t + 1)]$ is strictly increasing, strictly concave, and twice differentiable.

An exogenous aggregate endowment of time t goods of $Y(t)$ is available to the economy, $t \geq 1$. It is assumed that $Y(t)$ is nonstochastic. If in the aggregate $K(t) \geq 0$ is stored at time t, then $Y(t + 1) + x(t + 1)K(t)$ of time $(t + 1)$ goods are available. We let $K^p(t) \geq 0$ denote total private storage and $K^g(t) \geq 0$ denote government storage, so that $K(t) = K^p(t) + K^g(t)$.

At time 1, there are $N(0) > 0$ old people who are endowed in the aggregate with $M(0)$ units of unbacked and inconvertible fiat currency. At $t = 1$, old agent h is endowed after taxes with a quantity of time 1 consumption goods $w_0^h(1)$. An old agent h at time 1 acts to maximize time 1 consumption $c_0^h(1)$. We assume that $K^p(0)$ is nonnegative and given. We also assume that $K^g(0)$ is nonnegative and given.

Each household can transfer goods across time and states of nature on the following terms. First, by storing $k^h(t)$ at t, a household earns $x_i k^h(t)$ of time $(t + 1)$ goods when $x(t + 1) = x_i$. Second, at time t a household can purchase or sell one unit of consumption in state $x(t + 1) = x_i$ at a price of $s_i(t)$, measured in units of time t consumption good per unit of time $(t + 1)$ consumption good in state $x(t + 1) = x_i$. Third, if at time t when $x(t) = x_j$, the household invests $m^h(t)p_j(t)$ units of time t goods in currency, it receives $m^h(t)p_i(t + 1)$ of time $(t + 1)$ goods when the state x_i occurs at time $(t + 1)$. Here $p_j(t)$ is the value of money, the reciprocal of the price level, at time t when $x(t) = x_j$.[2] Thus the young consumer faces the budget constraints

$$c_t^h(t) + k^h(t) + \sum_{i=1}^{I} s_i(t)d_i^h(t) + p(t)m^h(t) \leq w_t^h(t)$$

$$c_{ti}^h(t + 1) \leq w_{ti}^h(t + 1) + k^h(t)x_i + p_i(t + 1)m^h(t) + d_i^h(t),$$
$$i = 1, \ldots, I,$$

2. Again, notice that this notation differs from that used in the previous chapter. The notation of the present chapter is chosen to agree with that of Wallace. The currency stock $M(t)$, tax collections $T(t)$, government purchases $G(t)$, and government investments $K^g(t)$ are each in general permitted to be functions of $\{x_t, x_{t-1}, \ldots, x_1, K^p(0), K^g(0), M(0)\}$. We will study

where $d_i^h(t)$ is the quantity of claims on $(t + 1)$ good contingent on state i purchased by agent h at time t. Multiplying the second inequality by $s_i(t)$, summing over i, and substituting the result into the first inequality gives

(8.0)
$$c_t^h(t) + \sum_{i=1}^{I} s_i(t)c_{ti}^h(t + 1)$$

$$\leq w_t^h(t) + \sum_{i=1}^{I} s_i(t)w_{ti}^h(t + 1) + k^h(t)\left[\sum_{i=1}^{I} x_i s_i(t) - 1\right]$$

$$+ m^h(t)\left[\sum_{i=1}^{I} p_i(t + 1)s_i(t) - p(t)\right].$$

Notice that, if $\sum_{i=1}^{I} x_i s_i(t) > 1$, then any household can attain unbounded consumption by storing sufficiently high amounts $k^h(t)$ and financing this by borrowing when young. That is to say, if $[\sum_{i=1}^{I} x_i s_i(t) - 1] > 0$, then arbitrage opportunities exist. Accordingly, for an equilibrium without arbitrage opportunities, it must be true that

$$\left[\sum_{i=1}^{I} x_i s_i(t) - 1\right] \leq 0.$$

Furthermore, if $\sum_{i=1}^{I} x_i s_i(t) < 1$, inspection of (8.0) verifies that it is optimal for each household to set $k^h(t) = 0$. We summarize with the condition

$$[x(t + 1)s(t) - 1] \leq 0, \qquad = \quad \text{if } K^p(t) > 0.$$

Here $x(t + 1)s(t)$ denotes the vector product $\sum_{i=1}^{I} x_i s_i(t)$. A similar argument demonstrates that absence of arbitrage opportunities requires

$$\sum_{i=1}^{I} p_i(t + 1)s_i(t) - p(t) \leq 0, \qquad = 0 \quad \text{if } \sum_{h=1}^{N(t)} m^h(t) > 0.$$

We can express this condition simply as

$$\sum_{i=1}^{I} p_i(t + 1)s_i(t) - p(t) = 0,$$

---

equilibria in which the equilibrium price of currency at $(t + 1)$, $p(t + 1)$, is a function of the history $(x_{t+1}, x_t, \ldots, x_1)$ and the initial conditions $K^p(0)$, $K^g(0)$, $M(0)$. Thus when we write $p(t + 1)$, it should be understood that we intend to connote a function $p[x_{t+1}, x_t, \ldots, x_1, K^p(0), K^g(0), M(0)]$. When we want to denote this function evaluated at $x_{t+1} = x_i$, we shall write $p_i(t + 1)$, which means $p[x_i, x_t, x_{t-1}, \ldots, x_1, K^p(0), K^g(0), M(0)]$. The notation $s(t)$ denotes the I-element vector whose ith component is $s_i(t)$. In equilibrium, $s_i(t)$ will turn out to be a function of $[x_t, x_{t-1}, \ldots, x_1, K^p(0), K^g(0), M(0)]$, where we should recall, $s_i(t)$ is the price in terms of the time t good of a claim on a unit of the time $(t + 1)$ good when $x_{t+1} = x_i$. Let us say, more compactly, that $x^t = (x_t, x_{t-1}, \ldots, x_1)$. In general, equilibrium values of both p_t and $s_i(t)$ are functions of $[x^t, K^p(0), K^g(0), M(0)]$.

because if it happens that $\Sigma_{h=1}^{N(t)} m^h(t) = 0$, then it must be true that currency is valueless now and in the future, so that $p_i(t + 1) = 0$ and $p(t) = 0$.

Using these results in Equation (8.0), we have that in an equilibrium each young household maximizes

$$\sum_{i=1}^{I} f_i u^h[c_t^h(t), c_{ti}^h(t + 1)],$$

$$\text{subject to} \quad c_t^h(t) + \sum_{i=1}^{I} s_i(t) c_{ti}^h(t + 1) \le w_t^h(t) + \sum_{i=1}^{I} s_i(t) w_{ti}^h(t + 1)$$

or

(8.1) $c_t^h(t) + s(t) c_t^h(t + 1) \le w_t^h(t) + s(t) w_t^h(t + 1).$

The maximization is over $c_t^h(t)$, $c_{ti}^h(t + 1)$, $i = 1, \ldots, I$. The first-order necessary conditions for this problem, assuming an interior solution, are

(8.2) $f_i u_2^h[c_t^h(t), c_{ti}^h(t + 1)] = s_i(t) \sum_{j=1}^{I} f_j u_1^h[c_t^h(t), c_{tj}^h(t + 1)]$

for $i = 1, \ldots, I$,   for all h,   for all $t \ge 1$.

Here u_j^h is the partial derivative of u^h with respect to the jth argument. We restate the no-arbitrage conditions as

(8.3) $s(t) x(t + 1) - 1 \le 0,$ $= \quad 0$ if $K^p(t) > 0,$ $t \ge 1$

(8.4) $p(t + 1) s(t) - p(t) = 0,$ $t \ge 1.$

Here $p(t + 1) s(t)$ denotes the vector product $\Sigma_{i=1}^{I} p_i(t + 1) s_i(t)$. This completes the description of the behavior of private agents.

The government purchases and consumes $G(t)$ units of the time t good. It purchases and stores $K^g(t)$ units of time t good. The government also expands or contracts the supply of currency, which is set at $M(t)$ at the beginning of period t. In the aggregate, the government collects taxes net of transfers in the real amount $T(t)$, measured in units of the time t good. The government's budget constraint is

(8.5) $K^g(t) + G_i(t) = T_i(t) + K^g(t - 1) x_i(t) + p_i(t)[M(t) - M(t - 1)],$
          for all i, $t \ge 1.$

In (8.5) $T(t)$ represents lump-sum taxes net of lump-sum subsidies, and satisfies[3]

---

3. The variables $T(t)$ and $G(t)$ are permitted to depend on $K^p(0)$, $K^g(0)$, $M(0)$, and $x^t = (x_t, x_{t-1}, \ldots, x_1)$. We denote these functions evaluated at $(x_i, x_{t-1}, \ldots, x_1)$ as T_i and G_i.

(8.6) $T_i(t) = Y(t) - \sum_h w_t^h(t) - \sum_h w_{t-1,i}^h(t)$,   for all i, $t \geq 1$,

when $x(t) = x_i$ at time t. The initial conditions $K^g(0)$, $w_0^h(1)$, $M(0)$ are regarded as given.

Equilibrium requires equality between the excess demand on the part of generation t for consumption in state $x(t + 1) = x_i$ and the excess supply on the part of generation $(t - 1)$ and the government. This condition can be expressed as

(8.7) $\sum_h [c_{ti}^h(t + 1) - w_{ti}^h(t + 1)] - K^p(t)x_i = p_i(t + 1)M(t)$,

   $t \geq 1$, $i = 1, \ldots, I$.

Equations (8.1)–(8.7) are the restrictions imposed by the model. Equations (8.1)–(8.4) summarize private agents' behavior, whereas Equations (8.5)–(8.6) restrict the government's behavior, and (8.7) is a set of equilibrium conditions. An *equilibrium* is a stochastic process for $\{c_t^h(t), c_t^h(t + 1),$ $w_t^h(t), w_t^h(t + 1), K^p(t), K^g(t), Y(t), N(t), M(t), G(t), T(t), p(t)$ and $s(t)\}_{t=1}^{\infty}$ that satisfies equations (8.1)–(8.7). This broad definition leaves open the matter of which variables are imagined to be exogenous (to be determined from outside the analysis) and which are to be viewed as endogenous (to be determined by the model). A variety of specifications of endogenous and exogenous variables can be imagined. A couple of alternative specifications will be used below.

Wallace (1981), for example, uses a particular definition of equilibrium, which incorporates a particular partitioning of variables into groups of exogenous and endogenous variables

DEFINITION. *Given $K^p(0)$, $K^g(0)$, $M(0)$, and $w_0^h(1)$ and stochastic processes for $[G(t), w_t^h(t), w_t^h(t + 1), Y(t), K^g(t), t \geq 1]$ an equilibrium is a set of stochastic processes $[c_t^h(t), c_t^h(t + 1), K^p(t), p(t), s(t), M(t)$ and $T(t)]$ that for all $t \geq 1$ solve Equations (8.1)–(8.7).*

In this definition, a given stochastic process for $[G(t), w_t^h(t), w_t^h(t + 1),$ $K^g(t), t \geq 1]$ can be regarded as reflecting the government's choice of a policy. In this definition, $M(t)$ and $T(t)$ are regarded as equilibrium outcomes that are mainly determined by the government's budget constraint. Under alternative breakdowns into exogenous and endogenous variables, $M(t)$ and $T(t)$ could themselves be exogenous.

8.2 Some Examples

It is useful to study several example economies that are special cases of the above economy.

EXAMPLE 8.1. *A Stationary Economy with No Government Storage*

We take $N(t) = N$ for all $t \geq 1$, $Y(t) = yN > 0$, $t \geq 1$, $w_t^h(t) = y$, for all h and $t \geq 1$; $w_{ti}^h(t+1) = 0$ for all h, t, i. Say that $I = 2$, and assume that $x_1 < 1 < x_2$ and that $Ex \equiv f_1 x_1 + f_2 x_2 > 1$ and that $Ex^{-1} > 1$. For government policy, assume that $M(t) = M > 0$ for all t and that $G(t) = K^g(t) = 0$ for all $t \geq 1$. As for preferences, assume that $u^h[c_t^h(t), c_t^h(t+1)] = \ln c_t^h(t) + \ln c_t^h(t+1)$.

Given the repetitive structure of the forcing variables of this economy, it is natural to seek a stationary equilibrium with positive private storage. In this example, by a stationary equilibrium, we mean one in which $p(t) = p$ and $K(t) = K$ for all $t \geq 1$ and for all i and $s_i(t) = s_i$, independent of t. Equations (8.1) and (8.2) become

(i) $$c_t^h(t) + c_{t1}^h(t+1)s_1 + c_{t2}^h(t+1)s_2 = y.$$

(ii) $$\frac{f_1}{c_{t1}^h(t+1)} = s_1 \frac{1}{c_t^h(t)}$$

$$\frac{f_2}{c_{t2}^h(t+1)} = s_2 \frac{1}{c_t^h(t)}.$$

Equations (i) and (ii) imply the demand functions

$$c_t^h(t) = \frac{y}{2}, \qquad c_{t1}^h(t+1) = \frac{yf_1}{2s_1}, \qquad c_{t2}^h(t+1) = \frac{yf_2}{2s_2}$$

for all h. Equations (8.3) and (8.4) become

(iii) $$s_1 x_1 + s_2 x_2 = 1$$

(iv) $$s_1 p + s_2 p = p \quad \text{or} \quad s_1 + s_2 = 1.$$

These equations have the solution

(v) $$s_1 = \frac{1 - x_2}{x_1 - x_2}$$

$$s_2 = \frac{x_1 - 1}{x_1 - x_2}.$$

Equation (8.7) becomes

$$Nc_{t1}^h(t+1) = Kx_1 + pM$$
$$Nc_{t2}^h(t+1) = Kx_2 + pM.$$

Substituting (v) and the demand functions for $c_{t1}^h(t+1)$ and $c_{t2}^h(t+1)$ into the above equations gives

(vi) $$N \frac{y}{2} \frac{f_1(x_1 - x_2)}{(1 - x_2)} = Kx_1 + pM$$

$$N \frac{y}{2} \frac{f_2(x_1 - x_2)}{(x_1 - 1)} = Kx_2 + pM.$$

These two equations are to be solved for positive (pM, K). Subtracting the second equation of (vi) from the first gives

$$N \frac{y}{2} \frac{f_1(x_1 - x_2)}{(1 - x_2)} - N \frac{y}{2} \frac{f_2(x_1 - x_2)}{(x_1 - 1)} = K(x_1 - x_2).$$

Dividing both sides by $(x_1 - x_2)$ and solving for K, we have

(vii) $$K = N \frac{y}{2} \left[\frac{f_1 x_1 + f_2 x_2 - 1}{(x_1 - 1)(1 - x_2)} \right],$$

which is positive, because $Ex > 1$. Substituting (vii) into either equation of (vi) and solving for pM, we have

(viii) $$pM = N \frac{y}{2} \left[\frac{f_2 x_1 + f_1 x_2 - x_1 x_2}{(x_1 - 1)(1 - x_2)} \right].$$

For $pM > 0$, we require that $f_2 x_1 + f_1 x_2 > x_1 x_2$ or $Ex^{-1} = f_1(x_1)^{-1} + f_2(x_2)^{-1} > 1$.

This example illustrates the following property, which occurs far more generally in models of this class: an equilibrium with valued fiat currency exists if and only if the gross risk-free rate of interest $[\Sigma s_i(t)]^{-1}$ in the equilibrium without valued currency is less than the gross growth rate, which in this case is unity. See Koda (1985) and Manuelli (1984) for development of some of the connections between conditions for existence of monetary equilibria and optimality of nonmonetary equilibria.

We invite the reader to calculate the equilibrium without valued currency and to verify that the condition $Ex^{-1} > 1$ is equivalent to requiring that the risk-free rate of interest in that economy is less than unity.

EXAMPLE 8.2. *A Stationary Economy with Government Storage and an Equilibrium Identical to That in Example 8.1*

We modify the Example 8.1 economy as follows. Let $\overline{K}$ be the equilibrium value of K given by (vii). For $t \geq 1$, we set $K^g(t)$ to satisfy $0 \leq K^g(t) \leq \overline{K}$. Let $\overline{M}$ be the currency stock of Example 8.1. We now assume that $p(t)M(t) = p(t)\overline{M} + K^g(t)$ for $t \geq 1$, where $p(t)$ is the equilibrium value of currency. Finally, we alter taxes for the Example 8.1 economy by taxing or subsidizing in the second period of life in order to pay out to people the government's earnings on its portfolio $K^g(t)$. In particular, we say that $w_{ti}^h(t + 1) = -(1 - x_i)K^g(t)/N$ for $t \geq 1$. All other features of the economy are as in Example 8.1.

We shall verify that a stationary equilibrium of this economy exists and is identical with that of Example 8.1. In particular, we seek an equilibrium in which $p(t) = p > 0$ and $K(t) = K > 0$ for all $t \geq 1$, and $s_1(t) = s_1$, $s_2(t) = s_2$ for all $t \geq 1$. As before, s_1 and s_2 then satisfy (iii) and (iv) and are given by (v). Note that the present value of a young agent's endowment is given by $y + s_1(x_1 - 1)K^g(t)/N + s_2(x_2 - 1)K^g(t)/N = y + [s_1 x_1 + s_2 x_2 - (s_1 + s_2)]K^g(t)/N = y$, by virtue of (iii) and (iv). Because the present value of a young agent's endowment equals its value in Example 8.1, an agent's demand continues to be given by

$$c_t^h(t) = \frac{y}{2}, \qquad c_{ti}^h(t + 1) = \frac{yf_i}{2s_i}, \qquad i = 1, 2.$$

Now equilibrium condition (8.7) becomes

$$N\left[c_{ti}^h(t + 1) + \frac{(1 - x_i)K^g(t)}{N}\right] = K^p(t)x_i + pM(t), \qquad i = 1, 2.$$

or $Nc_{ti}^h(t + 1) = [K^p(t) + K^g(t)]x_i + pM(t) - K^g(t), \qquad i = 1, 2.$

Substituting the demand schedules and the government's budget constraint on "open-market operations" $[p(t)M(t) = p(t)\overline{M} + K^g(t)]$ into the above equations gives

(ix) $$N\frac{yf_i}{2s_i} = [K^p(t) + K^g(t)]x_i + p\overline{M}, \qquad i = 1, 2.$$

Substituting (v) for s_i into the above equations gives the same two equations as encountered in (vi) in Example 8.1, with $K^p(t) + K^g(t)$ now playing the role of K. Therefore the two equations of (ix) have the same solution given by (vii) and (viii) of Example 8.1. Thus we have proved that $K^g(t) + K^p(t) = K$ and $p(t) = p$, $t \geq 1$, are equilibrium values for Example 8.2, where (K, p) are the equilibrium values for the Example 8.1 economy. It follows that variations of $K^g(t)$ and $M(t)$ are irrelevant insofar as consumption allocations and prices are concerned as long as they satisfy

(x) $M(t) = \overline{M} + K^g(t)/p(t), \qquad t \geq 1$

and

(xi) $w_{ti}^h(t + 1) = (x_i - 1)K^g(t)/N, \qquad t \geq 1.$

In performing variations of $M(t)$, $K^g(t)$ satisfying (x) and (xi), the government is acting as an intermediary that passes on to households a pro rata share of the net returns associated with government holdings of capital. Households adjust to these operations by modifying their own holdings of capital so as to leave total storage equal to its value in Example 8.1. This example illustrates a version of Neil Wallace's irrelevance theorem, which will be proved more generally below.

EXAMPLE 8.3. *An Economy with Government Storage and in Which Net Returns to Government Storage Are Used to Retire Currency*

Another modification of Example 8.1 leaves its equilibrium unaltered. The modification is designed to illustrate the irrelevance theorem of Chamley and Polemarchakis (1984).

We now set $K^g(t) = \hat{K}^g$ where $0 \le \hat{K}^g \le K$, where K is given by (vii). We continue to assume that $w^h_{ti}(t + 1) = 0$ and $w^h_t(t) = y$, so taxes are identical with those of Example 8.1. We continue to set $G(t) = T(t) = 0$ for all t. We let $\bar{p}$ and $\bar{M}$ be the values of $p(t)$ and $M(t)$ associated with the Example 8.1 equilibrium. We now set $\hat{M}(1) = \bar{M}$ and for $t \ge 2$,

(xii) $$\hat{p}_i(t)[\hat{M}_i(t) - \hat{M}(t - 1)] = (1 - x_i)\hat{K}^g,$$

where the caret denotes an equilibrium value for the current example. Equation (xii) is the government's budget constraint and describes the evolution of the stock of currency as a function of $\hat{K}^g$, x_i, and the equilibrium value of currency $\hat{p}_i(t)$.

We now verify that the equilibrium prices are given by $s_i(t) = s_i$ for $i = 1$, 2, $t \ge 1$ where s_i satisfy (iii) and (v). Also, it will be shown that the value of currency is given by

$$\hat{p}(1) = \bar{p}$$

(xiii) $$\frac{\hat{p}_i(t + 1)}{\hat{p}(t)} = \left(\frac{\bar{p}\bar{M}}{\bar{p}\bar{M} + \hat{K}^g}\right) + x_i\left(\frac{\hat{K}^g}{\bar{p}\bar{M} + \hat{K}^g}\right).$$

Notice that, according to (xiii), holders of currency receive a gross rate of return in state i, $\hat{p}_i(t + 1)/\hat{p}(t)$, that is a weighted average of unity (the equilibrium gross rate of return on currency in the Example 8.1 economy) and x_i (the gross rate of return on capital). The weights in (xiii) are simply the shares of unbacked currency $[\bar{p}\bar{M}/(\bar{p}\bar{M} + \hat{K}^g)]$ and backed currency $[\hat{K}^g/(\bar{p}\bar{M} + \hat{K}^g)]$ in the government's total liabilities. Thus Equation (xiii) prices government currency as though it were a mutual fund passing on its returns to its owners.

To verify that prices given by (xiii) and (v) are equilibrium ones, we need to show that (8.4) holds. Substituting (xiii) for $i = 1, 2$ into (8.4) gives

$$\frac{\bar{p}\bar{M} + x_1\hat{K}^g}{\bar{p}\bar{M} + \hat{K}^g}\, s_1 + \frac{\bar{p}\bar{M} + x_2\hat{K}^g}{\bar{p}\bar{M} + \hat{K}^g}\, s_2 - 1 = 0$$

or
$$\frac{(s_1 + s_2)\bar{p}\bar{M} + (x_1 s_1 + x_2 s_2)\hat{K}^g}{\bar{p}\bar{M} + \hat{K}^g} - 1 = 0.$$

Evidently this equation is satisfied if (iii) and (v) hold, that is, if $s_1 x_1 + s_2 x_2 = 1$ and $s_1 + s_2 = 1$. Therefore, when prices obey (xiii) and (v), conditions (8.3) and (8.4) hold.

Each private agent's budget set is unaltered relative to the equilibrium of Example 8.1. [Note the role of $\hat{p}(1) = \bar{p}$ in leaving unaltered the budget sets of the initial old.] Because s_1 and s_2 are the same as in the Example 8.1 equilibrium, the allocation to private agents is unaltered relative to Example 8.1. The condition (xii) assures that the government budget constraint is satisfied. Thus equilibrium allocations and relative prices s_1 and s_2 equal those of Example 8.1.

This example has very much of a "real bills" flavor. The stochastic process for the value of currency $p(t)$ *is* affected by the setting for $\hat{K}^g$, even though equilibrium allocations and state-contingent prices are not affected. The reason is that $\hat{K}^g$ determines the portfolio of assets "backing" the currency. The rate of return on currency reflects the rate of return on that portfolio. The Example 8.3 economy serves as a counterexample to the notion that government policies can be evaluated according to the price-level instability or uncertainty that they produce. The consumption allocations are identical between the economies in Example 8.1 and Example 8.3, even though the price level is constant in the Example 8.1 equilibrium and variable in the Example 8.3 equilibrium.

EXAMPLE 8.4. *An Economy with Periodic Government Purchases*
This example is identical to Example 8.1 except that we have

$$G(t) = \begin{cases} G_1 & \text{for } t \text{ odd} \\ G_2 & \text{for } t \text{ even.} \end{cases}$$

These expenditures are to be financed by taxes levied on the young, so that $w_t^h(t) = y - G_1/N$ for t odd, $w_t^h(t) = y - G_2/N$ for t even. Except for these differences, the economy is identical to that studied in Example 8.1. In particular, we have $M(t) = M$ for all t, and $K^g(t) = 0$ for all t.

We make the guess that an equilibrium solution can be found among the class of periodic solutions with

$$s_1(t) = \begin{cases} s_1(1), & t \text{ odd} \\ s_1(2), & t \text{ even} \end{cases}$$

$$s_2(t) = \begin{cases} s_2(1), & t \text{ odd} \\ s_2(2), & t \text{ even} \end{cases}$$

$$p(t) = \begin{cases} p(1), & t \text{ odd} \\ p(2), & t \text{ even.} \end{cases}$$

With these guesses, Equations (8.3) and (8.4) assume the forms

(xiv) $\qquad s_1(1)x_1 + s_2(1)x_2 = 1$
$\qquad\qquad s_1(2)x_1 + s_2(2)x_2 = 1$

(xv) $\qquad s_1(1)p(2) + s_2(1)p(2) = p(1)$
$\qquad\quad s_1(2)p(1) + s_2(2)p(1) = p(2).$

Dividing the first equation of (xv) by $p(2)$ and the second by $p(1)$ gives

(xvi) $\qquad [s_1(1) + s_2(1)] = \dfrac{p(1)}{p(2)}$

$\qquad\qquad [s_1(2) + s_2(2)] = \dfrac{p(2)}{p(1)},$

which shows that the risk-free rate of interest $[s_1(t) + s_2(t)]^{-1}$ oscillates periodically with period 2.

Equations (8.1) and (8.2) imply that

(xvii) $\qquad c_t^h(t) = \dfrac{y - G_1}{N} \dfrac{1}{2}$

$\qquad\qquad c_{t1}^h(t + 1) = \dfrac{y - G_1}{N} \dfrac{f_1}{2s_1(1)} \left. \begin{array}{} \\ \\ \\ \end{array} \right\}$ t odd

$\qquad\qquad c_{t2}^h(t + 1) = \dfrac{y - G_1}{N} \dfrac{f_2}{2s_2(1)}$

$\qquad\qquad c_t^h(t) = \dfrac{y - G_2}{N} \dfrac{1}{2}$

$\qquad\qquad c_{t1}^h(t + 1) = \dfrac{y - G_2}{N} \dfrac{f_1}{2s_1(2)} \left. \begin{array}{} \\ \\ \\ \end{array} \right\}$ t even.

$\qquad\qquad c_{t2}^h(t + 1) = \dfrac{y - G_2}{N} \dfrac{f_2}{2s_2(2)}$

We guess that $K(t) = K(1)$, t odd; $K(t) = K(2)$ for t even. With this and our other periodic-solution guesses, Equation (8.7) becomes

(xviii)
$$N c_{11}^h(2) = K(1)x_1 + p(2)M$$
$$N c_{12}^h(2) = K(1)x_2 + p(2)M$$
t odd

$$N c_{21}^h(1) = K(2)x_1 + p(1)M$$
$$N c_{22}^h(1) = K(2)x_2 + p(1)M$$
t even.

Equations (xiv), (xvi), (xvii), and (xviii) form fourteen equations in the fourteen variables $s_1(1)$, $s_2(1)$, $s_1(2)$, $s_2(2)$, $p(1)$, $p(2)$, $c_1^h(1)$, $c_{11}^h(2)$, $c_{12}^h(2)$, $c_2^h(2)$, $c_{21}^h(1)$, $c_{22}^h(1)$, $K(1)$, and $K(2)$. Under the regularity conditions that $Ex > 1$ and $Ex^{-1} > 1$, these equations have a unique solution with positive values of $p(1)$ and $p(2)$.

EXAMPLE 8.5. *An Economy with Growth*

This example is identical to Example 8.1 except that it assumes that $N(t) = n^t N(0)$, for $t \geq 1$, where $n > 1$, and that $Ex > n$, $Ex^{-1} > n^{-1}$. We invite the reader to verify that, for this example, an equilibrium exists with

$$p(t) = p(1)n^t,$$

$$s_1(t) = \frac{1 - n^{-1}x_2}{x_1 - x_2} \quad \text{for all } t$$

$$s_2(t) = \frac{n^{-1}x_1 - 1}{x_1 - x_2} \quad \text{for all } t$$

$$K(t) = \left[\frac{N(t)y}{2}\right]\left[\frac{n^{-1}(f_1 x_1 + f_2 x_2) - 1}{(1 - n^{-1}x_2)(n^{-1}x_1 - 1)}\right].$$

Notice that, for the claimed solution, $s_1(t) + s_2(t) = n^{-1}$ and $p(t+1)/p(t) = n$, so that the risk-free interest rate is n.

This example again illustrates the more general proposition in models of this class that an equilibrium with valued currency exists if and only if the gross risk-free interest rate in the equilibrium without valued currency is less than n, the gross rate of growth in the economy. We invite the reader to verify this proposition for this example.

EXAMPLE 8.6. *An Economy with Markov Government Purchases*

This example modifies Example 8.1 by permitting government expenditures to vary stochastically. The example falls somewhat outside the domain of the model formed by (8.1)–(8.7) because it adds an additional source of randomness, government expenditures, but the model is easily modified to handle this feature. In particular, we assume that $G(t)$ is governed by a Markov law, with

$$\text{prob}\{G(t+1) = G_j | G(t) = G_k\} = \Pi_{kj}$$

where $G_j > 0$, $j = 1, \ldots, m$. We continue to assume that expenditures are entirely financed by endowment taxation on the young. We have that

$$w_t^h(t) = y - \frac{G(t)}{N} \quad \text{for all } t \geq 1,$$

where we are assuming that $N(t) = N$ for all $t \geq 1$. We assume that $G(t)$ is observed at the beginning of period t, before the young make their decisions. We assume that the $G(t)$ process is statistically independent of the $x(s)$ process for all t and s.

We now let (i, j) index the state that occurs when $x(t) = x_i$ and $G(t) = G_j$ at the beginning of period t. In general, we would have to index endogenous variables at t by the values of (i, j) that have occurred at all dates prior to and including date t. In this case, however, it is natural to suppose a solution in which $p(t)$ depends only on the j part of the state. (Example 8.4 is the inspiration for this conjecture.) Thus we seek a solution in which $p(t) = p_j$ for all i and all t when $G(t) = G_j$, $s_{ij}(t) = s_{ij}(k)$ when $G(t + 1) = G_j$, $x(t + 1) = x_i$, and $G(t) = G_k$.

In this case, Equations (8.3) and (8.4) become

(xix) $\qquad \sum_i \sum_j s_{ij}(k)x_i = 1 \quad$ for all k.

(xx) $\qquad \sum_i \sum_j s_{ij}(k)p_j = p_k \quad$ for all k.

Equations (8.1) and (8.2) now give us

(xxi) $\qquad c_t^h(t, k) = \frac{y - G_k}{N} \frac{1}{2} \quad$ when $G(t) = G_k$

$$c_{t,ij}^h(t + 1, k) = \frac{y - G_j}{N} \frac{f_i \cdot \Pi_{kj}}{2s_{ij}(k)}.$$

If we use (xxi) and (8.7), equilibrium can be expressed as the requirement that

(xxii) $\qquad N\left[\frac{y - G_k N^{-1}}{2s_{ij}(k)}\right] f_i \Pi_{kj} = K_k x_i + p_j M \quad$ for all i, j, k.

where $K(t) = K_k$ when $G(t) = G_k$. Equations (xix), (xx), and (xxii) are $(m^2 I + 2m)$ equations in the $(m^2 I + 2m)$ variables $\{s_{ij}(k), p_j, K_k\}$. These equations are to be solved simultaneously. A solution with $p_k > 0$ exists, provided that $Ex^{-1} > 1$.

EXAMPLE 8.7. *The End of the World*

This example modifies the structure in the text by altering the source of randomness. The consumption good is now assumed to be nonstorable so that $x(t) = 0$ with probability 1 for all t. Randomness enters only because it is not certain when the world will end. At time 1, with certainty there are born $N(1) > 0$ young people. There are N_j people of type j, who are endowed with w_1^j when young and w_2^j when old. We permit $w_k^i \neq w_k^j$ for $k = 1, 2, i \neq j$, so that endowments are heterogeneous across young agents. We assume that $\Sigma_j N_j = N(1)$. At $t = 1$, there are also $N(1)$ old people who are endowed in the aggregate with M units of unbacked fiat currency, which they supply inelastically. There is no government activity.

For $t \geq 2$, the birth structure of the economy is as follows. If there are young people alive at $(t - 1)$, then with probability π, $N(1)$ young people are born at times t, with N_j people of type j being born; with probability $(1 - \pi)$, no people are born at t or ever thereafter. In this second event, the old simply live out their lives at t, and the economy expires. We assume that $0 < \pi < 1$.

We assume that young agents of each generation maximize $E[\ln c_t^h(t) + \ln c_t^h(t + 1)]$, where E is the mathematical expectation operator. Young agents are able to transfer income across time by trading claims contingent on the state of the world next period (whether young are born next period or not) and also perhaps by holding money. Let $s_1(t)$ be the time t goods price of a claim on one unit of time $(t + 1)$ good if young are born in $(t + 1)$, and $s_2(t)$ the price of a unit of time $(t + 1)$ good if no young are born at $(t + 1)$.

The reader is asked to verify the following proposition.

PROPOSITION. *A stationary equilibrium with valued currency exists if and only if $\pi - (\Sigma_j w_2^j N_j / \Sigma_j w_1^j N_j) > 0$.*

In this case, currency is valued according to the formulas

$$p(2) = 0$$

$$Mp(1) = \frac{\pi}{1 + \pi} \sum_j N_j w_1^j - \frac{1}{1 + \pi} \sum_j N_j w_2^j,$$

where $p(i)$ is the value of currency in state i; the state-contingent security prices are

$$s_1 = 1$$

$$s_2 = \frac{(1 - \pi) \sum_j N_j (w_1^j + w_2^j)}{(1 + \pi) \sum_j N_j w_2^j}.$$

In this equilibrium, the risk-free interest rate (on consumption loans) is given by $R^f = (s_1 + s_2)^{-1}$, or

$$R^f = \frac{(1 + \pi) \sum_j N_j w_2^j}{(1 - \pi) \sum_j N_j w_1^j + 2 \sum_j N_j w_2^j}.$$

The expected rate of return on currency is π. The preceding formula for R^f implies that $R^f < \pi < 1$.

Note that the realized rate of return on currency is unity so long as the economy continues. Furthermore, as long as the economy continues, the actual rate of return persistently overestimates the expected rate of return on currency. This example is related to the phenomenon known as "the peso problem," in which observations on the realized rate of return on a currency (for example, the Mexican peso from 1976 to August 1982) are believed persistently to overstate the expected return because people think that the government's current policy actions must eventually be reversed.

Notice that $\Sigma_j w_2^j N_j / \Sigma_j w_1^j N_2$ is the gross (risk-free) interest rate on consumption loans in the (Fisherian) economy without valued fiat currency. The preceding proposition requires that the probability of survival π exceed the Fisher equilibrium gross interest rate. This is a version of conditions for existence of an equilibrium with valued currency that we saw previously, which involved comparisons of a growth rate with the Fisher interest rate. In this regard, notice that π can be interpreted as the expected growth rate of the economy.

8.3 A General Irrelevance Theorem

By way of generalizing Examples 8.1, 8.2, and 8.3, it is useful to try to find an equivalence class of alternative government policies in which particular subsets of variables in equilibrium assume the same values. Following Wallace (1981), for example, we might ask whether there are alternative policies that lead to the same equilibrium stochastic processes for $c_t^h(t)$, $c_t^h(t + 1)$, $K(t)$, $s(t)$, and $p(t)$. Alternatively, in the spirit of uncovering conditions for "neutrality," we could follow Chamley and Polemarchakis and seek to characterize the class of all policies that lead only to the same equilibrium stochastic process for the real allocations, real interest rates, and aggregate investment rate $[c_0^h(1), c_t^h(t), c_t^h(t + 1), s(t), K(t)]$.

We begin in the spirit of Chamley and Polemarchakis. Our method is constructive. Let us assume that an initial equilibrium exists, then use Equations $(8.1)-(8.7)$ to determine the class of government policies that give rise to equilibria with the very same values of $[c_0^h(1), c_t^h(t), c_t^h(t + 1), K(t), s(t)]$.

Let a macron above variables denote the initial equilibrium, and let a caret above variables denote an alternative equilibrium. Given an initial macron-bearing equilibrium, we seek a caret-bearing equilibrium that satisfies:

(8.8) $\hat{c}_t^h(t) = \bar{c}_t^h(t)$ for all $t \geq 1$,   all h

(8.9) $\hat{c}_{ti}^h(t+1) = \bar{c}_{ti}^h(t+1)$ for all $t \geq 1$,   all h,   all i

(8.10) $\hat{s}_i(t) = \bar{s}_i(t)$ for all $t \geq 1$, all i

(8.11) $\hat{K}^g(t) + \hat{K}^p(t) = \bar{K}^g(t) + \bar{K}^p(t)$ for all $t \geq 1$
          $0 \leq \hat{K}^g(t) \leq \bar{K}^g(t) + \bar{K}^p(t)$ for all $t \geq 1$

(8.12) $\hat{G}(t) = \bar{G}(t)$.

In order to satisfy (8.8), (8.9), and (8.10) it is sufficient for private agents' budget sets to remain unaltered across the macron- and caret-bearing equilibria at the $\bar{s}(t)$ prices:

(8.13) $\hat{w}_t^h(t) + \bar{s}(t)\hat{w}_t^h(t+1) = \overline{w}_t^h(t) + \bar{s}(t)\overline{w}_t^h(t+1)$.

Sum (8.9) over h, then equate the market-clearing condition (8.7) for the caret-bearing equilibrium to (8.7) for the macron-bearing equilibrium and use (8.11) to obtain

(8.14) $\sum_h \hat{w}_{ti}^h(t+1) = \sum_h \overline{w}_{ti}^h(t+1) + [\hat{K}^g(t) - \bar{K}^g(t)]x_i$
$$+ \bar{p}_i(t+1)\overline{M}(t) - \hat{p}_i(t+1)\hat{M}(t).$$

Next multiply both sides of (8.14) by $\bar{s}_i(t)$ and sum over i to obtain

$$\sum_h \bar{s}(t)\hat{w}_t^h(t+1) = \sum_h \bar{s}(t)\overline{w}_t^h(t+1) + [\hat{K}^g(t) - \bar{K}^g(t)]\bar{s}(t)x(t+1)$$
$$+ \bar{p}(t+1)\bar{s}(t)\overline{M}(t) - \hat{p}(t+1)\bar{s}(t)\hat{M}(t).$$

We shall require both the macron- and caret-bearing equilibria to be such that (8.3) and (8.4) hold with equality and $p(t) > 0$. Under these conditions, the preceding equation becomes

(8.15) $\sum_h \bar{s}(t)\hat{w}_t^h(t+1) = \sum_h \bar{s}(t)\overline{w}_t^h(t+1) + [\hat{K}^g(t) - \bar{K}^g(t)]$
$$+ \bar{p}(t)\overline{M}(t) - \hat{p}(t)\hat{M}(t).$$

Substituting Equation (8.13) into (8.15) gives

$$\sum_h \bar{s}(t)[\hat{w}_t^h(t+1) - \overline{w}_t^h(t+1)]$$
$$= [\hat{K}^g(t) - \bar{K}^g(t)] + \bar{p}(t)\overline{M}(t) - \hat{p}(t)\hat{M}(t) = \sum_h [\overline{w}_t^h(t) - \hat{w}_t^h(t)].$$

Rearranging the second equality gives

(8.16) $\hat{p}(t)\hat{M}(t) = \bar{p}(t)\bar{M}(t) + [\hat{K}^g(t) - \bar{K}^g(t)] + \sum_h [\hat{w}_t^h(t) - \bar{w}_t^h(t)].$

Now rewrite (8.14) as

$$\sum_h \hat{w}_{ti}^h(t + 1) = \sum_h \bar{w}_{ti}^h(t + 1) + [\hat{K}^g(t) - \bar{K}^g(t)]x_i$$

$$+ \frac{\bar{p}_i(t + 1)}{\bar{p}(t)}\, \bar{p}(t)\bar{M}(t) - \frac{\hat{p}_i(t + 1)}{\hat{p}(t)}\, \hat{p}(t)\hat{M}(t).$$

Now use (8.16) in order to eliminate $\hat{p}(t)\hat{M}(t)$ from the above equation, thereby obtaining

(8.17) $\sum_h \hat{w}_{ti}^h(t + 1) = \sum_h \bar{w}_{ti}^h(t + 1) + [\hat{K}^g(t) - \bar{K}^g(t)]\left[x_i - \frac{\hat{p}_i(t + 1)}{\hat{p}(t)} \right]$

$$+ \left[\frac{\bar{p}_i(t + 1)}{\bar{p}(t)} - \frac{\hat{p}_i(t + 1)}{\hat{p}(t)} \right]\bar{p}(t)\bar{M}(t)$$

$$- \frac{\hat{p}_i(t + 1)}{\hat{p}(t)}\left[\sum_h \hat{w}_t^h(t) - \sum_h \bar{w}_t^h(t) \right].$$

We repeat (8.16):

(8.16) $\hat{p}(t)\hat{M}(t) = \bar{p}(t)\bar{M}(t) + [\hat{K}^g(t) - \bar{K}(t)] + \sum_h [\hat{w}_t^h(t) - \bar{w}_t^h(t)].$

Equations (8.16) and (8.17) result from our having imposed (8.8), (8.9), (8.10), (8.11), (8.12), (8.13), (8.7), (8.3), and (8.4). That is, (8.16) and (8.17) are implications of our having imposed identical allocations [Equations (8.8), (8.9), (8.11), (8.12)], identical state-contingent prices [Equation (8.10)], identical budget sets of private agents [Equation (8.13)], state-contingent market clearing [Equation (8.7)], and no arbitrage opportunities [Equations (8.3) and (8.4)]. Walras's law tells us that the government budget constraint [Equations (8.5) and (8.6)] are also satisfied, because market clearing and unaltered private agents' budget sets imply an unaltered budget set for the government. The reader is asked to prove this point in Exercise 8.4.

It follows that values of $\{\hat{w}_t^h(t), \hat{w}_{ti}^h(t + 1), \hat{K}^g(t), \hat{p}_i(t + 1), \hat{M}(t)\}$ that satisfy (8.13), (8.17), and (8.16) also satisfy (8.8), (8.9), (8.10), and (8.11). Thus all government policies $\hat{M}(t), \hat{w}_t^h(t), \hat{w}_{ti}^h(t + 1), 0 \le \hat{K}^g(t) \le \bar{K}^p(t) + \bar{K}^g(t)$ that satisfy (8.13), (8.17), and (8.16) are associated with equilibrium allocations $\bar{c}_t^h(t), \bar{c}_t^h(t + 1), t \ge 1$ and have the same equilibrium state-contingent prices $\bar{s}(t)$. These conditions leave open the consumption of the initial old, $\bar{c}_0^h(1)$, which depends on the value of currency at time $1, p(1)$. In order to assure that $\hat{c}_0^h(1) = \bar{c}_0^h(1)$ for all h, it is sufficient that $\hat{p}(1) = \bar{p}(1)$. To impose this condition, we set $\hat{p}(1) = \bar{p}(1)$ in (8.16) for $t = 1$ to obtain the following restrictions on $\hat{M}(1)$:

$$(8.18) \qquad \bar{p}(1)\hat{M}(1) = [\hat{K}^g(1) - \bar{K}^g(1)] + \bar{p}(1)\overline{M}(1) + \sum_h [\hat{w}_1^h(1) - \overline{w}^h(1)].$$

We summarize the results that we have constructed in the following theorem, special cases of which are the theorems of Wallace (1981) and Chamley and Polemarchakis (1984).[4]

THEOREM 8.1. *Let $K^g(0)$, $K^p(0)$, $w_0^h(1)$, and $M(0)$ be given. Let*

$$[\bar{c}_0^h(1), \text{ all } h], \{[\bar{c}_t^h(t), \bar{c}_t^h(t + 1), \text{ all } h], \bar{s}(t), \overline{K}(t) > 0, \bar{p}(t) > 0\}_{t=1}^{\infty}$$

and the government strategy

$$\{\overline{G}(t), \overline{K}^g(t) [\overline{w}_t^h(t), \overline{w}_t^h(t + 1), \text{ all } h], \overline{M}(t)\}_{t=1}^{\infty}$$

be an equilibrium. Suppose that the macron-bearing equilibrium satisfies (8.3) and (8.4) at equality. Then

$$[\bar{c}_0^h(1), \text{ all } h], \{[\bar{c}_t^h(t), \bar{c}_t^h(t + 1), \text{ all } h], \bar{s}(t), \overline{K}(t), \hat{p}(t))_{t=1}^{\infty}$$

and the government strategy

$$\{\overline{G}(t), \hat{K}^g(t), [\hat{w}_t^h(t), \hat{w}_t^h(t + 1), \text{ all } h], \hat{M}(t)\}_{t=1}^{\infty}$$

is also an equilibrium for any $\hat{K}^g(t)$ satisfying $0 \le \hat{K}^g(t) \le \overline{K}(t)$ if the government's strategy obeys the following conditions:

$$(8.13) \qquad \hat{w}_t^h(t) + \bar{s}(t)\hat{w}_t^h(t + 1) = \overline{w}_t^h(t) + \bar{s}(t)\overline{w}_t^h(t + 1) \qquad t \ge 1, \text{ all } h$$

$$(8.16) \qquad \hat{p}(t)\hat{M}(t) = [\hat{K}^g(t) - \overline{K}^g(t)] + \bar{p}(t)\overline{M}(t)$$
$$+ \sum_h [\hat{w}_t^h(t) - \overline{w}_t^h(t)], \qquad t \ge 1$$

$$(8.17) \qquad \sum_h \hat{w}_{ti}^h(t + 1) = \sum_h \overline{w}_{ti}^h(t + 1) + [\hat{K}^g(t) - \overline{K}^g(t)]\left[x_i - \frac{\hat{p}_i(t + 1)}{\hat{p}(t)}\right]$$
$$+ \left[\frac{\bar{p}_i(t + 1)}{\bar{p}(t)} - \frac{\hat{p}_i(t + 1)}{\hat{p}(t)}\right]\bar{p}(t)\overline{M}(t)$$
$$- \frac{\hat{p}_i(t + 1)}{\hat{p}(t)}\sum_h [\hat{w}_t^h(t) - \overline{w}_t^h(t)],$$
$$t \ge 1, \qquad i = 1, \dots, I,$$

4. In all of the theorems in this chapter, we assume that $\hat{w}_0^h(1) = \overline{w}_0^h(1)$ for all h, $\hat{K}^g(0) = \overline{K}^g(0)$, and $\hat{M}(0) = \overline{M}(0)$.

and provided that $\hat{M}(1)$ *obeys*

(8.18)　　$\bar{p}(1)\hat{M}(1) = [\hat{K}^g(1) - \overline{K}^g(1)] + \bar{p}(1)\overline{M}(1) + \sum_h [\hat{w}_1^h(1) - \overline{w}_1^h(1)].$

This statement completes Theorem 8.1.

With (8.13) Equation (8.16) can be rewritten as

$$\hat{p}(t)\hat{M}(t) = [\hat{K}^g(t) - \overline{K}^g(t)] + \bar{p}(t)\overline{M}(t)$$
$$+ \sum_h [\overline{w}_t^h(t+1)\bar{s}(t)] - \sum_h [\hat{w}_t^h(t+1)\bar{s}(t)].$$

This equation states a "real bills" property, namely, that the difference in the value of base money between the caret- and macron-bearing equilibria reflects the difference in the value of the "backing" $K^g(t)$ and the discounted future taxes between the caret- and macron-bearing equilibria.

Equation (8.18) is a version of (8.16) at $t = 1$, combined with the side condition $\hat{p}(1) = \bar{p}(1)$. As was mentioned above, this condition is imposed to assure that the initial old receive the same amount of the consumption good in the equilibria that are being compared. If we omit (8.18), a weaker version of the theorem evidently obtains in which the different equilibria assign equivalent consumption allocations to the young born at $t \geq 1$ but not to the initial old at $t = 1$.

Theorems of Wallace (1981), Chamley and Polemarchakis (1984), and Ricardo are special cases of Theorem 8.1. The theorem of Wallace emerges when we set $\hat{p}(t) = \bar{p}(t)$ and $\Sigma_h \hat{w}_t^h(t) = \Sigma_h \overline{w}_t^h(t)$ but permit the case that $\hat{K}^g(t) \neq \overline{K}^g(t)$ and that $\Sigma_h \hat{w}_{ti}^h(t+1) \neq \Sigma_h \overline{w}_{ti}^h(t+1)$. In Wallace's theorem, the government adjusts $\Sigma_h w_{ti}^h(t+1)$ as a means of paying out the earnings on its holding $K^g(t)$.

In the theorem of Chamley and Polemarchakis, $\Sigma_h \hat{w}_t^h(t) = \Sigma_h \overline{w}_t^h(t)$ and $\Sigma_h \hat{w}_{ti}^h(t+1) = \Sigma_h \overline{w}_{ti}^h(t+1)$. Still, $\hat{K}^g(t) \neq \overline{K}^g(t)$ and $\hat{p}(t) \neq \bar{p}(t)$. In Chamley and Polemarchakis's theorem, the price-level process adjusts in order to pay out the earnings on the government's holdings $K^g(t)$. A version of a Ricardian theorem can be obtained by setting $\hat{K}^g(t) = \overline{K}^g(t)$, $\bar{p}(t) = \hat{p}(t)$ but allowing the possibility that $\Sigma_h \hat{w}_t^h(t) \neq \Sigma_h \overline{w}_t^h(t)$ and $\Sigma_h \hat{w}_{ti}^h(t+1) \neq \Sigma_h \overline{w}_{ti}^h(t+1)$. These theorems will be described in more detail in subsequent sections.

8.4　Wallace's Modigliani-Miller Theorem for Open-Market Operations

Wallace's theorem is the special case that obtains when we also require that $\Sigma_h \hat{w}_t^h(t) = \Sigma_h \overline{w}_t^h(t)$ and that the price levels be identical across the two equilibria, so that $\hat{p}(t) = \bar{p}(t)$ for all $t \geq 1$. Substituting these conditions into (8.16) and (8.17) gives Wallace's theorem.

THEOREM 8.2 (WALLACE). *Let*

$$[\bar{c}_0^h(1), \quad \text{all } h], \{[\bar{c}_t^h(t), \bar{c}_t^h(t + 1), \quad \text{all } h], \bar{s}(t), \bar{K}(t) > 0, \bar{p}(t) > 0\}_{t=1}^{\infty}$$

and the government strategy

$$\{\bar{G}(t), \bar{K}^g(t), [\bar{w}_t^h(t), \bar{w}_t^h(t + 1), \quad \text{all } h], \bar{M}(t)\}_{t=1}^{\infty}$$

be an equilibrium. Then

$$[\bar{c}_0^h(1), \quad \text{all } h], \{[\bar{c}_t^h(t), \bar{c}_t^h(t + 1), \quad \text{all } h], \bar{s}(t), \bar{K}(t), \bar{p}(t)\}_{t=1}^{\infty}$$

and the government strategy

$$\{\bar{G}(t), \hat{K}^g(t), [\hat{w}_t^h(t), \hat{w}_t^h(t + 1), \quad \text{all } h], \hat{M}(t)\}_{t=1}^{\infty}$$

is also an equilibrium for any $\hat{K}^g(t)$ satisfying $0 \leq \hat{K}^g(t) \leq \bar{K}(t)$, if the government's strategy obeys the following conditions:

(8.13) $\hat{w}_t^h(t) + \bar{s}(t)\hat{w}_t^h(t + 1) = \bar{w}_t^h(t) + \bar{s}(t)\bar{w}_t^h(t + 1)$, $t \geq 1$,   all h

(8.19) $\bar{p}(t)[\hat{M}(t) - \bar{M}(t)] = [\hat{K}^g(t) - \bar{K}^g(t)]$, $t \geq 1$

(8.20) $\displaystyle\sum_h \hat{w}_{ti}^h(t + 1) = \sum_h \bar{w}_{ti}^h(t + 1) + [\hat{K}^g(t) - \bar{K}^g(t)]\left[x_i - \frac{\bar{p}_i(t + 1)}{\bar{p}(t)}\right],$

      $t \geq 1, \quad i = 1, \ldots, I$

This statement completes Wallace's theorem.

Equation (8.19) for $t = 1$ is equivalent to (8.18) because $\sum_h \hat{w}_t^h(t) = \sum_h \bar{w}_t^h(t)$. Equation (8.20) describes a scheme for distributing the net return on the government's holdings of capital. If $\hat{K}^g(t) > \bar{K}^g(t)$, the government increases it liabilities according to (8.19). It pays a gross rate of return of $\bar{p}_i(t + 1)/\bar{p}(t)$ on these liabilities and earns a gross rate of return of x_i in state i at $(t + 1)$. Equation (8.20) states that the government alters state-contingent taxes vis-à-vis the macron-bearing equilibrium in order to distribute the net return on $[\hat{K}^g(t) - \bar{K}^g(t)]$ to the public. By doing so and maintaining (8.13), the government insulates private agents' budget sets from any effects stemming from its altered holding of $\hat{K}^g(t)$.

8.5 Chamley and Polemarchakis's Neutrality Theorem

Chamley and Polemarchakis considered the case in which the government does not perform the kind of alterations in lump-sum taxes envisioned by

Wallace. Instead, Chamley and Polemarchakis rely on price-level fluctuations to alter the return on currency relative to the macron-bearing equilibrium, thereby distributing the net returns on the government's holdings of capital directly to holders of currency.

To obtain the theorem of Chamley and Polemarchakis (1984) from Theorem 8.1, we set $\Sigma_h \hat{w}^h_t(t) = \Sigma_h \overline{w}^h_t(t)$ and also $\Sigma_h \hat{w}^h_{ti}(t+1) = \Sigma_h \overline{w}^h_{ti}(t+1)$, so that no alteration in lump-sum transfers and taxes is permitted. We permit the case that $\hat{p}(t) \neq \overline{p}(t)$ for $t > 1$. Substituting these conditions into (8.17) and solving for $\hat{p}_i(t+1)/\hat{p}(t)$ gives

$$\frac{\hat{p}_i(t+1)}{\hat{p}(t)} = \frac{\overline{p}_i(t+1)}{\overline{p}(t)} \cdot \frac{\overline{p}(t)\overline{M}(t)}{\overline{p}(t)\overline{M}(t) + [\hat{K}^g(t) - \overline{K}^g(t)]}$$
$$+ x_i \frac{\hat{K}^g(t) - \overline{K}^g(t)}{\overline{p}(t)\overline{M}(t) + [\hat{K}^g(t) - \overline{K}^g(t)]}$$

or

(8.21) $$\frac{\hat{p}_i(t+1)}{\hat{p}(t)} = (1 - \alpha_t) \frac{\overline{p}_i(t+1)}{\overline{p}(t)} + \alpha_t x_i$$

where $$\alpha_t = \frac{\hat{K}^g(t) - \overline{K}^g(t)}{\overline{p}(t)\overline{M}(t) + \hat{K}^g(t) - \overline{K}^g(t)}.$$

This equation determines $\hat{p}(t)$, $t \geq 2$, while $\hat{M}(t)$, $t \geq 1$ is to be determined from a version of (8.18) and from a version of (8.5) all $t \geq 1$:

(8.22) $$\overline{p}(1)\hat{M}(1) = [\hat{K}^g(1) - \overline{K}^g(1)] + \overline{p}(1)\overline{M}(1)$$

(8.23) $$\hat{p}_i(t)[\hat{M}(t) - \hat{M}(t-1)] = \hat{K}^g(t) - x_i(t)\hat{K}^g(t-1) + \overline{G}_i(t) - \overline{T}_i(t),$$
$$t \geq 2, \quad i = 1, \ldots, I.$$

We now have the following theorem.

THEOREM 8.3 (CHAMLEY-POLEMARCHAKIS). *Let*

$$[\overline{c}^h_0(1), \quad \text{all } h], \{[\overline{c}^h_t(t), \overline{c}^h_t(t+1), \quad \text{all } h], \overline{s}(t), \overline{K}(t) > 0, p(t) > 0\}^\infty_{t=1}$$

and the government strategy

$$\{\overline{G}(t), \overline{K}^g(t), [\overline{w}^h_t(t), \overline{w}^h_t(t+1), \quad \text{all } h], \overline{M}(t)\}^\infty_{t=1}$$

be an equilibrium. Then

$$[\overline{c}^h_0(1), \quad \text{all } h], \{[\overline{c}^h_t(t), \overline{c}^h_t(t+1), \quad \text{all } h], \overline{s}(t), \overline{K}(t), \hat{p}(t)\}^\infty_{t=1}$$

and the government strategy

$$\{\overline{G}(t), \hat{K}^g(t), [\overline{w}_t^h(t), \overline{w}_t^h(t+1), \quad \text{all } h], \hat{M}(t)\}_{t=1}^{\infty}$$

is also an equilibrium for any $\hat{K}^g(t)$ satisfying $0 \le \hat{K}^g(t) \le \overline{K}(t)$ if $\hat{p}(t)$ and the government's strategy obey the following conditions:

(8.21)
$$\frac{\hat{p}_i(t+1)}{\hat{p}(t)} = (1 - \alpha_t) \frac{\overline{p}_i(t+1)}{\overline{p}(t)} + \alpha_t x_i, \quad t \ge 1, \quad i = 1, \ldots, I$$

$$\text{where} \quad \alpha_t = \frac{\hat{K}^g(t) - \overline{K}^g(t)}{\overline{p}(t)\overline{M}(t) + \hat{K}^g(t) - \overline{K}^g(t)}, \quad t \ge 1$$

(8.22)
$$\overline{p}(1)\hat{M}(1) = [\hat{K}^g(1) - \overline{K}^g(1)] + \overline{p}(1)\overline{M}(1)$$

(8.23)
$$\hat{p}_i(t)[\hat{M}(t) - \hat{M}(t-1)] = \hat{K}^g(t) - x_i(t)\,\hat{K}^g(t-1)$$
$$+ \, \overline{G}_i(t) - \overline{T}_i(t), \quad t \ge 2.$$

These equations are to be solved recursively as follows. First, (8.22) is solved for $\hat{M}(1)$. Then (8.21) is solved for the vector $\hat{p}(2) = [\hat{p}(2)/\overline{p}(1)]\overline{p}(1)$. Then (8.23) is solved for the state-contingent vector $\hat{M}(2)$. Then (8.21) can be solved for the vectors $\hat{p}(t+1)/\hat{p}(t)$, $t \ge 2$, whereas (8.23) can then be solved for the vectors $\hat{M}(t)$, $t > 2$. This statement completes the theorem.

In order to interpret the behavior attributed to the government in Chamley and Polemarchakis's theorem, consider the special case in which the government's budget on current account is always balanced so that $\hat{G}(t) = \hat{T}(t)$. In this case, (8.23) becomes

$$\hat{p}(t)[\hat{M}(t) - \hat{M}(t-1)] = [\hat{K}^g(t) - \hat{K}^g(t-1)]$$
$$+ \, [1 - x(t)]\hat{K}^g(t-1).$$

The sum of $\hat{K}^g(t) - \hat{K}^g(t-1)$ and $[1 - x(t)]\hat{K}^g(t-1)$ is the capital account deficit. The two terms on the right side of this equation indicate that currency is printed or retired in order both to augment the government's capital stock, at the rate $\hat{K}^g(t) - \hat{K}^g(t-1)$, and to "distribute" the net earnings on the initial stock $[1 - x(t)]\hat{K}^g(t-1)$. The interpretation is that, if $[1 - x(t)]$ $K^g(t-1) > 0$, the government sells off capital in this amount and uses the proceeds to retire currency. If $[1 - x(t)]K^g(t-1) < 0$, the government prints new currency to make up its losses. This policy in the end alters the rate of return on currency vis-à-vis the macron-bearing equilibrium, as described in Equation (8.21), in such a way that households confront the same opportunity sets as under the macron-bearing equilibrium. In effect, under Equations (8.23) and (8.21) the government is administering its holding of

$K^g(t)$ and its liabilities $M(t)p(t)$, so that its liabilities are priced as if they were claims on a mutual fund sharing the earnings on the government's portfolio.

8.6 Interpretation as a Constant Fiscal Policy

The preceding sort of interpretation can be extended to apply to the general setup of Theorem 8.1. In particular, Equation (8.17) can be interpreted as a condition that calls for holding fiscal policy constant across the caret- and macron-bearing equilibria. Following Wallace, define $E(t)$, the earnings on the government's portfolio held between $(t-1)$ and t, as

$$(8.24) \qquad E(t) = [x(t) - 1]K^g(t-1) - [p(t) - p(t-1)]M(t-1), \qquad t \geq 2,$$

where $[p(t) - p(t-1)]M(t-1)$ is the real capital gain to holders of currency. We require that

$$(8.25) \qquad \sum_h [\hat{w}^h_{t-1}(t-1) - \overline{w}^h_{t-1}(t-1)] + \sum_h \hat{w}^h_{t-1,i}(t) - \sum_h \overline{w}^h_{t-1,i}(t)$$
$$= \hat{E}_i(t) - \overline{E}_i(t) \qquad t \geq 2, \qquad i = 1, \ldots, I,$$

so that extra earnings on the government's portfolio in the caret-bearing equilibrium are rebated to households via alterations in lump-sum taxes. Substituting (8.24) for the caret- and macron-bearing equilibria into (8.25) gives

$$\sum_h \hat{w}^h_{t-1,i}(t) - \sum_h \overline{w}^h_{t-1,i}(t)$$
$$= [x_i(t) - 1][\hat{K}^g(t-1) - \overline{K}^g(t-1)]$$
$$\quad - [\hat{p}_i(t) - \hat{p}(t-1)]\hat{M}(t-1)$$
$$\quad + [\overline{p}_i(t) - \overline{p}(t-1)]\overline{M}(t-1) - \left[\sum_h \hat{w}^h_{t-1}(t-1) \right.$$
$$\quad \left. - \sum_h \overline{w}^h_{t-1}(t-1) \right], \qquad t \geq 2, \qquad i = 1, \ldots, I.$$

Substituting (8.16) into the above equation and rearranging gives

$$\sum_h \hat{w}^h_{t-1,i}(t) - \sum_h \overline{w}^h_{t-1,i}(t)$$
$$= \left[x_i(t) - \frac{\hat{p}_i(t)}{\hat{p}(t-1)} \right][\hat{K}^g(t-1) - \overline{K}^g(t-1)]$$
$$\quad + \left[\frac{\overline{p}_i(t)}{\overline{p}(t-1)} - \frac{\hat{p}_i(t)}{\hat{p}(t-1)} \right]\overline{p}(t-1)\overline{M}(t-1)$$
$$\quad - [\hat{p}_i(t)/\hat{p}(t-1)] \sum_h [\hat{w}^h_{t-1}(t-1) - \overline{w}^h_{t-1}(t-1)], \qquad t \geq 2.$$

This is simply Equation (8.17).

8.7 Indexed Government Bonds

It is straightforward to introduce "indexed government bonds" into the preceding setup. Indexed bonds are sure claims on future goods. A number of economists, including James Tobin (1963) and Milton Friedman (1972), have advocated that the government issue indexed debt, arguing that this would improve matters. Peled (1980, 1985) and Liviatan (1983) have described models in which, in and of itself, government issues of indexed debt are irrelevant, for reasons of a Modigliani-Miller variety. Peled's analysis can be presented in terms of a modification of model (8.1)–(8.7).

We modify the government budget constraint (8.5) as follows. At time t, the government now issues sure claims of $F(t)$ units of time $(t + 1)$ good. The price of these claims to $(t + 1)$ goods in terms of time t goods will be denoted $[1/R(t)]$, where $R(t)$ is the gross interest rate on indexed bonds between time t and $(t + 1)$, measured in sure time $(t + 1)$ good per time t good. With these conventions, the government budget constraint (8.5) becomes amended to

$$(8.5')\qquad G(t) + K^g(t) = T_i(t) + x_i(t)K^g(t - 1) + p_i(t)[M(t) - M(t - 1)]$$
$$+ \frac{F(t)}{R(t)} - F(t - 1), \qquad t \geq 1.$$

A household's problem is now to maximize $Eu^h[c_t^h(t), c_{ti}^h(t + 1)]$ subject to

$$c_t^h(t) + \frac{f^h(t)}{R(t)} + k^h(t) + m^h(t)p(t) + \sum_i s_i(t)d_i^h(t) \leq w_t^h(t)$$

$$c_{ti}^h(t + 1) \leq w_{ti}^h(t + 1) + m^h(t)p_i(t + 1) + d_i^h(t)$$
$$+ f^h(t) + k^h(t)x_i, \quad \text{all } i,$$

where $f^h(t)$ is the number of indexed bonds purchased or sold by the individual. Multiplying the second inequality by $s_i(t)$, summing over i, and substituting into the first inequality gives

$$c_t^h(t) + s(t)c_t^h(t + 1)$$
$$\leq w_t^h(t) + s(t)w_t^h(t + 1) + k^h(t)\left[\sum_{i=1}^{I} x_i s_i(t) - 1\right]$$
$$+ m^h(t)\left[\sum_i s_i(t)p_i(t + 1) - p(t)\right] + f^h(t)\left[\sum_i s_i(t) - \frac{1}{R(t)}\right].$$

The absence of arbitrage opportunities now implies (8.3) and (8.4) as well as

$$(8.26)\qquad \frac{1}{R(t)} = \sum_i s_i(t).$$

With (8.3), (8.4), and (8.26) imposed, agents' opportunity sets continue to be parameterized as in the original model. Thus they have the same demand functions that were given by the solution of (8.1) and (8.2). Introduction of government indexed bonds means that the equilibrium condition (8.7) must be modified to become

$$(8.7') \qquad \sum_h [c_{ti}^h(t+1) - w_{ti}^h(t+1)] = p_i(t+1)M(t) + x_i K^p(t) + F(t).$$

We assume that $F(0)$ is an initial condition. We now have the following broad definition.

DEFINITION. *An equilibrium with indexed bonds is a stochastic process for* $\{c_t^h(t), c_t^h(t+1), w_t^h(t), w_t^h(t+1), K^p(t), K^g(t), M(t), T(t), Y(t), F(t), p(t), R(t),$ *and* $s(t)\}$ *that satisfies (8.1), (8.2), (8.3), (8.4), (8.26), (8.5'), (8.6) and (8.7').*

It is straightforward to obtain the following theorem, which generalizes Theorem 8.1 in an evident way.

THEOREM 8.4. *Let*

$$[\bar{c}_0^h(1), \text{ all } h], \{[\bar{c}_t^h(t), \bar{c}_t^h(t+1), \text{ all } h], \bar{s}(t), \overline{R}(t), \overline{K}(t) > 0, \\ \bar{p}(t) > 0\}_{t=1}^{\infty}$$

and the government strategy

$$\{\overline{G}(t), \overline{K}^g(t), [\overline{w}_t^h(t), \overline{w}_t^h(t+1), \text{ all } h], \overline{M}(t), \overline{F}(t)\}_{t=1}^{\infty}$$

be an equilibrium. Then

$$[\bar{c}_0^h(1), \text{ all } h], \{[\bar{c}_t^h(t), \bar{c}_t^h(t+1), \text{ all } h], \bar{s}(t), \overline{R}(t), \overline{K}(t), \hat{p}(t)\}_{t=1}^{\infty}$$

and the government strategy

$$\{\overline{G}(t), \hat{K}^g(t), [\hat{w}_t^h(t), \hat{w}_t^h(t+1), \text{ all } h], \hat{M}(t), \hat{F}(t)\}_{t=1}^{\infty}$$

is also an equilibrium for any $\hat{K}^g(t)$, $\hat{F}(t)$ *strategy satisfying* $0 \le \hat{K}^g(t) \le \overline{K}(t)$ *if the government's strategy obeys the following conditions*

$$(8.13) \qquad \hat{w}_t^h(t) + \bar{s}(t)\hat{w}_t^h(t+1) = \overline{w}_t^h(t) + \bar{s}(t)\overline{w}_t^h(t+1), \qquad t \ge 1, \quad \text{all } h$$

$$(8.16') \qquad \hat{p}(t)\hat{M}(t) = \bar{p}(t)\overline{M}(t) + [\hat{K}^g(t) - \overline{K}^g(t)] + \frac{[\overline{F}(t) - \hat{F}(t)]}{\overline{R}(t)}$$

$$+ \sum_h [\hat{w}_t^h(t) - \overline{w}_t^h(t)], \qquad t \ge 1$$

(8.17') $$\sum_h \hat{w}_{ti}^h(t+1) = \sum_h \overline{w}_{ti}^h(t+1) + [\hat{K}^g(t) - \overline{K}^g(t)]\left[x_i - \frac{\hat{p}_i(t+1)}{\hat{p}(t)}\right]$$

$$+ \left[\frac{\overline{p}_i(t+1)}{\overline{p}(t)} - \frac{\hat{p}_i(t+1)}{\hat{p}(t)}\right]\overline{p}(t)\overline{M}(t)$$

$$+ [\hat{F}(t) - \overline{F}(t)]\left[\frac{\hat{p}_i(t+1)}{\hat{p}(t)}\frac{1}{\overline{R}(t)} - 1\right]$$

$$- \frac{\hat{p}_i(t+1)}{\hat{p}(t)}\sum_h [\hat{w}_t^h(t) - \overline{w}_t^h(t)],$$

$$i = 1, \ldots, I, \quad t \geq 1,$$

and provided that $\hat{M}(1)$ obeys

(8.18') $$\overline{p}(1)\hat{M}(1) = \overline{p}(1)\overline{M}(1) + [\hat{K}^g(1) - \overline{K}^g(1)]$$

$$+ \frac{\overline{F}(1) - \hat{F}(1)}{\overline{R}(1)} + \sum_h [\hat{w}_1^h(1) - \overline{w}_1^h(1)].$$

This statement completes the theorem.

Equations (8.16'), (8.17'), and (8.18') generalize equations (8.16), (8.17), and (8.18), respectively.

To prove Theorem 8.4, one mimics the steps used to prove Theorem 8.1. We shall simply display in order the equations that this process leads to, where a prime denotes the equation corresponding to Theorem 8.4:

(8.14') $$\sum_h \hat{w}_{ti}^h(t+1) = \sum_h \overline{w}_{ti}^h(t+1) + [\hat{K}^g(t) - \overline{K}^g(t)]x_i$$

$$+ \overline{p}_i(t+1)\overline{M}(t) - \hat{p}_i(t+1)\hat{M}(t)$$

$$+ \overline{F}(t) - \hat{F}(t).$$

(8.15') $$\sum_h \overline{s}(t)\hat{w}_t^h(t+1) = \sum_h s(t)\overline{w}_t^h(t+1) + [\hat{K}^g(t) - \overline{K}^g(t)]$$

$$+ \overline{p}(t)\overline{M}(t) - \hat{p}(t)\hat{M}(t) + \frac{\overline{F}(t)}{\overline{R}(t)} - \frac{\hat{F}(t)}{\overline{R}(t)}.$$

(8.16') $$\hat{p}(t)\hat{M}(t) = \overline{p}(t)\overline{M}(t) + [\hat{K}^g(t) - \overline{K}^g(t)]$$

$$+ \frac{\overline{F}(t) - \hat{F}(t)}{\overline{R}(t)} + \sum_h [\hat{w}^h(t) - \overline{w}^h(t)], \quad t \geq 1.$$

(8.17') $$\sum_h \hat{w}_{ti}^h(t+1) = \sum_h \overline{w}_{ti}^h(t+1) + [\hat{K}^g(t) - \overline{K}^g(t)]\left[x_i - \frac{\hat{p}_i(t+1)}{\hat{p}(t)}\right]$$

$$+ \left[\frac{\overline{p}_i(t+1)}{\overline{p}(t)} - \frac{\hat{p}_i(t+1)}{\hat{p}(t)}\right]\overline{p}(t)\overline{M}(t)$$

$$+ [\hat{F}(t) - \overline{F}(t)] \left[\frac{\hat{p}_i(t+1)}{\hat{p}(t)} \frac{1}{\overline{R}(t)} - 1 \right]$$

$$- \frac{\hat{p}_i(t+1)}{\hat{p}(t)} \sum_h [\hat{w}_t^h(t) - \overline{w}_t^h(t)], \quad \text{for all } i.$$

As with Theorem 8.1, the conditions of the theorem can be interpreted as requiring that fiscal policy be held constant in the face of an open-market exchange by the government. In particular, the natural definition of earnings on the government portfolio between $(t-1)$ and t is now

(8.24′) $E(t) = [x(t) - 1]K^g(t - 1) - [p(t) - p(t-1)]M(t-1)$
$\qquad\qquad - F(t-1)[1 - 1/R(t-1)].$

Holding fiscal policy constant amounts to requiring that (8.25) hold. Substituting (8.24′) for the caret- and macron-bearing equilibrium into (8.25) gives

$$\sum_h \hat{w}_{t-1,i}^h(t) - \sum_h \overline{w}_{t-1,i}^h(t)$$

$$= [x_i(t) - 1][\hat{K}^g(t-1) - \overline{K}^g(t-1)]$$
$$\quad - [\hat{p}_i(t) - \hat{p}(t-1)]\hat{M}(t-1) + [\overline{p}_i(t) - \overline{p}(t-1)]\overline{M}(t-1)$$
$$\quad - \hat{F}(t-1)\left[1 - \frac{1}{\overline{R}(t-1)} \right] + \overline{F}(t-1)\left[1 - \frac{1}{\overline{R}(t-1)} \right]$$
$$\quad - \left[\frac{\hat{p}_i(t)}{\hat{p}(t-1)} \right] \sum_h [\hat{w}_{t-1}^h(t-1) - \overline{w}_{t-1}^h(t-1)].$$

Substituting (8.16′) to eliminate $\hat{p}(t-1)\hat{M}(t-1)$ from the preceding equation and rearranging, we have Equation (8.17′).

When we set $\hat{K}^g(t) = \overline{K}^g(t)$ in Theorem 8.4, we obtain a result stating that government open-market exchanges of currency for indexed government debt are irrelevant for real allocations and real state-contingent prices.

8.8 A Ricardian Proposition

A Ricardian proposition emerges as a special case of Theorem 8.4 when we set $\hat{K}^g(t) = \overline{K}^g(t)$ and $\hat{p}(t) = \overline{p}(t)$.[5] We have

THEOREM 8.5. *Ricardian Proposition*
    Let

$[\overline{c}_0^h(1), \quad \text{all } h], \{[\overline{c}_t^h(t), \overline{c}_t^h(t+1), \quad \text{all } h],$
$\overline{s}(t), \overline{R}(t), \overline{K}(t) > 0, \overline{p}(t) > 0\}_{t=1}^{\infty}$

---

5. See Robert Barro (1974) for a discussion of a Ricardian proposition in an overlapping-generations model with bequests.

and the government strategy

$$\{\overline{G}(t), \overline{K}^g(t), [\overline{w}_t^h(t), \overline{w}_t^h(t+1), \quad \text{all } h], \overline{M}(t), \overline{F}(t)\}_{t=1}^{\infty}$$

be an equilibrium. Then

$$[\overline{c}_0^h(1), \quad \text{all } h], \{[\overline{c}_t^h(t), \overline{c}_t^h(t+1), \quad \text{all } h], \overline{s}(t), \overline{R}(t), \overline{K}(t), \overline{p}(t)\}_{t=1}^{\infty}$$

and the government strategy

$$\{\overline{G}(t), \overline{K}^g(t), [\hat{w}_t^h(t), \hat{w}_t^h(t+1), \quad \text{all } h], \hat{M}(t), \hat{F}(t)\}_{t=1}^{\infty}$$

is also an equilibrium for any $\hat{M}(t)$, $\hat{F}(t)$ *strategy satisfying*

(8.13) $\hat{w}_t^h(t) + \overline{s}(t)\hat{w}_t^h(t+1) = \overline{w}_t^h(t) + \overline{s}(t)\overline{w}_t^h(t+1), \qquad t \geq 1, \quad \text{all } h.$

(8.16″) $\displaystyle \overline{p}(t)\hat{M}(t) = \overline{p}(t)\overline{M}(t) + \frac{\overline{F}(t) - \hat{F}(t)}{\overline{R}(t)}$
$$+ \sum_h [\hat{w}_t^h(t) - \overline{w}_t^h(t)], \qquad t \geq 1$$

(8.18″) $\displaystyle \overline{p}(1)\hat{M}(1) = \overline{p}(1)\overline{M}(1) + \frac{\overline{F}(1) - \hat{F}(1)}{\overline{R}(1)}$
$$+ \sum_h [\hat{w}_1^h(1) - \overline{w}_1^h(1)].$$

To verify the theorem, write (8.17′) with $\hat{K}^g(t) = \overline{K}^g(t)$ and $\overline{p}(t) = \hat{p}(t)$:

(8.17″) $\displaystyle \sum_h \hat{w}_{ti}^h(t+1) = \sum_h \overline{w}_{ti}^h(t+1) + [\hat{F}(t) - \overline{F}(t)]\left[\frac{\overline{p}_i(t+1)}{\overline{p}(t)} \frac{1}{\overline{R}(t)} - 1 \right]$
$$- \frac{\overline{p}_i(t+1)}{\overline{p}(t)} \sum_h [\hat{w}_t^h(t) - \overline{w}_t^h(t)].$$

Multiplying both sides of this equation by $s_i(t)$ and summing over i simply give (8.13).

To interpret the theorem, notice that (8.13) and (8.16″) imply that

$$\overline{p}(t)\hat{M}(t) + \frac{\hat{F}(t)}{\overline{R}(t)} = \overline{p}(t)\overline{M}(t) + \frac{\overline{F}(t)}{\overline{R}(t)}$$
$$+ \sum_h \overline{s}(t)[\overline{w}_t^h(t+1) - \hat{w}_t^h(t+1)].$$

This equation asserts that the difference in the time t goods value of one-period government debt at time t between the caret- and macron-bearing equilibria equals the difference between the present value of time $(t+1)$ taxes on members of generation t in the caret- and macron-bearing equilibria. Thus alternative paths of government debt are being compared that leave unaltered the distribution of taxes and of wealth across agents and across generations. Because of the overlapping-generations structure and the resulting heterogeneity of agents with respect to time, it very much matters *when* taxes are levied. For this reason the present version of the Ricardian proposition is more restrictive in its hypotheses than some of our earlier versions, in which it was assumed that all agents, including the government, live over the same span of time.

8.9 Further Irrelevance Theorems

The "irrelevance theorems" studied in this chapter have all been constructed by working backward from an assumed initial equilibrium allocation to an equivalence class of government policies that support this same equilibrium allocation. Without doubt, there exist many more such irrelevance theorems. In Exercise 8.1, we ask the reader to formulate an irrelevance theorem for government trades in a foreign currency. Using the same structure of ideas, we also ask the reader to establish a general version of Kareken and Wallace's result that the exchange rate is indeterminate.

8.10 Conclusions

This chapter has described a model in which there is a class of government portfolio strategies and associated equilibrium stochastic processes for the price level that is consistent with the same consumption allocation. Government choices from among this class of portfolio strategies are said to be "irrelevant."

The existence of a class of open-market operations, of the kind described by Chamley and Polemarchakis, that affect the equilibrium stochastic process for the price level without affecting real allocations provides a counterexample to the notion that open-market strategies can be evaluated in terms of the price-level uncertainty or price-level variability that they imply. In these equilibria, price-level uncertainty simply reflects the uncertain nature of the claims "backing" the government's currency. It is easy to construct examples of economies in which open-market strategies exist that will completely eliminate price level uncertainty (see Examples 8.1 and 8.3). Because allocations are unaffected, however, there are no grounds for preferring such open-market strategies over others that permit price-level uncertainty to emerge.

The model of this chapter directs our attention to the backing behind a government's currency. In more general settings than those analyzed here, a government could be confronted with a range of alternative "investment projects" in which to conduct open-market operations. The price-level processes resulting from a given stochastic process for currency would in general depend on the composition of the government's portfolio of assets. Open-market purchases of less risky assets would generally cause the future value of currency to be less uncertain than open-market purchases of riskier assets. Theories such as this one have motivated informal interpretations of various historical episodes by Bruce Smith (1985) and Thomas J. Sargent (1983).

Exercises

Exercise 8.1. **A Version of Kareken-Wallace Exchange Rate Indeterminacy**

This problem concerns a two-country version of Wallace's model in his "A Modigliani-Miller Theorem for Open Market Operations." Residents in each country are free to hold assets issued by residents or the government of the other country. In each country, there is the same storage technology. If $k(t)$ units of the single good are stored at t, then $x(t + 1)k(t)$ become available at $(t + 1)$. It is assumed that $x(t + 1)$ for $t \geq 1$ is a positive and independently and identically distributed random variable. We assume that $\text{prob}\{x(t + 1) = x_i\} = f_i$. The same $x(t + 1)$ hits both countries. Agents have strictly increasing, strictly concave, and twice differentiable utility functions $u^h[c_t^h(t), c_{ti}^h(t + 1)]$. Agents maximize

$$\sum_{i=1}^{I} u^h[c_t^h(t), c_{ti}^h(t + 1)]f_i.$$

At time 1, old agents in the aggregate own $M^1(0)$ units of country 1's currency and $M^2(0)$ units of country 2's currency. Assume that there are $N_1(t)$ people born in country 1 and $N_2(t)$ born in country 2 at time t. Let $s(t)$ denote the vector of prices of one-period state-contingent commodities. Let $p^1(t)$ denote the value of country 1's currency at t (understood to be a function of the state of the economy at t) and let $p^2(t)$ denote the value of country 2's currency at t. Let superscripts denote country-specific values of the quantities defined in Wallace's paper. With this convention, the equilibrium conditions of the model can be expressed:

(1) $c_t^{hc}(t) + s(t)c_t^{hc}(t + 1) \leq w_t^{hc}(t) + s(t)w_t^{hc}(t + 1)$
        for all h and $c = 1, 2$ (c denotes country)

(2) $f_i u_2^{hc}[c_t^{hc}(t), c_{ti}^{hc}(t + 1)] = s_i(t) \sum_{j=1}^{I} f_j u_1^{hc}[c_t^{hc}(t), c_{tj}^{hc}(t + 1)]$

(3) $s(t)x(t+1) - 1 \leq 0,$ $= \text{if } K^{p1}(t) + K^{p2}(t) > 0$

(4a) $p^1(t+1)s(t) - p^1(t) = 0$

(4b) $p^2(t+1)s(t) - p^2(t) = 0$

(5) $K^{gc}(t) + G^c(t)$
$$= T^c(t) + K^{gc}(t-1)x(t) + p^c(t)[M^c(t) - M^c(t-1)],$$
$$c = 1, 2$$

(6) $T_i^c(t) = Y^c(t) - \sum_h w_t^{hc}(t) - \sum_h w_{t-1,i}^{hc}(t)$ $c = 1, 2$

(7) $\sum_c \sum_h [c_{ti}^{hc}(t+1) - w_{ti}^{hc}(t+1)] - [K^{p1}(t) + K^{p2}(t)]x_i$
$$= p_i^1(t+1)M^1(t) + p_i^2(t+1)M^2(t)$$

subject to $M^1(0) > 0,$ $M^2(0) > 0,$ $K^{g1}(0) = 0,$ $K^{g2}(0) = 0.$

a. Define an equilibrium for this economy.

b. Define an equilibrium with two valued currencies for this economy.

c. Assume that an equilibrium with two valued currencies exists, and let this equilibrium be denoted

$\{\overline{G}^1(t), \overline{G}^2(t), \overline{w}_t^{h1}(t), \overline{w}_t^{h2}(t), \overline{w}_t^{h1}(t+1), \overline{w}_t^{h2}(t+1), \overline{K}^{g1}(t),$
$\overline{K}^{g2}(t), \overline{K}^{p1}(t) + \overline{K}^{p2}(t) > 0, \overline{s}(t), \overline{p}^1(t) > 0, \overline{p}^2(t) > 0, \overline{M}^1(t) > 0,$
$\overline{M}^2(t) > 0, \overline{T}^1(t), \overline{T}^2(t)\}$ for $t \geq 1$.

Furthermore, suppose that, in this equilibrium, $\overline{p}^1(t) = \overline{e}\overline{p}^2(t)$ for all t and states of the world, where $\overline{e} > 0$ is a scalar constant.

Holding $M^1(0)$ and $M^2(0)$ fixed, prove that, for any $\hat{e} > 0$, there exists an equilibrium in which $\hat{p}(t) = \hat{e}\hat{p}^2(t)$, which is given by

$\{\overline{G}^1(t), \overline{G}^2(t), \overline{w}_t^{h1}(t), \overline{w}_t^{h2}(t), \overline{w}_t^{h1}(t+1), \overline{w}_t^{h2}(t+1), \overline{K}^{g1}(t),$
$\overline{K}^{g2}(t), \overline{K}^{p1}(t) + \overline{K}^{p2}(t) > 0, \overline{s}(t), \overline{T}^1(t), \overline{T}^2(t);$
$\hat{p}^1(t) > 0, \hat{p}^2(t) > 0, \hat{M}^1(t) > 0, \hat{M}^2(t) > 0\}$ for $t \geq 1$.

d. Are the allocations in the caret- and macron-bearing equilibria equal to one another? Does the answer depend on the distribution of $M^1(0)$ and $M^2(0)$ between old residents of countries 1 and 2?

e. State but do not prove a Modigliani-Miller-like theorem for government open-market operations in foreign currency. [Presumably you will have to modify (8.5) for one or both countries to state such a theorem.]

Exercise 8.2. **The Term Structure of State-Contingent Claims**

Consider the economy described in Wallace's "A Modigliani-Miller Theorem for Open Market Operations." Let $s^{(1)}(t, t+1; j, i)$ denote the price at time t when $x(t) = x_j$ of a claim to one unit of consumption at date $(t + 1)$ when $x(t + 1) = x_i$ [this is Wallace's $s_i(t)$]. Now suppose that there is opened a market in two-period-ahead state-contingent claims. Let $s^{(2)}(t, t + 2; j, i)$ denote the price at time t when $x(t) = x_j$ of a claim to one unit of consumption at date $t + 2$ when $x(t + 2) = x_i$.

Use an arbitrage argument to prove that

$$s^{(2)}(t, t + 2; j, i) = \sum_{k=1}^{I} s^{(1)}(t, t + 1; j, k)s^{(1)}(t + 1, t + 2; k, i).$$

Exercise 8.3. Walras's Law: 1

In the model of Section 8.2, prove that (8.2), (8.3), and (8.7) imply that

$$\sum_h w_t^h(t) - \sum_h c_t^h(t) = K^p(t) + p(t)M(t).$$

Interpret this equality.

Exercise 8.4. Walras's Law: 2

Verify that Equations (8.5) and (8.6) are satisfied for the caret-bearing equilibrium described in Theorem 8.1.

Exercise 8.5. Constancy of Fiscal Policy

In Proposition 5.1, in what sense is fiscal policy being held constant across equilibria?

Exercise 8.6. Altered Version of Logarithmic Preferences

Alter Example 8.1 as follows. Assume that

$$u^h[c_t^h(t), c_t^h(t + 1)] = \ln[c_t^h(t) + \alpha] + \ln[c_t^h(t + 1) + \gamma].$$

Assume that all other features of the example are the same.

a. Show that there is a stationary equilibrium in which s_1 and s_2 continue to be given by (v) and pM and K are given by

$$(1) \qquad K = N\left[\frac{f_1 x_1 + f_2 x_2 - 1}{(1 - x_2)(x_1 - 1)}\right]\left(\frac{y}{2} + \frac{y + \alpha}{2}\right)$$

$$(2) \qquad pM = N\left(\frac{y}{2} + \frac{y + \alpha}{2}\right)x_1 x_2\left[\frac{f_1 x_1^{-1} + f_2 x_2^{-1} - 1}{(1 - x_2)(x_1 - 1)}\right] - N\gamma.$$

b. In what sense are α and γ parameters indexing "risk" aversion?

c. How are variations in risk aversion across economies, as indexed by α and γ, reflected in the equilibrium values of the risky asset (K) and the safe asset (pM) that are saved?

References and Suggested Readings

Barro, Robert J. 1974. Are government bonds net wealth? *Journal of Political Economy* 82(6):1095–1117.

Chamley, Christophe, and Heraklis Polemarchakis. 1984. Assets, general equilibrium, and the neutrality of money. *Review of Economic Studies* 51(1):129–138.

Friedman, Milton. 1971. Purchasing-power bonds. *Newsweek,* April 12. (Reprinted in M. Friedman, *An Economist's Protest,* pp. 84–85. Glen Ridge, N.J.: T. Horton, 1972.)

Kareken, John, and Neil Wallace. 1981. On the indeterminacy of equilibrium exchange rates. *Quarterly Journal of Economics* 96(2):207–222.

Kihlstrom, Richard E., and Leonard J. Mirman. 1981. Constant, increasing, and decreasing risk aversion with many commodities. *Review of Economic Studies* 48(2):171–180.

Koda, Keiichi. 1985. A note on the existence of monetary equilibria in overlapping generations models with storage. *Journal of Economic Theory* 53(5):995–1046.

Liviatan, Nissan. 1983. On equilibrium wage indexation and neutrality of indexation policy. In *Financial Policies and the World Capital Market: The Problem of Latin American Countries,* ed. P. Aspe-Armella, R. Dornbusch, and M. Obstfeld. Chicago: University of Chicago Press for the National Bureau of Economic Research, 1983.

Manuelli, Rodolfo. 1984. A note on the relationship between existence of monetary equilibrium and optimality of the nonmonetary equilibrium in stochastic overlapping generations models. Northwestern University, Evanston, Ill.

Modigliani, Franco, and Merton Miller. 1958. The cost of capital, corporation finance, and the theory of investment. *American Economic Review* 48(3):261–297.

Peled, Dan. 1980. *Government Issued Index Bonds—Do They Improve Matters?* Ph.D.diss., University of Minnesota, Minneapolis.

——— 1985. Stochastic inflation and government provision of indexed bonds. *Journal of Monetary Economics* 15(3):291–308.

Sargent, Thomas J. 1983. The ends of four big inflations. In *Inflation: Causes and Effects,* ed. Robert Hall. Chicago: University of Chicago Press, for the National Bureau of Economic Research.

Smith, Bruce D. 1985. Some colonial evidence on two theories of money: Maryland and the Carolinas. Working Paper 245. Federal Reserve Bank of Minneapolis. (Reprinted in the *Journal of Political Economy* 93(6):1178–1211.)

Tobin, James. 1958. Liquidity preference as behavior towards risk. *Review of Economic Studies* 25(2):65–86.

——— 1963. An essay on the principles of debt management. In *Fiscal and Debt Management Policies,* ed. William Fellner et al., pp. 143–318. Englewood Cliffs, N.J.: Prentice-Hall. (Reprinted in James Tobin, *Essays in Economics,* 2 vols., vol. 1, pp. 378–455. Amsterdam: North-Holland, 1971.)

Wallace, Neil. 1981. A Modigliani-Miller theorem for open-market operations. *American Economic Review* 71(3):267–274.

Functional Analysis for Macroeconomics

The models studied in this book have solutions that are functions; for example, the solutions of difference equations are sequences, that is, functions mapping the integers into the real line. The solutions of dynamic programming problems are value functions and policy functions, both mapping elements of the state space into the real line. The equilibria of models for pricing assets are described by pricing functions that map elements of the state space into the nonnegative part of the real line.

The functions that solve our models are typically found by solving a set of first-order necessary conditions (for example, Euler equations and transversality and boundary conditions), together with a set of equations giving equilibrium conditions. These conditions assume the form of functional equations, being equalities involving unknown functions. In this book, we encounter a variety of examples of functional equations. They include nonstochastic difference equations (here sequences are the functions to be solved for), stochastic difference equations (here stochastic processes are the functions to be solved for), and Bellman's equation in dynamic programming (to be solved for a value function and policy function).

This appendix provides an introduction to the analysis of functional equations (functional analysis). It describes the contraction mapping theorem, which is applied to study a variety of functional equations that are encountered in this book. The goal is to convey the essential unity that underlies a variety of seemingly disparate results that are used in applied dynamic economics.

A.1 Metric Spaces and Operators

We begin with the definition of a metric space, which is a pair of objects, a set X and a function d.[1]

DEFINITION. *A metric space is a set X and a function d called a metric, d: $X \times X \to R$. The metric $d(x, y)$ satisfies the following four properties.*

(M1) *(Positivity)* $d(x, y) \geq 0$ *for all* $x, y \in X$.
(M2) *(Strict positivity)* $d(x, y) = 0$ *if and only if* $x = y$.
(M3) *(Symmetry)* $d(x, y) = d(y, x)$ *for all* $x, y \in X$.
(M4) *(Triangle inequality)* $d(x, y) \leq d(x, z) + d(z, y)$ *for all* x, y, *and* $z \in X$.

We give some examples of the metric spaces with which we will be working.

EXAMPLE A.1. $l_p[0, \infty)$. We say that $X = l_p[0, \infty)$ is the set of all sequences of complex numbers $\{x_t\}_{t=0}^{\infty}$ for which $\sum_{t=0}^{\infty}|x_t|^p$ converges, where $1 \leq p < \infty$. The function $d_p(x, y) = (\sum_{t=0}^{\infty}|x_t - y_t|^p)^{1/p}$ is a metric. Often we will say that $p = 2$ and will work in $l_2[0, \infty)$.

EXAMPLE A.2. $l_\infty[0, \infty)$. The set $X = l_\infty[0, \infty)$ is the set of bounded sequences $\{x_t\}_{t=0}^{\infty}$ of real or complex numbers. The metric is $d_\infty(x, y) = \sup_t|x_t - y_t|$.

EXAMPLE A.3. $l_p(-\infty, \infty)$ is the set of "two-sided" sequences $\{x_t\}_{t=-\infty}^{\infty}$ such that $\sum_{t=-\infty}^{\infty}|x_t|^p < +\infty$, where $1 \leq p < \infty$. The associated metric is $d_p(x, y) = (\sum_{t=-\infty}^{\infty}|x_t - y_t|^p)^{1/p}$.

EXAMPLE A.4. $l_\infty(-\infty, \infty)$ is the set of bounded sequences $\{x_t\}_{t=-\infty}^{\infty}$ with metric $d_\infty(x, y) = \sup|x_t - y_t|$.

EXAMPLE A.5. Let $X = C[0, T]$ be the set of all continuous functions mapping the interval $[0, T]$ into R. We consider the metric

$$d_p(x, y) = \left[\int_0^T |x(t) - y(t)|^p \, dt \right]^{1/p},$$

where the integration is in the Riemann sense.

EXAMPLE A.6. Let $X = C[0, T]$ be the set of all continuous functions mapping the interval $[0, T]$ into R. We consider the metric

$$d_\infty(x, y) = \sup_{0 \leq t \leq T} |x(t) - y(t)|.$$

---

1. General references on the mathematics described in this appendix are Luenberger (1969) and Naylor and Sell (1982).

We now have the following important definition:

DEFINITION. *A sequence $\{x_n\}$ in a metric space (X, d) is said to be a Cauchy sequence if for each $\epsilon > 0$ there exists an $N(\epsilon)$ such that $d(x_n, x_m) < \epsilon$ for any $n, m \geq N(\epsilon)$. Thus a sequence $\{x_n\}$ is said to be Cauchy if $\lim_{n, m \to \infty} d(x_n, x_m) = 0$.*

We also have the following definition of convergence.

DEFINITION. *A sequence $\{x_n\}$ in a metric space (X, d) is said to converge to a limit $x_0 \in X$ if for every $\epsilon > 0$ there exists an $N(\epsilon)$ such that $d(x_n, x_0) < \epsilon$ for $n \geq N(\epsilon)$.*

The following lemma asserts that every convergent sequence in (X, d) is a Cauchy sequence.

LEMMA. *Let $\{x_n\}$ be a convergent sequence in a metric space (X, d). Then $\{x_n\}$ is a Cauchy sequence.*

Proof. Fix any $\epsilon > 0$. Let x_0 be the limit of $\{x_n\}$. Then for all m, n one has

$$d(x_n, x_m) \leq d(x_n, x_0) + d(x_m, x_0),$$

by virtue of the triangle inequality. Because x_0 is the limit of $\{x_n\}$, there exists an N such that $d(x_n, x_0) < \epsilon/2$ for $n \geq N$. Together with the above inequality, this statement implies that $d(x_n, x_m) < \epsilon$ for $n, m \geq N$. Therefore, $\{x_n\}$ is a Cauchy sequence.   Q.E.D.

We now consider two examples of sequences in metric spaces. The examples are designed to illustrate aspects of the concept of a Cauchy sequence. We first consider the metric space $(C[0, 1], d_2(x, y))$. We let $\{x_n\}$ be the sequence of continuous functions $x_n(t) = t^n$. Evidently this sequence converges pointwise to the function

$$x_0(t) = \begin{cases} 0, & 0 \leq t < 1 \\ 1, & t = 1. \end{cases}$$

Now, in $\{C[0, 1], d_2(x, y)\}$, the sequence $x_n(t)$ is a Cauchy sequence. To verify this point, calculate

$$d_2(t^m, t^n)^2 = \int_0^1 (t^n - t^m)^2 \, dt = \frac{1}{2n + 1} + \frac{1}{2m + 1} - \frac{2}{m + n + 1}.$$

Clearly, for any $\epsilon > 0$, it is possible to choose an $N(\epsilon)$ that makes the square root of the right side less than ϵ whenever m and n both exceed N. Thus $x_n(t)$ is a Cauchy sequence. Notice, however, that the limit point $x_0(t)$ does *not* belong to $\{C[0, 1], d_2(x, y)\}$ because it is not a continuous function.

As our second example, we consider the space $\{C[0, 1], d_\infty(x, y)\}$. We consider the sequence $x_n(t) = t^n$. In $(C[0, 1], d_\infty)$, the sequence $x_n(t)$ is *not* a Cauchy sequence. To verify this point, it is sufficient to establish that, for any fixed $m > 0$, there is a $\delta > 0$ such that

$$\sup_{n>0} \sup_{0 \leq t \leq 1} |t^n - t^m| > \delta.$$

Direct calculations show that, for fixed m,

$$\sup_{n} \sup_{0 \leq t \leq 1} |t^n - t^m| = 1.$$

Parenthetically we may note that

$$\sup_{n>0} \sup_{0 \leq t \leq 1} |t^n - t^m| = \sup_{0 \leq t \leq 1} \sup_{n>0} |t^n - t^m| = \sup_{0 \leq t \leq 1} \lim_{n \to \infty} |t^n - t^m|$$

$$= \sup_{0 \leq t \leq 1} \lim_{n \to \infty} t^m |t^{n-m} - 1| = \sup_{0 \leq t \leq 1} t^m = 1.$$

Therefore, $\{t^n\}$ is not a Cauchy sequence in $(C[0, 1], d_\infty)$.

These examples illustrate the fact that whether a given sequence is Cauchy depends on the metric space within which it is embedded, in particular on the metric that is being used. The sequence $\{t^n\}$ is Cauchy in $(C[0, 1], d_2)$, and more generally in $(C[0, 1], d_p)$ for $1 \leq p < \infty$. The sequence $\{t^n\}$, however, is *not* Cauchy in the metric space $(C[0, 1], d_\infty)$. The first example also illustrates the fact that a Cauchy sequence in (X, d) need *not* converge to a limit point x_0 belonging to the metric space. The property that Cauchy sequences converge to points lying in the metric space is desirable in many applications. We give this property a name.

DEFINITION. *A metric space (X, d) is said to be complete if each Cauchy sequence in (X, d) is a convergent sequence in (X, d). That is, in a complete metric space, each Cauchy sequence converges to a point belonging to the metric space.*

The following metric spaces are complete:

$(l_p[0, \infty), d_p), \quad 1 \leq p < \infty$
$(l_\infty[0, \infty), d_\infty)$
$(C[0, T], d_\infty)$

The following metric spaces are not complete:

$(C[0, T], d_p), \quad 1 \leq p < \infty.$

Proofs that $(l_p[0, \infty), d_p)$ for $1 \leq p \leq \infty$ and $(C[0, T], d_\infty)$ are complete are contained in Naylor and Sell (1982, chap. 3). In effect, we have already shown by counterexample that the space $(C[0, 1], d_2)$ is not complete, because we displayed a Cauchy sequence that did not converge to a point in the metric space. A definition may now be stated.

DEFINITION. *A function f mapping a metric space (X, d) into itself is called an operator.*

Let us define continuity of an operator.

DEFINITION. *Let $f: X \to X$ be an operator on a metric space (X, d). The operator f is said to be continuous at a point $x_0 \in X$ if for every $\epsilon > 0$ there exists a $\delta > 0$ such that $d[f(x), f(x_0)] < \epsilon$ whenever $d(x, x_0) < \delta$. The operator f is said to be continuous if it is continuous at each point $x \in X$.*

We shall be studying a particular kind of operator, the application of which to any two distinct points $x, y \in X$ brings them closer together.

DEFINITION. *Let (X, d) be a metric space and let $f: X \to X$. We say that f is a contraction or contraction mapping if there is a real number k, $0 \le k < 1$, such that*

$$d[f(x), f(y)] \le kd(x, y) \quad \text{for all } x, y \in X.$$

It follows directly from the definition that a contraction mapping is a continuous operator.

We now state the following theorem.

THEOREM. *Contraction Mapping*

Let (X, d) be a complete metric space and let $f: X \to X$ be a contraction. Then there is a unique point $x_0 \in X$ such that $f(x_0) = x_0$. Furthermore, if x is any point in X and $\{x_n\}$ is defined inductively according to $x_1 = f(x)$, $x_2 = f(x_1)$, . . . , $x_{n+1} = f(x_n)$, then $\{x_n\}$ converges to x_0.

Proof. Let x be any point in X. Define $x_1 = f(x)$, $x_2 = f(x_1)$, . . . Express this as $x_n = f^n(x)$. To show that the sequence x_n is Cauchy, first assume that $n > m$. Then

$$d(x_n, x_m) = d[f^n(x), f^m(x)] = d[f^m(x_{n-m}), f^m(x)]$$
$$\le kd[f^{m-1}(x_{n-m}), f^{m-1}(x)]$$

By induction, we get

(*) $\qquad d(x_n, x_m) \le k^m d(x_{n-m}, x).$

When we repeatedly use the triangle inequality, the above inequality implies that

$$d(x_n, x_m) \leq k^m[d(x_{n-m}, x_{n-m-1}) + \ldots + d(x_2, x_1) + d(x_1, x)].$$

Applying (*) gives

$$d(x_n, x_m) \leq k^m(k^{n-m-1} + \ldots + k + 1)d(x_1, x).$$

Because $0 \leq k < 1$, we have

(†) $$d(x_n, x_m) \leq k^m \sum_{i=0}^{\infty} k^i d(x_1, x) = \frac{k^m}{1-k} d(x_1, x).$$

The right side of (†) can be made arbitrarily small by choosing m sufficiently large. Therefore, $d(x_n, x_m) \to 0$ as $n, m \to \infty$. Thus $\{x_n\}$ is a Cauchy sequence. Because (X, d) is complete, $\{x_n\}$ converges to an element of (X, d).

The limit point x_0 of $\{x_n\} = \{f^n(x)\}$ is a fixed point of f. Because f is continuous, $\lim_{n \to \infty} f(x_n) = f(\lim_{n \to \infty} x_n)$. Now $f(\lim_{n \to \infty} x_n) = f(x_0)$ and $\lim_{n \to \infty} f(x_n) = \lim_{n \to \infty} x_{n+1} = x_0$. Therefore $x_0 = f(x_0)$.

To show that the fixed point x_0 is unique, assume the contrary. Assume that x_0 and y_0, $x_0 \neq y_0$, are two fixed points of f. But then

$$0 < d(x_0, y_0) = d[f(x_0), f(y_0)] \leq kd(x_0, y_0) < d(x_0, y_0),$$

which is a contradiction. Therefore f has a unique fixed point. This statement completes the proof of the contraction mapping theorem.

We now restrict ourselves to sets X whose elements are functions. The spaces $C[0, T]$ and $l_p[0, \infty)$ for $1 \leq p \leq \infty$ are examples of spaces of functions. Let us define the notion of inequality of two functions.

DEFINITION. *Let X be a space of functions, and let $x, y \in X$. Then $x \geq y$ if and only if $x(t) \geq y(t)$ for every t in the domain of definition of the function.*

Let X be a space of functions. We use the d_∞ metric, defined as $d_\infty(x, y) = \sup_t |x(t) - y(t)|$, where the supremum is over the domain of definition of the function.

A pair of conditions that are sufficient for an operator $T: (X, d_\infty) \to (X, d_\infty)$ to be a contraction appear in the following theorem.[2]

THEOREM A.1. *Blackwell's Sufficient Conditions for T to Be a Contraction*
  Let T be an operator on a metric space (X, d_∞), where X is a space of

---

2. See Blackwell's (1965) theorem 5. This theorem is used extensively by Lucas, Prescott, and Stokey (forthcoming).

functions. Assume that T has the following two properties:

(a) *Monotonicity. For any x, y ∈ X, x ≥ y implies T(x) ≥ T(y).*
(b) *Discounting. Let c denote a function that is constant at the real value c for all points in the domain of definition of the functions in X. For any positive real c and every x ∈ X, T(x + c) ≤ T(x) + βc for some β satisfying 0 ≤ β < 1.*

Then T is a contraction mapping with modulus β.

Proof. Suppose that $x \geq y$ implies that $T(x) \geq T(y)$. We have $x = y + x - y$. It follows, because $x - y \leq d_\infty(x, y)$, that $x \leq y + d_\infty(x, y)$. Then by monotonicity property (a), $T(x) \leq T[y + d_\infty(x, y)]$. Applying the discounting property (b) to this inequality gives $T(x) \leq T(y) + \beta d_\infty(x, y)$ or $T(x) - T(y) \leq \beta d_\infty(x, y)$. It follows that $d_\infty(T(x), T(y)) \leq \beta d_\infty(x, y)$. Therefore T is a contraction.

We can also state the following alternative sufficient conditions for T to be a contraction.

THEOREM A.2. *Let T be an operator on a metric space (X, d∞), where X is a space of functions. Assume that T has the following two properties:*

(a) *Monotonicity. For any x, y ∈ X, x ≥ y implies T(x) ≤ T(y).*
(b) *Discounting. Let c denote a function that is constant at the real value c for all points in the domain of definition of the functions in X. For any positive real c and every x ∈ X, T(x − c) ≤ T(x) + βc for some 0 ≤ β < 1.*

Then T is a contraction mapping with modulus β.

Proof. Suppose $x \geq y$ implies that $T(x) \leq T(y)$. Suppose $x \geq y$. Note that $y \geq x - d_\infty(x, y)$. Monotonicity property (a) and discounting property (b) of T imply that $T(y) \leq T[x - d_\infty(x, y)] \leq T(x) + \beta d_\infty(x, y)$ for $0 \leq \beta < 1$. Therefore, $0 \leq T(y) - T(x) \leq \beta d_\infty(x, y)$. Therefore $d_\infty(T(x), T(y)) \leq \beta d_\infty(x, y)$. Therefore, T is a contraction.

A.2 First-Order Linear Difference Equations

Forward Solutions

Consider the difference equation

$$(A.1) \qquad y_t = \lambda y_{t+1} + \gamma x_t, \qquad |\lambda| < 1, \qquad t \geq 0,$$

where $\{x_t\}_{t=0}^\infty$ is an element of $(l_\infty[0, \infty), d_\infty)$. A sequence $\{y_t\}_{t=0}^\infty$ is said to solve the difference equation (A.1) if it satisfies (A.1) for all $t \geq 0$. We shall apply the contraction mapping theorem to prove that there exists a unique solution of (A.1) in the space $(l_\infty[0, \infty), d_\infty)$.

The difference equation (A.1) is associated with an operator on $(l_\infty[0, \infty), d_\infty)$. In particular, define the operator $T(y)$ by

(A.2) $[T(y)]_t = \lambda y_{t+1} + \gamma x_t$,

where $y = \{y_t\}_{t=0}^\infty$, and $[T(y)]_t$ denotes the tth element of the sequence $\{T(y)\}$. The operator T maps $(l_\infty[0, \infty), d_\infty)$ into itself. A solution of the difference equation (A.1) is evidently a fixed point of the operator, namely, a y that satisfies $y = T(y)$.

We have the following result.

PROPOSITION A.1. *The operator T defined by (A.2) is a contraction on $(l_\infty[0, \infty), d_\infty)$.*

Proof. First, suppose that $\lambda \geq 0$. We verify Blackwell's sufficient conditions for T.

(a) T is monotone. For $z_t \geq y_t$ for all $t \geq 0$, we have

$$[T(z)]_t = \lambda z_{t+1} + \gamma x_t$$
$$[T(y)]_t = \lambda y_{t+1} + \gamma x_t$$
$$[T(z)]_t - [T(y)]_t = \lambda(z_{t+1} - y_{t+1}),$$

which is ≥ 0 if $\lambda \geq 0$.

(b) T discounts. For any positive constant c and any $y \in (l_\infty[0, \infty), d_\infty)$ we have

$$[T(y + c)]_t = \lambda y_{t+1} + \lambda c + \gamma x_t = [T(y)]_t + \lambda c.$$

Because $0 \leq \lambda < 1$, we have condition (b) of Blackwell's theorem.

Now suppose that $\lambda < 0$. In this case, we appeal to the alternative version of Blackwell's conditions, Theorem A.2. We have

(a) T is monotone. For $z_t \geq y_t$ for all $t \geq 0$, we have

$$[T(z)]_t - [T(y)]_t = \lambda(z_{t+1} - y_{t+1}),$$

which is ≤ 0 if $\lambda \leq 0$.

(b) T discounts. For any positive constant c, and any $y \in (l_\infty, [0, \infty), d_\infty)$, we have

$$[T(y - c)]_t = \lambda y_{t+1} - \lambda c + \gamma x_{t+1} = [T(y)]_t - \lambda c.$$

Because $\lambda \leq 0$, set $\beta = -\lambda$, thereby establishing the fulfillment of condition (b) of Theorem A.2.

The space $(l_\infty[0, \infty), d_\infty)$ is complete. Because T as defined by (A.2) is a contraction, it follows that $y = T(y)$ has a unique solution in $(l_\infty[0, \infty), d_\infty)$. Furthermore, this solution is approached in the limit as $n \to \infty$ by iterations on T, namely by $y^n = T^n(y)$, where y is any point in $l_\infty[0, \infty)$. We illustrate such iterations by choosing as our initial point $\{y_t\}_{t=0}^\infty = \{0\}_{t=0}^\infty$. We have

$$y_t^1 = \gamma x_t, \quad t \geq 0$$
$$y_t^2 = \gamma x_t + \gamma\lambda x_{t+1}, \quad t \geq 0$$
$$y_t^3 = \gamma x_t + \gamma\lambda x_{t+1} + \gamma\lambda^2 x_{t+2}, \quad t \geq 0$$

.

.

.

$$y_t^n = \gamma \sum_{i=0}^{n-1} \lambda^i x_{t+i}, \quad t \geq 0.$$

Evidently, the solution $\lim_{n\to\infty} y_t^n$ is

(A.3) $$y_t = \gamma \sum_{i=0}^\infty \lambda^i x_{t+i}, \quad t \geq 0.$$

Equation (A.3) gives the unique solution of the difference equation (A.1) that lies in the space $l_\infty[0, \infty)$.

The difference equation (A.1), however, has many other solutions that fail to lie in the space $l_\infty[0, \infty)$. In particular, it can be verified directly that, for any constant g, a solution of (A.1) is given by

$$y_t = \gamma \sum_{i=0}^\infty \lambda^i x_{t+i} + g(1/\lambda)^t.$$

Only the solution for $g = 0$ lies in $l_\infty[0, \infty)$. If $g \neq 0$, $g\lambda^{-t}$ fails to converge as $t \to \infty$ because $|1/\lambda| > 1$. This example warns us that application of the contraction mapping theorem finds a unique solution within the metric space that we are studying. Other solutions may exist outside that space.

In many of the applications that follow, we shall restrict $\{x_t\}$ in (A.1) to lie in $l_2[0, \infty)$, and we shall desire a solution for $\{y_t\}$ that lies in $l_2[0, \infty)$. (The economics of the problem will dictate that we seek a solution belonging to $l_2[0, \infty)$, for reasons to be described below.) We note that the space $l_2[0, \infty)$ is included in the space $l_\infty[0, \infty)$. We have proved that (A.1) has a unique solution $\{y_t\}_{t=0}^\infty$ in $l_\infty[0, \infty)$, given by (A.3). When $\{x_t\}_{t=0}^\infty \in l_2[0, \infty)$, it can be verified directly that $\{y_t\}_{t=0}^\infty$ given by (A.3) belongs to $l_2[0, \infty)$. It follows since $l_2[0, \infty) \subset l_\infty[0, \infty)$, that (A.3) gives the unique solution for $\{y_t\}_{t=0}^\infty$ of (A.1) in $l_2[0, \infty)$ when $\{x_t\} \in l_2[0, \infty)$. We summarize this result in the following proposition.

PROPOSITION A.2. *If* $\{x_t\}_{t=0}^\infty \in l_2[0, \infty)$, *then the difference equation (A.1) has a unique solution* $\{y_t\}_{t=0}^\infty$ *belonging to the space* $l_2[0, \infty)$. *This solution is represented by (A.3).*

At this point, we introduce a metric space that is closely related to $(l_2[0, \infty), d_2)$. For $0 < b < 1$, we let X be the space $l_2^b[0, \infty)$ of sequences such that $\Sigma_{t=0}^\infty b^t x_t^2 < +\infty$. For a metric we choose $d_2^b(x, y) = [\Sigma_{t=0}^\infty b^t (x_t - y_t)^2]^{1/2}$. We denote this metric space $(l_2^b[0, \infty), d_2^b)$. This metric space is complete. The space $(l_2[0, \infty), d_2)$ is related to $(l_2^b[0, \infty), d_2^b)$ in the following way. Let $\{x_t\} \in (l_2^b[0, \infty), d_2^b)$. Then define $\{\tilde{x}_t\} = \{b^{t/2} x_t\}$. It follows that $\{\tilde{x}_t\}$ is in $(l_2[0, \infty), d_2)$. Conversely, let $\{\tilde{x}_t\} \in (l_2[0, \infty), d_2)$. Then $\{x_t\}$ is in $(l_2^b[0, \infty), d_2^b)$, where $x_t = b^{-t/2} \tilde{x}_t$ for all $t \geq 0$.

As an application, consider the difference equation (A.1), where we now assume that $x_t \in (l_2^b[0, \infty), d_2^b)$ for $0 < b < 1$ and that $|\lambda| < \sqrt{b}$. We can now state the following proposition.

PROPOSITION A.3. *The difference equation (A.1) with* $|\lambda| < \sqrt{b}$ *and* $\{x_t\} \in l_2^b[0, \infty)$ *has a unique solution* $\{y_t\}_{t=0}^\infty$ *belonging to* $(l_2^b[0, \infty), d_2^b)$. *The solution is given by (A.3).*

Proof. Set $\tilde{x}_t = b^{t/2} x_t$, and $\tilde{y}_t = b^{t/2} y_t$. Then the difference equation (A.1) becomes

$$b^{-t/2} \tilde{y}_t = \lambda b^{-(t+1)/2} \tilde{y}_{t+1} + \gamma b^{-t/2} \tilde{x}_t$$

or $\tilde{y}_t = \lambda b^{-1/2} \tilde{y}_{t+1} + \gamma \tilde{x}_t$

or

(A.4) $\tilde{y}_t = \tilde{\lambda} \tilde{y}_{t+1} + \gamma \tilde{x}_t, \qquad \tilde{\lambda} = \lambda b^{-1/2}$.

Because $|\lambda| < \sqrt{b}$, we have that $|\tilde{\lambda}| = |\lambda b^{-1/2}| < 1$, and because $\{\tilde{x}_t\}_{t=0}^\infty$ is in $l_2[0, \infty)$, it follows from Proposition A.2 that the unique solution of (A.4) in $l_\infty[0, \infty)$ is given by

$$\tilde{y}_t = \gamma \sum_{i=0}^\infty \tilde{\lambda}^i \tilde{x}_{t+i}.$$

We showed that $\tilde{y}_t$ is in $l_2[0, \infty)$, and it follows that the unique solution of (A.1) in $(l_2^b[0, \infty), d_2^b)$ is given by

$$y_t = \gamma \sum_{i=0}^\infty \lambda^i x_{t+i}.$$

Backward Solutions

Now suppose that, in (A.1), $|\lambda| > 1$. In this case, the operator T defined in (A.2) fails to be a contraction. Represent the difference equation (A.1) in the form

(A.5) $\qquad y_{t+1} = \delta y_t + \alpha x_t, \qquad t \geq 0,$

where $\delta = \lambda^{-1}$ and $\alpha = -\gamma\lambda^{-1}$. We have $|\delta| < 1$. Now define the operator

(A.6a) $\qquad [T(y)]_{t+1} = \delta y_t + \alpha x_t, \qquad t \geq 0.$

(A.6b) $\qquad [T(y)]_0 = \bar{y}_0,$

where $\bar{y}_0$ is a given initial condition. Note that unless we add (A.6b) (or something like it) to (A.6a), (A.6a) does not define an operator. The reason is that (A.6a) maps $\{\tilde{y}_t^1\}_{t=0}^{\infty}$ sequences into sequences $\{\tilde{y}_t^2\}_{t=1}^{\infty}$. We begin by supposing that $\{x_t\}_{t=0}^{\infty}$ belongs to $(l_\infty[0, \infty), d_\infty)$. We work in the metric space $(l_\infty[0, \infty), d_\infty)$.

We ask the reader to verify the following proposition by directly verifying Blackwell's sufficient conditions as given in Theorems A.1 and A.2.

PROPOSITION A.4. *The operator T defined by (A.6) is a contraction on the space $(l_\infty[0, \infty), d_\infty)$.*

Then as an application of the contraction mapping theorem, we immediately have the following results. The equation $T(y) = y$ has a unique fixed point in $l_\infty[0, \infty)$. This fixed point is the solution of the difference equation (A.5) or (A.1) and is approached by iterations on T starting from any $\{y_t\}_{t=0}^{\infty} \in l_\infty[0, \infty)$.

We calculate the solution of the difference equation starting from the initial point $\{y_t\}_{t=0}^{\infty} = \{y_0 = \bar{y}_0, y_t = 0, t \geq 1\}$. We have

$$y_0^1 = \bar{y}_0$$
$$y_1^1 = \alpha x_0$$
$$y_{t+1}^1 = \alpha x_t, \qquad t \geq 0$$

$$y_0^2 = \bar{y}_0$$
$$y_1^2 = \delta\bar{y}_0 + \alpha x_0$$
$$y_2^2 = \delta\alpha x_0 + \alpha x_1$$
$$y_{t+1}^2 = \delta\alpha x_{t-1} + \alpha x_t, \qquad t \geq 1$$

$$y_0^3 = \bar{y}_0$$
$$y_1^3 = \delta\bar{y}_0 + \alpha x_0$$
$$y_2^3 = \delta^2\bar{y}_0 + \delta\alpha x_0 + \alpha x_1$$
$$y_{t+1}^3 = \delta^2\alpha x_{t-2} + \delta\alpha x_{t-1} + \alpha x_t, \qquad t \geq 2.$$

.
.
.

Evidently, in the limit we will obtain

(A.7) $y_0 = \bar{y}_0$

$$y_t = \delta^t \bar{y}_0 + \alpha \sum_{i=0}^{t-1} \delta^i x_{t-i-1}, \qquad t \geq 1.$$

When $|\delta| < 1$, Equation (A.7) represents the unique solution of the difference equation (A.1) or (A.5) in the space $(l_\infty[0, \infty), d_\infty)$ that satisfies the initial condition $y_0 = \bar{y}_0$. (It also turns out to be the unique solution that satisfies the initial condition in the larger space R^∞, the space of infinite sequences of real numbers $\{y_t\}_{t=0}^\infty$.)

A.3 A Formula of Hansen and Sargent

Reconsider the difference equation

(A.8) $y_t = \lambda y_{t+1} + x_t, \qquad |\lambda| < 1, \qquad t \geq 0,$

where x_t is a sequence that satisfies

$$x_t = a_1 x_{t-1} + a_2 x_{t-2} + \ldots$$

or $$x_t = \sum_{j=1}^{\infty} a_j x_{t-j},$$

where the $\{a_j\}_{j=0}^\infty$ sequence is in $l_2[0, \infty)$ and $a_0 \equiv -1$. We assume that $\{x_t\}_{t=-\infty}^\infty \in l_2(-\infty, \infty)$. We have already proved that there exists a unique solution in $l_2[0, \infty)$ of Equation (A.8), for Equation (A.8) is the special case of (A.1) with $\gamma = 1$. The solution in $l_2[0, \infty)$ is represented by (A.3) with $\gamma = 1$.

We seek an alternative representation of the solution that is of the form

(A.9) $$y_t = \sum_{j=0}^{\infty} b_j x_{t-j},$$

where the sequence $\{b_j\}_{j=0}^\infty$ is in $l_2[0, \infty)$. We claim that there is a unique solution of (A.8) of the form (A.9) with $\{b_j\}_{j=0}^\infty$ in $l_2[0, \infty)$.

Define the operator associated with the right side of (A.8), which maps sequences $\{b_j^n\}_{j=0}^\infty$ into sequences $\{b_j^{n+1}\}_{j=0}^\infty$ as follows:

(A.10) $b_0^{n+1} = (\lambda b_0^n a_1 + \lambda b_1^n + 1)$
$b_j^{n+1} = (\lambda b_0^n a_{j+1} + \lambda b_{j+1}^n), \qquad j \geq 1.$

We obtain this operator by substituting $y_t = \sum_{j=0}^\infty b_j^n x_{t-j}$ into (A.8) to obtain

$$\sum_{j=0}^{\infty} b_j^{n+1} x_{t-j} = \lambda \left(\sum_{j=0}^{\infty} b_j^n x_{t-j+1} \right) + x_t.$$

Substituting $x_{t+1} = \sum_{j=1}^{\infty} a_j x_{t+1-j}$ into the above equation gives

$$(b_0^{n+1} x_t + b_1^{n+1} x_{t-1} + b_2^{n+1} x_{t-2} + \ldots)$$
$$= (\lambda b_0^n a_1 + \lambda b_1^n + 1) x_t + (\lambda b_0^n a_2^n + \lambda b_2^n) x_{t-1}$$
$$+ (\lambda b_0^n a_3^n + \lambda b_3^n) x_{t-2} + \ldots$$

Equating coefficients on x_{t-j}, $j \geq 0$, gives (A.10). Thus we have defined the operator T as

(A.11) $\qquad T(b)_j = \begin{cases} \lambda b_0 a_1 + \lambda b_1 + 1, & j = 0 \\ \lambda b_0 a_{j+1} + \lambda b_{j+1}, & j \geq 1. \end{cases}$

We seek the fixed point of $T(b)$ and want to show that the fixed point is unique. We set $b = T(b)$ in (A.11) to obtain the equations

(A.12) $\qquad b_0(1 - \lambda a_1) = 1 + \lambda b_1$

(A.13) $\qquad b_j = \lambda b_{j+1} + \lambda b_0 a_{j+1}, \qquad j \geq 1.$

From Section A.3, we have seen that (A.13) has a unique solution in $l_2[0, \infty)$, which is given by

(A.14) $\qquad b_j = b_0 \sum_{k=0}^{\infty} \lambda^{k+1} a_{k+j+1}, \qquad j \geq 1$

and in particular

(A.15) $\qquad b_1 = b_0 \sum_{k=0}^{\infty} \lambda^{k+1} a_{k+2}.$

Our problem reduces to one of solving the two equations (A.12) and (A.15) for (b_0, b_1).

Define the polynomials in the lag operator L as $a(L) = 1 - a_1 L - a_2 L^2 - \ldots$, $b(L) = \sum_{j=0}^{\infty} b_j L^j$. Here the lag operator L is defined by $Lx_t = x_{t-1}$. Notice that

$$a_2 \lambda + a_3 \lambda^2 + a_4 \lambda^3 + \ldots = \lambda^{-1} - a_1 - \lambda^{-1} a(\lambda).$$

Substituting this equation into (A.15) gives

(A.16) $\qquad b_1 = b_0[\lambda^{-1} - a_1 - \lambda^{-1} a(\lambda)].$

Solving (A.12) and (A.16) for b_0 gives

(A.17) $\qquad b_0 = a(\lambda)^{-1}.$

Finally, substituting (A.17) into (A.14) gives

$$b_1 = a(\lambda)^{-1}(\lambda a_2 + \lambda^2 a_3 + \lambda^3 a_4 + \ldots)$$
$$b_2 = a(\lambda)^{-1}(\lambda a_3 + \lambda^2 a_4 + \lambda^3 a_5 + \ldots)$$
$$\cdot$$
$$\cdot$$
$$\cdot$$

Using $b(L) = \sum_{j=0}^{\infty} b_j L^j$, we obtain the formula

(A.18) $$b(L) = a(\lambda)^{-1} \left[1 + \sum_{j=1}^{\infty} \left(\sum_{k=j+1}^{\infty} \lambda^{k-j} a_k \right) L^j \right].$$

This is a generalization for infinite-order $a(L)$ polynomials of a formula derived by Hansen and Sargent (1981, formula 8, p. 99).

In summary, the unique solution of the difference equation (A.8) in the space of square summable linear combinations of current and past terms x_t is given by

(A.19) $$y_t = a(\lambda)^{-1} \left[1 + \sum_{j=1}^{\infty} \left(\sum_{k=j+1}^{\infty} \lambda^{k-j} a_k \right) L^j \right] x_t$$

where $a(L)x_t = 0$.

These two equations display cross-equation restrictions characteristic of rational expectations models, reflected in the appearance of the parameters $a(L)$ from the law of motion of x_t in the formula for the parameters $b(L)$ depicting the dependence of y_t on current and lagged x_t. Hansen and Sargent (1980, 1981) use this formula repeatedly to characterize the econometric implications of a class of linear rational expectations models.

A.4 A Quadratic Optimization Problem in R^{∞}

Consider the problem of selecting a sequence $\{y_t\}_{t=0}^{\infty}$ to maximize

(A.20) $$J(\{y_t\}_{t=0}^{\infty}) = \sum_{t=0}^{\infty} [-(f/2)y_t^2 - (d/2)(y_t - y_{t-1})^2 + y_t x_t],$$
$$f > 0, \qquad d > 0,$$

subject to $y_{-1} = \bar{y}_{-1}$ given. Here $\{x_t\}_{t=0}^{\infty}$ is a given sequence in $(l_2[0, \infty), d_2)$. The maximization of (A.20) is over sequences $\{y_t\}_{t=0}^{\infty}$ belonging to R^{∞}.[3]

We first note that an optimum $\{y_t\}_{t=0}^{\infty}$, if it exists, necessarily lies in the space $(l_2[0, \infty), d_2)$. For if $\sum_{t=0}^{n} y_t^2$ diverges, then the term $-(f/2) \sum_{t=0}^{n} y_t^2$

---

3. This is a version of a problem studied in Sargent (1986, chap. 9).

diverges toward $-\infty$, making the value of the objective unbounded and negative. With $-(f/2) \Sigma_{t=0}^{n} y_t^2$ diverging toward $-\infty$, it can be established directly that the term $\Sigma_{t=0}^{n} y_t x_t$ cannot possibly diverge to $+\infty$ fast enough to prevent the objective J in (A.20) from going to $-\infty$ as long as $\{x_t\} \in l_2[0, \infty)$. Thus, without loss of generality, we restrict our search for a solution $\{y_t\}$ in (A.20) to the space $(l_2[0, \infty), d_2)$.[4]

Differentiating the right side of (A.20) with respect to y_t for $t = 0, 1, \ldots$, and equating to zero, we obtain the Euler equations:

$$-dy_{t+1} + (f + 2d)y_t - dy_{t-1} = x_t, \qquad t \geq 0$$

or

(A.21) $\qquad (1 - \lambda L^{-1})(1 - \lambda L)y_t = \dfrac{\lambda}{d} x_t, \qquad t \geq 0$

where

(A.22) $\qquad -dL^{-1} + (f + 2d) - dL = (1 - \lambda L^{-1})(1 - \lambda L)d/\lambda.$

Here L is the lag operator defined by $Lx_t = x_{t-1}$. In the factorization (A.22) of the characteristic polynomial of the Euler equation, $|\lambda| < 1$, and λ is the unique zero of the characteristic polynomial that lies inside the unit circle, that is, λ satisfies[5]

$$-d\lambda^{-1} + (f + 2d) - d\lambda = 0, \qquad |\lambda| < 1.$$

We seek a solution $\{y_t\} \in (l_2[0, \infty), d_2)$ that satisfies the Euler equation (A.21) and the initial condition $y_{-1} = \bar{y}_{-1}$ given.

We define $y_t^* = (1 - \lambda L)y_t = y_t - \lambda y_{t-1}$. Evidently $\{y_t^*\}_{t=0}^{\infty} \in (l_2[0, \infty), d_2)$ if and only if $\{y_t\}_{t=0}^{\infty} \in (l_2[0, \infty), d_2)$. Then the Euler equation (A.21) can be represented

(A.23) $\qquad y_t^* = \lambda y_{t+1}^* + \dfrac{\lambda}{d} x_t, \qquad |\lambda| < 1.$

This is the same difference equation studied above in Section A.3. From Proposition A.2, we know that (A.23) has a unique solution in $(l_2[0, \infty), d_2)$

---

4. The argument that the solution must lie in $l_2[0, \infty)$ replaces a "transversality condition." See Sargent (1986, chap. 9) for a treatment that appeals to a transversality condition. The condition that the solution lies in $l_2[0, \infty)$ generalizes to the detectability conditions in multivariate problems (see Sargent 1981).

5. See Sargent (1986, chap. 9) for discussion of lag operators, the characteristic polynomials associated with Euler equations, and their factorizations.

given by

(A.24) $y_t^* = \dfrac{\lambda}{d} \displaystyle\sum_{j=0}^{\infty} \lambda^j x_{t+j}.$

Now we get y_t from

(A.25) $y_t = \lambda y_{t-1} + y_t^*, \qquad t \geq 0,$

starting from the initial condition $y_{-1} = \bar{y}_{-1}$. As we saw in Section A.3, this equation has a unique solution. As an alternative to the form shown in Equation A.7, we substitute (A.24) into (A.25) and give this solution in the "feedback-feedforward" representation

(A.26) $y_t = \lambda y_{t-1} + \dfrac{\lambda}{d} \displaystyle\sum_{i=0}^{\infty} \lambda^i x_{t+i}, \qquad t \geq 0.$

Equation (A.26) and the initial condition for y_{-1} set forth the unique solution of the first-order necessary conditions (the Euler equations) that lie in $l_2[0, \infty)$. Because the optimum necessarily lies in $l_2[0, \infty)$, we have established that (A.26) represents the unique optimizer.

We add to the specification of problem (A.20) that x_t is a sequence in $l_2(-\infty, \infty)$ that obeys the difference equation $a(L)x_t = 0$, where $\Sigma_{j=0}^{\infty} a_j^2 < +\infty$. The results of Section A.4 then become applicable. Using formula (A.18) of Section A.3, we can represent solution (A.26) in the form

(A.27) $y_t = \lambda y_{t-1} + \dfrac{\lambda}{d} a(\lambda)^{-1} \left[1 + \displaystyle\sum_{j=1}^{\infty} \left(\sum_{k=j+1}^{\infty} \lambda^{k-j} a_k \right) L^j \right] x_t,$

where $a(L)x_t = 0$. Representation (A.27) is the unique optimizer of (A.20) in the space of square summable linear combinations of current and lagged x_t.

A.5 A Discounted Quadratic Optimization Problem

Consider the problem of selecting a sequence $\{y_t\}_{t=0}^{\infty} \in R^{\infty}$ to maximize

(A.28) $J(\{y_t\}_{t=0}^{\infty}) = \displaystyle\sum_{t=0}^{\infty} b^t [-(f/2)y_t^2 - (d/2)(y_t - y_{t-1})^2 + y_t x_t],$

$\qquad\qquad 0 < b < 1, \qquad d > 0, \qquad f > 0,$

subject to y_{-1} given. Here $\{x_t\}_{t=0}^{\infty}$ is a given sequence in $(l_2^b[0, \infty), d_2^b)$. By the same sort of reasoning applied in Section A.4, an optimal $\{y_t\}_{t=0}^{\infty}$ must lie in $(l_2^b[0, \infty), d_2^b)$. Sequences for y_t not lying in this space are associated with unbounded negative values for J.

We shall find the optimizer of (A.28) by first converting it to an undiscounted sum of some transformed variables. Note that (A.28) can be written

$$
\text{(A.29)} \quad \sum_{t=0}^{\infty} \{-(f/2)(b^{t/2}y_t)^2 - (d/2)(b^{t/2}y_t
$$
$$
- b^{1/2}b^{(t-1)/2}y_{t-1})^2 + (b^{t/2}y_t)(b^{t/2}x_t)\}
$$
$$
= \sum_{t=0}^{\infty} [-(f/2)\tilde{y}_t^2 - (d/2)(\tilde{y}_t - b^{1/2}\tilde{y}_{t-1})^2 + \tilde{y}_t\tilde{x}_t]
$$

where

$$
\text{(A.30)} \quad \tilde{y}_t = b^{t/2}y_t, \quad \tilde{x}_t = b^{t/2}x_t.
$$

Evidently, $\{\tilde{y}_t\}_{t=0}^{\infty}$ belongs to $l_2[0, \infty)$ if and only if $\{y_t\}_{t=0}^{\infty}$ belongs to $l_2^b[0, \infty)$. Thus our strategy is to find a maximizer $\{\tilde{y}_t\}_{t=0}^{\infty}$ of (A.29) in $l_2[0, \infty)$, then to recover y_t from $\tilde{y}_t$ by using (A.30).

The Euler equation associated with (A.29) is

$$
\text{(A.31)} \quad -db^{1/2}\tilde{y}_{t+1} + (f + d(1 + b))\tilde{y}_t - db^{1/2}\tilde{y}_{t-1} = \tilde{x}_t.
$$

We use the factorization of the characteristic polynomial in L

$$
\text{(A.32)} \quad \frac{db^{1/2}}{\tilde{\lambda}}(1 - \tilde{\lambda}L^{-1})(1 - \tilde{\lambda}L)
$$
$$
= \{-db^{1/2}L^{-1} + [f + d(1 + b)] - db^{1/2}L\},
$$

where $|\tilde{\lambda}| < 1$. Here $\tilde{\lambda}$ is the unique root less than unity in absolute value of the characteristic polynomial, that is, $\tilde{\lambda}$ satisfies

$$
\{-db^{1/2}\tilde{\lambda}^{-1} + [f + d(1 + b)] - db^{1/2}\tilde{\lambda}\} = 0, \qquad |\tilde{\lambda}| < 1.
$$

Substituting (A.32) into (A.31) gives the representation of the Euler equation

$$
(1 - \tilde{\lambda}L^{-1})(1 - \tilde{\lambda}L)\tilde{y}_t = \frac{\tilde{\lambda}}{db^{1/2}}\tilde{x}_t.
$$

We saw in Section A.4, that the unique solution of this functional equation in $l_2[0, \infty)$ satisfying $\tilde{y}_{-1}$ given can be represented as

$$
\tilde{y}_t = \tilde{\lambda}\tilde{y}_{t-1} + \frac{\tilde{\lambda}}{db^{1/2}} \sum_{i=0}^{\infty} \tilde{\lambda}^i\tilde{x}_{t+i}, \qquad t \geq 0
$$

With (A.30), this can be expressed in terms of (y_t, x_t) as

$$
\text{(A.33)} \quad y_t = \tilde{\lambda}b^{-1/2}y_{t-1} + \frac{\tilde{\lambda}}{db^{1/2}} \sum_{i=0}^{\infty} (\tilde{\lambda}b^{1/2})^i x_{t+i}, \qquad t \geq 0.
$$

Evidently, because $\{x_t\}$ belongs to $l_2^b[0, \infty)$, and because $|\tilde{\lambda}| < 1$, the right side of (A.33) belongs to $l_2^b[0, \infty)$. Note that, if we set $\hat{\lambda} = \tilde{\lambda}b^{-1/2}$, then (A.33) can be represented as

(A.34)
$$y_t = \hat{\lambda}y_{t-1} + \frac{\hat{\lambda}}{d} \sum_{i=0}^{\infty} (\hat{\lambda}b)^i x_{t+i},$$
$$t \geq 0, \qquad |\hat{\lambda}| < b^{-1/2}, \qquad |\hat{\lambda}b| < b^{1/2}.$$

which is the representation reported in Sargent (1986, chap. 9) for the solution of a discounted problem.

Now suppose that $\{x_t\}$ is an element of the space $l_2^b(-\infty, \infty)$, which is defined as the space of sequences $\{z_t\}_{t=-\infty}^{\infty}$ such that $\Sigma_{t=-\infty}^{\infty} b^t z_t^2 < +\infty$. Suppose that x_t satisfies the difference equation $a(L)x_t = 0$ where $\Sigma_{j=0}^{\infty} a_j^2 b^j < \infty$. Then the results of Section A.3 can be used to show that the solution (A.34) can be represented as

(A.35)
$$y_t = \hat{\lambda}y_{t-1} + \frac{\hat{\lambda}}{d} a(\hat{\lambda}b)^{-1} \left[1 + \sum_{j=1}^{\infty} \left(\sum_{k=j+1}^{\infty} (\hat{\lambda}b)^{k-j} a_k \right) L^j \right] x_t,$$

where $a(L)x_t = 0$. This equation represents the unique optimizer of criterion function (A.28).

We modify problem (A.28) as follows. Suppose that

(A.36)
$$a(L)x_t = \epsilon_t, \qquad t \geq 0,$$

where $\{a_j\}_{j=0}^{\infty}$ belongs to $l_2^b[0, \infty)$, and ϵ_t is a sequence of independently and identically distributed random variables satisfying

$$E\epsilon_t = 0 \qquad \text{for all } t \geq 0$$
$$E\epsilon_t x_{t-s} = 0 \qquad \text{for all } t \text{ and } s > 0$$
$$E\epsilon_t^2 = \sigma_\epsilon^2 > 0,$$

where E is the mathematical expectation operator. We assume that $(x_{-1}, x_{-2}, \ldots)$ is a given sequence satisfying $\Sigma_{j=1}^{\infty} b^j x_{-j}^2 < \infty$. We replace (A.28) with the criterion

(A.37)
$$E_0 \sum_{t=0}^{\infty} b^t[-fy_t^2 - (d/2)(y_t - y_{t-1})^2 + y_t x_t],$$

which is to be maximized subject to y_{-1} given and where E_0 is the conditional expectation operator. Consider the problem of maximizing (A.37) over the class of stochastic processes for $\{y_t\}_{t=0}^{\infty}$ that lies in the space of linear combinations of current and past x_t's, $\Sigma_{j=0}^{\infty} c_j x_{t-j}$, with $\Sigma_{j=0}^{\infty} c_j^2 b^j < +\infty$. Now this problem is a version of the stochastic optimal linear regulator problem described in Section 1.8. As an implication of the separation principle (or certainty equivalence) that obtains for such problems, it follows that representation (A.35) gives the solution of the problem of maximizing (A.37), subject to (A.36) and y_{-1} given, over the space of processes y_t expressible as b-square summable combinations of current and lagged x_t. This is the result that the optimal linear feedback rule is independent of the noise statistics.

A.6 Predicting a Geometric Distributed Lead of a Stochastic Process

Another approach may be used to derive the formula of Hansen and Sargent that was described above. Consider the stochastic expectational difference equation

(A.38) $y_t = \lambda \hat{E} y_{t+1} | X_t + x_t, \qquad |\lambda| < 1,$

where x_t is a covariance stationary stochastic process with Wold moving-average representation

$$x_t = \sum_{j=0}^{\infty} c_j \epsilon_{t-j} \equiv c(L)\epsilon_t,$$

where $\sum_{j=0}^{\infty} c_j^2 < +\infty$ and $\epsilon_t = x_t - \hat{E}(x_t | X_{t-1})$. Here $X_t = (x_t, x_{t-1}, \ldots)$ and $\hat{E}$ denotes the linear least-squares projection operator. We seek a solution of difference equation (A.38) that lies in the space of square summable linear combinations of current and lagged ϵ_t:[6]

(A.39) $y_t = \sum_{j=0}^{\infty} b_j \epsilon_{t-j}, \qquad \sum_{j=0}^{\infty} b_j^2 < +\infty,$

or $y_t = b(L)\epsilon_t.$

Given the process for x_t, and the process ϵ_t derived from x_t as $\epsilon_t = x_t - \hat{E}(x_t | X_{t-1})$, the space of random processes defined in (A.39) can be indexed by points in $l_2[0, \infty)$, the space within which $\{b_j\}_{j=0}^{\infty}$ is restricted to lie. We use the metric

$$d_2(f, g) = \left[\sum_{j=0}^{\infty} (f_j - g_j)^2 \right]^{1/2}.$$

The right side of (A.38) defines an operator from $l_2[0, \infty)$ into $l_2[0, \infty)$. For if $y_{t+1} = b_0 \epsilon_{t+1} + b_1 \epsilon_t + \ldots$, it follows that $\hat{E} y_{t+1} | X_t = \hat{E} y_{t+1} | \epsilon_t, \epsilon_{t-1}, \ldots = b_1 \epsilon_t + b_2 \epsilon_{t-1} + \ldots$. Thus if $y_t = b_0 \epsilon_t + b_1 \epsilon_{t-1} + \ldots$, then the

---

6. The linear space consisting of square summable linear combinations of $(\epsilon_t, \epsilon_{t-1}, \ldots)$ equals the linear space of square summable linear combinations of $(x_t, x_{t-1}, \ldots)$.

right side of (A.38) is

$$\lambda(b_1\epsilon_t + b_2\epsilon_{t-1} + \ldots) + (c_0\epsilon_t + c_1\epsilon_{t-1} + \ldots).$$

We define the operator $T(b)$ as

(A.40) $[T(b)]_j = \lambda b_{j+1} + c_j, \qquad j \geq 0.$

The operator $T(b)$ maps sequences b in $l_2[0, \infty)$ into sequences $T(b)$ in $l_2[0, \infty)$. A solution of the difference equation (A.38) is evidently a fixed point of T:

(A.41) $b = T(b).$

Rather than working directly in $(l_2[0, \infty), d_2)$, we begin by working in the larger space $(l_\infty[0, \infty), d_\infty)$, in order to avail ourselves of Blackwell's conditions.

PROPOSITION A.5. *The operator T defined by (A.40) has a unique fixed point $b \in l_\infty[0, \infty)$. The fixed point is approached by iterations on T starting from any initial $b_0 \in l_\infty[0, \infty)$.*

Proof. Note that if $b \in l_2[0, \infty)$, then b is also an element of $l_\infty[0, \infty)$. Consider the operator T defined by (A.40) on the metric space $(l_\infty[0, \infty), d_\infty)$. With Theorems A.1 and A.2, it can be verified that T is a contraction on the complete metric space $(l_\infty[0, \infty), d_\infty)$. Therefore T has a unique fixed point in $l_\infty[0, \infty)$, which is approached starting from any initial $b \in l_\infty[0, \infty)$ by successive iterations on T.

We note that, if the solution of $b = T(b)$ turns out to lie in $l_2[0, \infty)$, it is the unique solution in $l_2[0, \infty)$. The reason is that $l_2[0, \infty) \subset l_\infty[0, \infty)$. We shall show by construction that the solution b of (A.41) lies in $l_2[0, \infty)$.

We use iterations on T to calculate the solution of (A.40)–(A.41), starting from $\{b_j^0\} = \{0\}_{j=0}^\infty$. We obtain the following iterates by applying T defined by (A.41):

$$b_j^1 = c_j, \qquad j \geq 0$$
$$b_j^2 = \lambda c_{j+1} + c_j$$
$$b_j^3 = \lambda^2 c_{j+2} + \lambda c_{j+1} + c_j$$
$$\vdots$$
$$b_j^n = \lambda^{n-1} c_{j+n-1} + \lambda^{n-2} c_{j+n-2} + \ldots + c_j.$$

Evidently, the limit as $n \rightarrow \infty$ is

(A.42) $b_j = c_j + \lambda c_{j+1} + \lambda^2 c_{j+2} \ldots$

Using lag operators, we represent this solution as

$$
\begin{aligned}
b(L) &= \sum_{j=0}^{\infty} (c_j + c_{j+1}\lambda + c_{j+2}\lambda^2 + \ldots)L^j \\
&= \sum_{j=0}^{\infty} c_j L^j + \lambda \sum_{j=0}^{\infty} c_{j+1} L^j + \lambda^2 \sum_{j=0}^{\infty} c_{j+2} L^j + \ldots \\
&= c(L) + \lambda \left[\frac{c(L)}{L} - \frac{c_0}{L} \right] + \lambda^2 \left[\frac{c(L)}{L^2} - \left(\frac{c_0 + c_1 L}{L^2} \right) \right] \\
&\quad + \lambda^3 \left[\frac{c(L)}{L^3} - \frac{c_0 + c_1 L + c_2 L^2}{L^3} \right] + \ldots \\
&= \frac{c(L)}{1 - \lambda L^{-1}} - (1 + \lambda L^{-1} + \lambda^2 L^{-2} + \ldots) \\
&\quad \cdot \lambda L^{-1}(c_0 + c_1 \lambda + c_2 \lambda^2 + \ldots)
\end{aligned}
$$

or

(A.43) $b(L) = \dfrac{c(L) - \lambda L^{-1} c(\lambda)}{1 - \lambda L^{-1}}.$

It can be verified directly that $\{b_j\}_{j=0}^{\infty}$ given by (A.43) is in $l_2[0, \infty)$. Equation (A.43) is the formula associated with predicting a geometric distributed lead that was reported by Hansen and Sargent (1980).

Now suppose that $x_t = c(L)\epsilon_t$ has an autoregressive representation. This is equivalent to assuming that there exists an $a(L) = c(L)^{-1}$ where $\sum_{j=0}^{\infty} a_j^2 < +\infty$. In this case, (A.43) can be used to express y_t as

$$
y_t = \frac{c(L) - \lambda L^{-1} c(\lambda)}{1 - \lambda L^{-1}} \epsilon_t
$$

or

(A.44) $y_t = \dfrac{1 - \lambda L^{-1} a(\lambda)^{-1} a(L)}{1 - \lambda L^{-1}} x_t.$

It can be verified using the residue calculus (see Sargent 1986, chap. 11) that

(A.45) $\dfrac{1 - \lambda L^{-1} a(\lambda)^{-1} a(L)}{1 - \lambda L^{-1}} = a(\lambda)^{-1} \left[1 + \sum_{j=1}^{\infty} \left(\sum_{k=j+1}^{\infty} \lambda^{k-j} a_k \right) L^j \right].$

Thus the solution (A.44) agrees with the solution (A.18) in Section (A.3). As a result we see that the solution $y_t = \Sigma_{j=0}^{\infty} b_j x_{t-j}$ of the difference equation $y_t = \lambda y_{t+1} + x_t$, where $\Sigma_{j=0}^{\infty} b_j^2 < +\infty$, $a(L)x_t = 0$, $\Sigma_{j=0}^{\infty} a_j^2 < +\infty$, equals the solution of the stochastic difference equation (A.38) in the space to which we have restricted ourselves. This fact is at the heart of the certainty equivalence principle. In Chapter 1, we saw that the decision rule that solves the stochastic optimal linear regulator problem is independent of the variance matrix of the noises in the system. This fact reflects the equivalence of the above solutions of (A.1) and (A.38). The reason is that optimal linear regulator problems can be reformulated as stochastic calculus-of-variations problems, whose Euler equations assume forms that resemble (A.38) in essential ways. (See Hansen and Sargent 1981.)

A.7 Discounted Dynamic Programming

We study the functional equation associated with a discounted dynamic programming problem:

$$\text{(A.46)} \qquad v(x) = \max_{u \in R^k} \{r(x, u) + \beta v(x')\}, \qquad x' \leq g(x, u), \qquad 0 < \beta < 1.$$

We assume that $r(x, u)$ is real valued, continuous, concave, and bounded and that the set $[x', x, u : x' \leq g(x, u), u \in R^k]$ is convex and compact.

We define the operator

$$Tv = \max_{u \in R^k} \{r(x, u) + \beta v(x')\}, \qquad x' \leq g(x, u), \qquad x \in X.$$

We work with the space of continuous bounded functions mapping X into the real line. We use the d_∞ metric,

$$d_\infty(v, w) = \sup_{x \in X} |v(x) - w(x)|$$

This metric space is complete.

The operator T maps a continuous bounded function v into a continuous bounded function Tv. (For a proof, see Lucas, Prescott, and Stokey, forthcoming.)

We now establish that T is a contraction by verifying Blackwell's pair of sufficient conditions. First, suppose that $v(x) \geq w(x)$ for all $x \in X$. Then

$$\begin{aligned} Tv &= \max_{u \in R^k} \{r(x, u) + \beta v(x')\}, \qquad x' \leq g(x, u) \\ &\geq \max_{u \in R^k} \{r(x, u) + \beta w(x')\}, \qquad x' \leq g(x, u) \\ &= Tw. \end{aligned}$$

Thus T is monotone. Next, notice that for any positive constant c,

$$T(v + c) = \max_{u \in R^k} \{r(x, u) + \beta(v(x') + c)\}, \qquad x' \le g(x, u)$$

$$= \max_{u \in R^k} \{r(x, u) + \beta v(x') + \beta c\}, \qquad x' \le g(x, u)$$

$$= Tv + \beta c.$$

Thus T discounts. Therefore T satisfies both of Blackwell's conditions. It follows that T is a contraction on a complete metric space. Therefore the functional equation (A.46), which can be expressed as $v = Tv$, has a unique fixed point in the space of bounded continuous functions. This fixed point is approached in the limit in the d_∞ metric by iterations $v^n = T^n(v^0)$ starting from any bounded and continuous v^0. Convergence in the d_∞ metric implies uniform convergence of the functions v^n.

Lucas, Prescott, and Stokey (forthcoming) show that T maps concave functions into concave functions. It follows that the solution of $v = Tv$ is a concave function.

A.8 A Search Problem

We now study the functional equation associated with a search problem of Chapter 2. The functional equation is

(A.47) $\qquad v(w) = \max\left\{\dfrac{w}{1 - \beta}, \beta \int v(w') \, dF(w')\right\}, \qquad 0 < \beta < 1.$

Here the wage offer drawn at t is w_t. Successive offers w_t are independently and identically distributed random variables. We assume that w_t has cumulative distribution function $\text{prob}\{w_t \le w\} = F(w)$, where $F(0) = 0$ and $F(\overline{w}) = 1$ for some $\overline{w} < \infty$. In (A.47), $v(w)$ is the optimal value function for a currently unemployed worker who has offer w in hand. We seek a solution of the functional equation (A.44).

We work in the space of bounded continuous functions $C[0, \overline{w}]$, and use the d_∞ metric

$$d_\infty(x, y) = \sup_{0 \le w \le \overline{w}} |x(w) - y(w)|.$$

The metric space $(C[0, \overline{w}], d_\infty)$ is complete.

We consider the operator

(A.48) $\qquad T(z) = \max\left\{\dfrac{w}{1 - \beta}, \beta \int z(w') \, dF(w')\right\}.$

Evidently the operator T maps functions z in $C[0, \overline{w}]$ into functions $T(z)$ in

$C[0, \overline{w}]$. We now assert that the operator T defined by (A.48) is a contraction. To prove this assertion, we verify Blackwell's sufficient conditions. First, assume that $f(w) \geq g(w)$ for all $w \in [0, \overline{w}]$. Then note that

$$Tg = \max \left\{ \frac{w}{1 - \beta}, \beta \int g(w') \, dF(w') \right\}$$

$$\leq \max \left\{ \frac{w}{1 - \beta}, \beta \int f(w') \, dF(w') \right\}$$

$$= Tf.$$

Thus T is monotone. Next, note that for any positive constant c,

$$T(f + c) = \max \left\{ \frac{w}{1 - \beta}, \beta \int [f(w') + c] \, dF(w') \right\}$$

$$= \max \left\{ \frac{w}{1 - \beta}, \beta \int f(w') \, dF(w') + \beta c \right\}$$

$$\leq \max \left\{ \frac{w}{1 - \beta}, \beta \int f(w') \, dF(w') \right\} + \beta c$$

$$= Tf + \beta c.$$

Thus T satisfies the discounting property and is therefore a contraction.

Application of the contraction mapping theorem, then, establishes that the functional equation $Tv = v$ has a unique solution in $C[0, \overline{w}]$, which is approached in the limit as $n \to \infty$ by $T^n(v^0) = v^n$, where v^0 is any point in $C[0, \overline{w}]$. Because the convergence in the space $C[0, \overline{w}]$ is in terms of the metric d_∞, the convergence is uniform.

Exercises

Exercise A.1. **Periodic Difference Equation**
Consider the periodic linear difference equation

$$y_t = \lambda_1 y_{t+1} + x_t, \qquad t \geq 0, \qquad t \text{ odd}$$
$$y_t = \lambda_2 y_{t+1} + x_t, \qquad t \geq 0, \qquad t \text{ even.}$$

Suppose that $x_t \in l_\infty[0, \infty)$. Assume that $|\lambda_1 \lambda_2| < 1$.

a. Prove that the difference equation given above has a unique solution $\{y_t\}_{t=0}^\infty$ in $l_\infty[0, \infty)$.

b. Describe an algorithm for computing this solution.

c. Find the solution for $\{y_t\}_{t=0}^\infty$ that lies in $l_\infty[0, \infty)$.

Exercise A.2. Asset Pricing

Associated with Lucas's asset-pricing model (Chapter 3) is the functional equation

(1) $$w(x) = \beta \int w(x') \, dF(x', x) + g(x),$$

where $g(x)$ is a bounded and continuous function. We assume that $F(\cdot)$ is such that for every continuous and bounded function $h(x')$ the function $f(x) = \int h(x') \, dF(x', x)$ is a continuous function of x. This will be the case if, for example, the Markov process that x_t follows is generated by an equation of the form $x_{t+1} = g(x_t, \epsilon_{t+1})$, with ϵ_t a sequence of i.i.d. random variables and g a continuous function of x and a measurable function of ϵ.

   a. Prove that the functional equation has a unique continuous and bounded solution $w(x)$.

   b. Given a function $g(x)$, describe an algorithm for computing the unique continuous and bounded $w(x)$ that solves (1).

References and Suggested Readings

Blackwell, David. 1965. Discounted dynamic programming. *Annals of Mathematical Statistics* 36(1):226–235.

Hansen, Lars P., and Thomas J. Sargent. 1980. Formulation and estimating dynamic linear rational expectations models. *Journal of Economic Dynamics and Control* 2(1):7–46. (Reprinted in *Rational Expectations and Econometric Practice,* ed. R. E. Lucas, Jr., and T. J. Sargent, pp. 91–125. Minneapolis: University of Minnesota Press, 1981.)

———— 1981. Linear rational expectations models for dynamically interrelated variables. In *Rational Expectations and Econometric Practice,* ed. R. E. Lucas, Jr., and T. J. Sargent, pp. 127–156. Minneapolis: University of Minnesota Press.

Lucas, Robert E., Jr., Edward C. Prescott, and Nancy Stokey. Recursive methods for economic dynamics. Forthcoming.

Luenberger, David G. 1969. *Optimization by Vector Space Methods.* New York: Wiley.

Naylor, Arch, and George Sell. 1982. *Linear Operator Theory in Engineering and Science.* New York: Springer.

Sargent, Thomas J. 1981. Lecture notes on filtering, control, and rational expectations. University of Minnesota, Minneapolis. Unpublished.

———— 1986. *Macroeconomic Theory,* 2nd ed. New York: Academic Press.

Index